Introducing Global Englishes

Introducing Global Englishes provides comprehensive coverage of relevant research in the fields of World Englishes, English as a lingua franca, and English as an international language. The book introduces students to the current sociolinguistic uses of the English language, using a range of engaging and accessible examples from newspapers (*The Observer*, *The Independent*, *The Wall Street Journal*), advertisements, and television shows. This book:

- explains key concepts connected to the historical and contemporary spread of English;
- explores the social, economic, educational, and political implications of English's rise as a world language;
- includes comprehensive classroom-based activities, case studies, research tasks, assessment prompts, and links to extensive online resources;
- is accompanied by a companion website www.routledge.com/cw/galloway featuring further exercises, debate topics, and research tasks, audio and video clips.

Introducing Global Englishes is essential reading for students coming to this subject for the first time.

Nicola Galloway was an English language teacher for ten years. She currently works as a Lecturer in Education (TESOL) at the University of Edinburgh, where she teaches a course on Global Englishes. She is currently working on several publications related to Global Englishes, particularly in relation to English language teaching.

Heath Rose teaches applied linguistics at Trinity College Dublin, focusing on language teacher training. He holds a PhD from the University of Sydney and has taught for 17 years in Australia, Japan, and Ireland. Recent publications include articles in *Applied Linguistics* and *Modern Language Journal*.

Introducing Global Englishes

Nicola Galloway and Heath Rose

Routledge
Taylor & Francis Group

LONDON AND NEW YORK

First published 2015
by Routledge
2 Park Square, Milton Park, Abingdon, Oxon OX14 4RN

and by Routledge
711 Third Avenue, New York, NY 10017

Routledge is an imprint of the Taylor & Francis Group, an informa business

© 2015 Nicola Galloway and Heath Rose

The right of Nicola Galloway and Heath Rose to be identified as authors of this work has been asserted by them in accordance with sections 77 and 78 of the Copyright, Designs and Patents Act 1988.

British Library Cataloguing-in-Publication Data
A catalogue record for this book is available from the British Library

Library of Congress Cataloging-in-Publication Data
Galloway, Nicola (Linguist) author.
Introducing Global Englishes / Nicola Galloway and Heath Rose.
pages cm
Includes bibliographical references and index.
1. English language–Globalization. 2. English language–Variation–English-speaking countries
3. Test of English as a Foreign Language. I. Rose, Heath, author. II. Title.
PE1073.G35 2015
420.9–dc23
2014030469

ISBN: 978-0-415-83531-2 (hbk)
ISBN: 978-0-415-83532-9 (pbk)
ISBN: 978-1-315-73434-7 (ebk)

Typeset in Bembo
by Taylor and Francis Books

Printed and bound in Great Britain by
TJ International Ltd, Padstow, Cornwall

Contents

Figures

Tables

Preface

English is now a globalized phenomenon and the numbers of English speakers around the globe have risen dramatically. Today, non-native English speakers outnumber native English speakers (terms problematized in this book), and English has become the world's foremost lingua franca, dominating the world stage in a number of domains. The English language has transcended its original boundaries, resulting in more contact with other languages than any other language in the world. Of course, language change and variation is a natural occurrence and happens to all languages, but the spread of English is a rather unique phenomenon. English **language contact** is occurring on a global platform due to its inextricable connection to **globalization**, which is at the heart of the current spread of the language and its rise as a worldwide lingua franca. There has been an explosive growth in the number of English speakers, and this increased usage on a global level has resulted in **innovations** in its use as it is employed by speakers from diverse linguistic and cultural backgrounds and assumes distinct functions and forms in different contexts. It is no longer relevant to associate English purely with native-speaking nations; today, English is spoken by a global community and, therefore, is a language with a global ownership.

Such changes also have a number of implications for the way the language should be taught, given the fact that the majority of English learners will likely use the language as a lingua franca with fellow non-native English speakers, rendering models based on native English somewhat irrelevant for many. It is no surprise that the changing sociolinguistic uses of the English language have resulted in a wealth of research that investigates topics such as the history of English, language change, language variation, language **attitudes**, and English language teaching (ELT).

We both have experience in English language education in a traditionally 'English as a foreign language' setting. Over the years, our interest grew in the growth of English language users worldwide; the role of, and use of, the language in our teaching contexts; our students' needs as future users of the language; the relevance of traditional English language teaching approaches and materials; and our own roles as **native English-speaking teachers**. Such interest culminated in a series of research projects (Galloway, 2013; Galloway and Rose, 2013, 2014), including a PhD thesis on the topic of **Global Englishes** (Galloway, 2011). We were fortunate enough to be able to design and teach a university course on Global Englishes and to be able to integrate a global perspective into English language courses. It soon became apparent to us that the courses had a motivating influence on students, possibly better preparing them for their future use of English as a lingua franca. It also became clear that many colleagues shared an interest in the topic and desired to learn more. However, at the same time we realized that, whilst the pedagogical implications of the global spread of English are increasingly being discussed at the theoretical level, there is a severe lack of materials on Global Englishes available for teachers and students, and also for scholars in the field. Of course, a variety of reference materials have been published over the years on the historical spread of English, the current use of English, World Englishes, English as a lingua franca (ELF) and English as an international language (EIL) but, at the time of writing, there was no comprehensive introductory resource that covered the topic of Global Englishes, which we view as including all of the above. As teacher educators, we also desired a resource that could bring all of these strands together. And so this project was born.

Several key themes underpin this book's positioning of Global Englishes.

1 Language change is natural and normal.
2 Languages are in contact with one another, especially English which is used in more language-contact situations than any other.
3 Ownership of English should be viewed as a global concept.
4 English is adaptable, fluid, and ever changing; its code gets appropriated and adapted in varied contexts of use.
5 Many English users have a multilingual or translingual repertoire that they utilize to successfully communicate in English; knowledge of another language is a help, not a hindrance.
6 Meaning is achieved through communication and negotiation, not through adherence to a native English-speaking norm.

This book sets out to portray the English language as a malleable construct, bringing into question notions of English varieties or **Englishes** with linguistic boundaries. Readers will gain an understanding of the development of English in relation to historical, social, and economic forces, and will become familiar with key issues in the field of Global Englishes.

Terminology

It is important to clarify some of the terminology used in this book, beginning with the very term 'Global Englishes'. As defined elsewhere (Galloway, 2013), Global Englishes includes the concepts of World Englishes, which focuses on the identification and codification of national varieties of English, and ELF, which examines English use within and across such borders, as well as focusing on the global consequences of English's use as a world language. Global Englishes extends the lens of these fields to incorporate many peripheral issues associated with English, such as globalization, **linguistic imperialism**, education, and **language policy** and planning. We present World Englishes and ELF research separately in this book, given that the first focuses on the documentation of the distinct features of national varieties in the areas of phonology, lexis, grammar, and pragmatics in the 'New' Englishes while ELF research examines the use of English as a **contact language**, both within and across Kachru's (1985, 1992a) Inner, Outer and Expanding Circles. In ELF, communication is seen as a more fluid and changing phenomenon, used in 'communities of practice' (Lave and Wenger, 1991) as opposed to in fixed geographical settings, involving a process of ongoing linguistic accommodation where language is appropriated by speakers in response to situational demands. Despite their differences, there are similarities between the two research **paradigms**, based on a similar underlying ideology. Both:

- view English as a **pluricentric** notion;
- focus on the use of English by non-native English speakers, emphasizing the influence of linguistic contact;
- focus on the global ownership of English independent of native English **norms**;
- have implications for teaching the language.

Thus, ELF forms 'part of the wider WE [World Englishes] research community' (Seidlhofer, 2009a, p. 243). Because of these similarities and a 'shared endeavor' (Seidlhofer, 2009a, p. 243), together they form part of the broader Global Englishes paradigm.

We also see the shared ideologies of EIL falling under the Global Englishes umbrella term. At the Centre for Global Englishes launch at the University of Southampton in May 2012, Barbara Seidlhofer discussed two kinds of EIL: localized EIL, which includes World Englishes and nation-based varieties, and globalized EIL, involving international communication characterized by hybrid ways of speaking and de-territorialized speech events. However, given the definitions of EIL in the literature, which are often exclusionary of many concepts in ELF that we want to represent in this book, and which are discussed below, the term 'EIL' is avoided and 'Global Englishes' is used instead. Global Englishes, however, can also be viewed as including both localized EIL (World Englishes and nation-based varieties, thus including varieties from the Inner, Outer and Expanding Circles) and globalized EIL (henceforth 'ELF').

Our adoption of the term 'Global Englishes' does not mean that we are ignoring, or even underestimating, the importance of the work by scholars who choose to position their work within the field of EIL. In our opinion, what many EIL scholars have described as EIL fits within the Global Englishes framework, and we aim to be inclusive of such work. Sharifian (2009, p. 2), for example, defines EIL as referring 'to a paradigm for thinking, research and practice', as does Global Englishes in relation to the global spread of English. EIL also 'marks a paradigm shift in TESOL [Teaching English to speakers of other languages], SLA [second language acquisition] and the applied linguistics of English' (Sharifian, 2009, p. 2), as does Global Englishes or, more specifically, Global Englishes language teaching (GELT), introduced in Galloway (2011) and discussed in Chapter 9 of this book. Furthermore, Sharifian (2009, p. 2) notes that it 'does not refer to a particular variety of English'.

It is important to note that Global Englishes is a very different concept to 'Globish', which represents a reduced and simplified variety of English, different to the term Global English which represents an ideological world standard. 'One of the central themes of EIL as a paradigm is its recognition of World Englishes, regardless of which "circles" they belong to' (ibid, p. 2). Although we have pluralized English in our coverage of World Englishes, we also want to recognize that ELF research does not assume a single variety, and indeed challenges the very notion that such a thing exists. Further similarity between Global Englishes and EIL is found in the comment that, 'The EIL paradigm also emphasises the relevance of World Englishes to ELT' (ibid, p. 3).

However, EIL differs from Global Englishes in its understanding and treatment of ELF, which is problematic at times. In Sharifian's (2009) positioning of EIL, it is suggested that ELF research can 'broadly be associated with the EIL paradigm' (p. 6), but there is a misguided assumption that ELF researchers are only focused on the linguistic code and not the 'political/ideological dimensions of native/non-native distinction' (ibid, p. 6), which is, most certainly, not the case. Further problems stem from the fact that the term is often used differently. In the same book as Sharifian (2009), Holliday (2009, p. 21) suggests that EIL is synonymous with ESOL (English for speakers of other languages). Leung and Street (2012, p. 85) argue that EIL is 'closely related' to ELF and lingua franca English, and Gu (2012) uses EIL and ELF synonymously. Much EIL literature seems to dismiss ELF research, or to posit it as the study of English use in the Expanding Circle (e.g. Alsagoff, 2012b), or the study of 'short contact situations, such that fleeting English norms are in operation' (House, 2012, p. 187). It is for these reasons, among others, that we have not used the term 'EIL'. However, we hope that EIL scholars will find that their work fits nicely under the Global Englishes umbrella term.

We are not the first to use the term Global Englishes. The University of Southampton established a Centre for Global Englishes in 2007; Widdowson (2012, p. 22) noted that, 'ELF is part of the Global Englishes paradigm', concurring with our definition. Pennycook (2007, p. 18) has also written extensively on Global Englishes, which he notes 'might suggest a blend on the one hand of critical theories of globalization, where globalization is seen as an inherently destructive force homogenizing the world, and world Englishes on the other, where English is seen as a pluralized entity'. He posits that the term captures both of these polarities to a certain extent, that is a critical perspective of globalization and a pluralized concept of English. Here, we would agree with him. However, he also distances himself from both views, pointing out that the former could be seen as imperialist and the second as pluralist – these notions are also explored throughout our book and become increasingly relevant in our final chapter.

As will be discussed, the Global Englishes paradigm challenges the notions of geographic linguistic boundaries and distinct language varieties, and instead emphasizes the pluricentricity and fluidity of English. As Pennycook (2007, p. 5) points out, 'English is closely tied to processes of globalization: a language of threat, desire, destruction and opportunity. It cannot be usefully understood in modernist states-centric models of imperialism of world Englishes, or in terms of traditional, segregationist models of language'. Pennycook then feels that, while the pluralization strategy of World Englishes is useful, he prefers to locate Englishes 'within a more complex vision of globalization' (p. 5), that is one that views the role of English critically and in complexity.

Our definition of Global Englishes also resonates, in many ways, with Canagarajah's (2013) notion of translingual practice, which showcases the increasing linguistic hybridity. His points regarding the difference between the multilingual orientation (as an extension of the monolingual paradigm) and his translingual orientation (which conceives language in more dynamic terms) also resemble Global Englishes, as defined in this book. For example, amongst other things he points out that (summarized from Canagarajah, 2013, pp. 6–7):

- languages are in contact with others and the separation of languages with different labels needs to be problematized;
- users treat all available codes as a repertoire which are not separated according to their labels, and they don't have separate competences but an integrated proficiency;
- languages can complement each other in communication, allowing for more creativity;
- with such **linguistic diversity**, meaning arises through negotiation in local situations, not adherence to a common grammatical system or norm;
- grammatical norms are open to renegotiation and reconstruction, as users communicate in new contexts for varied purposes.

Thus, we believe our definition of Global Englishes complements previous publications that have used the term. However, it is important to point out that Canagarajah (2013) himself stresses the differences between his translingual approach and World Englishes, ELF, and EIL. Pennycook also distances Global Englishes from World Englishes when he states that,

> we need to move beyond arguments about homogeneity or heterogeneity, or imperialism and nation states, and, instead, focus on translocal and transcultural flows. English is a translocal language, a language of fluidity and fixity that moves across, while becoming embedded in, the materiality of localities and social relations.
> (Pennycook, 2007, pp. 5–6)

While our book endeavours to be inclusive of much World Englishes research, especially in Chapters 4 and 5, we do this as an acknowledgement of the important research conducted in World Englishes which has helped form the broader Global Englishes paradigm.

The problems regarding terminology are addressed throughout the book, and thus our adoption of certain terms does not always indicate our full compliance with them, especially regarding the following terms: the Inner, Outer, and Expanding Circles (see Section 1d for discussion); 'Standard' English; and 'Native' and 'New' Englishes. By the end of the book we have also questioned terms such as 'variety', 'language', 'culture', 'native English speaker' and 'non-native Englishes speaker'. Nevertheless, such terms are in common usage and so are used throughout this book, but not without question.

Book coverage and structure

The book is divided into 10 chapters, with each consisting of four subsections. This facilitates opportunities for a collaborative teaching approach. The companion website also contains lecture slides, audio materials, research tasks, tutorial worksheets and numerous links for students to find further information. We estimate there to be 70–80 hours of additional classroom materials.

Chapter 1 offers readers a historical perspective on the spread of English and describes how it is used today. Chapter 2 introduces key concepts and theories related to language change and variation as a backdrop for subsequent chapters. Our aim is to make readers aware that understanding some of the more recent changes in English use, as well as attitudes towards it, needs to be grounded in history. We aim to highlight that language change is both a natural and normal phenomenon, and that change to the English language is, most certainly, not a new occurrence. We also introduce the concept of standard language ideology, another concept that needs a historical perspective, to gain a full understanding of the attachments towards the concept of 'standard' English.

Chapter 3 takes the reader to the political side of the global spread of English, exploring the advantages and disadvantages of a global lingua franca. It also examines approaches to language policy and planning in varied contexts. Chapters 4 and 5 return to the topic of variation, the former focusing on variation in **'Native' Englishes** and the latter on the 'New' Englishes, or rather Kachru's Inner and Outer Circles. Chapter 5 showcases work in the World Englishes paradigm, although we acknowledge the inherent problems in the use of the terms 'native', 'non-native', 'Inner Circle', and 'Outer Circle', as well as the problems associated with whether or not it is even possible to establish a variety in today's increasingly global world where 'communities of practice' may be a more relevant term, something emphasized in the ELF research paradigm. To not cover the important research that has been conducted within the World Englishes paradigm would do our readers an injustice, as much of Global Englishes has been built on this foundation. This, however, does not assume that we claim to be geographically representative in our summary of World Englishes research: to do so would be an impossible and undesirable task. However, whilst it may not be a completely 'global' coverage, many of those that we have included are relevant beyond their specific contexts, and the reader is pointed to more comprehensive resources for further reading.

In Chapter 6, we move on to look at English in global contexts, or the Expanding Circle, where we focus more on the history of, the roles of, and attitudes towards English. We also introduce and define the notion of ELF, given that a lot of ELF usage takes place within this context. Chapter 7 then provides comprehensive coverage of ELF research. In Chapter 8 we move on to look at attitudes towards English and provide an overview of the various studies that have been conducted. Chapter 9 focuses on the debates surrounding English language teaching, outlining a new approach to ELT and GELT in depth. Chapter 10 ends the book with a look at the future of English, focusing on changing domains of English use in an emerging global culture and the internationalization of higher education, before looking at predicted directions of English language use as a world lingua franca.

Courses in World Englishes have been growing, and in recent years many universities are including Global Englishes components to their course offerings. We hope that this text on Global Englishes will be a useful resource. We are aware that reference materials have grown over the years, but this book differs in that it covers not only the theoretical and descriptive interest, but also the pedagogical interest. The very existence of a global language presents a number of challenges, and it is such challenges that this book hopes to address. The chapters are primarily addressed to researchers and undergraduate and graduate students in the field of applied linguistics and language teaching, but will also be of interest to those studying linguistics, international business, international relations, politics, or any field where English has made inroads as a contact language. We also believe it will serve as a foundation text for research students within the fields of Global Englishes, World Englishes, ELF, and EIL.

Acknowledgements

Firstly, our thanks go to Routledge, and in particular to Rachel Daw, Helen Tredget, and Nadia Seemungal, who have been continually supportive during our writing process and have offered advice at several stages. We also thank Irena Yanushevskaya and David Deterding for their detailed feedback on portions of the manuscript, as well as the other anonymous reviewers. Special thanks also go to Professor Jennifer Jenkins, particularly for her patient supervision of one of the authors during her PhD candidature and continued professional advice.

We have had the opportunity to try out some of the materials in teacher training courses at the University of Edinburgh and Trinity College Dublin. We would like to thank the students on these courses for their interest in the subject, and also for their feedback on many of the materials. Meanwhile, we remain incredibly fortunate to have supportive friends and family, who have been consistently patient during our writing process.

Acronyms

ASEAN	Association of South East Asian Nations
BELF	Business English as a lingua franca
EU	European Union
EFL	English as a foreign language
EIL	English as an international language
ELF	English as a lingua franca
ELT	English language teaching
EFL	English as a foreign language
ENL	English as a native language
ESL	English as a second language
ESOL	English for speakers of other languages
GELT	Global Englishes language teaching
RP	Received pronunciation
SLA	Second language acquisition
TESOL	Teaching English to speakers of other languages

Chapter 1

The history of English

Introductory activities

The following introductory activities are designed to encourage the reader to think about the issues raised in this chapter before reading it.

The spread of English

Discussion questions

1. As Figure 1.1 shows, English is the official language of many nations across the globe, in all continents.
   a. How, and why, did English become the official language of so many nations?
2. Mauranen (2012, p. 17) points out that English as a **lingua franca** is 'one of the most important social phenomena that operate on a global scale … The emergence of one language that is the default lingua franca in all corners of the earth is both a consequence and a prerequisite of globalisation.'
   a. How has globalization contributed to the spread of English to regions farther than those highlighted in Figure 1.1?
3. A number of frameworks to represent English speakers around the globe have been proposed, although it is difficult to categorize global English usage (e.g. as a native language or a second language).
   a. What difficulties might you encounter trying to categorize English speakers? Why is it difficult?
   b. How would you categorize English speakers from the countries shown in the box below?

> Australia, Singapore, Denmark, the USA, China, Hong Kong, the Philippines, Ireland, Brazil, South Africa, Iran, Kenya, India, Mexico.

Case study: problems with classifying English-speaking countries

English speakers are often divided into the **Inner Circle** (where English is a native language), the **Outer Circle** (where English plays an important role as an additional or

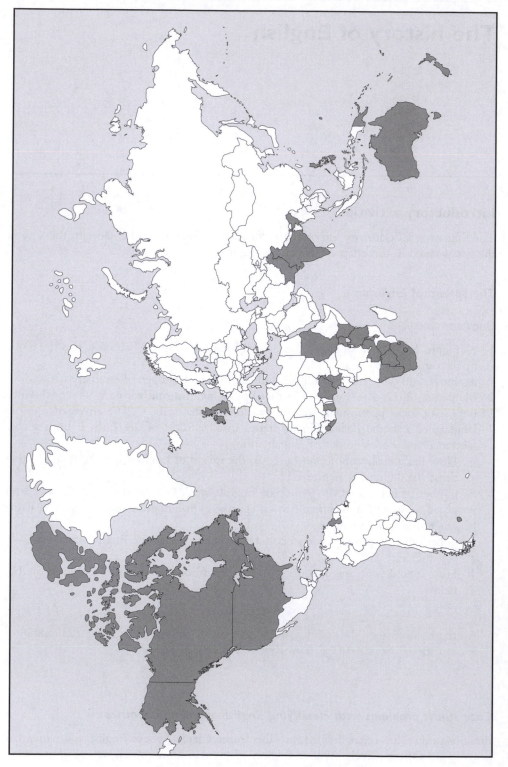

Figure 1.1 Countries where English is an official language

official language, including former Inner Circle colonies), and the **Expanding Circle** (where English has no official role and is learned as a 'foreign' language) (Kachru, 1985, 1992a). India is placed in the Outer Circle, because of its historic ties to the United Kingdom and English's official status, whereas the Netherlands is placed in the Expanding Circle because English has no official status. However, in India one-sixth of the population is estimated to speak English proficiently (Graddol, 2006), unlike in some Expanding Circle countries, such as the Netherlands and Scandinavian countries, which have much higher proportions of the population (up to 60 or 70 per cent) at a comparable level of proficiency.

Discussion

1 Why do some countries like the Netherlands have higher levels of English proficiency than countries such as India, where English is an official language? How is 'proficiency' defined?
2 According to this system of classification, Denmark would be placed in the same category as China, Singapore would be placed with Bangladesh, and Canada (including Quebec) would be placed with the UK. What are the inherent problems with categorizing countries based on colonial history or official use of English?
3 Can you make any suggestions for an alternative system of categorizing?

Further issues related to categorizing English use can be found in Section 1d.

Introduction

This chapter is devoted to exploring the history of English, tracking its development from a language of a small island in Europe to the global lingua franca it is today. Section 1a examines the roots of English in the Germanic languages spoken in the northern regions of Germany and Denmark. It explores the influences of other languages on English, including Old Norse, Latin, and French. Section 1b explores the early dispersal of English around the world, through **settler colonization**, **slavery** and **trade and exploitation** colonies. Section 1b also introduces the effects of this spread on English, a topic explored in greater depth in Chapter 2. Section 1c explores the more recent spread driven by globalization and the journey towards becoming a global lingua franca. Section 1d outlines the state of the English language today, focusing on the number of speakers and learners worldwide and categorization issues.

1a The origins of the English language

Much of this book looks at the implications of the spread of English around the world and the growing use of English as a global lingua franca. However, this first chapter begins with an examination of English through history. In fact, the modern English language has little resemblance to the language spoken in England 1,000 years ago, and almost no connection to the language spoken there 2,000 years ago. This section examines the influences of history and language contact on English, before looking at its dispersal around the world.

The roots of Old English

The people who lived in what is known today as England did not originally speak English. In fact, before the fifth century, the roots of English were not to be found in the languages spoken in Britain. The Ancient Britons, the original inhabitants of the region, spoke a Celtic language. Instead, English has its roots in the languages spoken in the northern areas of Germany and, possibly, the Jutland peninsula in Denmark, which were home to the Saxons, the Jutes, and the Angles (from whom the very word 'English' was derived). The spread of these languages to Britain was via the Anglo-Saxon invasion, when Germanic settlers flooded into the region.

However, this was by no means a single organized or unified attack on Britain. Germanic people had been living in England alongside the Britons and Romans for centuries beforehand. It was the power vacuum left there after Roman withdrawal that attracted a large number of invasions from CE 449 onwards, sometimes at the invitation of Celtic kings who were vying to fill the power void (Fennell, 2001). These invasions led to the establishment of seven kingdoms, each with communities of people who spoke vastly different dialects, which pushed the indigenous population into far-flung reaches of the island where remnants of the ancient Celtic languages remain today, including Welsh in the far west, Scottish Gaelic in the far north, and Cornish in the far south-west.

In the following centuries, the languages of these kingdoms were influenced by new settlers and invaders. Old Norse, for example, had a great influence in many parts of Britain due to Nordic invasions, and this influence eventually impacted on the language used throughout the whole region. Despite this variation, by the tenth century it could be claimed that a distinct language called **Old English** was spoken, albeit **unintelligible** to an English speaker today, as can be seen from the excerpt from *Beowulf*, an old heroic poem that is one of the most important works of Anglo-Saxon literature from this period (see Table 1.1).

Norman French and the emergence of Middle English

The English language underwent massive change after the Norman Conquest in 1066. This invasion of England by the Normans saw a French-speaking government established for the

Table 1.1 Excerpts from literature written in Old English, Middle English and Early Modern English

An excerpt from Beowulf from 900 AD	An excerpt from The Canterbury Tales from 1400 AD	An excerpt from The Hound of the Baskervilles from 1900 AD
Hwæt wē Gār-Dena in geār-dagum þēod-cyninga þrym gefrūnon hū ðā æþelingas ellen fremedon Oft Scyld Scēfing sceaþena þrēatum monegum mægþum meodo-setla oftēah egsian eorl syððan ǣ rest weorþan	His Almageste, and bookes grete and smale, His astrelabie, longynge for his art, His augrym stones layen faire apart, On shelves couched at his beddes heed; His presse ycovered with a faldyng reed And al above ther lay a gay sautrie, On which he made a-nyghtes melodie So swetely that all the chambre rong; And Angelus ad virginem he song;	Mr. Sherlock Holmes, who was usually very late in the mornings, save upon those not infrequent occasions when he was up all night, was seated at the breakfast table. I stood upon the hearth-rug and picked up the stick which our visitor had left behind him the night before. It was a fine, thick piece of wood, bulbous-headed, of the sort which is known as a 'Penang lawyer.'

following 300 years. As Old Norman (a variety of French) was the language spoken by the kings and nobles ruling England during this time, linguistic features of the language seeped into Old English. McIntyre (2009, p. 12) writes that, 'Of course, the language did not change overnight, but, gradually, French began to have an influence that was to change English substantially and lead it into its next stage of development – **Middle English**.' By 1205, Norman-French domination was replaced by Southern French domination. During the following centuries, English was viewed as the language of commoners, and the speaking of French held status in politics, law, government administration, and noble society.

During this period, English was an endangered language; the social restrictions on English were indicative of a dying language (Melchers and Shaw, 2011). However, in the later years of French rule, English grew in popularity as it was viewed as a positive symbol of national pride and, eventually, began to replace French as the official language of the nation from 1362, by which time French's influence on the language had been immense. During the middle ages, more than 10,000 French words entered the English language, particularly surrounding food, politics, and the judicial system (e.g. *mutton, pastry, soup, parliament, justice, alliance, court, marriage*). Massive grammatical changes also occurred, including the disposal of the gender-based grammatical differences that still remain in most Germanic languages. The result of such massive changes means that a speaker of English today could read a text written in Middle English in 1400 with some assistance, but would be incapable of doing so with a similar text written 400 years previously, as in the example of Old English (see Table 1.1).

The emergence of a 'standard' language

The concept of a unified English language began with an increasing need for a language of governance. In the early 1400s, **Chancery English** was chosen as the **'standard' English** for handwritten administrative documents in the courts. Chancery English was based on the Midlands variety of English at the time, but was historically influenced by the English used by King Henry V's private secretariat (Hogg and Denison, 2006). It was chosen as the standard, 'not only because the Midlands are located in the middle, but because the language was not as extreme as that of the innovative North or as conservative as in the South' (Gramley, 2012, p. 104). Hogg and Denison (2006) add a few more explanations for the rise of the Chancery English, which would later be referred to as the **Chancery Standard**. They state:

- the dialect was spoken by the largest number of people;
- the area was wealthy in agricultural resources;
- influential arms of government and administration were located there;
- the area was associated with education and learning, with Cambridge and Oxford universities in close proximity;
- it contained good ports;
- it had strong ties to the church and the Archbishop.

The emergence of a standard written English in the early 1400s, therefore, had much to do with political, social, religious, economic, and educational support. It will become clear in later chapters that such factors have also influenced notions of **'prestige** varieties' of English in more recent years, and the emergence of a standard language ideology.

Interestingly, the emergence of a definable English language from the late 1400s was, perhaps, less related to this political decision than to a commercial decision by a handful of printers of the time. The invention of Gutenberg's printing press in the mid-1400s saw Europe go through social and linguistic changes. The printing press saw an explosion of publications in vernacular languages, whereas previous publications were usually carried out in Latin, or in legal languages such as French. As Fennell (2001, p. 157) notes, 'it rapidly became obvious the English-language books sold better, so that market forces (a modern term applicable to this period) did much to strengthen the position of the vernacular language.' The printing press for the first time raised the question of what variety of vernacular language to publish in for a mass readership.

William Caxton was one of the first printers to publish texts in English once the printing press was introduced to Britain. In one of his publications he openly discussed the difficulties in choosing an English variety to publish in:

> And that common English that is spoken in one shire varies from another, so that, in my days, it happened that certain merchants were in a ship on the Thames to sail over the sea to Zealand, and, for lack of wind, they tarried at Foreland and went to land to refresh themselves. And one of them, named Sheffelde, a mercer, came to a house and asked for food, and, especially, he asked for egges, and the good woman answered that she could speak no French. And the merchant was angry, for he also could speak no French, but wanted to have egges, and she did not understand him. And then, at last, another said that he wanted eyren. Then the good woman said that she understood him well. Lo, what should a man in these days now write, egges or eyren? Certainly it is hard to please every man, because of diversity and change of language.
>
> (Caxton, *Boke of Eneydos*, 1490)

Caxton made a decision to settle on the Midlands variety of English, with added London inflections and expressions, because from a business perspective he wanted to print in a standard that could be most widely understood by those across Britain at the time, and the Chancery Standard had laid some of this groundwork. The inclusion of a London dialect in printing at the time might also have had a lot to do with the prevalence of London-based publishing houses.

Early Modern English

The acceptance of a written 'standard' English did not really occur until centuries after Caxton's first printed publications in the English vernacular language. During the next century, Britain saw massive writing and spelling reforms, and the publication of very influential English language dictionaries. Grammar and language dictionaries promoted conventions that were often based on the English used by wealthy merchants from the Midlands at the time, who were trading in London. McIntyre (2009, p. 22) states that 'the dialect was associated with powerful people and, as we have already seen, power equals prestige.' In these centuries, the Midland dialect had been adopted by printers, in Royal courts in London, and by the literate upper class. All of this impacted on the vernacular language, as spellings and grammar **standardizations** were reflected in speech. It could be said that modern English, then, was the result of a chain reaction which started with attempts at standardization of written English in the courts, gained wider momentum with the introduction of the printing press, and cemented itself in spoken English via the prestige associated with the Midland speakers, on whom the written standard was modelled.

In addition to this, during this time English went through the Great Vowel Shift, a phenomenon that involved changes in most long vowel sounds in English, and some short sounds. Gramley (2012) states the Great Vowel Shift may have been caused by an upper class distinguishing their 'correct' pronunciation from the lower class. This theory emphasizes the importance of the power and prestige associated with 'standard' English at the time. Other theories include upheavals in population mobility due to social changes at the time and in response to the Black Death (a bubonic plague). This theory points to the importance on language change of sudden contact with other dialects.

Needless to say, by the late 1600s a modern English had emerged that could be understood by an English speaker today. To track the history of English any further than this date becomes more challenging, as the English language underwent mass dispersal around the world due to an intense period of imperialistic activity. With the dispersal of English, the language could no longer be viewed as the language of one tiny island but as the seed of the global lingua franca that it is today.

1b   The early spread of English around the world

There have been many attempts to divide the spread of the English language into various stages, and one that is often cited in **World Englishes** literature is the **two diaspora** of the British Empire. The **first diaspora** involved large-scale migrations of English speakers from the British Isles to North America, Australia, and New Zealand in the seventeenth and eighteenth centuries (Jenkins, 2009). As people of various dialects mixed with each other, English underwent a number of linguistic changes in each of these regions, causing the emergence of new varieties of native Englishes. The **second diaspora** refers to the spread of English as a second or additional language to new communities due to contact with English colonizers. West Africa, for example, saw contact with English speakers due to trade colonies and port settlements, and English in Nigeria, Gambia, Ghana, Sierra Leone, and Cameroon was linked to the slave trade. English was also brought to South Asia (now India, Nepal, Pakistan, Bangladesh, and Bhutan), Hong Kong, and Singapore.

The problem with this two diaspora model is that it has very little to do with how the English language was introduced to each environment. In the first diaspora, for example, we see English dispersal by settlers to the Americas and Australia, causing new native Englishes to emerge. However, the spread of English to the Caribbean also saw the emergence of native Englishes, but via drastically different circumstances. Therefore, including the Caribbean and places such as Australia in one diaspora is problematic. Likewise, the way English was introduced in exploitation colonies (places controlled by Britain for trade purposes, rather than fully colonized by settlers) along the West African coast, or in places like India, is vastly different to the use of English in Caribbean nations where English has always been a native, and often only, official language.

Not only does the two diaspora model inadequately represent the actual spread of English and its use as a first or additional language, it also does not provide an accurate chronological account. The first diaspora is largely noted to occur in the eighteenth century, while the second diaspora 'took place at various points during the eighteenth and nineteenth centuries' (Jenkins, 2009, p. 7). However, British influence in India began in the early 1600s, well before the beginning of the spread of English to many parts of the world during the first diaspora (McCrum *et. al.*, 1992, p. 356).

Our intention is not to criticize the two diaspora model but to point out the inherent difficulty in categorizing the spread of English. Rather than examining the spread of English according to timing or region, as has been done in previous models, this book will examine the spread of English through four channels:

1   settler colonization;
2   slavery;
3   trade and exploitation colonies;
4   globalization.

The fourth channel of globalization mainly describes the spread of English via forces other than colonialism to regions with limited historical contact with the language.

Looking at the spread of English through these channels, rather than through geography or timing, can better describe the 'messy' spread of English. For example, the spread of English to English-speaking Canada occurred mostly through the channel of settler colonization (channel 1), but the more recent spread of English to French-speaking Canada is largely the result of globalization forces (channel 4). Likewise, the spread of English to Hawaii occurred initially through slavery plantations (channel 2), but the English widely spoken in Hawaii today has developed through more recent settler colonization (channel 1) from the English-speaking populations of the USA. By examining the spread of English through channels rather than through geographically defined locations or chronologically defined events we are better able to explain multiple types of spread in the same locations, and at the same points in time.

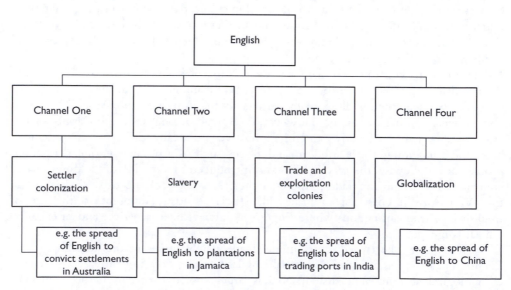

Figure 1.2 The four channels of English spread

'New' Englishes from historical spread

This part of the chapter explores Channels 1–3; Channel 4 is covered in Section 1c later in this chapter.

The first three channels of English spread were mostly the result of a popular economic theory from the 1500s called **mercantilism**, which viewed trade as a zero-sum game. That is, if one country benefited by trade, another country would lose. It was, therefore, in the best interests of a nation to increase its trading potential, to ensure economic growth. The resources of a country, in terms of its population and its natural resources, were paramount to benefiting from trade and, thus, increasing the strength of a nation. One way to rapidly expand the nation's resources, therefore, was seen to be the exploration of new territories, the colonization of new and already-known territories thought to be rich in resources, an increase in labour resources through slavery, and increased control of known lucrative markets and ports (like India, Singapore, and Hong Kong). During this era, England spread its territory into the Americas, Oceania, Asia, and Africa. With this spread came the dispersal in markedly different ways of the English language to new regions of the world.

Channel 1: Settler colonization

The dispersal of the English language through settler colonization brought English to the Americas, Africa, and the Pacific. Although there were a few settlements beforehand, expansion into North America really began in the early 1600s. During this same period, the Caribbean islands were being settled by English-speaking landowners, workers, and slaves (discussed next). From 1788, English spread to Australia and New Zealand, the former initially being through the establishment of penal colonies, the latter with the arrival of free English settlers. The spread of English through Channel 1 transplanted the English language via the movement of large populations of first-language English speakers (albeit from different dialectal regions) to new territories where, very quickly, they out numbered and out-powered local indigenous populations or other communities of different language backgrounds. For the indigenous populations, the introduction of the English language often resulted in the extinction of many local languages. Australia's 'white policy', for example, ran until 1969 and involved the removal of 6,000 aboriginal children from their parents for the purposes of 'white education'. Moreover, mixed race children were taken from their aboriginal communities and placed into 'white' homes for the purposes of assimilation. It was a hope of the policy that, eventually, the aboriginal race would slowly be 'bred out'. Indeed, most aborigines in Australia today speak English as a first and only language, and all but 20 indigenous languages have almost completely disappeared, with just 11 per cent of aboriginal and Torres Strait Islanders speaking an indigenous language at home (Australian Bureau of Statistics, 2012). In more remote areas of Australia, particularly in the far north, which was not heavily settled by European settlers, children and youth are far more likely to speak an aboriginal or Torres Strait Islander language (42 per cent compared to 4 per cent in non-rural areas, Australian Bureau of Statistics, 2012) due to a more limited historical contact with the English language. The impact of English on language loss will be discussed further in Chapter 3, but it is clear that settler colonization was a powerful channel in the spread of English around the world, replacing local languages in colonies far from English's geographic origins.

Channel 2: Slavery

This book, unlike others, treats the spread of English via the slave trade as a separate channel from colonization, even though the slave trade was a result of England's need for a workforce to develop newly acquired land resources in their new colonies. This is because, unlike settler colonies, where the English language spread into new areas of the world due to the migration of English language settlers from Britain, the slave trade elicited the spread of English through communities of displaced African populations from diverse linguistic backgrounds. For new slaves, the English language was used as a contact language for the purposes of communication but, for subsequent generations, this English became a first language. Therefore, slavery resulted in the emergence of English **pidgins** and **creoles**, which soon turned into native Englishes (a process that will be further examined in Chapter 2). The slave trade, therefore, spread English in vastly different ways than the migration of European communities via settler colonization. It also spread English in very different ways than the pidgins and creoles that developed as second languages in trade and exploitation colonies, discussed next.

Channel 3: Trade and exploitation colonies

In the third channel, English was spread throughout the world through international trade and British imposition on foreign lands. For areas where it was impractical or undesirable to establish full settlements or to claim territory, Britain aimed to control markets that would add to its trading power. This included the establishment of important ports along trade routes, such as in West Africa, as well as colonies in places such as Singapore and Hong Kong. It also saw heavy interest in India, evidenced by the early establishment of the East India trading company and Britain's heavy influence over India.

In some of these environments, English was a language used for the purposes of communicating for business and as a lingua franca for communities that had no other mutually **intelligible** language. For many involved in trade, English was used as a jargon, that is just enough vocabulary was known and used in order to complete business. If trade ceased, so, too, would the jargon. In places of more extended contact – usually through the establishment of British colonies, ports, or protectorates – the jargon developed into pidgins, extended pidgins (such as Tok Pisin, a superb example of English pidgin used widely throughout Papua New Guinea today), creoles (such as Sierra Leone Krio), or into Englishes (as in the case of Singaporean English and Indian English). In some countries, such as Singapore, the importance of English remained after British influence diminished, but in others, like Malaysia, other lingua francas, such as Bahasa Melayu, have taken over in terms of social importance and everyday use.

The important difference in the spread of English to places like these compared with those mentioned under the earlier heading of settler colonization is that, even though colonial control was often established and English was introduced as the language of administration and education, these were areas where few **native English speakers** settled, and thus English was mostly (but not always) used as an additional language to the local languages.

Summary

The historical spread of English was the direct result of the expansion of the British Empire to parts of the world through settler colonization, slavery, and trade and exploitation colonies. The spread caused the emergence of 'new' types of Englishes where English was in substantial contact with other languages, and linguistic difference was then further enhanced when colonies became independent (Strevens, 1992), or trading settlements increased or decreased in importance. The end of slavery also established formerly fringe varieties of English as eventual national languages (although, as Chapter 2 will explain, this was not an automatic process). An explanation of these varieties will be explored in later chapters (namely Chapters 2, 4, and 5), as will attitudes towards them (Chapter 8).

The fourth channel of globalization (discussed in the next section) occurred on the back of the first three channels, and was spurred on by the economic strength of the USA after the Second World War.

1c   Globalization and the rise of the world's lingua franca

The previous section outlined the historical spread of English to many parts of the world, causing English to become a native or second language of many communities. However, this historic account does not explain how English rose to be the world lingua franca it is today in countries as diverse as Japan, Denmark, and Thailand. A fourth channel of the spread of English has been the force of globalization, defined as the strengthening of worldwide interconnectedness in terms of society, culture, economy, politics, spirituality, and language (McIntyre, 2009). The strengthening of international connections through globalization saw the need to connect the world linguistically, and English filled this need. This section examines English's status as the world's first truly global language, before exploring the driving forces that placed it there.

English: a truly global language

Many lingua francas have existed in history and enjoyed their days of power and influence, such as Sanskrit, Arabic, Aramaic, Latin, and Greek. Despite their use as a lingua franca and their influence at the time, none of these were truly global languages. No matter where you travel around the globe today, English is heard often in daily use, especially in large cities. It has become part of the daily lives of many people from diverse linguistic and cultural backgrounds, and this is also true in countries where it is not a primary language but functions as either a second language or has a supranational function. For example, in many countries where English is not an official language, road signs are often written in both the local language and in English, shop fronts may have English signs, and several products in these shops also have English names. English has permeated into pop culture, resulting in English use in song lyrics, band names, and product marketing. It is used as the language of business, not only with foreign clients and colleagues but also as an official working language within the company itself. Further evidence of its rise to a truly global language is outlined in the box.

- 88 countries (60 sovereign and 28 non-sovereign states) give English official status (British Council, 2014).

- English is the language of international diplomacy and plays an official or working role in the proceedings of most major political gatherings, including the United Nations, the Association of South East Nations (**ASEAN**), and the European Union (EU).
- English is used as the working language in many international organizations. In Asia and the Pacific, about 90 per cent of international bodies carry out their proceedings entirely in English. 'The overriding assumption is that, wherever in the world an organisation is based, English is the chief auxiliary language' (Crystal, 2003, p. 89).
- English radio programmes are received by 150 million people in over 120 countries, and 100 million receive programmes from the BBC World Service (Crystal, 2008, p. 4).
- Some 75 per cent of the world's mail and the world's electronically stored information is in English (McArthur, 2002, p. 3).
- English dominates popular culture and the entertainment industry, and in 2002 over 80 per cent of feature films released in cinemas were in English (Crystal, 2003, p. 99).
- English is the lingua franca of air traffic control, airports, and civil aviation, and of hotels and shipping lanes.
- English is more widely taught as a foreign language than any other and is the foremost language of international scholarship (Coulmas, 2005).
- English is involved in more language-contact situations than any other language.
- English is now universal in many academic disciplines, workplaces, international communications, and publications, and the leading language of science, medicine, and technology.

As the statements in the box show, English is a truly global lingua franca, used for a varied range of activities across a varied range of contexts. The majority of English speakers have, for a long time now, been people who use it as a second (or additional) language, making it a language that has come into contact with a range of other languages and cultures like no other language before it.

Why English became the world's lingua franca

English as a lingua franca (ELF) on a worldwide scale is a relatively new phenomenon and, as Mauranen (2012, p. 3) points out, 'on this count, we are living in the first generation of ELF'. As discussed in Section 1b, the worldwide spread of English has continued from the early seventeenth century through different phases and for different reasons. Exploration, trade, and conquest were clearly important factors, but these alone are not sufficient to explain how English has become a world lingua franca. Portuguese, for example, is a language that was spread around the world in the fifteenth and sixteenth centuries by a dominant European trading nation. However, despite wide geographical distribution it is almost solely used as a mother tongue language by people in Portugal and Brazil, and not as a lingua franca for other populations. So why is English different? Why has English developed as a language used on a global scale?

Inherent linguistic qualities

Many people have speculated over the reasons why English has become the world's lingua franca, and many different explanations have been put forward. Some believe that it relates to its linguistic qualities, making it an easier language to learn, or its attractiveness, simplicity, and logical structure. For example, English has few complex grammatical endings and learners do not have to remember the difference between masculine, feminine, and neutral gender. As Section 1a illustrated, English also has a historically mixed vocabulary, derived from both Romance language and Germanic roots, which allows speakers of many language backgrounds to make associations. It can also be described as a flexible language (e.g. as a **borrowing** language, taking the names of ideas and things from other cultures it comes into contact with and expressing them in English; it has a great range of rules for the formation of new words). It welcomes new words, in contrast to other languages such as French, giving it a somewhat cosmopolitan character.

But do these characteristics have anything to do with its rise as a global lingua franca? Latin, with its many inflectional endings and gender differences, became an international language. French, with its masculine and feminine nouns, also achieved international status. Greek, Arabic, Spanish, and Russian, all with their inflectional endings, have also been widely used across linguistically diverse regions. In fact, the characteristics of English have little to do with the rise of English as a global language, and claims that it is easy to learn would be disputed by many English learners around the world. In fact, English grammar and syntax is actually rather complex, and language-internal qualities of English are not attributable to its spread.

Language-external factors

The main reasons for the spread of English via the fourth channel and its current status as the world's leading language are more to do with language-external factors. That is, the special position of English in a worldwide perspective is related to political/economic power and historical coincidence. By the mid-twentieth century, most of England's former colonies had become independent but many continued to use English for several internal purposes. Because of its colonial past, English was already in a good position to become a useful language for global business and trade, and it was the language of the leading economic power – the USA. Gramley (2012, p. 175) explains that 'this aspect of spread most likely runs parallel to, first, the rise of Britain and then the United States as the major global players from the late eighteenth century on.' At that time, the USA's population was larger than any of the countries in Western Europe, and its economy was the most productive and fastest growing in the world.

The modern spread of English was due not only to American economic and political power, but also to the volume of native English speakers from America, and the initial dominance of America at the time globalization forces gathered speed. With globalization came economic developments on a global scale, new communication technologies, the emergence of huge multinational organizations, a growth in competitive international business, increased power of the press to cross national boundaries, increasingly global popular culture, and increased mobility of the world's population. Globalization brought new linguistic opportunities and caused the need for a lingua franca for use in these diverse domains. English found itself in the midst of all of the changes and soon became the leading language. Therefore, it was simply a matter of the English language being 'in the right place at the right time' (Crystal, 2003, p. 78).

English speakers around the world

English speakers are commonly divided into three categories: **English as a native language (ENL)**, **English as a second language (ESL)** and **English as a foreign language (EFL)**. Speakers of ENL, also often called native English speakers (a concept problematized in Chapter 9) mainly include the populations of the UK, the USA, Canada, Australia, and New Zealand, which have been referred to as 'the traditional cultural and linguistic bases of English' (Kachru, 1992a, p. 356). ESL speakers come from former British colonies, such as India, Bangladesh, Nigeria, and Singapore. EFL speakers, who are on the rise, come from countries such as China and Japan, where traditionally English has no internal purposes and they historically learned English to use with native English speakers. This division is commonly used to refer to the worldwide distribution of English speakers, even though categorizing speakers is problematic (fully discussed in Section 1d). For example, many people defined as ESL speakers in fact speak English as a native language. Moreover, in EFL settings, as Chapter 6 will show, the English language has clearly become more than a mere 'foreign' language. Many people may not actively travel to a 'traditional' English-speaking country, but it is increasingly likely that they will need to write and carry out negotiations in English, particularly if they are working in the globalized business arena. Today, English is used to communicate with other **non-native English speakers** more than with native English speakers. Therefore, the term 'EFL' has become a bit of a misnomer, and these speakers would now be better described as 'speakers of ELF'.

Despite the problems with grouping speakers into overly simplistic categories such as this, and problems in finding reliable estimates of English speakers who fit within these categories, it is estimated that today:

- there are between 320–380 million people who speak English as a first language;
- there are between 300–500 million people who speak English as a second language;
- there are nearly one billion people who speak English as a foreign language, or as a lingua franca.

(Crystal, 2003, p. 61)

Because there is no single source of statistical information on language totals, Crystal used the UNESCO statistical yearbook, the *Encyclopaedia Britannica Yearbook*, Ethnologue: Languages of the World, and census data to calculate the above estimates. These figures are not uncontroversial and EFL estimates are particularly difficult to assess due to problems in identifying how to determine proficiency. For example, functional proficiency in English is low in populous Asian nations, such as China, Japan, Indonesia, and Vietnam, and therefore may give a false impression of actual English use in these regions (Gil, 2010). Today, more people are adding English to their linguistic repertoire and using English alongside one (or two, or more) other languages. The British Council has recently estimated that over 1 billion people are learning English worldwide, 750 million of whom are learners who are traditionally defined as EFL speakers (British Council, 2014). If this is the case, there are now more non–native English speakers than there are native English speakers – a gap that will increase as English continues to grow as a global lingua franca.

1d Representing English speakers

It is clear from the previous section that what makes English different from other lingua francas of the past is the sheer diversity of people using the language. As a result of such diversity, a number of attempts have been made to 'capture' and categorize English speakers through various models. These are, mostly, pluralist constructs that seek to capture the diversity in the English-speaking population. Several of these models are discussed in this section.

Strevens' World Map of English

One of the first attempts to categorize the world's English speakers was Strevens' World Map of English (Strevens, 1980 – see Figure 1.3). The aim of the upside-down tree diagram superimposed onto a world map is to highlight that the form of English by a certain group does not exist in a vacuum, but exhibits similarities with other varieties of English. It shows, for example, that West African English is more similar to the English spoken in East Africa than in Australia. It also aims to show that every variety of English is aligned with one of the two main branches of English (British or American), and to illustrate the historical and geographical relationships between them and their various 'children' in different parts of the world. The model, however, is quite America-centric in that it positions American English *with* British English, and does not represent the origins of American English *in* British English. Other Englishes, such as Irish English (which is much older than American English), are relegated to smaller branches, so historical representation is also somewhat confused. This model promotes a stereotype that American English and British English are somehow the fundamental central Englishes of the world (a notion that will be revisited in Section 2d on standard language ideology).

McArthur's Circle of World English

McArthur's Circle of World English (McArthur, 1987 – see Figure 1.4) places **World Standard English** at the centre, or 'hub', of the wheel. (Debate about the existence of a World Standard English will be discussed in subsequent chapters and returned to in the final chapter of this book.) In this model, the existence of regional varieties is highlighted, including both 'standard' and other forms, and then eight regions are represented by various spokes that encircle the hub. These include the standard and other forms of African English, American English, Canadian English, and Irish English. Beyond these, but linked to them by spokes marking off eight regions of the world, are the 'subvarieties', such as Aboriginal English, Inuit English, Ugandan English, and Singapore English.

While this is a tidy attempt at illustrating the world's Englishes based on geographic location, it is not indicative of the true historic, political, and linguistic ties that exist in

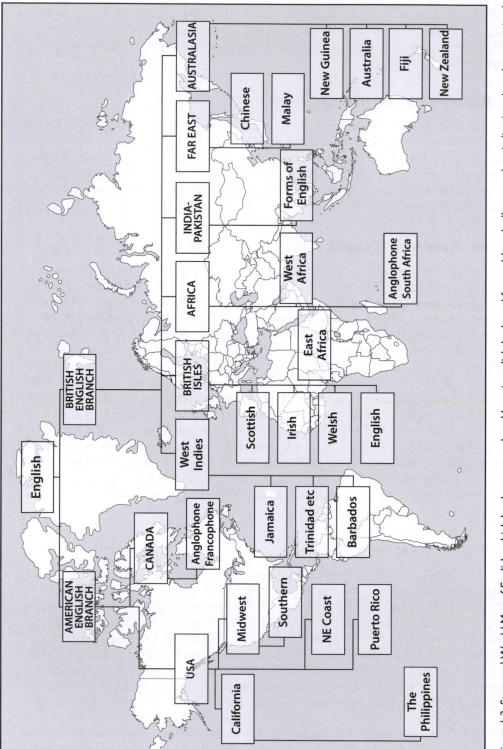

Figure 1.3 Strevens' World Map of English, which has been reproduced here in a slightly altered form, although all text and capitalizations have been retained. (For the original see Strevens, 1980, p. 86)

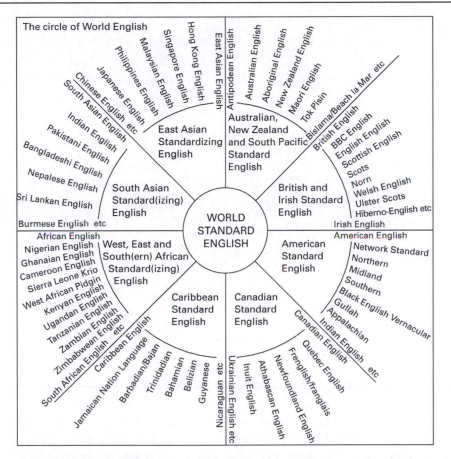

Figure 1.4 McArthur's Circle of World English (© Cambridge University Press, reproduced with permission)

the varieties of English represented. For example, Hong Kong English has much more in common historically, politically, and linguistically with British English than Japanese English, which is included in the same category. The same could be said for the Philippines, which is much closer to American English, due to its historical development, than to Chinese English.

Kachru's Three Circle Model

In Kachru's Three Circle Model (Kachru, 1992a – see Figure 1.5), varieties of English (or countries in which it is used) are presented as three overlapping circles (which were concentric circles in earlier diagrams) that are labelled 'Inner Circle', 'Outer Circle', and 'Expanding Circle'. This classification largely follows the categorisation of ENL, ESL, and EFL speakers respectively, as discussed in Section 1c. This classification dates back to a proposal by Barbara Strang in 1970, who labelled them as 'a', 'b', and 'c' speakers. This tripartite model was adopted and then developed further two years later by Randolph Quirk and his co-authors of the reference grammar of English book, *A Grammar of Contemporary English*, and by Manfred Görlach in several books in the 1990s. However,

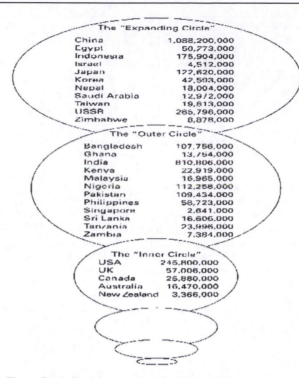

The "Expanding Circle"
China	1,088,200,000
Egypt	50,773,000
Indonesia	175,904,000
Israel	4,512,000
Japan	122,620,000
Korea	42,593,000
Nepal	18,004,000
Saudi Arabia	12,972,000
Taiwan	19,813,000
USSR	285,796,000
Zimbabwe	8,878,000

The "Outer Circle"
Bangladesh	107,756,000
Ghana	13,754,000
India	810,806,000
Kenya	22,919,000
Malaysia	16,965,000
Nigeria	112,258,000
Pakistan	109,434,000
Philippines	58,723,000
Singapore	2,641,000
Sri Lanka	16,606,000
Tanzania	23,996,000
Zambia	7,384,000

The "Inner Circle"
USA	245,800,000
UK	57,006,000
Canada	25,880,000
Australia	16,470,000
New Zealand	3,366,000

Figure 1.5 Kachru's Three Circle Model, reproduced with permission

instead of using Strang's letter categories, speakers were labelled as 'ENL', 'ESL', and 'EFL' speakers. Kachru (1985, p. 2) explains in an earlier publication that the Inner Circle is often viewed as 'norm-providing' in its projection of perceived norms of language use; the Outer Circle is 'norm-developing' in that **'New' Englishes** are developing their own norms independently from the Inner Circle; and the Expanding Circle is 'norm-dependent' in that it looks to the Inner Circle to provide such norms.

This model has been very influential in raising awareness of the existence of different Englishes, and the terms are commonly used. Yano (2001, p. 121) refers to it as the 'standard framework of World Englishes studies' and, in all current discussions around Global Englishes, this is probably the model that is most widely referred to. Thus in this book the terms 'Inner Circle', 'Outer Circle', and 'Expanding Circle' are also used. An updated version of this model is depicted (see Figure 1.6) with population data as of 2014. As with the original model, total national populations are shown as opposed to estimated numbers of English speakers.

Criticism of Kachru's model

Despite its usefulness and this book's conformity to Kachru's terminology, it is important to note that the model is severely flawed in a number of aspects. (For an overview of the criticism of the tripartite model see McArthur, 1998, pp. 43–46, and for an overview of criticisms of Kachru's model separately see Bruthiaux, 2003 and Jenkins, 2009.) The most prominent criticisms will each be discussed in turn.

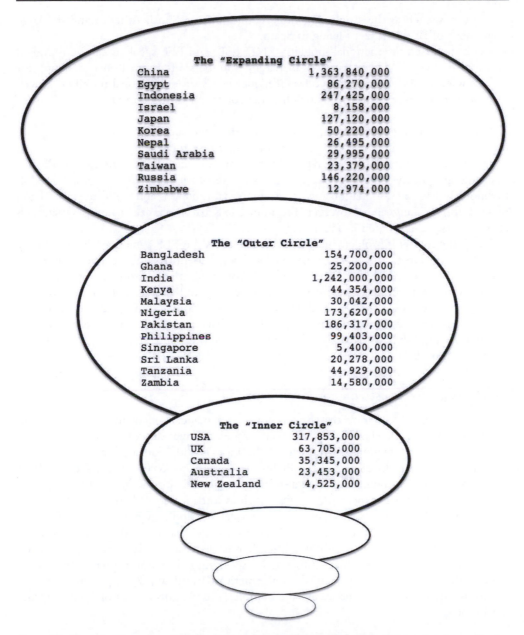

The "Expanding Circle"
China	1,363,840,000
Egypt	86,270,000
Indonesia	247,425,000
Israel	8,158,000
Japan	127,120,000
Korea	50,220,000
Nepal	26,495,000
Saudi Arabia	29,995,000
Taiwan	23,379,000
Russia	146,220,000
Zimbabwe	12,974,000

The "Outer Circle"
Bangladesh	154,700,000
Ghana	25,200,000
India	1,242,000,000
Kenya	44,354,000
Malaysia	30,042,000
Nigeria	173,620,000
Pakistan	186,317,000
Philippines	99,403,000
Singapore	5,400,000
Sri Lanka	20,278,000
Tanzania	44,929,000
Zambia	14,580,000

The "Inner Circle"
USA	317,853,000
UK	63,705,000
Canada	35,345,000
Australia	23,453,000
New Zealand	4,525,000

Figure 1.6 An updated version of Kachru's Three Circle Model of World Englishes using data reflecting estimated national population figures in 2014

THE MODEL OVERLY EMPHASIZES GEOGRAPHIC AND HISTORIC FACTORS

First, the tripartite model fails to account for those ENL speakers who live in ESL and EFL territories. For example:

- Large numbers of Anglo-Indians live in India and large numbers of British expatriates live in Hong Kong. Furthermore, there are also several ENL communities in EFL territories, such as the Anglo-Argentine community in South America and the large number of British citizens living in Spain.

• With increased international mobility, ENL, ESL, and EFL speakers can be found all over the world. There are also increasing numbers of international students, for example, in ENL countries, because of higher levels of international mobility, as well as increased desires to gain an English education in an ENL country.

Thus, by focusing on historical events rather than the sociolinguistic uses of English, the model does not give a realistic picture of English use today.

Second, the historical and geographical focus conceals the fact that the role of English is changing quickly in many Expanding Circle territories. In these regions, English traditionally had few intranational users, little internal function, and was often considered to be a foreign language. However, the model fails to emphasize that this situation is changing fast, as illustrated in Figure 1.7.

Third, the model is problematic when one considers the ELF paradigm, discussed fully in Chapter 7, due to the focus on nationally defined identities and varieties within the circles, without acknowledging the use of ELF both within and across these three circles or categories. Therefore, this 'superficially appealing and convenient model conceals more than it reveals' (Bruthiaux, 2003, p. 165). Pennycook (2007, p. 22) calls models of World Englishes an 'exclusionary paradigm' that 'does little more than pluralize monolithic English'. The topics of variety recognition and status are discussed in Chapters 2 and 5.

THE MODEL IS TOO FOCUSED ON COLONIAL HISTORY

The model fails to recognize that Britain also had a mandate in many countries not in Kachru's Outer Circle. For example, Britain occupied Egypt after 1882 and it officially became a British protectorate at the end of the First World War, a period much longer than the American colonization of the Philippines (Bruthiaux, 2003). Nevertheless, Egypt is placed in the Expanding Circle while the Philippines is placed in the Outer Circle. Britain also had a brief mandate in countries such as Jordan, Iraq, Palestine, and Kuwait.

Bruthiaux (2003) also points out that the model overlooks regions in countries that have heavy colonial influences, such as Cameroon, which has more than 6 million non-native English speakers. Furthermore, English represents a prestige language in many countries that were never subjected to English-speaking colonization, such as the multi-ethnic Ethiopia and various parts of Central America (Bruthiaux, 2003, p. 166). Colonial history is not sufficient to understand the complex sociolinguistic uses of English in the world today.

THE MODEL FAILS TO CAPTURE THE TRUE ROLE OF ENGLISH IN MULTI-ETHNIC AND MONOLINGUAL TERRITORIES

Kachru's three-way categorization also distracts from complex realities and fails to acknowledge the changing status of English in many regions over the last few decades. For example, Canada and South Africa are very multilingual, yet in this model they are categorized as ENL/Inner Circle speakers, ignoring the French Canadians and Zulu (among others). Strongly multilingual Nigeria, Mauritius, and Singapore use English in a

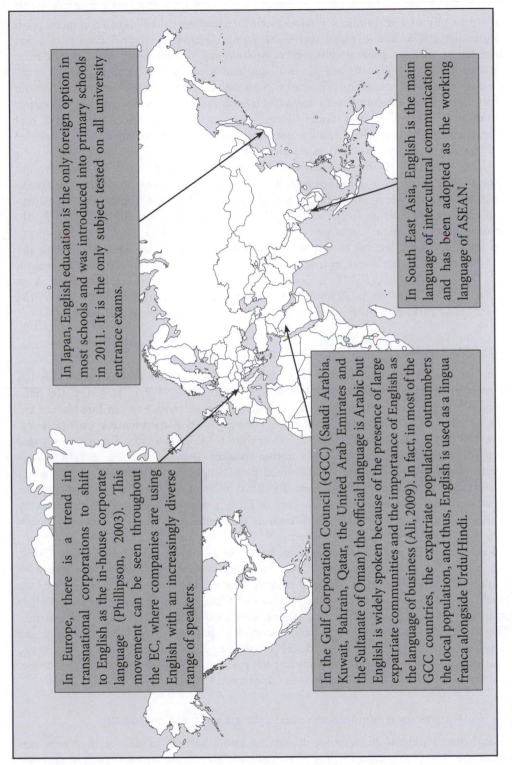

In Europe, there is a trend in transnational corporations to shift to English as the in-house corporate language (Phillipson, 2003). This movement can be seen throughout the EC, where companies are using English with an increasingly diverse range of speakers.

In Japan, English education is the only foreign option in most schools and was introduced into primary schools in 2011. It is the only subject tested on all university entrance exams.

In the Gulf Corporation Council (GCC) (Saudi Arabia, Kuwait, Bahrain, Qatar, the United Arab Emirates and the Sultanate of Oman) the official language is Arabic but English is widely spoken because of the presence of large expatriate communities and the importance of English as the language of business (Ali, 2009). In fact, in most of the GCC countries, the expatriate population outnumbers the local population, and thus, English is used as a lingua franca alongside Urdu/Hindi.

In South East Asia, English is the main language of intercultural communication and has been adopted as the working language of ASEAN.

Figure 1.7 English use around the globe

variety of official and unofficial roles in both international and internal communication (Bruthiaux, 2003). And in places such as Singapore speakers may speak English as a first language or, perhaps, grow up bilingual or multilingual. On the other hand, despite their colonial history, Bangladesh and Hong Kong tend to limit English internally for commercial, legal, and educational functions. South Africa meets all of the criteria for the Inner Circle, but English is only a native language for a minority of the population (Bruthiaux, 2003). Thus, the model conceals the fact that many Inner Circle/ENL territories are not homogeneous and are not 'ENL only', strictly speaking.

Canagarajah (2006a, p. 590) notes that 'diaspora communities have brought their Englishes physically to the neighbourhoods and doorsteps of American families' and elsewhere in migrant communities around the world. For example, 51 million Americans speak Spanish as their main language, according to the 2009 US Census Bureau American Community Survey. In the United Kingdom, many speakers speak Gaelic, Welsh, or one of several Asian languages as their first language. In fact, in 2013 Polish was reported to be the second most commonly spoken language in England, putting the 500,000 native Polish speakers ahead of Punjabi (273,000), Urdu (269,000), Bengali (221,000), and Gujarati (213,000), which account for 1 million speakers combined. A lot of the world is now bilingual, multilingual or translingual. Thus, the model ignores the co-existence of English with other languages in today's increasing globalized world.

THE MODEL ASSUMES A MONOLITHIC STANDARD

First, the model assesses proficiency using the Inner Circle as a **native–speaker yardstick** of measurement. Both Jenkins (2009, p. 20) and Bruthiaux (2003, p. 169) note the difficulty in using the model to define speakers in terms of their proficiency in English, and the lack of an attempt to differentiate between degrees of **communicative competence**. 'The fact that English is somebody's second or third language does not, in itself, imply that their competence is less than that of a **native speaker**' (Jenkins, 2009, p. 20). In this tripartite model, 'native-speakership' is defined by birthright and is assumed to be superior to a 'foreign' user, no matter how inept the native or adept the foreigner. In this sense, the tripartite model assumes a monolithic view of English, and English is seen as the property of the ENL speakers. This simplistic dichotomy between native and non-native speakers is controversial and is returned to in Chapter 9.

Kachru's (1985, p. 2) 'norm-providing' Inner Circle, 'norm-developing' Outer Circle, and 'norm-dependent' Expanding Circle has been criticized in light of the spread of English as a world language, where the native English speakers represent a minority. As Bruthiaux (2003, p. 162) points out, 'by over simplifying in this manner, the model offers an incomplete and potentially misleading representation of one of its major components.' The model also insufficiently represents variation within and across ENL countries, and gives the impression that Inner Circle/ENL/native English is a single variety of English, which Chapter 4 will illustrate is clearly not the case. Levels of variation within, and across, Kachru's three circles will be discussed in Chapters 2, 4, 5, and 6.

THE MODEL DISTRIBUTES PIDGINS AND CREOLES ACROSS ALL THREE CATEGORIES

English-based pidgins and creoles do not fit into Kachru's model, as they may run across the three categories. Pidgins and creoles are also found in ENL settings (e.g. the

Caribbean), they are also used in several ESL settings, such as in West Africa. As will be explored further in Chapter 2, pidgins and creoles are problematic; some people call them varieties of English and others call them separate languages, particularly creoles, due to their distinctiveness. Thus, they do not fit neatly into this simple three-way categorization.

SUMMARY OF CRITICISMS

Despite having an inclusionary political agenda in an attempt to have the 'New' Englishes acknowledged as varieties of English, the three circle model is, in effect, exclusionary. Canagarajah (1999a, p. 180), for example, states that, in Kachru's

> attempt to systematise the periphery variants, he has to standardise the language himself, leaving out many eccentric, hybrid forms of local Englishes as too unsystematic. In this, the Kachruvian paradigm follows the logic of prescriptive and elitist tendencies of the center linguists.

Kachru's model 'is a twentieth-century construct that has outlived its usefulness' (Bruthiaux, 2003, p. 161). English speakers do not fit nicely into one of the three circles and globalization, and its associated increased interconnectedness, has had a tremendous influence on how people communicate today, particularly true of ELF which does not fit neatly into the model at all. As Bruthiaux (2003, p. 175) states, 'much is to be gained by focusing less on where speakers of English come from and more on what they do – or don't do – with the language.'

Despite these problems, the three circle model has been very influential in raising awareness of varieties of English. The term *expanding*, for example, implies a process of growth. It also raises awareness of the notion of variety and opens up possibilities for research. The model is used with World Englishes scholars to challenge the predominance of native English and the Inner Circle, and to raise awareness of variations in English and issues of ownership, discussed more fully in Section 2d. Despite its limitations, 'This model has, thus, instilled increasing self-confidence in localized varieties of English and strongly influenced language teaching and applied linguistics in countries of Asia and Africa in particular' (Schneider, 2011, p. 32).

A note on alternative models

A number of alternative models have been proposed, including Görlach's Circle of International English (Görlach, 1990), and Modiano's Centripetal Circles of International English (Modiano, 1999a) and English as an International Language (EIL) (Modiano, 1999b), shown in Figures 1.8 and 1.9 respectively. Further information on Görlach's model in relation to other models can be found in Mesthrie and Bhatt (2008), but this model has not been discussed at length here due to the authors' assessment that it succumbs to the same criticism as McArthur's Circle of World English. A more detailed discussion of Modiano's model is outlined on this book's companion website.

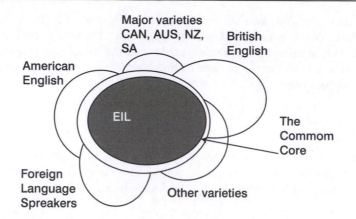

Figure 1.8 Modiano's Centripetal Circles of International English

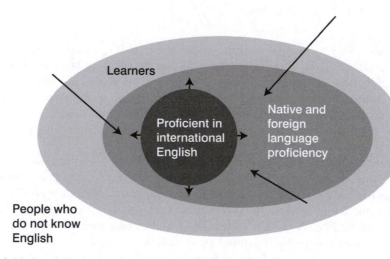

Figure 1.9 Modiano's English as an International Language (EIL)

Chapter summary

This chapter has outlined the spread of English from its roots in the Germanic languages spoken by the Anglo-Saxons 1,500 years ago to the global lingua franca it is today. The historical overview of English has shown that the one consistent element of English over time is that it is not a monolithic entity, but one that adapts and changes according to its surroundings. English has changed dramatically over the last ten centuries, since its emergence from the Old Norse-influenced Anglo-Saxon languages of the first millennium. Furthermore, history has shown other huge influences by later languages, such as Norman French.

This chapter has also investigated the more recent history of English's emergence from British imperial influences to becoming the world's foremost language and a global lingua franca. With the historical forces of mercantilism and the recent driving force of globalization, English has reached a position where it is spoken as a native, or second, language by more than 700 million people, and is a foreign language to more than one billion. Non-native speakers now outnumber native speakers, which has extraordinary implications for the ownership of English, a notion explored further in Chapter 2.

Due to the messy spread of English around the world via various channels, it has become increasingly difficult to categorize the world's speakers of English, as Section 1d has shown. While this book continues to use Kachru's Three Circle Model, the limitations of this model of categorization have been brought to the forefront. Difficulties of categorization and exceptions to these labels will be highlighted in further detail when the Englishes of the Inner Circle, Outer Circle, and Expanding Circle are outlined in Chapters 4, 5, and 6 respectively.

Further reading

On the history of the English language and its historical spread:

- McIntyre, D. (2009). *A History of English: A Resource Book for Students*. London: Routledge.

On the rise of English as a lingua franca:

- Crystal, D. (2003). *English as a Global Language*. Cambridge: Cambridge University Press.

On evaluations of models of World Englishes:

- Bruthiaux, P. (2003). 'Squaring the circles: issues in modeling English worldwide.' *International Journal of Applied Linguistics*, 13(2), pp. 159–78. doi: 10.1111/1473–4192.00042

Closing activities

Chapter discussion questions

Section 1a

1 Discuss the influences of German, French, and Latin on the English language. In what ways have other languages influenced the development of the modern English language?
2 Do you see any parallels between the influence of the printing press and the influence of modern communication technologies?
3 Describe the history of the language in a context you are familiar with. What were the influences that affected how it is spoken and written today?

Section 1b

1 What are the difficulties in categorizing the early spread of English around the world?
2 This section examined the early spread of English through colonization, slavery, and trade up until the nineteenth century. In what ways has English continued to spread since this time? What are the driving forces?
3 Describe the spread of another language you are familiar with. Where did it spread to and what were the driving forces behind its spread? Will it continue to spread in the future?

Section 1c

1 'Although the history of world English can be traced back 400 years, the current growth spurt in the language has a history of less than forty years' (Crystal, 1995, p. 110). What are the main reasons for the recent spread of English?
2 Some have argued that English has grown to be a worldwide language because of its language-internal features. Is English an 'easier' language to learn than other languages?
3 Although it is the pre-eminent world language of our time, English is far from being the only world language. Discuss the presence of other languages in the world.

Section 1d

1 What are the main criticisms of Kachru's Three Circle Model? Can you think of any other problems?
2 Canada, India, and the Netherlands have been called English-speaking countries. How would you explain the different status and role of English in these countries?
3 In what way has increased ELF usage on a worldwide basis made it even more difficult to categorize English speakers?

Debate topics

1 Although it is the pre-eminent world language of our time, English is far from being the only world language. Other world languages are just as important and influential, and could dethrone English in the future.
2 'The result of this rapid spread has meant that speakers of English, who learn and use it as an additional language to their own mother tongues, now considerably outnumber those who speak English as their L1 [first language]' (Alsagoff, 2012b, p. 109). Today, native English speakers are irrelevant.
3 Kachru's model of English speakers is the best we can make of organizing the messy spread and use of English.

 ## Writing and presentation prompts

Below are ideas for writing and presentation tasks to apply the knowledge learned in Chapter 1. Additional assignment prompts can be found on the companion website.

	Assignment topics
Personal account	We now have a global lingua franca with more non-native English speakers than native English speakers. Whether English is being used at an airport in London or Delhi, at a hotel in Tokyo, or on a Skype conference call between Hamburg and Beijing, everyone needs to communicate. Provide an account of your own personal encounters with English.
Research task (see website for worksheet)	Take a 200-word piece of English text from a source of your choice (such as a book, a newspaper, or a menu). Isolate all the nouns, verbs, and adjectives, and delete proper names and grammatical items. Using an etymology dictionary, look up the origin of each word and the time of its introduction to the English language. Present your findings using charts and graphs to highlight the influences of other languages on English.
Basic academic	English's global spread was not due to internal-linguistic properties of the language, but to external reasons. Discuss the special position of English worldwide in relation to political/economic power, as well as historical coincidence.
Advanced academic	When criticizing the tripartite model, McArthur (1998, pp. 43–46) points out that, 'It is, therefore, risky to classify a territory as ENL and leave it at that, the ENLhood of a place being no guarantee whatever of unhampered communication in English. There are, also, noticeable variations in "standard" English in many territories, most especially the UK and Australia.' What does he mean? What are the other problems?

Chapter 2

Language change and variation

 Introductory activities

The following introductory activities are designed to encourage the reader to think about the issues raised in this chapter before reading it.

Variation in English

Discussion questions

Some examples of variation in English are given in the box.

> • Hawaii: *mahalo* (thank you), *aloha* (hello/goodbye), *haole* (foreigner), *keiki* (children).
> • America: *sidewalk*; UK: *pavement*.
> • Australia: *outback* and *bush* (countryside), *barbie* (barbeque), *arvo* (afternoon).
> • India: *fifty students have applied for freeship this year* (tuition-free place).
> • ELF context: *we should not wake up any dogs* (let sleeping dogs lie) (Pitzl, 2009).

1 Why do you think English vocabulary is often different in different parts of the world?
2 What is the origin of the words in the box below? Do you know of any other examples? (Answers can be found in Section 2a.)

> passport, rucksack, coffee, mathematics, castle, skipper, cliché, shampoo, hamburger, pyjamas.

3 Lexical change does not only involve single words, but can involve longer phrases and idioms – *lucky money* or *red envelope* (the money given to children from their parents and grandparents as a New Year gift in Hong Kong) is an example. Are you familiar with any others?
4 How is variation in the Englishes around the world perceived?

Case study: English as a business lingua franca

On 22 March 1995, there appeared in *The Wall Street Journal* a feature article by Barry Newman. It was entitled 'Global chatter: the reality of "business English"', and its focus was on just how much business is done through 'broken English'. Commenting on the fact that more non-native English speakers use the language than native English speakers, he assumes that, 'They must have gotten the hang of it by now.' However, he refers to Satoshi Nishide, the managing director of Daihatsu Auto in Prague, who has studied English for ten years and been using it at work for nine, as an example of someone struggling to get 'the hang of it'. At Daihatsu in Prague, English is the only common language. One manager, Mr Moravec, noted that,

> If I don't understand very well, so I can expect what my boss want to say. We have special vocabulary ... If you hear two English person, they discussing their problem, it's other language than we use.

This 'language' is referred to as 'broken English', 'foreigner talk', 'Czechlish-Japlish', 'Auto-lish', and 'Daihat-Praglish'. The author then states that, 'The global chatter explosion, it seems, is blowing the language to smithereens.'

(Reprinted in *English Today*, 46(12), 2 April and cited in McArthur, 2002, p. 419)

Discussion

1 What do you think of Newman's assessment that the global chatter 'explosion' has 'blown the language to smithereens'?
2 What do you think of Moravec's description that their usage is different to native English speakers?
3 In your opinion, what language does Prague Daihatsu use: broken English, foreigner talk, Czechlish-Japlish, Auto-lish, Daihat-Praglish, or something else?

Introduction

Following on from Chapter 1, which discussed the development of English as a global lingua franca and how the language is used today, this chapter introduces language change, language variation, and standard **language ideology**, as well as the concepts of ownership and identity. It also briefly introduces the World Englishes and ELF. It begins with the various reasons why languages change, following on from the historical changes introduced in Section 1a. It is clear from Chapter 1 that English speakers are mostly bi- or multilingual people, coming into contact with a wide range of languages and cultures. This chapter also explores the influence of such contact on English. Section 2b provides an introduction to the various Englishes before they are examined in detail in Chapters 4, 5, and 6. This section also examines variation in language in terms of grammar, syntax, phonology, and vocabulary and idiom usage. Section 2c examines pidgins and creoles, looking at theories of how creoles developed, and their historical and changing place in the World Englishes paradigm. Finally, Section 2d looks at **language standardization** and the concepts of ownership and identity. The chapter will exemplify how variation in language is multidimensional, being influenced by social structure, geographical variation, and language contact.

2a Language change and contact

An inevitable consequence of the globalization of English documented in Chapter 1 has been linguistic change. English has taken root in many new territories, and today it consists of a myriad of **dialects**, **accents**, and **varieties**.

Language change

All languages are in a constant state of change, which can affect multiple facets including pronunciation, orthography, grammar, vocabulary, and **pragmatics** (language in use), examples of which are given in Section 2b. The rate of change can vary; it can be substantial or small, sudden or gradual, on one occasion or incremental. Chapter 1 highlighted that many changes to English have been incremental over a long period of time, termed diachronic change, and, because of changes in syntax and morphology over centuries, speakers of modern English have difficulty understanding Middle English and find Old English completely unintelligible.

The use of inflection in English, for instance, has reduced slowly over centuries, and the inflectional system of the present tense is now much simpler. For example, centuries ago the past tense of *work* was *wrought*, although this irregularity has been dropped and the past tense is now *worked*. The rule for forming plurals has also changed. In Old English, plurals were formed in many ways, for example the plural of *cwen* (meaning *queen*) was *cwene*, but *scip* (meaning *ships*) was *scipu*, and *hund* (meaning *dogs*) was *hundas*. However, around 1600 the choice of forming the past tense was made simpler, to mainly-(*e*)*s* and-(*e*)*n*. Regularizing the foreign plural systems has also occurred in English. For example, the plural of *formula* is *formulas*, not *formulae*, and *data* is now used more regularly as the singular and the plural rather than *datum is* and *data are*.

In discussions about the phases, or processes, through which change occurs, a distinction is usually made between **internally driven changes** from the language system (**endogenous**) and **externally driven changes** caused by the speakers (**exogenous**). Internal causes include things such as making optimal use of the available articulatory space, stabilization, regularization, and simplification, and giving distinct formal expression to distinct meanings. In addition to the grammatical simplifications discussed above, English has also undergone pronunciation changes. The Old English word *hlafordum*, for example, was very difficult to pronounce and was simplified to *lord*. In more recent years, change is also related to the difficulty some speakers with certain language backgrounds have pronouncing things like inflections, especially when they occur as **consonant clusters**, meaning that the third-person singular -*s* is often dropped in many of the 'New' Englishes, discussed in Section 2b.

Attitudes are also important as people have different attitudes to language change, and the desire to stop it has led to the notion of 'correct' or 'acceptable' and 'incorrect' or 'unacceptable' usage, further discussed in Section 2d as well as in subsequent chapters (particularly Chapter 8). Chapter 1 introduced the Great Vowel Shift, which resulted in some long vowels changing to **diphthongs** (two vowel sounds combined). For example, the word *time* was originally pronounced with a long vowel sound (similar to how many modern day speakers would say *team* [tiːm]), but this sound was replaced by a diphthong for many speakers, as in [taɪm].

Language change is closely related to social prestige and desirability, and therefore to identity. For example, some communities and their linguistic style may seem attractive to others, and may also be considered to be prestigious or correct, or even trendy. This is particularly the case with American English, discussed further in Chapter 4, where Englishes such as the then non-**rhotic** New York accent changed in the 1940s, when the rhotic accent was associated with prestige (see Labov, 1972). A rhotic accent is one where the /r/ is pronounced in all positions of a word (e.g. in *rat, tar*, and *tartan*), and a non-rhotic accent is one where /r/ is pronounced only when it precedes a vowel (e.g. in *rat*, but not in *tar* or *tartan*). In most accents, the /r/ is realized as the alveolar approximate [ɹ], as opposed to the trilled [r] in Scottish English accents. The change from a non-rhotic to rhotic accent in the case of New York clearly connects to communication **accommodation** theory, which involves the adaptation to an **interlocutor**'s communicative behaviour to help communication (Giles and Coupland, 1991). When speakers wish to increase the social proximity to their interlocutor, perhaps to ease communication, they often converge towards each other. On the other hand, when they want to do the opposite, perhaps to show authority in a particular situation, they may diverge, that is adapt their language to make it sound linguistically different. Giles and Powesland (1975) also discussed this in relation to the desire to be understood, and the accommodation theory also provides a good framework for analysing ELF talk, as discussed in Section 7b.

Language contact

Linguistic variation and change is the result of many factors, but one of the most influential factors is the degree of contact with speakers from different language backgrounds or speakers of a different dialect, and this is particularly the case with English. In addition to diachronic change, language contact can cause sudden periods of language change known as synchronic change, which results in the transference of words, sounds, and structures from one language to another. As discussed in Chapter 1, in some ways 'standard' English is a mixed language with Germanic origins but strong contact influences from French, Latin, Old Norse, and Celtic languages, and loan words from many other languages. For example, English syntax has been influenced by Celtic languages, such as in the use of continuous tenses which are absent in other Germanic languages. Examples of words that have been borrowed from other languages include: French (*army, nationalism, passport*); Latin (*agenda, March, September, mile*); Greek (*gymnasium, mathematics, democracy*); Old Norse (*sky, troll*); Norman (*castle*); Dutch (*skipper, keel*); Spanish (*guerrilla warfare*); Italian (*piano, balcony, umbrella*); Hindu/Urdu (*pyjamas, bungalow, shampoo*); German (*hamburger, rucksack*); and Arabic (*coffee, muslin*).

Language change also happens when new realities require description. The rise of science and empiricism, for example, led to the need to describe new terms which involved borrowing from other languages, for example Latin (*altitude*), Arabic (*alcohol, algebra*), and Greek (*diagonal*). New realities can include physical or social objects, the environment, cultural traditions, etc. Examples are provided in Section 2b. It is important to point out that it is often difficult to determine if an item is a loan word or a result of code-mixing or code-switching, which is common in multilingual settings.

- **Code-switching** occurs when multilingual speakers switch between different languages or varieties, e.g. Person A: 'Would you mind passing my sweater to me?' Person B: 'This one?' Person A: '*Iya. Sochhi.* [No. That one!]'
- **Code-mixing** is the transfer of linguistic items from one language into another in multilingual speech, usually within the phrase level, e.g. Person A: 'Pass my sweater, *onegaishimasu* [please].' Person B: '*Kochhi*? [This one?]' Person A: 'No. *Socchi!* [That one!]'
- Borrowing is when items from another language, or variety, might begin to be used with increased frequency and undergo some kind of assimilation into the new language.

More recent notions of translingual practice (see Preface) also add a further dimension to language use with others, blurring the borders between languages even further. Language contact can come in a range of intensity. 'Light, superficial contact' (Schneider, 2011, pp. 27–28), for example when one culture admires and is influenced by another, often leads to lexical borrowing. However, more intense contact, such as when a minority population lives in a majority's territory, may lead to changes in morphology and syntax. Intense contact can also result in the birth of new language systems with the emergence of pidgins and creoles, as introduced in Chapter 1, which are important examples of synchronic change through intense language contact.

Contact-induced change: the 'New' Englishes and World Englishes

Most languages are in contact with others, but English more than any other. It has now become customary to use the plural **Englishes**, and central to the World Englishes paradigm is acceptance of the fact that English is a dynamic, multifarious, and pluricentric entity. World Englishes scholars have focused on the investigation and description of various national varieties, which have been described in the areas of phonology, lexicon, syntax, pragmatics, discourse, and literary creativity, in order to identify characteristics distinct from native or '**standard**' norms, i.e. 'accepted' norms. Such attempts at **codification** provide a formal record of a variety, and thus are a significant process in legitimizing World Englishes' varieties.

What are often termed 'New' Englishes resulted from Channel 3 spread outlined in Chapter 1. 'New' Englishes have, therefore, been shaped by contact with the indigenous languages of the population where they became 'localized', or '**nativized**', by adopting some unique language features. (The use of the term 'nativized' has been debated and is discussed later in this section.) According to Platt, Weber and Lian (1984), these 'New' Englishes are far from uniform in their characteristics and current use, although they do share certain features. They usually developed through the education system in places where English was not the main language. In these postcolonial territories, English was, initially, only spoken by the colonizers. However, once schools were established and English was used as a medium of instruction, and as time went on, local English teachers were recruited who used varieties of English influenced by their mother tongue, the differences became more widespread.

Kachru discusses three phases that non-native, institutionalized varieties of English pass through, which are not mutually exclusive (Kachru, 1992a, p. 56). In the initial phase, there is 'non-recognition' of the local variety and conscious identification with native speakers. They are prejudiced against the local variety, seeing the native version as superior. After this, the local variety then exists side by side with the imported one, beginning to be used in a wide range of situations for varied purposes. However, it is still viewed as 'inferior'. In the third phase, the local variety becomes recognized as the norm, and becomes socially accepted and used as a model in education. 'New' Englishes are a prime example of contact-based language change. As colonial settlements increased, and when these nations subsequently became independent, these varieties became even more distinct.

Schneider's (2007) Dynamic Model of Postcolonial Englishes is another attempt to show the evolution of the 'New' Englishes in postcolonial territories and the various 'phases' they pass through. These include:

Phase 1   Foundation – English arrives;
Phase 2   **Exonormative** stabilization – extensive English usage, particularly amongst the native English-speaking settler community;
Phase 3   Nativization – the English used by native English speakers is used alongside a more indigenous one;
Phase 4   **Endonormative** stabilization – the indigenous variety takes root and becomes more widely accepted by the local community;
Phase 5   Differentiation – speakers of the indigenous variety take pride in their variety.

As with Kachru's model, we see the importance of local attitudes towards and acceptance of the local, indigenous variety. Schneider gives examples of varieties that have completed the 'cycle', including Australia, Canada, and New Zealand, and is a tidy attempt to show the similar historical path that many new varieties of English have taken.

The status of 'New' Englishes

In addition to the development of the 'New' Englishes, there is also a lot of debate on their status (see the Quirk/Kachru debate in Chapter 5). Widdowson (1997, p. 139) points out that English 'is not *distributed* as a set of established encoded forms, unchanged into different domains of use, but it is *spread* as a virtual language'. It is this virtual language (explained in Section 7b and in Figure 7.10) that has been spread. As he points out, 'The distribution of the actual language implies adoption and conformity. The spread of virtual language implies adaptation and non-conformity. The two processes are quite different' (p. 140). English is not a 'franchise language' (p. 140) and, as the language spreads, 'it gets adapted as the virtual language gets actualized in diverse ways, becomes subject to local constraints and controls' (p. 140). In discussing this variation, Widdowson discusses the emergence of language varieties and points out that Englishes across the globe have developed in different ways to those spoken in Inner Circle countries. In fact,

> They have sprung up in a relatively unplanned and expedient way in response to the immediate communicative needs of people in different communities with quite different ancestors. There is no comparable developmental continuity. The status of dialects in England as variant actualizations of the same virtual language is confirmed by their common history. To the extent that other varieties do not have such a history, one may hesitate to call them dialects.
>
> (Widdowson, 1997, p. 141)

Thus, Widdowson proposes that some varieties, e.g. Ghanaian and Nigerian English, should be seen as different languages. This raises the question of the status of the 'New' Englishes and whether they are varieties, Englishes, dialects, or languages.

Other scholars (e.g. Kirkpatrick, 2007; Mufwene, 2001; Schneider, 2003) argue that all varieties of English develop in similar ways. Varieties are seen to reflect the cultural realities of their speakers, as well as being adaptable enough for their speakers to engage in international communication. This highlights the problems with labelling the 'New' Englishes as 'nativized', due to such influence from local language and culture, unlike 'native' Inner Circle varieties which are not seen to have been influenced in such ways. Does classing British English as a 'native' variety ignore the existence of languages that preceded it, such as the Celtic language? Varieties of English are often classed as 'native' if they have been around for a long time and have influenced younger varieties of English in some way (Kirkpatrick, 2007). However, 'a long time' is rather vague, and British English pre-dates Australian English but they are both classified as being native. Indian English also pre-dates Australian English but is considered non-native. Kirkpatrick (2007, p. 6) suggests that a third criterion may relate to prejudice and one's image of a 'native speaker', a topic discussed in Section 2d and Chapter 9. He prefers to classify all varieties as 'nativized', since they have all been influenced by the local cultures and languages of the people who have developed the variety. Thus, varieties of British English are as nativized as varieties of Filipino English (Kirkpatrick, 2007, p. 7). The topic of status and ownership will also be revisited in Section 2d.

Variation in the Expanding Circle and ELF usage

It is also important to point out that, in addition to problems with terminology, the various Englishes of the world, whatever circle they belong to, are not internally uniform. While there is an abundance of literature describing the features of varieties of English, discussed in Chapters 4 and 5, and while it is necessary to document such characteristics in a book such as this, the contribution of ELF to the field cannot be ignored. English has also taken root in a number of Expanding Circle countries and, as a result of globalization, it is now used across all of the three circles in more fluid contexts.

While the World Englishes paradigm focuses on the identification of varieties of English in specific geographical regions, ELF researchers do not focus on such 'fixed' speech communities but examine how English is used in more virtual and transient contexts worldwide. English is viewed as a contact language, where 'both the community of speakers and the location can be changing and are often not associated with a specific nation' (Cogo and Dewey, 2012, p. 97), and speech communities are ever-changing. ELF research will be discussed at various points throughout this book, but it is clear that the Global Englishes paradigm (with its incorporation of ELF research) questions whether one can actually classify varieties of English at all.

2b   Levels of variation

English is tremendously varied at all levels of language, including spelling, grammar, vocabulary, phonetics/phonology, and pragmatics. More specific variation is discussed in subsequent chapters, but here we provide an introduction to variation in English. There is some debate over terminology and whether we should use the term 'language' or 'variety'. Hence, we begin with an examination of such terms.

Dialect, accent, variety or language?

When discussing language change and variation, the large number of terms can cause confusion. 'Dialect' denotes a geographical subdivision of a language form and is usually associated with a region ('regional-dialect'). However, in addition to regional distinctions, dialect variation can also be influenced by a number of factors including class, social group, ethnic group, age group, and gender.

For example, we can talk of a Welsh regional dialect, or an upper-class social dialect of British English. 'Accent' relates to pronunciation (the sounds speakers produce and other **prosodic** variation that accompanies sound), but dialect includes its grammar and vocabulary. However, the two often go hand in hand; if a person speaks in a regional dialect, such as Scottish, then their accent is also likely to be particular to that area. However, dialect often comes with negative connotations and, in addition to negative connotations, dialect cannot be used to describe the various Englishes worldwide. Thus, in this book, the more neutral term 'variety' is preferred to denote group-specific and region-based language forms.

'**Register**' is also important and refers to stylistically defined language varieties, or situational contexts, and is often associated with jobs. For example, we can talk of a spoken or written register, or context-specific registers such as in the medical and law professions.

Sounds

In terms of sounds, the Englishes of the world differ markedly from each other. Written English is not a good indicator of the sounds of the English language as it is not always easy to predict how a word is pronounced from its spelling. The same sounds are written using a variety of conventions, and many have no corresponding symbol in written English. The International Phonetic Alphabet (IPA) is a language-neutral system of phonetic symbols that has been developed to describe sound variation in a systematic and unambiguous way, and this will also be used here. A subset is provided for reference at the end of this book. In this table reference is made to **General American**, among others. However, this should not suggest that General American is a 'norm', as it is instead used as a convenient illustration of sounds as they are widely understood. Audio is provided on the companion website to this book to illustrate many of the examples in this section.

Phonemic variation

Most differences in the sounds of Englishes are related to the realization of vowels. For example, in terms of Inner Circle difference, there are many examples of **vowel mergers** and **splits**. In most British accents (except south-west England), the stressed vowel in *bother* and *lot* is an open back rounded vowel, symbolized as /ɒ/. This vowel is distinct from the open back unrounded long /ɑː/ in *father* and *palm*. However, in most varieties of English in North America no distinction is made, so that *bomb* and *balm* have identical pronunciations, and *bother* rhymes with *father* (Siegel, 2010, p. 14). Even within smaller regions mergers exist, such as the *buck–book* merger in some Englishes in the British Isles (e.g. found in Irish English, Scottish English, and Northern English accents), and the *Mary–merry–marry* merger in the USA (pervasive across North America but not in the north-east).

Variation also exists in the Outer Circle and the Expanding Circle. An example is the *trap–strut* vowel merger, characteristic of Caribbean varieties (though both are also found in Africa and elsewhere). In the Outer Circle and Expanding Circle, Kachru and Smith (2008, p. 81) point out that many varieties simplify the diphthongs of the many Inner Circle varieties, e.g. /eɪ/ to [eː] in *paid* and /əʊ/ to [ɔː] in *boat*. Here, 'simplification' refers to the realization of a complex vowel articulation [eɪ] in *paid* (in which the vowel quality changes from the first to the second vocalic component) to a single elongated vowel such as [eː]. In many African Englishes (e.g. in Kenya) and Asian Englishes (e.g. the Philippines) there is no difference between the vowels of *bit* (/ɪ/) and *beat* (/iː/) (Schneider, 2011, p. 20).

Individual consonants are also pronounced differently by speakers of English throughout the world. In America, for example, the /t/ in word medial position often sounds like a [d] in words like *butter* and *little*, and in India it may not be aspirated and is frequently realized as **retroflex**. Kachru and Smith (2008, pp. 80–81) note that the voiceless **plosives** /p t k/ lose their aspiration when realized word-initially before a vowel (e.g. *pike*, *time*, *kite*) so that the speakers of Inner Circle varieties often perceive them as /b d g/. In Singaporean-Malaysian English, /b/, /d/, and /g/ are often devoiced in the final position of a word. Thus, words such as *pig* and *pick* may not be differentiated as much as in other varieties. In many varieties of English, the **phonemes** /θ/ and /ð/ (as in *think*, *they*) are realized differently. For example, they can be realized as **dental fricatives** (with the tongue between the teeth) [θ] and [ð], as **alveolar plosives** (as in [t] and [d], producing *tink* and *dey*), or as **labiodental fricatives** (as in [f], producing *fink* and [v] in place of [ð] in the middle or end of words like *smooth,* producing *smoov*). In addition, several speakers of African Englishes (e.g. Zambian) and in the Expanding Circle (e.g. Japan) do not distinguish between /r/ and /l/, and these may be substituted for each other freely. Thus, *flight* and *fright*, or *rice* and *lice*, may sound similar.

In fact, many 'New' Englishes operate on a smaller set of vowels than 'native' Englishes, leading many to describe them as reductive and 'simpler'. However, there are numerous cases where the phonemic inventory of 'New' Englishes includes sounds not found in accents like **Received Pronunciation (RP)** and General American (such as retroflex sounds in Indian English, e.g. [ʈ]), thus 'New' Englishes could as easily be deemed as richer and more complex by this same logic.

Prosodic variation

Variation also exists in the domains beyond individual segments/sounds, such as the syllable and the utterance, in relation to prosodic (suprasegmental) features. For example, Japanese speakers adapt foreign loan words to the sound structure of their native language by adding epenthetic vowels to consonant clusters (e.g. *sutopu* [stop] and *aisukurimu* [ice cream]). The addition of vowels to consonant clusters is also found in Inner Circle varieties, such as the Scottish and Irish English pronunciation of *film*, where an extra vowel is added in order to pronounce the consonant cluster (making it sound more like *fillum*).

Wells (1999, p. 91) points out that certain British accents, including Birmingham, Liverpool, Newcastle, and Glasgow, have some tendency to use **rising tones**, where most other accents have falling tones. In Australian English there is also a tendency to use rising pitch contours in declaratives and *wh*-questions (*who?*, *what?*, *where?*, *when?*, *why?*), whereas most other accents have falling pitch. In Irish English, the tendency appears to be to prefer falling pitch contours in all communicative types.

Shifts in lexical stress patterns and rhythmic organization of speech may also occur. In Outer Circle and Expanding Circle varieties of English, lexical stress placement is often different to Inner Circle varieties, for example *suc*cess for suc*cess* in Nigeria (Kachru and Smith, 2008, p. 74). In other Englishes, stress may not be used to differentiate between verb and noun forms of words, such as *con*duct (noun) and con*duct* (verb).

Many 'New' Englishes are characterized by perceptually syllable-timed speech, whereas Inner Circle varieties are perceptually stress-timed. In syllable-timed English, the rhythm of speech can be likened to a machine gun, where syllables are perceived as occurring at equal intervals of time. On the other hand, the rhythmic pattern of stress-timed speech can be likened to Morse code, where stressed syllables are perceptually evenly spaced, regardless of the number of unstressed syllables between them. It will become clear in Chapters 5 and 6 how Outer Circle and Expanding Circle varieties of English do not utilize stress in the same way as Inner Circle speakers. Research carried out into phonology in the ELF paradigm will be discussed in Chapter 7.

Vocabulary

Lexical variation, and word choice and usage are commonly known differences in the Englishes of the world. Some examples include the following.

- **Variety-specific compounds**, such as *salary man* (company employee) in Japan.
- **Same meaning, different words**, such as *jumper* in the UK and *sweater* in North America.
- **Conversion**, a shift of a word class with retention of meaning, such as *off* meaning *to switch off* in West Africa (Melchers and Shaw, 2011, p. 24).
- **Semantic extension**, where terms are assigned new meanings in addition to their original one – for example in Malawi the verb *to move* takes on various meanings, e.g. *Suzagao is moving with my cousin* (dating) or *He is moving with bad boys* (socializing) (Kamwangamalu, 2001, p. 57).
- **Semantic narrowing**, where words take on a more restricted meaning, such as in Middle English where a *girl* was a young person of either sex, but now only refers to a female.
- **Compounding/specialized meaning**, where new words are formed by compounding or giving a specialized meaning to a combination of words – e.g. in South Africa the end of apartheid led to the creation of compound *rainbow x,* referring to either 'the coming together of people from previously racially segregated groups' or 'something that affects or benefits these people', resulting in compound nouns such as *rainbow nation*, *rainbow swimming pool*, *rainbow gathering*, *rainbow school* etc. (Kamwangamalu, 2001, p. 54).
- **Derivation**, where new words are created by adding prefixes or suffixes to an old one, such as in Ghana where *enstool* and *destool* are used, since a king sits on a *stool* not a *throne* (Jenkins, 2009b, p. 30).

- Abbreviation, where words are shortened, such as *afternoon* to *arvo* and *barbeque* to *barbie* in Australia.
- **Blending**, where parts of words are combined, such as *distripark* (a distribution park or a warehouse complex) in Singapore.
- Acronyms, such as *MC* (medical certificate) in Singapore and Malaysia.
- **Coinages**, where new words are formed such as *killer litter* (rubbish discarded from high-rises which may end up killing someone by accident) in Singapore.
- Borrowing, where words are taken from another language to describe new phenomena, local environments, or culture (as discussed in Section 2a), especially in newly settled areas – examples include:
  - physical landscape, e.g. to name places, rivers, mountains, flora, and fauna;
  - physical objects, e.g. *boomerang* in Australia;
  - food, e.g. *sushi* (Japan), *vodka* (Russia), *pizza* (Italy), and *alcohol* (Arabic);
  - clothing, e.g. *sarong* (Malaysia) and *sari* (India);
  - social standing and customs, e.g. *Nawabs* (Pakistan – an Indian ruler during Mogul empires) and *Sahib* (Pakistan – used to address a man, especially one with some status);
  - animals, e.g. *kangaroo* in Australia;
  - cultural traditions, e.g. *Melas* (Pakistan – a cultural festival).
- Variety-specific compounds and derivatives, e.g. *sheep station* (New Zealand), *careers master* (Kenya), and *democrator* (India). (Schneider, 2011, p. 24)

It is important to point out that, when words are borrowed, they often gradually change to fit the phonological and morphological structure of the borrowing language (e.g. the plural of *pizza* is *pizze* in Italian, but *pizzas* in English). Borrowed terms also result in **hybrid forms** that are a combination of English and borrowed terms, such as *lathi-charge* (a charge by the police with batons) in India.

Vocabulary differences do not only include individual words, but also phrases and idioms. Some examples include **locally coined idioms** and word-by-word translations of indigenous phrases. The term *long legs* is used in West Africa, meaning to have influence in high places (Melchers and Shaw, 2011, p. 25), while *to shake legs* in Malaysia, coming from the Malay idiom *goyang kaki*, means 'to be idle' (Jenkins, 2003, p. 27). There is also variation in the use of native English-speaker idioms (e.g. *to eat your cake and have it* in Singapore, instead of the British *to have your cake and eat it* (Jenkins, 2009b, p. 27)). In relation to ELF research, Pitzl (2009) shows how idioms are expressed rather differently and how speakers coin idiomatic language that has gone through what she calls **re-metaphorization** (Seidlhofer and Widdowson, 2009). This research is important, especially as she shows how such usage does not inhibit, and may even enhance, communicative ability. One example of such innovative metaphorical use of language is *we should not wake up any dogs* [let sleeping dogs lie].

Spelling

As discussed in Chapter 1, the process of standardization in English spelling was greatly influenced by the printing revolution and the spread of English dictionaries. This was further influenced by the American lexicographer, Noah Webster, who proposed an

Table 2.1 Differences in British and American spelling

American	British
Center	Centre
Traveling	Travelling
Favor	Favour
Defense	Defence

'American Standard' in 1789, and today there are many differences between British and American spellings, shown in Table 2.1.

However, despite these well-known differences, most published written texts, at least those published in 'standard' English, exhibit little variation in spelling. However, Melchers and Shaw (2011, p. 15) point out that, 'In some transported Englishes, especially Canadian English, which is generally characterised by conflicting loyalties, that is to Britain vs. the USA, there is great variability in spelling, and usage varies for regional, social and political reasons.' English-based pidgins and creoles, discussed in Section 2c, also often do not have standardized orthographies (Romaine, 1988, p. 111).

Grammar/syntactic variation

Variation also exists in grammar (or syntax), and differences include the following.

- **Subtractive differences** – for example, in the Caribbean speakers often omit their verbal *-s* endings, as in *he go* (Schneider, 2011, p. 24). This is also a common feature of ELF usage, for example *he sing* instead of *he sings* (Seidlhofer, 2005, p. 92).
- **Additive differences** – where many Outer Circle and Expanding Circle speakers turn uncountable nouns into countable ones (e.g. *informations, staffs*). Once again, this is a common feature of ELF usage.
- **Tense and aspect** – where speakers use different forms. For example, where Americans may use the simple past tense *Did you eat yet?*, British speakers may use the present perfect *Have you eaten?* Similarly, Indian English speakers may use the present continuous or progressive *I am knowing very well*, while British speakers may use the present simple *I know very well* (Kirkpatrick, 2007, p. 23).
- **Question formation** – where patterns may be used differently. For example, tag questions like *He is coming, isn't it?* are found in some contexts (e.g. India). This is also common in ELF usage (see Seidlhofer, 2005, p. 92).
- **Article omission** – for example, *He is very good person* is common in Outer Circle and Expanding Circle varieties, and is also a common feature of ELF conversations.
- **Concord with collective nouns** – for example *the government is/are*. Melchers and Shaw (2011, p. 23) note that 'the plural is used much less frequently in American English than in English English'.
- **Use of auxiliaries** – for example variation in the use of *shall* and *should* with first-person subjects and the development of new auxiliaries, e.g. *gotta* (Melchers and Shaw, 2011, p. 24).
- **Levelling of irregular verb forms** – for example, in America *spoiled* is used for the past tense instead of *spoilt* in the UK.

Pragmatics

It is also important to point out differences in pragmatics, which involves how language is used and conventions on how to behave. For example, greetings and address vary (e.g. in some Asian countries, people may greet you by asking *Have you eaten?*). Non-verbal communication also varies, such as Indians signal *yes* by nodding their head sideways, which is often mistaken for a *no* elsewhere. Conventions of formality also vary.

Intelligibility

There is clearly a lot of variation in English, leading many people to worry that speakers will not be able to communicate with each other. Concern over such variation is inevitable and will be discussed further in subsequent chapters. However, it is important not to forget that English speakers have for hundreds of years spoken varieties that have been mutually unintelligible (for example, review the excerpt from Caxton in Chapter 1). There is no evidence to suggest that variation today is any greater to that of the past; thus we need to raise awareness that deviations from 'the standard' are natural and normal. Chapters 4, 5, 6, and 7 will provide further descriptions in relation to the Inner Circle, Outer Circle, Expanding Circle, and ELF usage, highlighting further diversity in how ELF speakers use adaptive accommodation skills and employ various strategies to achieve communication. However, a purely linguistic description is insufficient, and attitudes towards such change will be explored in Chapter 8.

2c Pidgins and creoles

Pidgins and creoles arise in situations where two communities of people do not speak a common, mutually intelligible language. A pidgin is usually defined as a language that emerges in situations where a simple language is needed to communicate between the two communities. Singh (2000) outlines a misconception of a pidgin as a 'broken' English, where two people speak a language that is not their own and thus the language used follows no structural or grammatical rules. While pidgin English is 'one outcome of language contact between speakers of different languages who need to communicate', Singh states that 'a lack of linguistic structure is not a characteristic of pidgin' (Singh, 2000, p. 2).

The distinction between a pidgin and a creole lies in the usage of the language. A creole usually develops via a generation of speakers for whom the contact language is a first and primary language of communication. As a result, the language develops more grammar and vocabulary, forming a complete working creole. The process of language development from a contact language to a creole is called **creolization**. Depending on the environment in which the language is used, creolization might be as short as a single generation of speakers, or be developed slowly from a pidgin over decades of use. Sometimes, a pidgin might never move beyond an **extended pidgin**, lacking the grammatical and lexical complexity and stability to be defined as a creole.

The world's English pidgins and creoles

English pidgins and creoles can be found worldwide, but are mostly concentrated in the Caribbean, along the west coast of Africa, and, to a lesser extent, in Australasia.

Most history divides the world's creoles (and pidgins) into two categories based on their historical origin: **fort creoles** and **plantation creoles**. An English fort creole is typical of those found in regions where English was the contact language used for communication with local communities who traded with, worked for, or were colonized by English speakers. Most of the world's fort creoles can be found along the west coast of Africa – an important and historical shipping and trade route that caused the need for English to be used as a contact language with communities of people living and stationed along these routes. An English plantation creole is typical of those found in the Caribbean and Central America. These creoles developed through the mass-displacement of slaves into New World plantations in the area. English was the contact language between the African slaves and the English-speaking masters.

The fundamental difference between a fort creole and a planation creole is that the plantation creole quickly developed into a first language in these communities, as it was not only used between slaves and their masters but as a lingua franca within the community itself, which had been displaced from linguistically diverse regions of Africa. Members of these displaced communities had less contact with the minority of Europeans who spoke the language, and creolization occurred without passing through a stage of a pidgin. On the other hand, fort creoles were developed in closer proximity to Europe and served as a lingua franca for communication (alongside other languages). The fort creoles of West Africa involved English being imposed on groups of people for trade purposes and during colonization, resulting in the language being 'diluted' into the local communities very quickly, and 'indigenous people in fort situations became Europeanised to varying degrees' (Gramley, 2012, p. 216).

Characteristics of pidgins and creoles

Even though pidgins and creoles developed around the world in very diverse situations, there are some characteristics that most of the world's pidgins and creoles share. It is the similarities more than the differences between the world's pidgins and creoles that continue to fascinate linguists today, unlike varieties of English where differences attract attention. According to McIntyre (2009), one key precursor to the emergence of a pidgin is the existence of a **superstrate language** and a **substrate language**. A superstrate language is usually the contact language, or imposed language, such as the English language along coastal trading routes of West Africa or plantations in the Caribbean. The substrate language is the local language, such as the West African languages spoken along these trading routes and the numerous African languages on the plantations.

A key feature of a pidgin is the simplification of grammatical features of the superstrate language, such as verb irregularities (*throwed* instead of *threw*) and superfluous grammatical

Table 2.2 Sranan Tongo Creole

Sranan Tongo Creole	Literal meaning	Meaning
Wrokoman	Work + man	Worker
Wakaman	Walk + man	Drifter
Wrokosani	Work + thing	Tool

features, such as the third-person 's' (*she say* instead of *she says*). In addition, the word order may also be simplified, such as *You see her?* instead of *Did you see her?* (Sebba, 1997, p. 54). Morphological simplification is also a recurring feature of pidgins, as too is vocabulary reduction (Singh, 2000), such as in the case of Sranan Tongo Creole, as illustrated by Sebba (1997, p. 50) (see Table 2.2).

The example below is taken from Winford (2008, p. 416) and illustrates the grammatical and morphological structure of Belize Creole English (BCE).

> *A don gat evriting redi, inoo, mis B.*
> I already have everything ready, you know, Miss B.
> *I mi gat plees op ya we me an hi mi liv.*
> There was a place up here where he and I lived.

In these examples, we can see grammatical simplification of verb tenses in the verb *gat* [get], being modified by additional words *don* [completive preverbal marker] and *mi* [past tense marker], rather than the original verb conjugation in English [have gotten].

How did pidgins and creoles develop?

There is very little documentation on the development of historical pidgins and creoles and, as such, little is known regarding how they developed. For example, it is still debated whether many creoles developed out of pidgins, or via separate processes due to the unique circumstances of the language contact. Nevertheless, there have been a number of theories regarding the origins of creoles, three of which are outlined below.

Theory 1: Influence of the superstrate language via 'baby-talk'

This theory dates back to the nineteenth century French observations of creoles (Mufwene, 2008), arguing that the grammatical simplification of pidgins and subsequent creoles was due to the original simplification of the language by those introducing it in contact language situations. That is, the European traders, for example, used grammatically reduced forms to communicate with locals. There was a view that African languages were more 'primitive' than European languages, and thus simplification was necessary to communicate, hence the 'baby-talk' tag attached to this theory (Mufwene, 2008).

Theory 2: Parallel development of the substrate and superstrate language

In the development of a pidgin, the substrate language usually provides the grammatical structure, while the superstrate language usually provides the vocabulary of the resulting pidgin (McIntyre, 2009). However, this mixing of the two languages is not so black and white, because numerous cases have shown vocabulary of the substrate to also be incorporated into the pidgin. Winford (2008, p. 414) gives some examples of vocabulary in West African substrate languages found throughout creoles in the Caribbean, such as *bakra* (white man) and *nyam* (eat). Furthermore, analysis of pidgins and creoles usually shows a heavy influence of substrate languages. For example, Gramley (2012, p. 230) argues that, even though 'no African language survived more than two or three generations in the New World ... language influence is said to be present in underlying structures'. Mufwene (2008) argues it is an obvious phenomenon that African languages influenced the structures of new Creole languages, but this does not detract from the influence of the superstrate language, which is also obvious.

Theory 3: The effect of universal grammar

Theories of universal grammar have been used to explain children's innate ability to master language that is too structurally complex to learn through limited input and imitation alone. According to the theory, a child makes sense of a language through a universal understanding of grammar, which is why it is common to hear children say the following, despite never hearing them: *sawed* instead of *seen*, and *foots* instead of *feet*. A universal grammar theory sees the development of a creole as affected by humans' innate understanding of language universals. Gramley (2012) argues that these phenomena can be observed more clearly in creoles that emerged very quickly, sometimes within a single generation. However, Mufwene (2008) questions this theory on a number of factors – the most pertinent, perhaps, is his observation that some pidgins, which developed over long periods of time in more naturalistic second-language acquisition environments, have a lot in common with creoles that were abruptly developed in a generation.

De-creolization and attitudes to creoles

If a creole develops in a way that it loses those characteristics that defines it as a creole, it can be said to undergo **de–creolization**. Because of a mistaken view of pidgins and creoles as 'broken English', there has been a push in the education systems of creole communities to promote 'standard' English, which is viewed as 'correct'. This is a further example of how attitudes towards language and the notions of prestige discussed in Section 2a can influence language change. It is also an example of the importance of prejudiced attitudes towards 'native' and 'nativized' varieties discussed in Section 2b.

Singh (2000) outlines real examples of recent changes in policy in the creole communities, which pushed for the use of 'standard' English in schools and governance but have more recently adopted a more open stance. While early policy tried to 'fix' creole Englishes, recent policies take a much more positive view of creoles and encourage them to be embraced and recognized as languages in their own right. In Caribbean communities, for example, the creoles spoken are much more positively viewed as symbols of national identity and pride than they were in the past. Winford (2008, p. 419) states,

> Changes in attitudes have been due to several factors: the growing sense of nationalism in these communities since independence; the emergence of a substantial body of scholarship that demonstrates the validity of the creoles as languages in their own right; the growing tendency to use creole in literary works; and the readiness of the powers-that-be to allow use of creole in contexts such as education.

This movement in scholarship towards the recognition and value of variation in English is the topic of much of this book. A linguistic description of Caribbean creoles is discussed in Chapter 4, and those found in other parts of world in Chapter 5. Attitudes toward 'standard' and 'non–standard' Englishes will be revisited in Chapter 8.

2d Standard language ideology, ownership, and identity

Thus far, this chapter has highlighted the linguistic variation and change in English. This final section examines standard language ideology that has emerged in reaction to the variation and change. Despite the fact that English has changed over the years, often in an unregulated and haphazard way, it is also tightly regulated. According to Seargeant (2009, p. 26), 'Language ideology can be defined, in broad terms, as the structured and consequential ways we think about language', and standard language ideology thus relates to the way society thinks about language standards. As Chapters 1 and 2 thus far have shown, the global spread of English gave rise to a wide variety of Englishes, and debate and argument for and against there being a 'standard' English has grown.

Standard language ideology in ENL countries

The belief in the existence of a 'standard' English, and the promotion of standardization towards this 'ideal' language, is deeply rooted in history. In fact, there is a record of very early attempts to standardize language during the reign of King Alfred (849–901), when policies aimed at making West Saxon English the official language of the court, education, and scholarship (Nevalainen and van Ostade, 2006). West Saxon began to permeate other regions of England both in its written form and through the prestige associated with its spoken form. The next movement of language standardization came centuries later, with the establishment and promotion of the Chancery Standard (outlined in Chapter 1), coupled with the impact of the printing press, which helped sow the seeds of an ideology of a standard written English.

The first target of language regulation was spelling and, in pursuit of consistency, printing houses sought spelling standardization. The first dictionaries of English came at the turn of the eighteenth century, soon followed by books of prescribed grammar usage aiming to establish a set norms of 'standard' English. To this day, American and British versions of prescribed spelling and grammar conventions differ because of different conventions chosen in the publication of these early dictionaries in each nation, namely Samuel Johnson's (1755) *A Dictionary of the English Language* and Noah Webster's (1828) *American Dictionary of the English Language*. In other parts of the Inner Circle, it is important to note, codification of English and prescription of grammar usage in books was not the only means of language standardization, and standard language ideology also emerged through accepted usage. As Kachru and Smith (2008, p. 3) explain:

> Codification is not a prerequisite for legitimizing a language. For instance, Australians spoke Australian English for years before a dictionary of Australian English (*The Macquarie Dictionary*, 1981) was compiled and a grammatical description of Australian English (Collins and Blair, 1989) appeared.

In terms of vocabulary standardization, even the first dictionaries recognized that the English language was always changing, and thus that the dictionary would not be an ever lasting account of English (see Samuel Johnson's dictionary of 1755, for example).

However, this did not stop some people from advocating the standardization of voca-bulary, such as author Jonathan Swift who wrote 'A Proposal for Correcting, Improving and Ascertaining the English Tongue' (1712) in which he purported the value in 'fixing' English, and stopping the flow of vocabulary in and out of the English language (see the companion website for a case study of Swift). However, Swift's proposal is not unique to history, as Milroy (2007, p. 138) writes, 'there is usually a tradition of popular complaint about language, bewailing the low quality of general usage and claiming that the lan-guage is degenerating'. This notion certainly rings true today.

Nevalainen and van Ostade (2006, p. 275) write, 'For a long time, the history of standard English is, indeed, a history of standard written English.' Indeed, ideology of a 'standard' English is more concretely associated with grammatical forms in *written* English than with spoken forms, or vocabulary usage, which stayed regionally and socially contained. However, the establishment of compulsory schooling in the UK facilitated increased contact between the wealthier and the middle classes, which caused the emergence of a desirable wealthy accent. Eventually this accent was referred to as RP, in which 'received' pronunciation referred to the 'accepted' pronunciation. With the introduction of radio and the founding of the British Broadcasting Company in 1921, RP became even more prevalent as the 'standard'. McIntyre (2009, p. 29) writes that 'the prestige associated with it [RP] led to many people adapting their own accents (either consciously or subconsciously), in order to avoid the stigma that was increasingly associated with regional pronunciations.' The attraction to RP even extended beyond the borders of the UK, to the point that RP still holds prestige in most of the Expanding Circle and Outer Circle countries, and even in America where people still assign prestige value to the RP accent (Wolfram and Schilling-Estes, 2006). It is unusual that an accent only spoken by 3 per cent of the population in the UK came to be thought of as the 'standard' English (McIntyre, 2009).

In America, standardization of spoken English was less intense. Unlike Britain, where RP is still associated with prestige and class, there is no standard American English that now holds the same prestige value. Wolfram and Schilling-Estes (2006, p. 13) write:

> For the most part, Americans do not assign strong positive, or prestige, value to any particular dialect of American English. The basic contrast in the USA exists between negatively valued dialects and those without negative value, not between those with prestige value and those without.

However, in both America and Britain gravitation toward a spoken standard American English or British RP has considerably diminished, particularly in the latter half of the twentieth century. This is true of most Englishes found in Kachru's Inner Circle, where national varieties of English are often viewed with pride, as can be seen in the Jamaican example in the previous section.

Standardization, the 'New' Englishes, and the Expanding Circle

Despite the increasing acceptance of national and regional varieties of native Englishes, 'New' Englishes are still often viewed as 'deficient' or 'fossilized' versions. Bamgbose (1998) argues that, while native English-speaker-led language change is often seen as a sign of creativity and innovation, non–native English-speaker-led change is labelled as an error. Mufwene (2001, p. 107) adds that the indigenized Englishes of the Outer Circle are treated as the 'illegitimate' offspring of English, while native English-speaker varieties are regarded as the 'legitimate' offspring, because of the (mistaken) belief that they have evolved from Old English without 'contamination'.

Furthermore, the idea of a 'standard' English exists across the Expanding Circle in regions as diverse as East Asia, South America, and Europe, and the education policy of countries in these regions continues to promote a 'standard' English ideology by providing to students a limited range of models of English that usually adhere to General American or British RP norms. Standard language ideology often exists because ownership of English is placed on ENL countries. Galloway (2011, 2013) highlighted that, in Japan, native English speakers are seen as the 'owners' of English and speakers of a 'legitimate' variety. However, this study also highlighted that, despite being attached to the idea of 'standard' English, participants could not define it and were also unable to explain their strong attachment to it in relation to learning the language. Stereotypes are also important, stemming from information about the target language and culture portrayed through the mass media, advertising, experiences, and also the use of native English as a yardstick of comparison. Stereotypes do not develop suddenly but develop over a longer period of time. Dominant ideologies, such as standard language ideology, can render certain aspects of sociolinguistic usage invisible (such as the use of English in non-native English-speaking contexts). Unfortunately, in many contexts non-native English, and also non-native English speakers, are ideological outliers and are not given prominence.

In addition to stereotypes and ideas of ownership, it is possible that in places like China and Japan attitudes are related to a standard language ideology of their own national language (see Galloway, 2011 on Japan). These countries are both language conscious nations, and their move to a standard national language was an attempt to override the multiplicity of dialects and unite the nation to foster a national identity. Thus, a strong essentialist view of the national language exists and, with the integration of ethnic minority groups into the majority culture, language standardization created the ideology that a nation is formed of one ethnic group, sharing one language. There is, therefore, a possibility that a monolithic view of linguistic diversity persists in countries such as these, which may have implications for attitudes towards English and, at least, partly explain positive attitudes towards standards of native English.

The future of standard English ideology

This chapter has shown language standardization occurs through sources of authority, which include books, policy, and the education system. Beliefs about 'standard' English also stem from the way in which English is taught, stereotypes surrounding English, and attachment of ownership of English to native English-speaking countries. Widdowson (2003, pp. 41–42), for example, notes that, 'The very idea of a standard implies stability, but language is of nature unstable.' Others assert that Inner Circle varieties are only the 'source of a world language, not the world language itself' (Brutt-Griffler, 2002, p. 179), and that English 'belongs to everyone who speaks it, but it is nobody's mother tongue' (Rajagopalan, 2004, p. 111). Moreover, support of the notion of 'standard' English is incompatible with the complex reality of how English is used worldwide (Saraceni, 2009). As Milroy and Milroy (1999, p. 45) state, 'standardisation is never complete because, ultimately, a language is the property of the communities that use it ... It is not the exclusive property of governments, educators or prescriptive grammarians, and it is arrogant to believe that it is.'

ELF research is central here, where ownership is removed from native English speakers, who do not provide a linguistic reference point, and instead an expert user of ELF is preferred. Within the ELF paradigm, it has been increasingly recognized that native English speakers do not speak a standardized version, and furthermore it is increasingly difficult and irrelevant to define a 'native speaker' in multilingual societies (Kirkpatrick, 2007). Mauranen (2012, p. 6) has the following to offer:

> Imposed standards are different from the natural norms that arise in groups and communities primarily in face-to face interaction to regulate interaction in the interests of **mutual intelligibility** and smooth communicative progress. Natural norms arise from what a speech community adopts, tolerates, or rejects ... Although ELF is typically associated with fleeting encounters between strangers, it is also the working language of more long-lasting communities, for example business, trade or academia. Spontaneous norms arise in communities of these kinds; they can, thus, become endonormative for their own duration and purposes. In the absence of linguistic authority, other than communicative efficiency, group norms are negotiated internally.

Thus, to return to the introductory case study of this chapter, the Daihat-Praglish English that drew scorn from Newman (1995) is an antiquated and Inner Circle-centred view of English, which is precisely the type of standard language ideology Global Englishes is trying to move away from.

Chapter summary

This chapter has highlighted key issues in variation and change in English. From Section 2a, it is clear that language is always changing, and thus a view that English is a monolithic entity that is impervious to variation is an incorrect assumption. English does not live in a vacuum, nor is it preserved like many of the dead languages of the world existing in its last recorded state; it is a living entity which feeds off other languages, speakers, cultures, and societies. Such contact has caused massive variation worldwide in terms of grammatical structures, vocabulary, syntax, and phonology, as Section 2b has illustrated. In areas of extreme contact with speakers of other languages, English has undergone massive change, such as the pidgins and creoles that developed in such contexts.

Negative attitudes toward variation and change are not new to society, and a standard language ideology of English has existed for a millennium and, throughout time, regional variations of English have been subjected to stereotypes on whether they constitute 'correct' usage. Standard language ideology remains strong, especially in the Expanding Circle where learners maintain stereotypes of English as a monolithic entity, placing importance on the idea of a 'standard' English and placing ownership of it within the Inner Circle. However, ELF researchers have done much to highlight the fact that ownership of the English language no longer rests with native English speakers.

Further reading

On language variation and change:

- Chambers, J. K., Trudgill, P. and Schilling-Estes, N. (2004). *The Handbook of Language Variation and Change*. Malden, MA: Blackwell.

On variation in World Englishes:

- Chapters 4, 5, 6, and 7 of this book.

On pidgins and creoles:

- Singh, I. (2000). *Pidgins and Creoles*. London: Hodder Arnold.

On standard language ideology:

- Milroy, J. and Milroy, L. (1999). *Authority in Language: Investigating Standard English*. London: Routledge.

Closing activities

Chapter discussion questions

Section 2a

1   What have been the main driving forces behind change in the English language?
2   Why (and in what ways) do you think contact with other languages has influenced English? Think of the varying levels of language contact, e.g. superficial contact and more intense contact.
3   What is your opinion on Widdowson's (1997, p. 43) comment that 'the very fact that English is an international language means that no nation can have custody over it'?

Section 2b

1   Some English phonology does not match English spelling, e.g. the phoneme /ʃ/ in *shut* and *champagne*; pronunciation of *bow* as /bəʊ/ or /baʊ/; and the pronunciation of *aren't* and *aunt* both as /ɑːnt/. What other inconsistencies exist? Can you think of any ways to regularize spelling?
2   Crystal (1997, p. 116) points out, 'the need for intelligibility and the need for identity often pull people and countries … in opposing directions'. Do the demands of mutual intelligibility point to a need to decrease such variation?
3   'Postcolonial Englishes' is a term used by Schneider (2007) that attempts to investigate common trajectories of change in the Englishes spoken in countries colonized by Britain. What are your opinions of this way of viewing English variation? What about the term 'nativized'?

Section 2c

1   Which of the three theories of how pidgins and creoles developed seems most likely, based on what you have read?

2   When does a language cease to be a creole and be considered its own language?

3   Pennycook (2007) debates the inclusion of creoles in the World Englishes paradigm. Exclusion impacts on the identity of creole speakers, but inclusion impacts on what is understood by language in general and English in particular. Expand on the arguments for and against inclusion of creoles as a variety of English.

Section 2d

1   How has a 'standard' English ideology for the English language developed and changed over history?

2   Why is standard language ideology more prevalent in the written form of the English language than the spoken form?

3   What are your views on the idea of a 'standard' English? What are your experiences of 'standard' English (or language) ideology?

Debate topics

1   Creoles are languages in their own right and should not fall in the World Englishes paradigm. Placing creoles with other World Englishes is equivalent to placing Modern English in a paradigm of 'World Frenches', seeing as Middle English emerged through contact with Norman French.

2   'New' Englishes will continue to be negatively evaluated until they are fully described, and in a position to identify and codify their standard forms.

3   Language change and variation enriches the expressive potential of English. It is inevitable and should be encouraged.

Writing and presentation prompts

Below are ideas for writing and presentation tasks to apply the knowledge learned in Chapter 2. Additional assignment prompts can be found on the companion website.

	Assignment topics
Personal account	Which variety of English do people in a context you are familiar with associate with prestige? Explore the topic of linguistic prejudice, and your own experiences, in this context. Think about the national language(s), if relevant, and English.
Research task (see website for worksheet)	Collect data on people's 'standard' English ideology using the questionnaire and/or interview agenda from the companion website. Analyse the data and present your findings. Comment on how your findings compare to historical and current perspectives of 'standard' English.
Basic academic	Research and present about one of the world's pidgins or creoles. Explain its historical emergence and its current features, using examples to illustrate your points.
Advanced academic	Choose two Inner Circle or Outer Circle World Englishes that emerged at a similar point in history. Describe the current phonologic, lexical, grammatical, and syntactic differences between the two, and why this variation has occurred. Discuss influences on the languages in accordance to their variation and change.

Chapter 3

English as a global language

Issues and attitudes

 Introductory activities

The following introductory activities are designed to encourage the reader to think about the issues raised in this chapter before reading it.

> ### Spread of English: the winners and losers
>
> #### Loser: languages other than English
>
> - Number of languages that currently die out every year: four (ELCat, 2014).
> - 40 per cent of the world's 7,000 languages are in danger of disappearing (ELCat, 2014).
> - Percentage of languages that have fewer than 1,000 speakers: 25 (Crystal, 2002).
>
> #### Winner: English-medium education
>
> - Increase in programmes taught in English in Europe in the past decade: 1,000 per cent (Brenn-White and Faethe, 2013).
>
> #### Loser: foreign-language education in the UK
>
> - German language enrolment at universities in 1998: 2,288 students.
> - German language enrolment at universities in 2008: 610 students.
> - Students taking a foreign-language GCSE qualification in the UK in 1999: 71 per cent.
> - Students taking a foreign-language GCSE qualification in the UK in 2010: 43 per cent.
>
> (Above statistics from Garner, 2008.)

Winner: the UK and US educational sectors

- Annual income generated by 586,000 international students in the USA: $12 billion (Braine, 2005).
- Number of UK and US universities in the top 10 of the QS World University Rankings: ten (2013).

Winners and losers: international communities

- Money spent by the EU in 2006 on translation and interpreting services: $1.3 billion (USD).

Discussion questions

1 Which of these statistics were most surprising to you?
2 The following statement is from *The British Council Annual Report (1987–88)*: 'Britain's real black gold is not North Sea oil but the English language. It has long been at the root of our culture and now is fast becoming the global language of business and information. The challenge facing us is to exploit it to the full' (cited in Seidlhofer, 2011, p.29).
   a In what ways do ENL nations exploit the English language as an economic resource?
   b Is it fair that the UK benefits financially because it is an ENL nation?
3 Why is foreign language learning declining in the UK? What will be the long-term effects of native English speakers not choosing a foreign language in their education?
4 Do financial savings from translation and interpreting services justify decisions to switch to a single working language in an international company or organization?

Case study: the death of Alaskan indigenous languages

The following case study is taken from Dauenhauer and Dauenhauer (1998), with more up-to-date statistics from Krauss (2007).

Alaska is currently home to approximately 20 indigenous languages. In 1995, 14 of these languages had no speakers younger than 40 and, by 2007, each of these had fewer than 50 speakers, and only two had more than 1,000 speakers (Krauss, 2007). This decline has been linked to laws, policies, and practices of English-speaking Americans. In Alaska, an **English-only policy** in schools and political administration affected native languages, strictly and forcibly replacing them with English. The switch to English also occurred in Native Alaskan organizations, seen as necessary to legally fight the US government on issues of Native rights and land reforms. In more recent years, as such policy has eased, the loss of Native languages continues, with younger generations reluctant to learn or use them, and parents reluctant or unable to teach them. Factors at play include the following:

- Christian ideals associated with English as the language of God;
- An older generation who remember harsh educational policies that punished the use of native languages;

- Negative socio-economic stigmas attached to native languages;
- Mixed messages on the value of learning native languages in the community.

As a result of these factors, 19 of 20 languages are not being passed down to younger generations and face extinction (Krauss, 2007).

Source: Dauenhauer and Dauenhauer (1998)

Discussion

1 Who/what is responsible for the decline in Native Alaskan languages: American policy; the education system; Native Alaskan community leaders; speakers of Native Alaskan languages; the Anglo-American community; speakers of the English language; or the English language itself?
2 In what ways can policy improve the value of learning Native Alaskan languages?
3 Do you know of other examples where languages have been negatively affected by the arrival and imposition of the English language?

Introduction

This chapter examines the issues and attitudes surrounding the global spread of English, with the aim of providing a balanced and objective view of the advantages and disadvantages of English's rise as a world lingua franca. Section 3a examines the uses of English in relation to some of the world's previous and concurrent lingua francas, and examines the advantages of having a global lingua franca. Section 3b looks at the disadvantages of the global spread of English, including language loss and language death. It particularly focuses on indigenous languages in former British colonies, but also examines the impact it has had on foreign language learning around the world as more and more people turn to English as a study option. Section 3c continues to explore the role of English in creating social inequalities around the world, and whether this was an intentional or incidental outcome. Section 3d examines the reality of English in the world today, and the language policies that have aimed to limit and/or accelerate its intrusion into nations around the world.

3a   The advantages of the global spread of English

The why and how of languages becoming a lingua franca

The history of language spread and rise of lingua francas has usually gone hand-in-hand with historical migrations of communities, or the conquering of new lands by those wielding military power at the time. The adoption of one language over another is usually the case of needing a common language for communication. However, the process by which this is achieved is quite complex and many factors are at play. Therefore, before we examine the advantages of having a common language, it is first necessary to examine the processes by which the need for a common language emerges.

The spread of language by those in power has not always meant the replacement of the languages spoken in the conquered communities. There are many factors that come into play regarding whether languages of intervening powers result in the death, reduction, integration, or adoption of the languages of subordinate communities. These include the following.

- The expectations of the ruling power. The Ottoman Empire, for example, permitted communities in their wide-ranging empire to keep their ethnic identities and language use (Dorian, 1998).
- The geographical distance from the home territory. It has been argued that in the past, if communities felt isolated from their home territory, the need to maintain the native language diminished, which could sometimes result in the adoption of local languages. For example, the Vikings who settled in far-flung territories (e.g. southern Italy in the eleventh century) eventually adopted the local language.
- The loss of home territory. The French-speaking Normans, for example, eventually made the switch to English after 300 years of rule in England. This decision could be related to the fact that the Normans had lost control over their lands in Normandy, and thus the focus of their new life and rule was entirely in the English-speaking nation.
- Population size. The ratio of the population of the ruling power and the subordinate communities has a large effect on whether a language is replaced, integrated, or adopted. In places like India, for example, the ruling English speakers of the British colony were far outnumbered by the local population, and thus English existed alongside local languages. The same can be said for most of England's exploitation colonies. In countries such as Australia and North America, however, the British settlers soon outnumbered Native American communities and Australian aboriginal communities, resulting in the reduction and extinction of many local languages.
- The prestige attached to the language. As Chapter 2 outlined, prestige attached to a language influences its spread. This is certainly true in places where knowledge of prestigious languages is seen to represent a certain level of education and class. In more recent times of globalization, the impetus to learn languages is linked to greater opportunity for employment and economic success.
- Policy. Educational policy encourages the use of a language over another among a new generation of speakers. Religious policy has been instrumental in the destruction of language, especially when packaged as the language of god (see the introductory case study in this chapter). It has also been instrumental in language preservation. Welsh, for example, may not have survived had the Bible not been translated into it, making Welsh a tool to deliver religious messages to non-English-speaking communities. Government policy can also reduce or increase language in the public domain, from media regulations to road signs.

Thus, to answer the question of why languages are adopted, it is first important to understand that not all languages are adopted for the same reasons. The reasons why English was adopted in various parts of the world relate to a mixture of many of these factors.

Advantages of a global lingua franca

There are a number of clear advantages to adopting a lingua franca, stemming from the benefit of having a shared language for communication. These are outlined below.

Advantages for international relations

A global lingua franca breaks down barriers between nations. As highlighted in Chapter 1, English is now an official, or co-official, language in one third of the world's countries and plays a significant role in 90 countries in total (McArthur, 2002, p. 3). This benefits international diplomacy and major political gatherings. Delegates from countries as diverse as China, Russia, the USA, and Japan can discuss major political issues without the need for multiple interpreters. It is also said to have created a genuinely pan-European space for political debate: 'It has never been easier for other Europeans to know what Poles think about the credit crunch, Germans about the Middle East or Danes about nuclear power' (*The Economist*, 2009). As the official working language of ASEAN, English allows cost-cutting measures, unlike in the EU which provides a costly translation service in an attempt to promote linguistic equality among member countries (although the latter is starting to scale down the costs spent on translation, discussed in Chapter 6). Chapter 6 will also highlight that increasing emphasis is being placed on developing English proficiency by ASEAN countries as they prepare for the ASEAN Economic Community (AEC) in 2015.

Advantages for business

Many international companies have also noticed the benefit to productivity of having a global lingua franca. Whereas previously communications between company head-quarters and their foreign branches, factories, subsidiaries, and various connected institutional bodies had to be translated (along with company policy documents, meeting minutes, etc.), the use of a single working language means that this can be streamlined, and if this language is the same as the global lingua franca it also streamlines communication outside the company. Thus many international firms have decided to use English as their working language, even though the company might be based entirely in non-English-speaking countries. The switch is usually led by written communication. For example, a study of Swedish-based companies found that half of the engineers wrote in English every day, because it had become the main mode of written communication in emails and technical reports (Apelman, 2010).

The use of English in the business arena is, in fact, attracting the attention of many ELF researchers, and has given rise to a new field of study, termed **BELF (business English as a lingua franca)** – a term introduced by Louhiala-Salminen *et al.* (2005) to describe the use of English in international business, and discussed in Chapter 7 of this book. Kankaanranta and Planken (2010), in their study of European multinational companies, found that about 70 per cent of the English communication among internationally operating business professionals could be characterized as BELF. Gil (2010), however, draws attention to a number of studies in Asia that show, while English is used on a daily basis in many companies, its use is not only limited to a small percentage of company employees but was often confined to faxes, memos, minutes of meetings, and forms.

Advantages for communication

It can be argued that a global language makes international communication more efficient. The use of a global lingua franca means access to wider sources of information, and the growth of internet-based media also means that English has remained the preferred language of most electronically stored information. English proficiency has resulted in the outsourcing of a number of different types of call-centres in places like India and the Philippines, meaning that people in Scotland may end up discussing their finances with someone in Delhi. Although information in other languages has risen in recent years, there is an implicit understanding that, if information is written in English, it can be more widely accessed. A 2009 UNESCO report stated that English comprised 45 per cent of the content on the Internet, which was down from previous estimates in the 80–90 per cent range but still substantial considering English speakers represent just 10 per cent of the world's population (UNESCO, 2009, p. 25). The same report showed that other world languages, such as Spanish and French, had less than 10 per cent of the information on the Internet (UNESCO, 2009, p. 28).

The growth of a global lingua franca also means faster and more efficient access to popular media, such as music, films, and literature. English speakers no longer need to wait for local translations of literature, while movie houses in Germany increasingly screen original versions of English films, without having to wait for dubbed or subtitled versions to be released.

A global lingua franca also aids communication for the transportation industries, and English has been instigated as the lingua franca for air traffic control and shipping to ensure smooth communication with pilots and ship captains and maintain safety. To minimize miscommunication, guidelines stipulate that fixed 'phraseology' be adhered to and, if this does not suffice, specific and explicit 'plain English' should be employed (ICAO, 2004, pp. 3–5).

Advantages for education and scientific advancement

Another advantage of a global lingua franca is that scientific knowledge and discovery can be communicated widely and speedily. This reduces the historical uses of languages as a barrier of access to information, when knowledge and power was guarded by those with literacy in the language in which it was stored. For example, in Europe prior to the invention of Gutenberg's printing press, knowledge was only available to those who had access to books and the ability to read in Latin (or other languages, such as French). The emergence of a global lingua franca as the language of science and scientific scholarship has meant wider access to knowledge and new scientific discoveries, which are often printed for the first time in English. Translations are, nowadays, uncommon, as English is further cemented as the language of international scholarship.

Today, half of the world's international students are learning through English, and English-medium programmes in non-native English-speaking countries are becoming greater in number, a topic discussed further in Chapter 10. English is now universal in many academic disciplines, and key information is now only made available in English. The Web of Science database of 12,000 'top tier' journals, for example, places great emphasis on using English as the medium of publication, stating that in order for a journal to be listed 'full text English is highly desirable, especially if the journal intends to serve an international community of researchers' (Thomson-Reuters, 2012).

Advantages for political unity

Another advantage of a global lingua franca is its use in contexts where the use of another language might unfairly favour certain populations. As Chapter 5 will highlight,

English is sometimes seen as a neutral language, one that spans linguistic, cultural, and religious boundaries. In this sense, it can be viewed as a mechanism for political unity. English has become the primary language of education in Singapore, for example, partially because of the role it played in colonial times, but also due to its mediatory capacity across the linguistically diverse populations that live there. English is a unifying language for the Chinese-speaking, Tamil-speaking and Bahasa-Melayu-speaking populations of Singapore and, by conducting education and political administration in English, no single group is theoretically disadvantaged. Rubdy *et al.* (2008, p. 44) point out:

> Hence, whether as a key to the nation's economic survival or to an individual's social mobility, as the primary language of global communication and international trade and commerce, or because of its 'neutrality' with regard to diverse ethnic groups, wherein no single group is privileged above the rest, along several dimensions, English alone has the ability to function as a unifying language for Singaporeans.

English has played a similar role in India, where historically discriminated-against minority language speakers were denied access to certain tiers of society and politics. The use of English has, in some ways, levelled this playing field (although access to English education is still a barrier faced by many).

Furthermore, it can be argued that a lingua franca allows for greater pursuit of egalitarian global justice, enabling the rich and the poor, the powerful and the powerless to communicate across formerly insurmountable linguistic boundaries and national borders (Van Parijis, 2011). An illustration of this is the use of English when demonstrating for or against political causes, where protesters use English on their placards to ensure that they reach a wider audience. English has also enabled citizens of rather totalitarian regimes to voice their cause and reach the world at large, such as the role of social media in the Arab uprising of 2011. In this sense, having a global language means that news can travel fast, as well as over a long distance.

Later in this chapter, and in Chapter 5, the notion that English can be a tool for economic development and upward social mobility will be discussed. There are many other factors at play when discussing this 'advantage', including the creation of linguistic inequality in the first place, which is discussed at length in Section 3c.

Advantages for society

Finally, a global lingua franca serves a social purpose. It is involved in more language-contact situations than any other language and, therefore, is becoming more essential as a language to communicate with people across linguistic communities. H.E. Lê Lu'o'ng Minh, Secretary General of ASEAN, noted that,

> English enables us to interact with other ASEAN colleagues in our formal meetings, as well as day-to-day communications. From these interactions, we are able to get to know better our regional neighbours, their interests, their concerns, as well as their dreams and aspirations. Through English, we are raising our awareness of the ASEAN region and, with the many characteristics we share and hold dear, further strengthening our sense of an ASEAN Community.
>
> (Quoted on www.asean.org, 2013)

In addition to its benefit to the social relationships of neighbouring countries, English provides advantages to fostering relations between mobile populations around the globe. Chinese tourists may use English to communicate with hotel staff in Norway, Italians may use English to talk to Polish taxi drivers in Germany, and Australians may use English to communicate with store owners in Chile. ELF usage is on the rise and, without a lingua franca, globalization would be a lot more difficult and a lot less successful.

3b The dark side of the global spread of English: is English a killer language?

While there are clear advantages of a global lingua franca, there are also numerous disadvantages including: language death; reduced diversity of global languages; homogenization of cultures; and a reduction in learning other foreign languages. A further disadvantage is the creation of socio-economic inequalities, which will be explored in Section 3c.

Language death and the reduced diversity of global languages

There are between 5,000 and 6,000 languages spoken in the world today. The precise figure is difficult to estimate due to fuzzy boundaries between languages and dialects. Based on these figures, however, it has been predicted that 3,000–4,000 may cease to exist by 2100 (Grenoble and Whaley, 1998). It has also been argued that those that do not perish in the coming decades will be severely limited by their number of surviving speakers, with just 600 languages having more than 100,000 speakers (Hale, 1998). Indeed, 10 per cent of all known languages are already extinct, and a further 10 per cent have fewer than 10 speakers remaining. More recent statistics have shown that the oft-cited statistic that languages are disappearing at a rate of one language every two weeks is incorrect (ELCat, 2014). Based on the Endangered Languages Project's catalogue, languages are dying out at a rate of four a year, but the future looks more grim with 40 per cent of the world's languages currently endangered. The arrival of new languages into a region has a tremendous impact on the death of a language, and is often the primary cited cause of language death. In the USA and Canada alone, of the 270 documented mutually intelligible indigenous languages, one-third have already disappeared and all but several are expected to be extinct within the next few generations (Mithun, 1998).

With the recent spread of English via Channel 4 (globalization), attention has been drawn to the threat that English poses to foreign languages. For example, in most of Europe secondary-level students learn English in their modern foreign language class, often in place of traditional neighbouring European languages, a point discussed further in Chapter 6. Motivation to study and interest in languages such as Russian and German have dramatically dropped in Hungary, replaced by motivation to learn English (Dörnyei and Csizér, 2002). As an integral part of the curriculum from primary schools, English is now taught at the expense of other major ASEAN languages in ASEAN countries (Kirkpatrick, 2009), also discussed further in Chapter 6. And as will be discussed in Chapter 5, in the case of Singapore the increased use of English has resulted in decreased use of other languages, particularly by the younger generations. Thus, English certainly appears to fit the description as a 'killer language', and seems to have many parallels with other historical language destroyers, but with an added dimension of destroying foreign languages due to the new reach afforded by globalization.

In response to the reduction of global linguistic diversity, some scholars have made pleas to the wider community to become more compassionate over what is lost when languages die. With the growth of English, the world not only loses languages, but also the cultures, traditions, and knowledge that surround them. The loss of language is also a mental loss for society, as it loses a perspective to look at things differently (Mithun, 1998). And it is a scientific and intellectual loss for humanity (Hale, 1998) because 'in the death of any language comes the irreplaceable loss of a picture of human creativity' (Grenoble and Whaley, 1998, p. xiv).

Homogenization of cultures

English is viewed as not only a destroyer of languages but also of the culture and traditions associated with them, although defining culture can be problematic in today's society (the issue of culture is explored further in section 10b). Language can be seen as a symbol of culture, and the strong connection between the two means that the worldwide spread of English has resulted in the worldwide spread of Western and, more specifically, American culture. There is reference to the 'Americanization' of local cultures in public discourse worldwide. It is difficult to assess to what extent language detracts from cultural identity, and to what extent the language has been absorbed into local cultures, but one thing is certain: language, culture, and identity are inextricably intertwined, each exerting influence on the other. The promotion of Western culture through English language teaching has received a lot of attention. Thus, not only are students increasingly expected to be proficient in English but also to know about Western culture. Textbooks continue to be filled with static depictions of Western culture and learners are often expected to adhere to such cultural identities when using the language. As Pennycook (1994, p. 21) points out, 'Access to prestigious but often inappropriate forms of knowledge is often only through English, and, thus, given the status of English both within and between countries, there is often reciprocal reinforcement of the position of English and the position of imported forms of culture and knowledge.' As will be discussed in Chapter 6, such a fear of Westernization has characterized language policies in East Asia, where the promotion of English has often been side by side with promotion of national culture.

Reduction in learning foreign languages by English speakers

Not only have the effects of the spread of English been felt by those nations that English has spread to, but globalization and the importance of English is also deterring native English speakers from studying other languages. The number of students taking a language for their GCSE qualifications in the United Kingdom, for example, has been reported to be in steady decline, as shown in the introductory activity to this chapter. This decline has also had a knock-on effect in higher education, which has seen even more dramatic drops, such as French which has declined by more than 30 per cent. Furthermore, it is not the case that other world languages are being taken up in favour of traditional European languages. In Australia, where Asian language education has been typically strong, a report released by the Department of Education, Employment and Workplace Relations in 2010 found that the number of Australian students studying the big four Asian languages (Chinese, Indonesian, Japanese, and Korean) in Australian schools had significantly decreased since 2000.

In the UK, some media sources link the decline in the learning of foreign languages to UK policy, which no longer makes the learning of foreign languages a compulsory component of teenage education. However, in light of community criticism over this decline, foreign languages have been promoted in UK policy in recent years, in the form of lessons in primary education and inclusion of languages in some performance measures of UK schools. However, this does not detract from the fact that students are no longer viewing foreign languages as a worthy pursuit, which is, perhaps, indicative of the myth perpetuated by globalization – that knowing English will be sufficient for future international communication and careers. Sharifian and Clyne (2008, p. 28) state, 'What seems to be boosting the decline of other languages is not so much the widespread use of an international language as the monolingual mindset.' Unfortunately, many studies have highlighted that this mindset is not correct, and that the monolingual employee will be at a disadvantage in the job force and recruitment pool. As Gil (2010, p. 55) notes,

> Adding English to their existing linguistic repertoires will allow such bi/multilingual people to compete for any employment or other opportunity for which English is a requirement, as well as those for which proficiency in other languages is a requirement. Monolingual English speakers, on the other hand, will not be able to do the same.

This is a sentiment shared by many linguists, who have argued that the complacent monolingual English speaker will not be able to compete in the international job market on the basis of their native English-speaking capabilities.

Is English a killer language?

Reference to the English language has often been analogous to monsters and other beasts that bring death and destruction (Wilton, 2012). Phillipson (2008), for example, describes ELF as a 'lingua Frankensteinia', and others have described the spread of English as 'hydra' (Rapatahana and Bunce, 2012) and 'Tyrannosaurus Rex' (Tardy, 2004). Cooke (1988) also described it as a 'Trojan horse', as a language of imperialism. Are such analogies to the English language warranted? Is English truly a killer language?

In English's defence, it has been argued that Spanish was the cause of much more language death, replacing most indigenous languages of South America and other places where it spread (Spolsky, 2004), whereas English was often used alongside other languages that still persist today. At the same time, however, the spread of English and colonialism wiped out indigenous languages and cultures, but can we lay blame on the English language, or on linguistic policy, or on another not-yet-mentioned source? It could be possible that name-calling and reference to English as a mythical beast or monster distracts from the real enactors of language death.

Mufwene (2002, p. 12) makes an important argument 'that languages don't kill languages, their own speakers do, in giving them up.' This is not to belittle the victims of the spread of colonial power, but history has shown that, even after centuries of repression and rule, when people wish to maintain their language then the language survives. It is speakers themselves who hold the ultimate decision to abandon or continue a language. Perhaps the biggest reason languages die, or are abandoned, is connected to the prestige attached to a language, an issue that Nancy Dorian discusses at length. She states that, 'because the standing of a language is so intimately tied to that of its speakers, enormous reversals in the prestige of a language can take place in a very short time span' (Dorian, 1998, p. 4). If the standing of a language in a community is considerably less than other languages that surround it, parents become more reluctant to pass their own language on to their children if they believe that it will disadvantage them in their future due to the low prestige status attached to it.

Opinion on the role of English in the destruction of other languages and culture is polarized. One camp views the intentional destruction of language as a top-down decision by English-speaking powers, and others see it as a bottom-up decision by speakers turning to English for their own purposes and gains. As Wilton (2012, p. 339) notes,

> Linked to those two extreme positions are conceptualisations of language as an evil and threatening creature, or as a simple tool, almost clinically devoid of anything that enables a language to express the linguistic and cultural identity of its speakers.

So what role did other language speakers play, and what role did the policy of English speakers play? This is a debate that is discussed at length in the following section.

3c Linguistic imperialism and the creation of inequalities by the global spread of English

Linguistic imperialism

Many linguists refer to the ideological, cultural, and elitist power of English, and the immense economic advantage it offers to the dominant nations of America and the UK. English is associated with colonialism and corporate multinationals, and has been labelled a form of 'linguistic imperialism' (Phillipson, 1992b). Linguistic imperialism is seen by many academics as a globally organized form of **linguicism**, which is defined as 'the intentional destruction of a powerless language by a dominant one' (Spolsky, 2004, p. 79). The notion that the spread of English was a form of linguistic imperialism was widely written about by Phillipson in the 1990s and early 2000s, who examined who benefited from the spread of English in order to establish who was responsible for it (Spolsky, 2004). Phillipson argued that it was in the interests of the UK and the USA to have English spread, and that policies reflected this. Furthermore, he makes the case that these (and other) ENL countries are unfairly benefiting today because of English's position as a global lingua franca. In a recent publication on the topic in 2012 (after 20 years of intense academic debate over the notion), Phillipson (2012, p. 214) stated that he sees linguistic imperialism:

- as a form of linguicism which manifests in favouring the dominant language over another, along similar lines as racism and sexism;
- as a structurally manifested concept where resources and infrastructure are provided to the dominant language;
- as being ideological in that it encourages beliefs that the dominant language form is superior to others, and is thus more prestigious – he also argues that such ideas are internalized by society as being 'normal';
- as being intertwined with the same structure as imperialism in culture, education, the media, and politics;

- as having an exploitative essence that causes injustice and inequality between those who use the dominant language and those who do not;
- as having a subtractive influence on other languages, in that learning the dominant language is at the expense of others;
- as being contested and resisted because of these factors.

Creation of socio-economic inequalities

There is much evidence that what Phillipson defines as the characteristics of linguistic imperialism is true of the spread of English around the globe. Linguicism has been seen in the education policy in former UK colonies around the world. In many colonies, it was expected that English would be the dominant language at the expense of all others, and in many of these contexts an elite English-speaking class has often emerged who use English proficiency as a means to determine inclusion or exclusion. In a sense, then, these English-speaking members of the elite class have adopted the position of their former colonizers. Globalization may be seen to have a number of advantages, but not everyone benefits from it. As Blommaert (2010, p. 197) notes, 'Globalization is something that has winners as well as losers, a top as well as a bottom, and centres as well as peripheries.' While knowing English may be an asset, it is not a benefit afforded to everyone due to unequal access to language education. Within countries where the UK had a colonial presence, English is clearly the favoured language, even if it is not the language most commonly used by its citizens. Social, political, and educational disadvantages exist for those who do not speak it. English, then, functions as a gatekeeper for upward social mobility. Non-English speakers also face discrimination in government policy: English language tests are used in the USA and Australia for people to become naturalized citizens, despite these countries' claims to embrace linguistic diversity.

Such inequality also occurs on a micro-level in nations where English played no historical role. Kim and Elder (2009), for example, note that in 2003 the International Civil Aviation Organization (ICAO) implemented English language proficiency requirements for aviation personnel, leading the Korean government to develop an English language test. The authors note that, while all Korean airline pilots and controllers involved in international flights passed the test before the enforcement date of 2008, 97 per cent 'attained no more than the minimum required level' (p. 23.2), meaning they will have to take the test again after three years. Various objections to the test were put forward, including the fact that miscommunication does not solely result from lack of English proficiency on the part of the non-native English speaker. Implications of this policy might also mean that highly experienced, less-proficient air traffic controllers might be replaced by less-experienced proficient ones, which begs the question: does language proficiency trump knowledge of regulations and experience in the industry?

Discrimination also occurs in education around the world, with English proficiency necessary to enter most world-class institutions. In postcolonial India, prestigious schools offer courses through the medium of English, while indigenous languages are tied to schools in poorer communities. A similar situation is found in Hong Kong (discussed in Chapter 6). In areas of the world where there was no colonial presence, the spread of English through globalization has had an impact. Brock-Utne (2012) argues that there is an inherent inequality in movements towards English as a language for education, in that many children are forced to learn in a language they do not use outside of school and have not mastered.

There are also innumerable financial and social benefits afforded to the native English speaker because of the spread of English. They can more easily be accepted into the world's top universities (most of which have an English language entrance requirement), be hired into top-paying international firms, be published in world-reputed journals (which have strict language requirements), and claim political positions (in many countries where English language has an administrative role). Seidlhofer (2011, p. 34) further observes an inequality between non-native and native English speakers in terms of the perceived acceptableness of the English they use:

> Non-native speakers just cannot win: either they subject themselves to native-speaker authority and obediently strive to meet the norms of the hegemonic language, or they try to assert themselves against the hegemony, only to then be told that they got it wrong because they have the misfortune not to be native speakers. So the primacy accorded to NS norms puts the NNS user of English in an inescapable double bind.

Thus there is evidence from all tiers of society of a socio-economic inequality stemming from language use, supporting Phillipson's notion of linguistic imperialism.

Bottom-up and top-down perspectives

Despite evidence supporting the existence of inequality created by English, there is debate as to whether this result was intentional or incidental to the spread of English. Phillipson's view is, certainly, a **top-down perspective**, where it was the intent of ENL nations to spread English for their own gains to create social and economic inequality. Other scholars take more of a **bottom-up perspective**, arguing that the spread of English was merely a consequence of the spread of British and American power, which went hand-in-hand with first colonization and later globalization. For example, it has been argued that, if such top-down intent existed, it would be one of the most successful examples of language policy management the world had ever seen (Spolsky, 2004). Instead, Spolsky (2004, p. 90) argues that the development of English as a global language 'reflects local and individual language acquisition decisions, responding to changes in the complex ecology of the world's language system'. Evidence to attest this claim includes the fact that the spread of English, especially in countries where English settlers were a minority, is a recent phenomenon that happened in the postcolonial era. Unlike colonization of territories by other nations (e.g. Japan of Taiwan, the USSR of Ukraine, Poland, and Latvia) where the colonizers took an aggressive stance in the promotion of language through education, politics, and society, English was not always pushed in regions where British presence existed for exploitive reasons. Indeed, British colonial powers tended to deny language education to local populations as it was thought that English language acquisition might lead to organized resistance to colonial rule (Ferguson, 2006). By this logic, then, the denial and control of the English language, rather than its promotion and spread, would be considered to be in the best interest of colonial powers – an idea that existed centuries beforehand with the safeguarding of information and power by literacy in Latin.

Organizations such as the British Council and the United States Information Agency certainly have a top-down approach to promoting the English language. However, Ferguson (2006) argues that such organizations exist for most nations that invest considerable sums of money to promote national languages. Thus, the reason for the success of English language learning around the world has little to do with the success of such organizations. Canagarajah (1999b, p. 41) has argued that,

> What enables dominance are 'ideologies, structures and practices' that are considered extra-linguistic. In other words, language does not affect this inequality – it is just an arbitrary construct exploited by politico-economic structures to carry out their own agenda of dominance.

History has shown that an aggressive language policy, like that of the USSR, has not eventuated in the adoption of language – what is needed is a lack of resistance to the promoted language, coupled with a perceived personal advantage to adopting the language (Ferguson, 2006).

Thus, the initial spread of language has occurred due to its inseparable connection to other key factors, such as politics, culture, education, and the media, which concurs with Phillipson's view. However, this spread was incidental to the spread of power by dominant forces, and was not a matter of language planning and policy. Nevertheless, because inequality of political power, economic power, media reach, and access to education still remains in the postcolonial era, language is seen as a door to access this power. The success of the spread of English, therefore, is due to the adoption of English by non-English speakers, driven by personal advantage for those who speak it.

Levelling inequality

If language is viewed as a door to access the advantages afforded to English speakers, then it can also be seen as a vehicle for upward social and economic mobility. Accordingly, there is a belief at the macro level that policy that promotes English language education will help to leverage economic benefits. However, it is important to note that knowledge of English alone is not a means, in itself, for a nation to develop politically or economically. Kirkpatrick (2010a) argues that the economic stagnation of Laos and Burma are due to political systems, rather than to their level of English proficiency, and that Vietnam and Indonesia are enjoying much economic success while maintaining strong national languages. He argues that 'it would appear, then, that economic progress and political development can be successfully achieved without mass recourse to English' (Kirkpatrick, 2010a, p. 64). Such evidence supports notions that language is not a 'food aid' package, and thus that the introduction of English language education will not automatically result in economic upward mobility. In relation to the point that a lingua franca language is **levelling** inequality, Phillipson (2008, p. 250) staunchly disagrees, saying, 'Labelling English as a lingua franca, if this is understood as a culturally neutral medium that puts everyone on an equal footing, does not merely entail ideological dangers – it is simply false.' Shifts are also found at the local level where discussions of Englishes, and individual decisions to engage in code-mixing and code-switching, 'challenge the ideologies and institutions which undergird the dominance of English' (Canagarajah, 1999b, p. 42).

Linguistic imperialism and the World Englishes paradigm

As will become evident in upcoming chapters, both the World Englishes and ELF research paradigms, which together form the Global Englishes paradigm, seek to challenge the dominance of native English by emphasizing that English is pluricentric. Despite acknowledging its usefulness in helping one to understand the variability in English today, as well as opening up a large field of study, Pennycook (2007) critiques the World Englishes framework, noting that it holds back full exploration of global Englishes due to a rigid political framework that avoids the broader political impact of the global spread of English. Pennycook argues that nationalism is at the core of the World Englishes framework, with its focus on the identification of distinct varieties of English within strict national boundaries. He notes that, 'By focusing centrally on the development of new national Englishes, the world Englishes approach reproduces the very linguistics it needs to escape' (Pennycook, 2007, p. 21). He suggests a move away from arguments centring on homogeneity, heterogeneity, imperialism, and nation states, towards a focus on translocal and **transcultural flows** (points that are discussed in more depth in Chapter 7). We examined the problems with World Englishes' models in Chapter 1, and agree with Pennycook's assertions. Several 'varieties' do not fit neatly into this framework and it may be seen as being more exclusionary than inclusionary for this reason. Canagarajah (1999b) points out that in Kachru's attempt to systematically categorise all Englishes, he had left out many hybrid forms of local Englishes because they were unsystematic, and thus the 'Kachruvian paradigm follows the logic of the prescriptive and elitist tendencies of the center linguists' (p.180).

Nevertheless, Global Englishes, in building on fields like World Englishes alongside ELF, provides us with an alternative means of looking at language spread today. Concepts such as linguistic decay and linguistic imperialism are still important, but we must also acknowledge new ways of viewing the spread of English in its political, economical, and social contexts.

3d The politics of the spread of English: influences on language policy and planning

In light of divisions in the treatment of English and other languages in both postcolonial nations and those nations affected by globalization in more recent years, this section looks at a number of scenarios where English policy has been implemented to either promote or contain the use of English.

English-only policy in the Inner Circle

The historical economic wealth of ENL countries such as the USA, the UK, Australia, and Canada attracted waves of immigrants in search for a better life (or, in the case of the USA, 'the American dream'). This migration was either met with enthusiasm or disdain (Ferguson, 2006), but increasingly the latter toward the end of the twentieth century. As a result, many predominantly English-speaking nations are seeing a political backlash against other languages that are seen as a threat to the status of English, often in the form of anti-immigrant discourse in politics and society but also in the form of language policy.

For years, the USA followed a **submersion** education policy, sometimes referred to as a 'sink or swim' policy. The policy involved the placement of newly arrived immigrants into schools with no language support. The modest **Bilingual Education Act** of 1968 was introduced to address the difficulties faced by learners who had a poor command of English, and the re-authorizations of this act in the period from 1974 to 1994 established programmes to better cater for immigrant children. However, the policy was criticized for its purpose of integrating children into mainstream English-speaking programmes as quickly as possible, which was further emphasized in the 1980s under the leadership of Ronald Reagan (Ferguson, 2006). Many of the teachers within this programme were monolingual English-speaking teachers whose goal was to wean students off their home languages. Bilingualism, therefore, was not the goal at all. Matters only fared worse in the 1990s with Proposition 227 in California instructing that all children 'be taught English by being taught in English'. In 2002, George W. Bush's **No Child Left Behind Act** further cemented an emphasis on the development of English language skills at the expense of children's home languages.

The English-only movement was also occurring at the political level. No state constitutions prior to the early 1980s declared an official language, with the exception of Hawaii which declared English and Hawaiian as co-official state languages in 1978. Unlike Hawaii, where this decision was based on an inclusive ideology, in the 1980s and 1990s a slew of states declared English to be the only official language. This move was driven by exclusive ideology that saw immigrant languages as a threat to American ideals and culture. The English-only movement has been spearheaded by prominent figures, such as US Senator Ichiye Hayakawa and Californian businessman Ron Unz, who have lobbied English-only policy at state and federal levels with a great deal of success (Spolsky, 2004). The movement has caused debate in the media and backlash in court rulings, which have overturned policy as unconstitutional in certain states due to the policy's violation of human rights. Public discourse about this movement is still heated in the USA today, but it is important to emphasize that the USA is not alone: many other nations have engaged in a similar debate.

Minority language policy in the Inner Circle

Other ENL nations have made a political effort to maintain and revitalize indigenous minority languages that suffered from centuries of British colonial rule. Prominent in this category are New Zealand, Ireland, and Wales. **Language maintenance** is defined as 'denoting the continuing use of a language in the face of competition from a regionally and socially more powerful language' (Mesthrie *et al.*, 1999, p. 253), the powerful language in this case being English. In Wales, the Welsh Language Act of 1993 was a result of increasing pressure to revitalize the Welsh language in the educational, public, and political spheres. The introduction of the Welsh language into public education has been instrumental in the revitalization of the language, and to raising the prestige of the language in the UK as a whole.

In the case of Ireland, Irish has been the first official language of state since the Republic was formed in 1922. However, English remains as the prominent language of the country. The emphasis for the revitalization of Irish has been placed on the educational system and, with few exceptions, all children undertake study in Irish for their entire schooling (up to 14 years). However, census data shows that Irish is rarely used outside of the classroom context and, although people claim to be fluent, it is not used on a frequent basis. Native speakers are mostly isolated to a few regions on the island. Thus, it has been argued that the lack of use of Irish in other areas of Irish society has not provided opportunity to apply the Irish skills studied in class, bringing its real success into question. Nevertheless, Irish receives political and community support, and thus remains an important example of language maintenance of minority languages in postcolonial ENL policy.

In New Zealand, language policy saw Māori instigated as an official language with the passing of the Māori Language Act of 1987. Moreover, in 2006 New Zealand Sign Language joined Māori and English as the official languages of this nation. Such acts sought to undo decades of English-only policy that plagued the nation during and after colonial rule. Since the passing of the Māori Language Act, a number of other provisions have been made for the revitalization of the Māori language and its further prominence in everyday life in New Zealand (on signs, in policy documents, and on the radio and television). Unlike the cases of Wales and Ireland, however, Māori is treated as a minority language, tied to the Māori community. As such, it has not been integrated into mainstream schools as a compulsory language. According to New Zealand Ministry of Education data, 79.3 per cent of students have no language education in Māori, apart from a handful of cultural words and expressions, 18.5 per cent have Māori language education in English-medium schools, and 2.2 per cent have Māori language immersion where the majority of classroom instruction occurs in the Māori language (Education Counts, 2014).

Language policy in the Outer Circle

In most postcolonial territories, where settlers from England did not outnumber indigenous populations or other communities of migrants, English has been maintained in an official capacity alongside other languages. In countries like Nigeria, where English is seen as the sole official language, education policy has dictated that primary-school-aged students can elect to learn in their home language. In reality, because Nigeria is a nation of over 400 languages, many parents elect (or have no choice) to have their child learn in one of the handful of dominant languages, English being one of them. Singapore acknowledges four official languages but, in education, English is the medium of instruction, along with education in one home language (see Chapter 5 for more on the English +1 policy). For the most part, English is a theoretical 'second language' of Singapore's population, with the 'home' language being tied to the three main ethnic groups that comprise the nation's population (Chinese, Indian, and Malay). It therefore acts in a politically mediatory role by theoretically not favouring any of these communities. Other nations in regions like the Philippines and Malaysia also have an official capacity for English, although in the latter Bahasa Malayu has encroached on English's former status as the language of political administration and education. However, as English makes inroads into ASEAN, Kirkpatrick (2012, p. 122–23) warns that,

Handling the relationship between English and other languages is perhaps the most important language policy issue facing politicians and language planners in today's world. A series of particular questions need to be addressed:

(i)   How can the apparently insatiable demand for English be married with the need to provide mother tongue education for children?

(ii) How can English complement local languages in the school curriculum (especially the primary curriculum) rather than replace them?

(iii) How can schools create an ethos which values multilingualism in languages other than English?

Thus, language policy in multilingual nations like Malaysia, Singapore, and Nigeria is a sensitive subject, and one that continues to challenge politicians and policy makers.

Language policy in the Expanding Circle

With the spread of English via Channel 4 (globalization), English is becoming increasingly predominant, prompting changes in language policy. Rwanda, for example, is transitioning from French to English as the main official language, despite being a former Belgian colony, and despite already having a unifying national language in Kinyarwanda. The government has stated that English will help Rwanda economically and improve relations with its East African English-speaking neighbours, which are part of the powerful East African Community. (See the Rwandan case study on the companion website for more information.) Similar movements are happening in Eritrea and Sudan which have also switched in recent years to English in an official capacity, despite the colonial Italian history of the former and the mixed history of colonial control of the latter. Georgia, which has a tumultuous history with Russia, is also talking of switching from Russian to English as an official language. The move is thought to be intended partly as a way to distance themselves from their northern neighbour, but also to leverage economic advantages by increasing ties with economically powerful nations with which English (not Russian) will be the lingua franca for communication. In the realm of business, multinational corporations are turning to English, as seen by the examples at the beginning of this chapter.

In more bottom-up policy approaches, nations such as Demark, Finland, and Sweden have turned to learning from and studying in English, as it is seen as a useful language for academia and scientific research. Because of this seemingly uncontrolled intrusion of English into education, these nations have actually introduced policy to strengthen the role of the national languages (Ferguson, 2012). English is appearing more and more in pop media, print media, and everyday communication. In Japan recently, an older man sued the national broadcasting station for 'mental distress' over 'an excessive use of words borrowed from English' (BBC, 2013), illustrating social resistance to this intrusion.

Perhaps the movements of English in countries affected by its spread due to globalization can best be summed up with the European example:

> The current role of English in Europe is, thus, characterized by the fact that the language has become a lingua franca, a language of wider communication, and has entered the continent in two directions as it were, top-down by fulfilling functions

in various professional domains and, simultaneously, bottom–up by being encoun-
tered and used by speakers from all levels of society in practically all walks of life.

(Seidlhofer, 2006, p.5)

The use of ELF in the European context will be explored further in Section 6a and
Chapter 7.

The ebb and flow of English policy

This section has outlined the politics surrounding English's rise as a lingua franca around
the world. First we can see two trends in English-speaking countries in regards to policy.
One trend, illustrated by the USA, is the promotion of the English language through
nationalistic ideology and policy, which aims to cement English as the national language in
response to waves of immigration from non-English-speaking countries. Another trend is a
more inclusive policy that aims to maintain, or revitalize, indigenous languages of the
nation. In other nations where English is predominantly used alongside other languages,
English-language policy has centred on it being a lingua franca of education and administration, alongside a number of home languages. Singapore's English +1 policy is a prime
example. Other postcolonial nations like Malaysia, however, have reduced emphasis on
English in recent years, although the increased status of English as the language of ASEAN
is likely to reverse this flow. Other policy has centred on the promotion of English in
order to leverage the benefits of it as a lingua franca of trade and business, as illustrated by
national policy in Georgia and Rwanda. In nations where English has seeped in other than
through policy, such as many Scandinavian countries, there is evidence of a growing
backlash to the threat it might pose to the national languages.

In sum, English is making a splash in nations around the world, and has been met
either with policies to increase this trend or with a backlash of policies to curb it.

Chapter summary

This chapter has examined the issues and attitudes surrounding the spread of English as a
global lingua franca. Section 3a examined the advantages brought to nations. However,
the spread of English and the adoption of it as a lingua franca come at a cost, discussed in
Section 3b. The spread of English has caused a reduction in global linguistic diversity. In
many contexts, the loss of language means a loss of identity, traditions, and practices that
are tied to that language. With the death of languages comes the hegemony of global
cultures and the notion of Americanization of ideals and practices. The question of blame
for the adoption of English and abandonment of local languages was the subject of
Section 3c, which examined arguments for and against linguistic imperialism – a notion
that states the spread of English and destruction of other languages was the direct result
of policies connected to colonialism and the pursuit of power through inequality.
Arguments against linguistic imperialism take a more bottom–up perspective, in that
languages were abandoned by speakers in favour of English as an indirect consequence of
colonialism and globalization, and that partial blame for its current status be attributed to
speakers, who are driven by personal gain.

Section 3d put aside the argument of blame in an examination of current policy connected with how languages are promoted and curbed. In some places, policies promoted

English at the expense of other languages (American bilingual education policy) and others actively revitalized languages (e.g. Wales and New Zealand). We also examined policy in light of globalization, which promotes English education and use through a top-down policy (such as Georgia's switch from Russian to English), and which aims to curb the bottom-up intrusion of English into educational domains (such as in Sweden).

Issues and attitudes surrounding English are a complex mix of factors that can be measured in terms of policy and social discourse, but also subtler factors such as the prestige attached to the language and opportunities afforded by speaking some languages over others.

Further reading

On the effects of the spread of English:

- Crystal, D. (2003). *English as a Global Language*. Cambridge: Cambridge University Press.
- Crystal, D. (2002). *Language Death*. Cambridge: Cambridge University Press.

On linguistic imperialism:

- Phillipson, R. (1992b). *Linguistic Imperialism*. Oxford: Oxford University Press.
- Canagarajah, S. (1999b). *Resisting Linguistic Imperialism*. Oxford: Oxford University Press.

On language policy:

- Spolsky, B. (ed.). (2012). *The Cambridge Handbook of Language Policy*. Cambridge: Cambridge University Press.

Closing activities

Chapter discussion questions

Section 3a

1 Of all the benefits of having English as a lingua franca, which is the most persuasive, and which is the most disputable?
2 Which of the factors that affect whether a language is rejected or adopted figure heavily in determining the use of English in postcolonial nations today?
3 Do you think, as these factors change, we will see expansions or reductions in the way English is used in nations in the future?

Section 3b

1 What is lost when languages die?
2 What issues surround the Americanization of cultures around the world?
3 Do you see English as a killer language?

Section 3c

1 In a context you are familiar with, what has been the impact on languages of the spread of English, from either a top-down or a bottom-up perspective?
2 What are the arguments for and against linguistic imperialism?
3 Canagarajah (1999b) argues that, in periphery communities (in everyday communication and local contexts), people are resisting the spread of English by using it in a manner that suits their needs. He argues that practices of code-switching and engaging in discourse on the spread of English are subtle ways to challenge the dominance of English. What is your view on this?

Section 3d

1 Do you believe policies to maintain or revitalize minority languages in ENL countries are effective?
2 Do you know of policies similar to the English-only policy of the USA in countries where speakers of languages other than English have been disadvantaged and encouraged to abandon home languages in favour of English?
3 The section ends with a quote from Seidlhofer (2006) on the spread of English in Europe. Do you think the benefits of the spread of English outweigh the negative effects?

Debate topics

1 The spread of English at the expense of other languages is the clear result of linguistic imperialism.
2 Organizations, such as the EU, must switch to a single working language in order to leverage the advantages provided by a lingua franca.
3 **Language revitalization** policies, such as in New Zealand, Ireland, and Wales, will not save languages in the long run, but only prolong their death.

Writing and presentation prompts

Below are ideas for writing and presentation tasks to apply the knowledge learned in Chapter 3. Additional assignment prompts can be found on the companion website.

	Assignment topics
Personal account	Write a short reflection on the pros and cons of English's rise as a lingua franca. What are the most salient issues to your community at the moment? How has this rise affected you?
Research task (see website for worksheet)	Using the worksheet and documents on the companion website, analyse English language policy in the USA. Examine whether the support and criticisms of this policy in public discourse can be supported or refuted by evidence in the No Child Left Behind Act.
Basic academic	Research a language that has fewer than 100,000 speakers. Discuss the factors leading to its possible demise and what will be lost if it becomes extinct. Have there been any efforts to maintain or revitalize it?
Advanced academic	Explore the linguistic imperialism debate. Evaluate the evidence provided by proponents and those who are more sceptical about its involvement in the spread of English (a bottom-up perspective).

Chapter 4

Variation in 'Native' Englishes

Introductory activities

The following introductory activities are designed to encourage the reader to think about the issues raised in this chapter before reading it.

Look at the list of grammar-syntactical variations in English grammar below.

Example sentences

1 I done eat the ice-cream.
2 I seen something strange.
3 She's a nice car, that is.
4 I went to town for to see a doctor.
5 You joking!
6 Is it half eight already? I best be going.
7 I was sat here when he came in.
8 The children sings beautifully.
9 I didn't say nothing.
10 I never knew he had a brother.
11 He swim in that river every day.
12 You sing real good.

Discussion questions

1 Based on the ideas presented in Chapter 2 of a 'standard' English, discuss and record on a scale of 1–4 whether the sentences above fit into an ideology of acceptable English. (1 = completely acceptable; 2 = acceptable; 3 = unacceptable; 4 = completely unacceptable.)
2 Are there any forms that you, personally, believe are completely acceptable, but that standard language proponents might not?
3 Are there any forms that might be more acceptable in certain regions of the world?
4 All the above sentences are typical of native English speakers around the world. How do you think such differences emerged?

Case study: South Africa – Inner or Outer Circle?

South Africa's placement in Kachru's Three Circle Model is highly problematic, as discussed in Chapter 1. The use of English in South Africa meets the criteria of the Inner Circle, and South Africa is considered by many to be an ENL nation. English is the main language for government, administration, and commerce, and is widely understood alongside Afrikaans. However, English is a first language for only 9.6 per cent of the population, and is an official language alongside 10 other languages of which Zulu, Xhosa, and Afrikaans all have more native speakers. Thus, for many English is a second language, as in Outer Circle countries like Singapore. While some forms of South African English resemble other 'native' new world varieties (Bowerman, 2008), other forms have many features that resemble 'New' Englishes, such as the existence of **acrolect** and **mesolect** forms and a reduced vowel set (van Rooy, 2008). This is most likely the result of different channels of spread to the region, via both Channel 1 (settler colonization) and Channel 3 (trade and exploitation colonization), unlike most other British colonies where it was predominately one or the other.

Discussion

1   Where would you place South Africa in Kachru's model?
2   What role did apartheid play in the problematic placement of South Africa in the Three Circle Model? Without apartheid, what would have been the hypothetical result of language use in South Africa?
3   How can the four-channel dispersal of the English language, outlined in Chapter 1, better describe the processes by which the Englishes in South Africa were formed?

Introduction

This chapter is devoted to exploring variations of 'Native' Englishes in nations that are often placed in the first diaspora of the spread of English, or the Englishes that emerged from Channel 1 (settler migration) and Channel 2 (slavery plantations). As Chapter 1 points out, categorizing Englishes into neat categories is an impossible task. This chapter looks at 'Native' Englishes, rather than Inner Circle Englishes, as we understand that not all native speakers of English live in the Inner Circle and not all speakers living in the Inner Circle are native English speakers. The term 'Native', then, is in inverted commas to indicate that this term is also problematic, in that many speakers of the 'New' Englishes are also native English speakers. As outlined in the *Preface*, Global Englishes prefers to examine language use as a fluid construct, and thus problematizes the very notion that borders can be drawn around malleable constructs as illusive as 'varieties' and 'dialects'. Nevertheless, the Global Englishes paradigm is built on the foundations provided by World Englishes research, and thus to ignore this important research would be doing a disservice to the understanding of the global use of English today. Therefore, this chapter (and Chapter 5 on 'New' Englishes) will present variation in the English language according to geographically defined 'varieties', with the explicit understanding that the English language is not bound by geographic or linguistic boundaries. It is also important to note that we are not geographically representative in our summary of variation in 'Native' Englishes and merely provide illustrative examples.

In Section 4a we examine the Englishes typical of the British Isles, including England, Wales, Scotland, and Ireland. We include linguistically codified varieties across the British Isles from Ireland to East Anglia. In Section 4b the Englishes of North America are discussed, with reference to regional and socio-economic divisions across this continent. In Section 4c the Englishes of Australia and New Zealand are explored, followed in Section 4d by the Englishes of the Caribbean. Each section of this chapter is divided into identical subsections, examining the history and role of English, followed by an outline of variation in phonology, lexis, grammar, and pragmatics. Each section then concludes with a discussion of issues surrounding variation in that region.

Much research into native varieties of English is based on **corpus**-based studies, which aim to investigate authentic language use. Well-known corpora of native English speaker usage include:

- COBUILD (at www.mycobuild.com/about-collins-corpus.aspx), a corpus of 4.5 billion words that is updated monthly to include new coinages;
- The British National Corpus (BNC, at www.natcorp.ox.ac.uk);
- The Michigan Corpus of Academic Spoken English (MICASE, at http://quod.lib. umich.edu/m/micase/).

4a English language variation in the British Isles

The history of English in the British Isles

The history of English and the spread of language *from* the UK has been outlined in great length in Chapter 1. It is important to note, however, that colonization elsewhere had an effect on language *within* the UK, too. For example, there has been mass migration of the Irish population into parts of England, Scotland, and Wales, which heavily influenced the English spoken in these regions. Over 400,000 people living in England and Wales were born in Ireland, and those with Irish ancestry living in the UK are in the millions. Cities such as Liverpool are places of known continued historical Irish settlement, and there have been links made between the distinctive accent spoken in that city and Irish English.

Populations from colonies such as India were brought to the UK to fill labour needs, as were people from African colonies. Later, before the Commonwealth Immigration Act of 1962, citizens of Commonwealth nations could enter the UK freely, bringing in large populations from India, the Caribbean, and the further-afield Australia and New Zealand. Since then, other agreements between these nations, and citizenship granted to those of British ancestry, has maintained a continuous stream of immigrants from former colony nations. According to the National Census for 2011, for example, 694,148 people in the UK were born in India, a further 482,137 people were born in Pakistan, and 211,500 people were from Bangladesh. In addition to migration from Commonwealth nations, the region has seen a sharp increase in the mobility of populations from Europe due to its participation in the EU. Two million people living in the UK in 2011, for example, were from EU countries, many of whom were from post-2001 accession countries, like Poland, which accounted for more than 570,000 of this total.

The role of English today in the British Isles

English is the only official language of England, although Cornish is a recognized regional language, and Welsh is the co-official language of Wales. In Scotland, English is the sole official language, although Scottish Gaelic is given equal respect as a recognized regional language under the Gaelic Language (Scottish) Act of 2005. Irish is the first official language in Ireland, although in practice English takes this role. According to 2011 census data, 92.3 per cent of the population in the United Kingdom speak English as the only language in the home. In the Republic of Ireland, English is the main language of the household, and Polish is the second most widely used language (2.5 per cent of the population), followed by Irish (41 per cent of the population can speak Irish, but only 1.8 per cent use it outside educational contexts).

Features of English in the British Isles

The divisions between the variation of Englishes spoken in the British Isles (the islands of Great Britain and Ireland) depend greatly on what aspect of linguistic variation is used as the benchmark for such divisions.

Sounds

PHONEMIC VARIATION

Based on this dimension of variation, Hughes, Trudgill and Watt (2012) claim there are five accent groups of the British Isles:

1   Scotland and the north of Ireland;
2   south of Ireland;
3   Wales;
4   north of England;
5   south of England.

The south of England is also commonly broken into two sub-groups: the south-west and south-east. As has been seen in this book thus far, it is not easy to categorize Englishes into neat categories, and exceptions and deviations can be found in and across these five categories. Nevertheless, it is a useful starting point to begin the investigation of regional variations.

VOWELS

A number of studies have been carried out over past decades that aimed to codify variation in vowels. This sections draws on a list of common words used by Wells (1982), which were selected because of their representation of English vowel sounds. Wells used RP and General American as reference accents to compare pronunciation differences within this lexical set. For example, using the lexical set, it can be stated that the vowel in *strut* is realized the same in RP and General American [ʌ], unlike the vowel in *bath*, which is different.

Variation and conformity exists across and within these accent groups, depending on the phonological features one is examining. For example, there appears to be great conformity between Irish and northern accents in terms of the pronunciation of the *strut* vowel. However, further examination finds that fundamental differences occur in other pronunciations, such as the vowel sounds in *bath* and *palm*. Some of the more notable differences in British Isles accents include the following.

- Vowel mergers of /ʌ/ and /ʊ/ – much research has focused on the *strut–foot* vowel merger. The /ʌ/ vowel does not appear in north of England accents (including the Midlands) and some Irish accents, where the [ʊ] vowel is realized in both words, making the words *strut* and *foot* rhyme due to a historical phonemic split of /ʌ/ and /ʊ/ (Hughes *et al.*, 2012), which did not take place in northern England or Ireland.
- Long–short vowel mergers – Scottish speakers make little distinction between length in /ʊ/ and /uː/, or in /ɒ/ and /ɔː/, causing *pool–pull* and *cot–caught* to be homophonous (Hughes *et al.*, 2012).
- Lexical distribution of /a/ and /ɑː/ – a distinction in north and south England can also be made with the vowels /a/ and /ɑː/. Northern accents have /a/ or /æ/ in *bath*, but southerners say /ɑː/. This feature also causes the word pairs of *pam–palm* to sound homophonous.

CONSONANTS

Notable variation of consonant pronunciation includes the following.

- Differences in /ŋ/ – within the group of north of England accents, a strong division exists even between neighbouring varieties, such as the addition of a distinct final /g/ sound in *sing* in Central Lancaster English, as opposed to a final nasal /ŋ/ in the neighbouring areas north of Lancaster and elsewhere.
- Dental fricatives realized as **alveolar plosives** – dental consonants (as in *think* and *they*) may be realized in Irish English as fricatives [θ ð], or as dental or alveolar plosives [t d]. An Irish speaker may switch between [θ] and [t] or [ð] and [d] to accommodate various interlocutors. As a general rule, however, the further north one goes in Ireland, the more likely one is to encounter [θ] and [ð] as the norm.
- Dental fricatives realized as labiodental – the realization of labiodental fricatives [f v] in place of RP accent dental fricatives [θ ð] also exists across the British Isles, and often has developed independently in regions as diverse as Scotland, Yorkshire, London, the south-west, and the south-east. It has been reported, for example, that [v] has been used in place of [ð] in words like *smooth* in Glasgow, far from its historical origins (Stuart-Smith, 2008).

As Chapter 2 has shown, the English language is always changing, and there have been numerous historical instances where this change has occurred in a short space of time (e.g. the Great Vowel Shift). Phonological shifts have occurred in recent times; an example is the realization of /t/ as the glottal stop in words such as *butter*, which was only observed in Scotland and the north of England in the first half of the century but can be now found in most urban areas of Britain (Beal, 2008a).

PROSODIC VARIATION

Some accents found in Newcastle, Belfast, and Dublin have a distinct rising tone in declarative sentences (Beal, 2008a), and thus mimic the intonation of a question. Orkney English and Welsh speech (Upton, 2008) are also impressionistically referred to as having a 'sing-song' lilt (Beal, 2008a, p. 140), although linguistic evidence to support this is weak. In Irish English there is a falling pitch in yes/no questions. In many accents across the region, schwa is also inserted in consonant clusters, as in words like *film*, being realized as [ləm], a feature that is particularly distinct in both Scotland and across Ireland.

Vocabulary

Lexical variation has received less attention than variation in phonology. However, substantial variation exists. Notable lexical variation includes the following.

- Borrowing from indigenous languages – contact with the Celtic language in various parts of the British Isles has resulted in the adoption of borrowed lexical items. In Scotland, there has been minimal borrowing, as seen from everyday words like *glen* (valley) and *loch* (lake), and in Ireland some Irish terms are used in English language, e.g. *gardai* (police) and *the craic* (a good time).
- Borrowing from foreign languages – English was also influenced heavily by historical invaders, free settlers, and immigrants. Old Norse influenced heavily settled areas of Scotland, as did French due to the 'Auld Alliance' between Scotland and France from 1295 to 1560. For example, Old Norse influence in Scotland can be seen in the use of words such as *bairn* (child).
- Same meaning, different words – local words for livestock, fish, and fauna, for example, differ even over small geographic distances, with small fishing villages in close proximity adopting different words for the fish caught and sold in their local areas (although, with the centralization of markets in recent decades, a levelling of vocabulary has occurred). Specific words, like *splinter* (wooden shard), can vary considerably. *An Atlas of English Dialects* (Upton and Widdowson, 1996), for example, offers nine alternative words (*spell, spelk, speel, spill, splie, spool, splint, shiver,* and *silver*) for *splinter* in England alone, as shown in Figure 4.1.

Grammar-syntactic variation

As with phonological variation, morphological and syntactical variation in the British Isles is immense. This section draws heavily from Kortmann and Upton (2008), and illustrative examples are taken from the following sources, which cover six regions of the British Isles, and further examples can be found within them: Irish English (Filppula, 2008), Welsh English (Penhallurick, 2008), the north of England (Beal, 2008b), Scottish English (Miller, 2008), south-west England (Wagner, 2008), and south-east England (Anderwald, 2008). These regions are not exhaustive or exclusive, and further variation exists within and across these regions. For example, in some parts of the UK there is conformity across urban–rural and socio-economic lines, rather than pure geography.

Figure 4.1 Lexical variation in England (adapted from Upton and Widdowson, 1996)

- Aspect – the use of progressive aspects (verb + *-ing*) in a wider range of applications is observable in Scotland and Ireland, such as: *Barbara is knowing the answer* (Barbara knows the answer), and is also observable in Wales (Kortmann, 2008).
- Irregular verb variation – irregular verbs occur in Scottish English, such as *brung* instead of *brought*, *writ* instead of *wrote*, and *selt* instead of *sold*. In northern England, a levelling of past and present participle forms is observed, sometimes occurring with the present particle replacing the past form (*do–done–done* instead of *do–did–done*), and at other times the past form replacing the present participle (*bite–bit–bit* instead of *bite–bit–bitten*).
- Adverbs – adverbs frequently take the same form as the adjective and this is pervasive across all regions in the British Isles, as in *I did good* (I did well) and *I won that easy* (I won that easily).
- Plurality and concord with collective nouns – in Scotland, the following may be heard: *the windies wiz aw broken* ('was' replacing 'were' in stating 'the windows were all broken'); and *the lambs is oot the field* ('is' replacing 'are'). In Ireland, statements like *the town is changed and improved in recent years* ('is' replacing 'has') and *there was four of us* ('was' replaced 'were') are common. Similar examples of subject–verb disagreement are found in the south-east of England. Of interest is the **Northern Subject Rule**, which dictates that 'a verb takes an -s in the plural, where the subject is a noun or noun phrase, but not when it is a pronoun' (Beal, 2008b, p. 381). The rule dictates that *the children sings beautifully* would be acceptable, but not *they sings beautifully*. In other areas associated with northern syntax, such as Ireland, examples of language that break this rule have been observed, such as *they learns it* and *we bakes it* (Filppula, 2008).

- **Negation** – we see variation in Scottish English, such as *she's no leaving* (she isn't leaving) and 'none' used to indicate an absence of ability, as in *Rab can sing nane* (Rob cannot sing). *Never* is often used as a term of negation across regions, such as in statements like *I never knew he had a brother*. Double negation also exists across the British Isles in examples like *it didn't make no sense*, although it is more widespread in the south than in the north of England (Kortmann, 2008). Statements such as *he's not been well lately* are frequent in Irish English and northern English, among other regions.
- Auxiliary verbs – this varies considerably, and each region is subject to different rules. For example, *want* is used instead of *should* or *ought* in both Scotland and northern England, such as in the example *you'll want to see a dentist about that tooth!* Double modal use occurs in these same two regions, such as in the examples *he'll can help us in the morning* (Scotland) and *I might could change it* (northern England).
- Pronouns – in Wales, a greater array of pronouns is used than in other regions, with *thee, thou, thy, thine,* and *yourn* still in use, although traditional dialects in northern England have also retained the use of *thee* and *thy*. The south-west of England sees substitution of pronouns, such as the use of *I* instead of *me* in cases like *she did give I an earful*. Substitution, to a lesser degree, can also be seen in the south-east in the cases of: *me* used widely instead of *my* (as in *let me grab me coat*); *us* used instead of *we* (as in *us kids can ride for free*); and *us* used instead of *me* (as in *give us a go* in place of 'give me a go'). The south-west also sees gender-neutral pronouns replaced by **gendered pronouns** when referring to inanimate objects (*she's a beautiful car*), although this feature is receding to the point of being used in just 1 per cent of cases (Wagner, 2008).
- Word order – numerous variations can be found, including the placement of predicates at the front of sentences in Wales, as in the example *right you are* (referred to as 'predicate fronting'). Another syntactic feature referred to as 'dislocation' occurs in the north of England, as in the example of *he's got his head screwed on, has Dave* (Beal, 2008b).

As a general observation, when certain features of morphology and syntax are compared across regions, a north–south divide is evident. Kortmann (2008) compares these features in a table, which has been condensed and summarized in Table 4.1. In this table, a single check mark indicates that use has been observed, although it might not be frequently used, and a double check indicates that use has been observed in a more prevalent manner.

Attitudes toward English variation in the British Isles

In modern times, there seems to be a dichotomy of movement towards, and away from, standardization. While RP seems alive and well in UK political circles, in pop culture regional varieties of English are thriving. The Beatles' popularity did much to raise the international profile of the Liverpool accent. Likewise, celebrities like Cheryl Cole (a singer and a judge on a popular UK television show) have done much to raise the profile of the Newcastle accent. However, grammar-syntactical variation from the 'norm' is still heavily associated with a lack of education, and thus attracts more negative social evaluation. While geography plays a major role in determining an accent in the UK, social boundaries also play a pivotal role; an RP accent can be found in almost any region of the UK, and is determined by socio-economic factors rather than geographic boundaries.

Table 4.1 Kortmann's (2008, p. 491) synopsis of variation in parts of the British Isles

	North			South		
	Scottish English	Irish English	Northern English	Welsh English	South-West English	South-East English
Second person plural pronouns: *youse, y'all, you guys*	✓	✓✓	✓✓	✗	✗	✗
Progressive tense widening: *She's knowing that well*	✓	✓✓	✓	✗	✗	✗
Be as perfect auxiliary: *They're not finished yet*	✓	✓✓	✓	✗	✓	✗
Double modals: *I tell you what we might should do*	✓✓	✗	✓✓	✗	✗	✗
Must for conclusions drawn: *This mustn't be true*	✓✓	✓	✓✓	✗	✗	✓
What you doing?	✓	✓✓	✓✓	✗	✗	✗
You get the point?	✓	✓✓	✓✓	✓✓	✗	✗
Ain't for negative 'be'	✗	✗	✓	✓	✓	✓
Ain't for negative 'have'	✗	✗	✗	✗	✓	✓
I wasn't a doing nothing	✗	✗	✗	✓	✓	✓
They had them in their hair, innit?	✓	✗	✗	✓✓	✓	✓
What in relative clauses: *This is the man what painted my house*	✗	✓✓	✗	✓	✓	✓

4b   English language variation in Canada and the USA

The history of English in North America

English was brought to North America in the form of permanent English-speaking settlements from the early 1600s, and the historic patterns of settlement lend much to the differences in dialects spoken there today. The first regions to be settled were the eastern parts of the USA and, due to a historic lack of mobility across these regions, variation in these areas tends to be strongest. With the Louisiana purchase of 1803 and the California gold rush soon afterwards, the population spread across the continent rapidly. From a linguistic perspective, these later-settled areas saw more dialect mixing and thus more conformity across them. For example, a Seattle resident and a Los Angeles resident might have indistinguishable accents, despite living 2,000 kilometres apart; however, a Boston accent and a New York accent are completely distinguishable, as are a Philadelphian accent and a Virginian accent, despite being less than 300 kilometres apart.

The emergence of a standard American English did not happen in the same way as in the British Isles. In fact, Kretzschmar (2010, p. 101) argues that standard American English is an institutional construct, with 'no native speakers'. Standard American is characterized by speech that avoids marked accent features, rather than conforming to a given 'standard'. This does not mean that it is neutral, but that it is devoid of characteristics usually associated with particular *regional* American accents. Thus, a speaker could pronounce the vowel in *cob* as [kɑb] or [kɔb] yet still be considered a speaker of standard American, as this variation is not associated with a marked accent (Kretzschmar, 2008). Thus, the basis of a standard American accent is its avoidance of features that make marked accents like those of Boston, New York, Philadelphia, or Minnesota distinct.

The role of English today in North America

In the USA, English is the de facto official language for most political, administrative, and educational functions. According to 2011 census data, it is the main language of 79.4 per cent of the population. Spanish speakers constitute half of the 21 per cent of the population who speak another language at home.

In Canada, English is the official language alongside French, and 17.4 per cent of the population are bilingual in both official languages. More than 20 per cent of the Canadian population reported a mother tongue other than English or French, but only 6.2 per cent reported this language as being the sole language of the household.

Features of English in North America

This section illustrates variation in English usage, with illustrative examples from Canada and the USA, although limited space has resulted in an uneven coverage of variation (especially for Canada). It might be useful to first crudely summarize some distinctive features that differentiate American English from British English, and this is done in Table 4.2.

Sounds

PHONEMIC VARIATION

Phonological variation sometimes manifests in a geographic distinction, sometimes in an urban–rural division, and at times according to ethnicity. Because of this, it is difficult to categorize into neat groups. For example, a small geographic region of the USA, such as New Orleans, may contain speakers of a variety of accents, including an urban southern accent, a rural southern white accent, an African American Vernacular accent, a Cajun creole accent, and a standard American accent. But in crude terms, the continent can be divided into the following accents: Newfoundland; Atlantic

Table 4.2 Differences between American English and British English

	American English	British English (RP)
Rhoticity	Rhotic, e.g. /ɹ/ in car	Non-rhotic
Vowels	/ɒ/ in *lot* and /æ/ in *bath*	/ɑ/ in *lot* and /ɑː/ in *bath*
Word stress	First syllable stress in *locate*	Second syllable stress in *locate*
Spelling	*Color; center; canceled*	*Colour; centre; cancelled*
Lexis	*Sweater*	*Jumper*
Grammar	*I have a car*	*I've got a car*

Provinces/Maritimes; east New England; west New England; New York; Western Pennsylvania; Canada (southern regions of British Columbia to Ontario); the north; inland north; mid-Atlantic; mid-Western; and the south, including the inland south and Texas south. This, of course, is not without the inherent difficulties of drawing geographic boundaries around a notion as fluid as language variation. A geographical map of accents is provided on the companion website.

VOWELS

- Vowel mergers – a vowel shift occurred in Canadian English, causing /ɔ/ to be realized as [ɒː].
- Vowel lengthening – the above-mentioned shift, when coupled with a vowel lengthening prevalent across much of North America, has resulted in homophonous pairing of words like *cot* and *caught*, and *don* and *dawn* (Levey, 2010).
- Diphthong shift – the phenomenon of **Canadian rising** has also received much attention, and describes a tendency to raise the diphthongs /aʊ/ and /ai/ (that is, to realize the first vocalic components of these diphthongs as more close vowels), but this phenomenon is also found in many parts of the USA. The famous example is the raising of /aʊ/ to [ʌʊ] in words like *about*, erroneously mimicked by Americans as *a boot*.
- Vowels are realized as diphthongs – a distinct property of southern American English is the diphthongization of short vowels, e.g. the /i/ vowel in *think* is realized as vowels in the range of [ɛi~æi] (Thomas, 2008).
- Vowel mergers – splits on some vowel pairs, with a famous example being the *Mary–merry–marry* lexical set. For most of the USA and Canada, the vowels before the intervocalic /r/ have been levelled, to be equivalent of the vowel in *square*. Thus, in standard American, these three words are all pronounced /'meɪri/ or /'mɛəri/, depending on accent. However, in the New York City, New Jersey, and Boston vicinity a three-way distinction is still present (/'mɛəri/, /'mɛri/, and /'mæri/), and in parts of Pennsylvania a two-way distinction is observed (with *marry* being distinct). Linguists have stated that this levelling was not historically prevalent across the USA, with it being more noticeable in younger generations than older generations in the south (Thomas, 2008). It is possible that this difference may become levelled entirely across the North American continent in the future. The mobility of population in the USA is causing greater conformity in recent years, attested by the fact that Florida accents are closer to the accents of the north-east than to those of the south.

CONSONANTS

- Deletion of phonemes in consonant clusters – in many varieties, the deletion of the final sound in a consonant cluster occurs at the end of words, resulting in words like *tas'* (task) and *help'* (helped).
- Dental fricatives – the realization of /θ/ and /ð/ to produce [t] and [d] is less common across North America than we saw in the British Isles. However, it does happen infrequently in accents such as Newfoundland and African American Vernacular. The labiodental, replacing dental, fricatives (e.g. /v/ for /ð/) in intervocalic environments occurs even less frequently.

Vocabulary

Lexical variation includes the following.

- Borrowing from indigenous languages – Canadian English originally adopted more borrowings from indigenous languages, resulting in words like *kayak* and *toboggan*, which have since spread to other parts of the world. In general, indigenous languages have made minimal impact on the English spoken in the USA.
- Borrowing from non-indigenous languages – in French-speaking regions, French has infiltrated the language, as is the case for Montréal, Quebec, and Louisiana. Many African words also entered the English language through the creole languages and have since spread to English worldwide, such as *tote* (to carry by hand) via Gullah and *mojo* (a magical, effective power) via Louisiana Creole. Some areas of the USA have seen modern lexical borrowing in recent decades, due to immigration from Spanish-speaking linguistic communities.
- Same meaning, different words – words attributed to everyday objects differ greatly. For some, we can see a historical trend, with *tennis shoes* used as the pre-ferred term in the earlier settled north-eastern part of the USA, but *sneakers* used elsewhere. For other words, there is a more-or-less north–south divide, such as *crayfish* used in the north but *crawfish* preferred in the south and most of the west (with large pockets of speakers who prefer *crawdad*). Other words show an east–west split, such as the use of the phrase *drinking fountain* in the west and *water fountain* in the east (with *bubbler* the preferred term in pockets). A carbonated drink poses a bigger challenge, with *soda* being the preferred term in the historical north-east and the cities of Chicago and St. Louis, but also in areas including and sur-rounding California. *Pop* is the preferred term in the north of the USA and Canada, and *coke* in the south.

Grammar-syntactic variation

As with other regions, grammar-syntactic variation in North American Englishes is immense, with illustrative examples provided as follows.

- Adverbs – the use of adverbs without -ly is pervasive across the North American continent (*she runs quick*).
- Negation – double negation is pervasive throughout the continent (*he didn't do nothing*).
- Pronouns – gendered pronouns (*she's a beautiful table*) are noted across many regions of the continent.
- Tense and aspect – the levelling of tenses has followed a similar pattern to that of the British Isles, with tenses being levelled to include a broader range of meaning. In many cases, the past participle has been replaced with the past form and vice versa. Examples from colloquial American are: *we have swam there*; *she'd sung*; *I seen something strange*. Unlike British Isles Englishes, the plain verb, in place of the past and past participle in American English, is much more prevalent, such as in the following examples from Murray and Simon (2008): *he swim in that river just about every day of his life* and *he come in about 15 minutes late*. The bare root used in

the past tense is particularly pervasive throughout African American Vernacular and Gullah.

At times, there is also a tendency for grammar-syntactic features to be observed in ethnic or social varieties. For example, the perfective *done* is observed in pockets across the continent (e.g. *that squirrel was done eat* in Appalachian English (Montgomery, 2008)), and is also pervasive in African American Vernacular. In African American Vernacular, the perfective 'done' is also constructed differently, using the past tense (e.g. *they done used all the good ones*), and it is also used to describe a future conditional state, as in *my ice cream be done melted by the time we get there* (Wolfram, 2008).

There is also a north–south division. For example, the second person plural pronoun *y'all* is used pervasively in the south, in favour of *you guys* in the north and the west (although geographic pockets prefer alternative terms such as *yous* in Newfoundland).

Thus, morphological and syntactical variation in North American English is complex. At times, variation occurs on geographical dimensions (such as the use of *y'all*), but often urban–rural factors, socio-economic factors, linguistic influence, and historical factors are more important in determining the morphological and syntactic composition of the Englishes used today across North America.

Attitudes toward English variation in North America

Milroy and Milroy (1999, p. 160) state,

> In the USA, bitter divisions created by slavery and the civil war shaped a language ideology focused on racial discrimination, rather than on the class distinctions characteristic of an older monarchical society, like Britain, which continue to shape language attitudes.

North American Englishes that stray from standard American English generally attract negative societal views, such as a commonplace distasteful public disparagement of African American English (Milroy and Milroy, 1999). Appalachian accents are often used to depict uneducated characters, such as in *The Simpsons* (an American TV Show), where linguistic variation is used to make a social distinction between Cletus's family (a poor, rural family) and the rest of the townspeople. When the movie *Star Wars: The Phantom Menace* was first released, there was controversy that the bumbling, idiotic character of Jar Jar Binks used speech patterns reminiscent of African American Vernacular Englishes.

On the other hand, some marked accents are associated with positive values, notably southern ones which are often more favourably viewed in the south than the standard American accent. Much of this view is based in the bitter history of the North and the South, which has created separate cultural identities. In recent American politics, it seems that a standard American accent (Barrack Obama, Ronald Reagan) or a southern accent (George H. W. Bush, Bill Clinton, George W. Bush) are preferred for presidential candidates. The politics of standard language ideology permeate deep in US history, which perhaps explains why standard American is created from avoidance of features that deviate from such ideals.

4c   English language variation in Australia and New Zealand

The history of English in Australia and New Zealand

The Englishes that emerged in Australia and New Zealand were the result of a mixing of contact dialects from numerous parts of the British Isles. This type of mixing of dialects is referred to as **koineization**, which involves wide-scale levelling of mutually intelligible dialects. The koineization processes in New Zealand and Australian accents were very similar, and largely occurred during heavy periods of colonization around the turn of the nineteenth century. This might explain why some untrained ears might confuse these accents. However, the variables, such as proportions of dialects in each of the country's koineization mix and contact with other languages, have in fact created quite distinct variation across and within each of the regions.

Burridge (2010) discusses a number of stages in the formation of new dialects in the koineization process that involve initial levelling of minority features, followed by variation among speakers, then stabilization, and finally nativization of local patterns in language. In the cases of Australia and New Zealand, there is evidence that the first generation of those born in these new colonies adopted their parents' accents, with considerable mixing and variation, but that the accents began to stabilize with the following generation.

New Zealand is a unique case because it is the youngest 'Native' English variety of the British settler colonies and audio recordings exist to document its full development. A distinct variety of English is noticeable in such recordings as early as 1870 (Maclagan, 2010), a variation that is also referred to in written documents at the time, which report a 'colonial twang'. This is quite remarkable because it indicates that the process of stabilization happened within a couple of generations of heavy settlement.

In Australia, koineization occurred with a mix of accents from across Great Britain and Ireland, with London-based accents being the dominant type (Burridge, 2010). New Zealand, on the other hand, comprised settlers from the rural south-east of England, as well as from Scotland and Ireland. Irish English is not thought to have had a huge impact in the region, despite being well represented, and it has been argued that the Irish accent was easily distinguishable and identifiable at the time, and thus effort may have been undertaken to avoid rather than emulate it, meaning that features of a distinctly Irish accent receded rather than becoming adopted (Hickey, 2010). This might partially explain the notable absence of the rhotic post-vocalic /r/ across this region, except in the Southland region of New Zealand.

There were great differences in the make up of settlers in each region. For example, Scottish immigrants in 1871 in the Southland region of New Zealand constituted 61 per cent of the population, but less than 10 per cent in the Taranaki region (Gordon and Maclagan, 2008), which, naturally, caused quite distinct accents to originally develop (and may partially explain the rhotic accent that is found in the region today). However, the mobility of the population over the years caused a levelling of accents throughout most of New Zealand, so that far fewer differences in accent are found today.

The role of English today in Australia and New Zealand

English is the de facto official language of Australia, which has no stated official language. It is an official language in New Zealand, alongside Māori and sign language. In

New Zealand, English is spoken in 95 per cent of homes, although it is often used alongside other community languages in migrant populations. In Australia, it is the main language spoken in 80 per cent of homes, with others using a variety of community languages, such as Mandarin, Italian, Greek, Vietnamese, and Cantonese, often alongside English in bilingual families and communities.

It is worth noting that English plays a major role in other nations in this region of the world. English is the official language of Micronesia, Fiji, Kiribati, Nauru, Palau, Papua New Guinea, Samoa, the Solomon Islands, Tonga, Tuvalu, and Vanuatu. Apart from Micronesia, where English is the sole official language, in other nations English is used to varying degrees alongside native languages (e.g. Fijian, Tongan), non-native languages (e.g. Hindi in Fiji, French in Vanuatu), and creoles (e.g. Tok Pisin in Papua New Guinea).

Features of English in Australia and New Zealand

As with previous sections, in this section we will examine phonemic and prosodic variation, lexical variation, grammar-syntactic variation, and pragmatic variation.

Sounds

PHONEMIC VARIATION

Famous differences in vowel pronunciation across these regions include the following.

- Vowel mergers – the merger of the vowels found in the words *near* and *square* to the /iə/ diphthong in the New Zealand region causes *bear* and *bare* to be pronounced the same as *beer*.
- Vowel distinctions – the *kit* vowel in New Zealand English is 'notoriously centralized, to such an extent that it is parodied by Australians using their *strut* [ʌ] vowel' (Bauer and Warren, 2008, p. 46). Australians take delight in mimicking the New Zealand accent in pronouncing *fish and chips* as [fʌʃ ən tʃʌps], and New Zealanders do the same to Australians, using their [iː] vowel in saying [fiːʃ ən tʃiːps]. In reality, New Zealanders' pronunciation is closer to [fəʃ ən tʃps], and Australians use the short /ɪ/ sound.
- Vowel distinctions /æ/ and /aː/ – there are class and regional differences in the pronunciation of certain vowels, such as /æ/ or /aː/ in words like *chance* and *castle* (Bradley, 2008), with middle classes favouring the latter. There is also a geographic distinction here, with some cities that are known to project pride in the fact that they were not established as a convict settlement, such as Adelaide, also favouring the latter. (Note: the *bath* vowel in Australian [aː] and British [ɑː] differs slightly.)

CONSONANT VARIATION

Unique differences in consonant pronunciation include the following.

- Rhoticity – speech is generally non-rhotic across the region, except in some pockets like the Southland region of New Zealand. However, it has been noted that in New

Zealand words like *Ireland* include a [ɹ] in order to semantically differentiate it from *island* (Bauer and Warren, 2008).

- /t+j/ and /d+j/ sequences in Australian English (in words like *Tuesday* and *due*) are realized as **affricates** [tʃ dʒ] when they precede the /ʊ/ and /u/ vowels, resulting in homophonous realization of words like *dune* and *June*. This feature is also common in RP.

PROSODIC VARIATION

Australian English has been the subject of a number of studies that highlight the high rising tone of declarative sentences, mimicking the pitch pattern of a question. This is particularly noticeable in younger generations, and especially teenage girls. As it is particularly common in descriptions and narratives, it has been thought to have developed from a need to seek verification that the listener is following what is being said (Horvath, 2008), and not from insecurity, as others have proposed in the past.

Vocabulary

- Borrowing from indigenous languages – lexical borrowing from indigenous languages was much more prevalent in New Zealand than in Australia. In Australia, lexical borrowing mainly occurred in the naming of aboriginal or local environmental items, such as *boomerang* (hunting weapon), *billabong* (waterhole), *kangaroo*, and *coolabah* (an indigenous tree), and half of Australian place names (e.g. *Geelong*, *Bondi [Beach]*, *Wollongong*, *Toowoomba*). In New Zealand, borrowing extends further than items associated with indigenous culture, and in recent years there has been a resurgence of Māori language borrowing into the English language. Many Māori words now appear in public written discourse without English glossing, much to the confusion of first-time visitors to New Zealand (Maclagan, 2010).
- Same meaning, different word – despite the mobility of the population, which caused a great deal of levelling of pronunciation across the continent of Australasia, lexical variation within the region has persevered. Walking in the woods is called *hiking* in Australia and *tramping* in New Zealand; light footwear are *jandals* in New Zealand and *thongs* in Australia; and a sweater is a *jumper* in Australia and a *jersey* in New Zealand. Differences are not always defined by country. The preferred term for swimwear is *togs* in Queensland and New Zealand, but *bathers* in southern parts of Australia and *swimmers* in New South Wales.
- Preserved vocabulary and idiomatic expressions – a note of interest here is the preservation of lexis that have been largely dropped from use in their UK origins. Examples include *billy* (a pot for boiling water) from Scotland, *fair dinkum* (authentic) from Derbyshire, *cobber* (mate) from Suffolk, and *stone the crows* (expression of surprise) from cockney (Burridge, 2010).
- Abbreviation – another common feature is lexical shortening, including the addition of the famous –o and –ie suffixes, typical of Australian English. The result is words like *tellie* (television), *chrissie pressies* (Christmas presents), *barbie* (barbeque), and *journo* (journalist). These features are also found in New Zealand English.

Grammar-syntactic variation

Much of the variation in Australia and New Zealand mimics some of that found in the previous two sections of this chapter on North American and British Isles Englishes. Common variations, such as tense levelling, pronounce substitution, double negatives, and subject–verb (dis)agreement are all widely found across these regions. Rather than rehash such examples, this section will note some areas of difference.

- Tense and aspect – studies have shown younger speakers in Australia are levelling irregular verbs, with 76 per cent of those aged 65 maintaining a *spring–sprang–sprung* distinction, compared with 24 per cent of those aged 10–24 who made a *spring–sprung–sprung* distinction (Collins and Peters, 2008). New Zealand English is more conservative in terms of the regularization of irregular verbs (Hundt *et al.*, 2004), maintaining distinctions that have been levelled elsewhere.
- Modal verbs – in other areas, however, Hundt *et al.*, 2004 show that New Zealand English has changed more quickly than the Englishes of Australia, such as the shedding of the modal *shall*. Modals in Australia and New Zealand are also of interest. In addition to the decline of *shall* in favour of *will*, and *should* in favour of *ought*, the region also sees *better* or *gotta* instead of *have to* or *should* (e.g. *we better go* and *we gotta go*).
- Pronouns – gendered pronouns in Australia attract the attention of some linguists (e.g. Pawley, 2004) who note inconsistency of use of gendered pronouns, as well as a division between objects that are consistently masculine (e.g. plants, animals) and objects that are consistently feminine (e.g. environment, buildings). Interestingly, a vehicle with an unknown driver is masculine (e.g. *a truck came flying out in front of me and he was swerving all over the place*), but vehicles themselves are feminine (e.g. *she's a beautiful car, that one*).

Pragmatics

A famous example in recent years of pragmatic variation of Australian English is the use of swear words. In a 2006 campaign, the Australian tourism board adopted the slogan 'Where the bloody hell are you?' in television spots and billboards, which was censored in the UK for use of the word *bloody*, and flagged in Canada for use of the word *hell*. The case serves as a good example of differences in the subtle pragmatic weight of terms between English-speaking cultures.

Attitudes toward English variation in Australia

The Australian media has been very active in bringing the accents of politicians to the forefront. The *Courier-Mail* newspaper, for example, has remarked how former prime minister, Julia Gillard, had 'a wonderful Australian accent and a genuinely democratic one', associating broad accents with political prowess. This was something Gillard was acutely aware of, as illustrated in her address to an international audience in Brussels where she drew attention to her accent by stating, 'Perhaps I should start by saying that, with my broad Australian accent, even the English speakers in the room may want to access the translation to make sure they're understanding my words.' Other politicians, such as Alexander Downer, have suffered due to their 'cultivated' Australian accent towards which the Australian media have been less forgiving, labelling it 'posh' and 'plummy'. In 2013, the then opposition leader, Tony Abbott, stated that his political party would 'always speak with a strong Australian accent' when targeting a member of the prime minister's cabinet, who spoke with a broad Scottish accent, as not being 'local' or 'home grown' (Farr, 2013). Ministers then singled out Belgian-born Mathias Cormann as a member of Abbott's cabinet who media pundits stated sounded 'more like Arnold Schwarzenegger than Slim Dusty [an Australian country singer]' (Farr, 2013). Because of such public attitudes, 'posh' Australian accents are very likely to vanish in the following decades as they are seen as the remnant of a colonial past (Moore, 2007).

4d English language variation in the Caribbean

This section looks at variation in English in the Caribbean separately from the rest of the North American continent, as English not only spread via different channels but the linguistic developments in the regions were also very different.

> Most importantly, in the present linguistic perspective, different settlements patterns have resulted in North American varieties of English being characterised by dialect transmission (with some degree of koineization, but also innovation), as against Caribbean forms of English being shaped by process of creolization.
>
> (Schneider, 2008a, p. 23)

For this reason, this chapter looks at variation of English in the Caribbean separately, while acknowledging the inherent dangers in making any geographic or historical division of linguistic boundaries. A prime example is the English of the Bahamas, which was also a settler destination for Anglo-Bahamian British loyalists who escaped the US after the Revolutionary War (Childs and Wolfram, 2008), and for Gullah-speaking Afro-Bahamians moving from South Carolina and Georgia. Similarly, Barbados developed very differently to other plantation colonies in the Caribbean, due to its long 300-year British colonization history, and the fact that settlers outnumbered slaves in the first 25 years of its settlement, marking a huge difference in language exposure in the creolization process (Blake, 2008).

The history of English in the Caribbean

In Chapter 2, the development of creoles and pidgins was discussed, giving the example of plantation creoles of the Caribbean. Creolization occurred in contexts where uprooted and linguistically diverse populations on new plantations needed to use English as a lingua franca to communicate with English-speaking masters and with each other. As a result, the creolization process occurred rapidly and other languages were abandoned, leaving English as the sole native language of new communities. The history of English use is quite different from the 'New' Englishes in trade and exploitation colonies (see Chapter 5), where the creolization process was much more drawn out and where English was (and still is) used alongside other languages. The history of English across the Caribbean is not uniform: while nations like Jamaica earned independence early, others, like Barbados, were British colonies until 1966. Likewise, unlike most Caribbean islands, the Bahamas was not a stable plantation colony from the outset due to its infertile soil, and was a haven for pirates and then British loyalists, only later becoming a colony of mostly unsuccessful plantations. Such differences all affect language development, and have given birth to variation in English throughout the region.

The role of English today in the Caribbean

English is the official language of a number of Caribbean nations, including Antigua and Barbuda, the Bahamas, Barbados, Dominica, Grenada, Jamaica, Saint Kitts and Nevis, Saint Lucia, Saint Vincent and the Grenadines, Trinidad and Tobago, and Belize. Only Jamaica lists its English creole (Patois) alongside English as a co-official language, although Bajan is a recognized regional language in Barbados. In most nations an official distinction is not made between the creole English and the official language. As mentioned in Chapter 2, the distinctions between an English creole and the English language are blurry, with the language taking on **basilect** and acrolect forms. Simmons-McDonald (2010) makes a distinction throughout much of the region between foreign English and 'radio and television' English, compared with colloquial English and creole English, indicating that a more standard form of English is used in the public sphere and that creole English is used in the social spheres.

Features of English in the Caribbean

This sections aims to introduce notions of English variation in the Caribbean, providing illustrative examples from the most populous regions, namely Jamaica, Trinidad and Tobago, the Bahamas, and Barbados.

Sounds

PHONEMIC VARIATION

Vowels   Vowel differences worth noting in the Caribbean region are often used to group Caribbean Englishes with either American or British accent families.

- Vowel mergers – in Trinidadian English, vowel mergers appear, such as the vowels in minimal pairs, *bird–bud, body–buddy, cut–cot–caught, bit–beat*, and *harm–ham*. Words like *hat* and *heart* are only distinguishable by vowel length (James and Youssef, 2008).
- Bahamian English vowels are more similar with North American than Caribbean varieties in the cases of their *goat* and *lot* vowels (Childs and Wolfram, 2008).
- The open-mid central vowel /ʌ/ in *strut* is prominent in Bajan English, but is rare in North American Englishes. Anglo-Bahamian Englishes are often compared with UK varieties of English (Childs and Wolfram, 2008).
- Bajan English has a distinctive pronunciation of the *price* and *prize* diphthong as [ʌɪ], which causes visitors to comment that Bajan English is somewhat 'reminiscent of the west of England, or an Irish brogue' (Blake, 2008, p. 315).

PHONEMIC VARIATION IN CONSONANTS

Consonant variation in the Caribbean worth noting includes the following.

- Dental fricatives – the stopping of voiced and voiceless dental fricatives is characteristic of Caribbean English, with /θ/ realized as [t], as in *think*, and /ð/ realized as [d], as in *these*. In Jamaican Patois, this realization is the norm, but not always in Jamaican English, indicating a point of distinction between the two. In the Bahamas, stopping of voiced dental fricatives is common, but stopping of voiceless dental fricatives is less common. Unlike some UK Englishes and African American Vernacular English, [v] rarely replaces /ð/ in words like *father*, nor does [f] replace /θ/ in words like *tooth*.

- [v] is used in place of /w/ in Bahamian English, and is especially prominent among the Anglo-Bahamian community (Childs and Wolfram, 2008).
- Rhoticity – Caribbean accents tend to be non-rhotic across most of the region, except in Bajan which is fully rhotic across all communities of speakers. This ties most Caribbean Englishes closer to UK varieties than those found in North America.
- There is a tendency in the Bahamas to delete the initial /h/ phoneme in words like *harm*, *hat*, *hurry* (to produce *'arm*, *'at*, *'urry*). Tobagonian English also omits the /h/ sound in most words where it is the initial sound (James and Youssef, 2008). The Anglo-Bahamian have been noted to add an initial [h] sound in words like *eggs* (to produce *heggs*), perhaps due to over-correction (Childs and Wolfram, 2008).
- Consonant clusters – in Togonian English, sounds are omitted in consonant clusters, such as *from* becoming *fom* and *smell* becoming *mell* (James and Youssef, 2008).

PROSODIC VARIATION

Prosodic variations in Caribbean English worth noting include the following.

- High rising tone – a high rising intonation tends to be a long-running characteristic of Bahamian English, linking it with more recent (unrelated) phenomenon occurring in Australia (Childs and Wolfram, 2008).
- Vowel assimilation in Jamaican English occurs across syllables, as in *see it* pronounced [siːt], and syllable amalgamation occurs across syllables like *do it*, pronounced [dwiːt] or *go on*, pronounced [gwaːn] (Devonish and Harry, 2008).
- Pitch – Jamaican Creole and Tobagonian English use difference in pitch to differentiate homonyms. Pitch is used to differentiate between *father* (meaning parent) and *father* (meaning priest) (Devonish and Harry, 2008; James and Youssef, 2008).

Vocabulary

Due to the process of creolization, many African words from the substrate languages entered the superstrate language. Examples include Bahamian words like *obeah*, meaning witchcraft. Because of the links between the USA and the Bahamas, some lexical items entered Bahamian English through Gullah, such as *hoe-cakes* (cornmeal cake), *gulin* (greedy), and *ninny* (breast) (Reaser and Torbert, 2008).

Grammar-syntactic variation

The grammar-syntactic innovation in Caribbean Englishes is the subject of intense linguistic study, and to illustrate some features of the Englishes in this region we draw on the following: Reaser and Torbert (2008) on Bahamian English; Patrick (2008) on Jamaican Creole English; and James and Youssef (2008) on Trinidad and Tobagonian English.

Grammar-syntactical features indicative of Caribbean English include the following:

- Tense and aspect – in the Bahamas (and, to a lesser extent, Jamaica), it is common to omit the verb *to be* in certain constructions, such as *you [are] fat, I [am] smart*, and *he [is] over there*. The levelling of verbs to the present tense is also pervasive throughout the Caribbean (e.g. *he swim yesterday*). Tense is often indicated in Caribbean creole Englishes through use of markers preceding verbs (e.g. past tense indicated with the addition of *ben* in *I ben run*). The completive *done*, as in *he done eat it* in Bahamian and Jamaican, is used in place of the past perfect tense.
- Auxiliary verbs – double-modals (*he might could come*) are common in Jamaican English, but not in Bahamian.
- Pronouns – like many British varieties of English discussed in Section 4a, substitution of pronouns is pervasive across the Caribbean. Gendered pronouns (e.g. *she's a good boat*) are also pervasive, perhaps due to the influence of seafarers in the islands.

Attitudes toward English variation in Jamaica

Jamaica makes an interesting case of attitudes towards variation in English, with its distinction between English and Patois as co-official languages, creating a political view that they are two languages. Literature on Jamaica often refers to speakers who are proficient in both varieties as bilingual, and those fluent in just Patois or English as monolingual. While English is used in formal public settings and in written discourse, Patois is used in informal private settings and in oral discourse. The lines between the two languages, however, are not as distinct as policy indicates, and, as education in Jamaica has traditionally moved speakers towards Jamaican English and away from Patois, features of Jamaican English regularly make their way into spoken Patois. Therefore, language use, education, and social class are very intertwined in Jamaican speech patterns.

Devonish and Harry (2008) argue that, for many Jamaicans, English is a second language, acquired through education as the language of formal speech and writing, and that the creole is spoken as a native language. However, we claim that the same argument can be made for perceived 'illegitimate' varieties around the world. For example, speakers from the Appalachian area of the USA learn to shed characteristics of their native speech in their learning of the target 'idealized' language through formal education. However, due to a political process of legitimizing Patois in Jamaica, which has not happened to Appalachian English in the USA, a Jamaican speaker is considered bilingual and can be proud of the knowledge of both languages, while an Appalachian English speaker is viewed by society as deficient in language education.

In Jamaica, 'recent years have seen the "functional dethronement" of Standard English as the exclusive language of public-formal domains and there is a shift toward a local variety as the new standard' (Melchers and Shaw, 2011, p. 123). Such is the power of legitimizing English varieties in politics and society, highlighting the importance of World Englishes research.

Chapter summary

This chapter has outlined variation of the 'Native' Englishes found in Inner Circle countries, which were spread via Channels 1 and 2. It is clear that English varieties carry different political weight and prestige in various parts of the Inner Circle. In the UK, an RP accent is considered an indicator of social class, and it can be argued that an RP accent advantages speakers of it in politics, business, and society.

In the USA, the standard American accent (whether northern or southern) permeates across America in a similar way, but unlike RP this accent is viewed as being unmarked. American Englishes sees divisions in power and language that are based along race and regional lines, rather than class and regional lines as seen in the UK.

In Australia, due to the youth and mobility of the population, there is far less regional variation than in the UK and the USA, and lines are drawn almost entirely according to 'broad' and 'cultivated' lines, with a standard lying somewhere between the two. While the broad accent is, at times, associated with the working class, and the cultivated associated with the educated and the rich, in practice this does not entirely hold true, with many successful politicians, businessmen, and highly educated members of society sporting the broad Australian accent.

Other members of the Inner Circle show divisions of power and standardizations along the lines of these three examples. In Ireland and New Zealand, for example, there are similarities with postcolonial Australia, which shows a movement away from RP-influenced accents, which are seen to mark class and unwanted associations with the British monarchy. Canada follows a similar line to the USA, with an unmarked standard English, although racial lines are far less pronounced than in the USA due to a very different history of racial tensions. The Caribbean sees movements like those witnessed in the UK, where regional varieties are becoming a source of pride and identity, rather than seen as deviations.

In summary, politics, power, and language are a very complex network, and are subject to quick changes in attitudes that will be explored further in Chapter 8.

Further reading

On Englishes of the British Isles:

- Kortmann, B. and Upton, C. (eds). (2008). *Varieties of English: The British Isles*. Berlin: Mouton de Gruyter.
- Hughes, A., Trudgill, P., and Watt, D. (2012). *English Accents and Dialects: An Introduction to Social and Regional Varieties of English in the British Isles*. New York: Routledge.

On the Englishes of North America and the Caribbean:

- Schneider, E. W. (ed.). (2008). *Varieties of English 2: The Americas and The Caribbean*. Berlin: Mouton de Gruyter.

On the Englishes of Australia and New Zealand:

- Kortmann, B., Burridge, K., Mesthrie, E., Schneider E. W., and Upton, C. (eds). (2008). *Varieties of English 3: The Pacific and Australasia*. Berlin: Mouton de Gruyter.

Closing activities

Chapter discussion questions

Section 4a

1 Do you know of any other examples of phonemic, grammar-syntactical, lexical, and pragmatic variation across the British Isles?
2 Do you think policies that aim to push and strengthen ties with indigenous languages can undo centuries of English language imposition across the British Isles?
3 This book mentions that the realization of /t/ as the glottal stop in words like *butter* is spreading into urban centres across the British Isles, even though it was limited to a small geographical area two decades ago. What do you think is the cause of such historically unprecedented spread?

Section 4b

1 Do you know of any other examples of phonemic, grammar-syntactical, lexical, and pragmatic variation across North America?
2 Section 4c discusses koineization in the Australian and New Zealand context, but it does not report on koineization in the North American context. What mixes of immigrants do you think produced distinct varieties of North American Englishes, such as those found in Minnesota, New York, Boston, and Newfoundland?
3 Do you agree that language in the USA is racially divided? Compare and contrast with other 'Native' English-speaking countries.

Section 4c

1 Do you know of any other examples of phonemic, grammar-syntactical, lexical, and pragmatic variation across Australia and New Zealand?
2 Why do the regions of Australia and New Zealand not have the same degree of variation within their national borders as the British Isles and North America do?
3 In 2011, the UK prime minster David Cameron publicly mimicked the Australian prime minister's broad accent for comedic purposes. UK newspapers reported the impersonation as received in good humour, but Australian newspapers were very critical. Why do you think the impersonation was viewed so differently in the two contexts?

Section 4d

1 Do you know of any other examples of phonemic, grammar-syntactical, lexical, and pragmatic variation across the Caribbean?
2 Do you agree that Caribbean creoles should be legitimized in their own right and regarded as separate languages (such as is the case in Jamaica)? Consider what it means for national identity, but also the ramifications of labelling many creole speakers as 'non-native English speakers'.
3 Many Caribbean nations are moving away from former prestige accents, as political power becomes more centred in local varieties. How does this compare with movements in prestige accents across Inner Circle countries?

Debate topics

1 Due to increases in mobility and the mixing of speakers of varieties of English, we will see more koineization, and the eventual levelling of English across and beyond national boundaries.
2 The argument that a standard American accent is 'unmarked', and thus is distinguished by 'no accent', is a fallacy.
3 While Australia has seen a slew of regional accented 'broad Australian' politicians, America will not see a president in the foreseeable future who uses a 'deviant' variety of English (e.g. Appalachian).

Writing and presentation prompts

Below are ideas for writing and presentation tasks to apply the knowledge learned in Chapter 4. Additional assignment prompts can be found on the companion website.

	Assignment topics
Personal account	Provide an account of the type of English you use, providing examples of unique phonemic variation, grammar-syntactic variation, lexical variation, and pragmatic variation compared with a 'standard' in your local context/country.
Research task (see website for worksheet)	Get two or three speakers of different varieties of English to read the list of words containing key vowel sounds used by Wells (1982). Using IPA symbols, analyse the vowel sounds and write a short report comparing the phonemic variation of these speakers.
Basic academic	Choose one 'Native' English and write about the historical, cultural, and social processes by which this English emerged. How did this variety develop its distinctive features?
Advanced academic	'In the US, bitter divisions created by slavery and the civil war shaped a language ideology focused on racial discrimination rather than on the class distinctions characteristic of an older monarchical society like Britain, which continue to shape language attitudes' (Milroy and Milroy, 1999, p. 160). Discuss how history shapes ideas of standard English in an ENL country of your choice.

Chapter 5

The 'New' Englishes

Introductory activities

The following introductory activities are designed to encourage the reader to think about the issues raised in this chapter before reading it.

Variation in the Outer Circle

Look at the map in Figure 5.1 that shows some uses of English around the world.

Discussion questions

1 Figure 5.1 shows how English has adapted to its surroundings in various contexts around the world. Are you familiar with any of these examples? Do you know of any others?
2 In what ways do you think language contact has been influential in the development of 'New' Englishes? Are you familiar with the English spoken in Singapore?

Case study: creativity in South Asian Englishes

English has been adapted in various Outer Circle contexts in diverse ways. Kachru (1985, p. 20) uses the term 'bilinguals' creativity' to describe 'those creative linguistic processes which are the result of competence in two or more languages'. Creativity in writing showcases the pluricentricity of English today as these writers adapt the language and make it their own. Several writers of 'New' Englishes in various contexts have made names for themselves across the English-speaking world. Kachru (1997, pp. 222–23, cited in Kachru and Nelson, 2006, p. 32) presents a list of world-class literary prize-winners that includes the following:

Nobel Prize in Literature

Wole Soyinka (Nigeria), 1986
Derek Walcott (Trinidad), 1992
V. S. Naipaul (Trinidad), 2001

Neustadt Award

Raja Rao (India), 1988

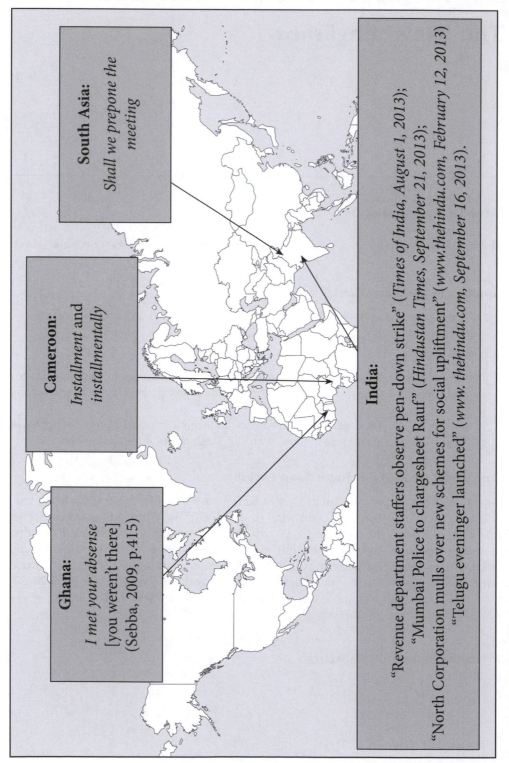

Figure 5.1 Uses of English around the world

Man Booker Prize

Chinua Achebe (Nigeria), 1987
Michael Ondaatje (Sri Lanka), 1992
Ben Okri (Nigeria), 1991
Salman Rushdie (India), 1995
Arundhati Roy (India), 1997

Discussion

1   Despite the long history of English in places like India, and despite the fact that creative writing in South Asian English has gained stature in recent years, the English used in such contexts continues to be viewed by some as inferior to 'standard' English. Why do you think such attitudes persist? Can the writers listed above claim 'ownership' of the English language?
2   Are you familiar with any of the work shown above? Do you know of any other bilingual writers who use things like code-mixing, code-switching, and borrowing in their work?
3   In what ways can the development of postcolonial literature help the status of the 'New' Englishes? Does winning a prize give them a certain kind of legitimacy? Does this growing body of postcolonial literature have any implications for the study of English literature?

Introduction

This chapter focuses on the 'New' Englishes spoken as an official or recognized second language in Kachru's Outer Circle. Used in a variety of domains, even after gaining independence, English has been appropriated in these 'new' contexts to suit the needs of those living there. However, a number of questions arise. What is a 'New' English? Can it be used in the classroom? Are their features innovations or errors? Is it even appropriate to talk of 'varieties' today, given the rapid spread of English as a lingua franca? This last question is tackled in the subsequent two chapters but the others are tackled here, in our examination of the diversity of English. We explore the systematic description of features in an attempt to show their legitimacy.

A useful starting place is to return to the definition introduced in Chapter 2. According to Platt *et al.* (1984, pp. 2–3), a 'New' English is one that fulfils the following criteria:

1   It has developed through the education system.
2   It has developed where a native variety of English was *not* the language spoken by most of the population.
3   It is used for a range of functions *among* those who can speak or write it in the region where it is used (e.g. in literature, the government, and the media).
4   It has become 'localized' or 'nativized' by adopting some language features of its own.

These points, as well as Kachru's three phases discussed in Chapter 2, will be discussed throughout this chapter and more fully in Section 5d, where we examine the status of the 'New' Englishes.

This chapter has been divided into Sections 5a (covering South Asia), 5b (South-East Asia), 5c (Africa), and 5d (Hong Kong as well as looking at status). While the 'New' Englishes do share some features, they are far from uniform in their characteristics. Much work has been conducted in the World Englishes paradigm (see Kachru *et al.*, 2006), and scholars have made tremendous progress documenting the core grammatical, lexical, and phonological forms that are distinct from 'standard' varieties of English. However, by documenting such features, we are not ignoring the use of ELF either within or across these regions. As introduced in the Preface, the term 'World Englishes' not only refers to a research paradigm but also an ideology, and is based on an inclusive philosophy that emphasizes the pluricentricity of English. Thus, topics such as creative writing, pedagogy, and legitimacy are all discussed. In essence, this chapter exemplifies the variation in the use of English today within the World Englishes paradigm. It is also important to note that, while we refer to 'standard' Inner Circle varieties when we document the distinctive features of the 'New' Englishes, this does not indicate a superior status.

5a   English in South Asia

This section focuses on India, Nepal, Pakistan, Bangladesh, and Sri Lanka. It is worth noting that the 'use of the term South Asian English is not to be understood as indicative of linguistic homogeneity in this variety nor of a uniform linguistic competence' (Kachru, 1986, p. 36). We begin with the historical background, the role of English today, and the general features of these regional varieties, and end with an examination of the status of English in South Asia.

The history of English in South Asia

Contact with English can be traced to 1579 with the arrival of Father Thomas Stephens in India. British involvement grew in the seventeenth century through trade and subsequent British rule with the East India Company. The East India Company gained more power, eventually taking over the civil government, and education and government in 1858. British Christian missionaries, who used English as a medium of instruction, were also influential in the early nineteenth century. English was also desirable for modernization and economic development. Policy makers gave it a superior status, evident in the Minute on Indian Education (1835), which made a plea for a Western mode of education and the creation of 'a class of persons, Indian in blood and colour, but English in taste, in opinion, in morals and in intellect' (Kachru, 1983, p. 22). English was seen as necessary for career advancement as it was becoming a language of the elite, and an English literature was also emerging. Three English-medium universities were established in 1857 in Bombay/Mumbai, Calcutta/Kolkata, and Madras/Chennai, followed by two more in Allahabad and Punjab by the end of the century.

As internal functions grew, English became dominant in politics, education, administration, the legal system, and the media. An elite class of Indians who were proficient in English emerged and, when Indian independence was granted in 1947, English had already established a dominant role in the emerging nations of India, Pakistan, and Bangladesh. The 1950 constitution made Hindi the official language, yet, after unrest amongst the non-Hindi-speaking populations and the language riots of the 1960s, the Official Language Act, passed in 1963 and amended in 1967, made English co-equal with Hindi. The Three Language Formula was then introduced in 1964–66, requiring that Hindi, English, and a regional language be taught in every state.

There have been attempts to diminish the role of English in India and elsewhere in South Asia. In Pakistan, the position of Urdu has been strengthened in constitutional amendments over the years. Sri Lanka's three-language policy (English, Sinhalese, and Tamil) also attempted to replace English, although it was unsuccessful and English was reinstated. Nevertheless, the dominant role of English in South Asia today is an undisputed fact.

The role of English today in South Asia

Today, there are more English speakers in South Asia than there are in Inner Circle countries, although numbers are difficult to estimate and proficiency varies. Speakers of an educated variety of Indian English are estimated to be around 35–50 million, making Indian English the third largest 'variety' of English worldwide, after British and American English (Mukherjee, 2010, p. 167), if such linguistic lines can be drawn.

Many different languages are spoken in India and the constitution recognizes 22 official languages, including English. Hindi is the major language, with upward of 422 million speakers if all dialects are included (although in the south of India Dravidian languages are more prominent). In Sri Lanka, Sinhala and Tamil are the main local languages. However, many continue to use English on a daily basis and code-mix with local languages. It is also the language of choice by many 'to show off or as a mark of their age or position', and some upper class urban families may have adopted English almost entirely (Melchers and Shaw, 2011, p. 146).

In India, English has become the language of administration, politics, education, and academia. Several English newspapers are published, English news is broadcast, and a growing number of books are published in English. It is also used as a lingua franca within the country, among people from different linguistic backgrounds. The situation is similar in Pakistan, where English assumes a dominant role in science and technology, the media, and international communication.

Features of English in South Asia

Lengthy historical contact with other languages in South Asia's multilingual mosaic landscape has led to a lot of variation, which has attracted the attention of a number of scholars.

Sounds

A lot of research has been conducted on variation in the accents of South Asian Englishes (Gargesh, 2006; Kachru and Nelson, 2006; Kirkpatrick, 2007; Melchers and Shaw, 2011; Platt *et al.*, 1984). A few illustrative examples are outlined in the following subsection.

PHONEMIC VARIATION

Vowels

It is widely reported that many Englishes linked to South Asia have a **reduced vowel system** when compared with the Englishes covered in Chapter 4. Some distinctive features include the following.

- Vowel mergers – as a result of a reduced vowel set, some vowels are merged. The RP vowels /ɑː/ and /ɔː/ are merged as [ɑː] in many Indian accents, and the /ɒ/ and /æ/ differences in some accents are not maintained with the vowels often merged as [a] (Trudgill and Hannah, 2008).
- Diphthongs are realized as simple vowels – this results in many diphthongs being reduced to monophthongs, as in the examples of /eɪ/ becoming [eː] (e.g. *day* realized as [deː]) and /əʊ/ becoming [oː] (*coat* pronounced [koːt]).
- Absence of schwa /ə/– in Pakistani English, the schwa found in RP and other South Asian varieties in *letter*, *horses*, and *comma* is realized as a more open and retracted [ʌ] vowel.
- Initial front vowels are sometimes preceded by a [j] glide – thus, in India, *inner* is pronounced as 'yinner' (Kachru and Nelson, 2006, p. 157), and in Southern India *eight* as [jeːt] (Trudgill and Hannah, 2008).
- Back vowels are sometimes preceded by [w] – in southern India, *own* may be pronounced as 'wown' (Trudgill and Hannah, 2008) and *open* as 'wopen' (Kachru and Nelson, 2006, p. 157).
- The merging of **sibilants** – there is considerable merging of sibilants in India, resulting in homophonous realization of words like *same* and *shame*, in which both initial consonants are realized as [s]. Likewise, this occurs with the /dʒ/ (as in *major*), /z/ (as in *razor*), and /ʒ/ (as in *measure*), which are all realized as [dʒ] (Kachru and Nelson, 2006, p. 157).

Consonants

- Rhoticity – Englishes found in South Asia are rhotic. The trilled /r/ is pronounced in Indian English wherever the letter 'r' appears in English spelling (e.g. the 'r' in *dart* and in *door*), differentiating it from most non-rhotic British colony accents.
- Retroflexed /t/ and /d/ – the alveolar /t/ and /d/ tend to be realized as retroflex [ʈ] and [ɖ], which are articulated with the underside of the tongue making firm contact with the alveolar ridge or palate. Such sounds are typical of Indo-Aryan and Dravidian languages, but uncommon in most English accents. This feature gives Indian English a distinctively recognizable quality.
- The dental fricatives – the /θ/ and /ð/ phonemes are realized as dental [t̪] and [d̪] or alveolar [t] and [d] plosives (e.g. *think* as 'tink').
- Various phonemic distinctions may not be maintained – distinctions are not made between /v/ and /w/ in Sri Lanka and some parts of India, and /p/ and /f/ plus /s/ and /ʃ/ may also not be distinguished. There is often no distinction between some voiced and voiceless consonants. For example, the voiceless plosives /p/, /t/, and /k/ at the beginning of words tend to be unaspirated, e.g. *time* and *dime*, and *ten* and *den* may not be differentiated.

- **Postalveolars** – /tʃ/, /dʒ/, /ʃ/, and /ʒ/ may be pronounced with contact between the blade of the tongue and the roof of the mouth (rather than its tip, as in other varieties) (Melchers and Shaw, 2011).
- Consonant clusters are broken up – as discussed in Chapter 2, speakers of the 'New' Englishes often employ a number of strategies to deal with consonant clusters. Gargesh (2006, p. 102) notes the following: Punjabi and Haryana speakers may insert a schwa in word initial clusters (e.g. *sport* as 's[ə]port', *school* as [səkuːl]). In northern India, word-initials /sk/, /st/, or /sp/ tend to receive a preceding /ɪ/ (e.g. *speak* [ɪspiːk]. Hindi-Urdu speakers in the east may also add a /ɪ/ (e.g. *speech* [ɪspiːtʃ]).

PROSODIC VARIATION

South Asian Englishes tend to be perceived as syllable-timed, not stress-timed, and word stress is not prominent. Function words that are reduced when unstressed in other varieties of English (*of* /əv/, *to* /tə/, etc) tend not to undergo reduction in India (Trudgill and Hannah, 2008). Intonation is 'characterised by rather short intonation units (so that the placement of sentence stress may seem uninformative)' (Melchers and Shaw, 2011, p. 147).

Vocabulary

Gargesh (2006) notes that lexical variation is the area where divergence is most noticeable, and this has received the attention of many World Englishes scholars (Bamgbose, 1992; Kachru and Smith, 2008; Kirkpatrick, 2007; Gargesh, 2006; Melchers and Shaw, 2011; Platt *et al.*, 1984; Trudgill and Hannah 2008). Some examples include the following.

- Variety-specific compounds – *shoe-bite* (blister), *head-tie* (woman's head dress), *chalk-piece* (piece of chalk), and *key-bunch* (bunch of keys).
- Same meaning, different words – *bogey* (railway carriage), *cracker* (firework), *biodata* (curriculum vitae), and *colony* (residential area). Some older British English lexical items are also still used in India (e.g. *thrice*).
- Conversion – *to off/on* (to switch off/on).
- Semantic extension – *hotel* (a restaurant or café not necessarily with lodgings).
- Compounding/specialized meaning – *pen-down-strike* (workers present at work, but refusing to work).
- Derivation – *upliftment* (uplift), *prepone* (to bring forward in time).
- Abbreviations – *funda* (fundamental).
- Coinages – *co-brother* (one's wife's sister's husband), *cousin-brother* (as opposed to a sibling), *eve-teasing* (sexual harassment of women), *inskirt* (petticoat), *love marriage* (marrying someone of one's own choice, as opposed to someone chosen by the family), and *eveninger* (evening newspaper in India and Pakistan).
- Borrowing – *goonda* (hooligan), *mela* (crowd), *lathi* (bamboo stick), *dosa* (Indian crepe), *channa* (chick peas), *sari* (traditional dress), and *melas* (gathering).
- Hybrid forms – *lathi-charge* (an attack by the police using lathis) and *congresswallah* (member of congress).
- Locally coined idioms and word-by-word translations of indigenous phrases – *I bow my forehead* and *I fall at your feet* as popular greetings in India, and phrases such *cherisher of the poor* meaning someone who is cherishing of or kind to the poor.

Grammar-syntactic variation

Unlike the lexicon, syntax is more stable, although some distinctive features have been documented (Baumgardner, 1987; Kachru, 1983; Gargesh, 2006; Kirkpatrick, 2007; Mukherjee, 2010; Platt *et al.*, 1984; Seargeant and Swann, 2012; Trudgill and Hannah, 2008).

- Plurality – countable nouns are not always marked by -s to show plurality, while uncountable nouns are sometimes marked for plurality, so many uncountable nouns often become countable (e.g. *I saw him dropping a lot of litters*).
- Tense and aspect – in India, the present continuous, or progressive, with stative verbs (the be + verb + -ing) construction, is extended, as in *I am having a stomach ache* (I have a stomach ache) and *where is our new teacher coming from?* (where does our new teacher come from?). The present tense is also often used for durational phases, e.g. *I am here on holiday since Tuesday* (I have been here on holiday since Tuesday). The perfective may be used instead of the simple past (especially with past-time adverbs), e.g. *I have been in Italy twenty years ago* (I was in Italy twenty years ago). Future forms are used in temporal and conditional clauses, e.g. *when will you get there, open the present* (when you get there, open the present). Finally the verb 'be' is often omitted.
- Question formation – tag questions may be invariant, e.g. *you know it, isn't it?* and *you went there yesterday, no?* The subject and the verb may not be inverted in direct questions, e.g. *where you are going?*
- Yes/no – the use of yes/no responses may not conform to Inner Circle conventions, with 'yes' used to agree with a negative assertion, as in the enquiry *You have no question?* being responded to with *Yes, I have no question*.
- Adverbs – may be positioned differently, e.g. *always I drink coffee*.
- Articles – the rules for the use of the definite article ('the') and the indefinite article ('a'/'an') are different. For example, there is a tendency to omit the article for non-specific objects, e.g. *do you want apple?*
- Reduplication – repetition of words is used for emphasis, e.g. *it was a big big cake*.
- Prepositions – phrasal and prepositional verb constructions may differ. In India, prepositions may be dropped, e.g. *to dispense* (to dispense with), or added, e.g. *to accompany with* (to accompany) and *to air out one's views* (to air one's views), or used differently, e.g. *to pay attention on* (to pay attention to).
- Auxiliary verbs – in India, *could* and *would* may be used instead of *can* and *will* (being seen as more polite), e.g. *we hope that you could join us* and *the lecture would begin at 2:00*. *Could* may also be used instead of *able to*, e.g. *he could just only finish it before we left*. *May* can be used for politeness, e.g. *this furniture may be removed tomorrow* (this furniture is to be removed tomorrow).

Pragmatics

Distinct communicative styles can also be identified.

- Gestures vary – Indians may signal 'yes' by nodding their head sideways, often mistaken for a 'no' by those unfamiliar to the context.

- Formality – increased formality is common, e.g. *what is your good name, sir?*, and honorific suffixes (e.g. *ji* or *sahib*) may be added to names to indicate respect. Matrimonial advertisements, which feature heavily in newspapers, are a prime example of culturally specific use of the language and reveal a lot about the domains in which English is used in India.

Attitudes toward English variation in South Asia

The creative nature of South Asian English is evident in the innovative and creative ways South Asian poets and novelists have exploited English. However, despite such work, a lot of which is internationally acclaimed, and the wealth of World Englishes work, the use of English by speakers in this region continues to be viewed as 'illegitimate' and 'inferior' by some, and the topic becomes particularly controversial in relation to classroom models. Adherence to native-speaking norms isn't always a choice, and Cowie's (2007) report on 'accent training' for a 'neutral' accent in the call centre training industry highlights occurrences of call centre agents taking 'elocution lessons' to gain a British or American accent.

In addition to the 'type' of English used, debate has also arisen over the status of English in India, as discussed in Chapter 3. For some, it is a neutral language that cuts across cultural and religious boundaries, a vehicle for political unity and a tool for economic advancement. For others, it is something that creates and perpetuates societal divisions. Kachru and Nelson (2006, p. 163) discuss three dominant views, which include: support for the use of English from a Westernization/technological progress view; a rejection of English; and a neutral position, which sees English being retained as one of several foreign languages, but not in competition with local languages. Attitudes are complex and, as will be discussed in Chapter 8, are subject to change. An article in *The Telegraph* on 10 October 2012, for example, pointed out that British diplomats to India are being advised to learn 'Hinglish' to avoid being left out of the loop in conversations. They are also being urged to learn Hindi to aid communication. In fact, the notion of 'Hinglish' has become popularized in India through Bollywood, where film titles increasingly blend Hindi and English, indicating a move away from 'standard' norms. Thus on the one hand we have call centre agents attempting to 'neutralize' their accents to sound more British, while British diplomats are being urged to learn more about the local usage of English.

5b English in South-East Asia

This section examines English in South-East Asia, where it is spoken as an official second language (Singapore, Malaysia, Brunei, and the Philippines). Other ASEAN nations are discussed in Chapter 6. Once again, we begin with a historical overview, followed by the current role of English and an examination of research that has been conducted within the World Englishes paradigm, ending with a closer examination of Singapore.

The history of English in South-East Asia

English has a long history in South-East Asia, albeit shorter than in South Asia. Colonialism, which affected all countries except for Thailand (see Chapter 6), can be traced back to the acquisition of Penang in Malaysia by the East India Company in 1786. A trading settlement was established in Singapore in 1819, and in 1826 the 'Straits Settlements' were created, consisting of Singapore, Malacca, and Penang, used as trading centres by the East India Company. Malaysian states maintained their royal families, under the influence of the British Empire, but Singapore was colonized and British colonial rule lasted for nearly 140 years. In 1946, the Malaya federation was established although Singapore stayed as a separate crown colony. Malaya became independent in 1957 and was joined in its federation by Singapore in 1963. However, in 1965 Singapore was expelled from the federation and became an independent state.

English in Singapore

After independence, language policies in Singapore were related to a desire to construct a unified nation among a highly multilingual and multi-ethnic population, alongside a desire for economic advancement. In 1965, equal status in education was given to all four national languages (English, Malay, Mandarin, and Tamil). Since 1987, English has been the major language of education at all levels, and the bilingual policy of English +1 requires citizens to learn English as well as their mother tongue. However, English is the medium of instruction in education, and the other three languages have been assigned second or 'mother tongue' language status. This has led to increased use of English in the country and almost 80 per cent of the population now has some command of the language (Rubdy *et al.*, 2008, p. 40). Census figures note that English is routinely used in 32.6 per cent of Chinese homes, 17.0 per cent of Malay homes, and 41.6 per cent of Indian homes. Today, many young Singaporeans learn English as a first language, and this brings us back to the problems with Kachru's simplistic model discussed in Chapter 1.

English in Malaysia

As a result of colonialism, English education was introduced in the Straits Settlements from the early nineteenth century, albeit approached cautiously due to fears of nationalism. Until the 1960s, English was an important language in Malaysia in a number of domains, including the government, administration, and education. However, with independence, Malaysia replaced English with Malay (Bahasa Maleyu). The National Language Act of 1976 made this the official language and it became the main language of education in 1982, although English was also compulsory. Today, Malay is the sole language of administration and Malaysia has reduced the role of English.

In the twenty-first century, the importance of English was recognized and it was re-introduced as the language of science in secondary education. In 2002, it became the medium of instruction for mathematics and science from primary one, followed by the tertiary sector. This policy was, however, reversed in July 2009, and since 2012 mathematics and science have been taught in Malay, although the policy stated that **English-medium instruction** would continue at the pre-university and tertiary levels. Today, all university undergraduates are required to study English and it is increasingly used in the business arena.

Thus, in Malaysia there appears to be a 'back-and-forth movement, which is quite indicative of the ambivalent attitudes toward English in the country: it shouldn't get too strong, but it is equally unthinkable to let it go' (Schneider, 2011, p. 153), points that were raised in Chapter 3.

English in the Philippines

A Spanish expedition in 1521 began colonization of the Philippines, which resulted in 400 years of Spanish rule. In 1896, unrest led to American intervention and America defeated Spain in 1898, beginning American colonization. English replaced Spanish as the official language and became the sole medium of instruction in 1901. With independence in 1946, English continued to be the official language of schools and government, although, in 1973, English and a modified version of Tagalog, known as Filipino, were made the two official languages.

More than 70 different local languages and dialects are used in the Philippines, but the constitution places emphasis on Filipino as a medium of instruction, although Bautista and Gonzalez (2006) point out that English has taken centre stage in recent years due to the demands of globalization. Today, about three-quarters of the population can read or understand English, and more than half are said to be able to speak it (Schneider, 2011, p. 155). It has also become dominant in business, politics, and education, and most official government publications and legal documents are published in English (Friginal, 2007). It is also associated with career advancement and social mobility, particularly evident in the growing call centre industry, although as Schneider (2011, p 156) notes, this is a 'double-edged process', since such jobs, despite being well paid, result in unsociable working hours to meet the time lag with US-based customers, points that were raised in Chapter 3.

English in Brunei

Brunei became a British protectorate in 1888. Malay was adopted as the medium of instruction and was designated as the official language in 1959. Independence was granted in 1984 and, in 1985, the national education system was implemented, accompanied by a bilingual policy. This bilingual education policy introduced Malay as a medium of instruction for the first three years of primary school, after which English was to be used. However, since 2011 subjects such as mathematics and science are taught in English from the first year of primary education, which is different compared with Malaysia, as discussed above, which shifted back to Malay for these subjects. Kirkpatrick (2010a, p. 35) notes that this language education policy has, perhaps, been the most successful in ASEAN. The University of Brunei Darussalam offers English-medium degrees as well as Malay-medium ones. The CfBT Education Trust, a UK-based educational organization, also employs a large number of native English-speaking teachers in primary and secondary schools throughout the country. The education system is based on the British system, and Brunei students study for British General Certificate of Education A and O levels.

Features of English in South-East Asia

As in South Asia, English comes into contact with a number of other languages in South-East Asia.

Sounds

While examples of distinct features are given below, once again differences do exist. In addition, the examples given can substantially differ from the English used in formal settings. For this section, a number of sources have been consulted (Bautista and Gonzalez, 2006; Kachru and Nelson, 2006; Kirkpatrick, 2007; Low, 2010; Melchers and Shaw, 2011; Platt *et al.*, 1984; Schneider, 2003, 2011; Trudgill and Hannah, 2008).

PHONEMIC VARIATION

Vowels

- Vowel mergers – due to a reduced vowel set, there are a number of vowel mergers in South-East Asian Englishes. For example, /æ/ and /ɑ/ (*cat–cot* /kat/), and /ɔ/ and /ou/ (*caught–coat* /kot/) are merged in the Philippines (Trudgill and Hannah, 2008), and in Singapore the *dress* and *trap* vowels are merged as /e/, resulting in homophonous word sets of *set–sat* and *man–men* (Kirkpatrick, 2007).
- Lack of vowel quality/length distinction – due to a reduced vowel set, coupled with a lack of vowel quality/length distinction, some vowel pairs in certain regions of South-East Asia are not differentiated:
  - *kit* and *fleece* vowels are realized as /i/;
  - *goose* and *foot* vowels are realized as /u/;
  - *palm* and *strut* vowels are realized as /ɑ/;
  - *north* and *lot* vowels are realized as /ɔ/.
- Diphthongs are realized as monophthongs/simple vowels – this results in /eɪ/ in *face* being realized as [eː] (e.g. *day* as [deː] and the /əʊ/ in *goat* as [oː], resulting for example in *coat* as [koːt]).
- Absence of schwa [ə] – similar to the Pakistani English example in Section 5a, there is an absence of a schwa in Malaysia and the Philippines, where it is realized as a more open variant.
- In Singapore, triphthongs may be treated as two syllables with a glide insertion (e.g. [aɪ.jə] and [aʊ.wə] instead of [aɪə] and [aʊə] in words like *fire* and *hour*).

Consonants

- Rhoticity – Philippine English is rhotic, but Singaporean and Malaysian English are non-rhotic.
- Dental fricatives – where other accents of English have dental fricatives, /t/ or /d/ are realized word-initially, e.g. thin (*tin*), three (*tree*), think (*tink*), then (*den*). In the word-final position, /f/ is realized and voicing contrast is neutralized (e.g. *breath* as [brɛf] and *breathe* as [brif]).
- Less distinction between some voiced and voiceless consonants – the voiceless plosives /p/, /t/, and /k/ at the beginning of words tend to be unaspirated, thus the /t/ in *time* might be mistaken as a /d/ to an untrained ear, e.g. *time* as *dime*. Likewise, the voiced consonants at the end of words may be devoiced, creating similarly pronounced word pairs such as *knees–niece*, *leaf–leave*, *rope–robe*, *bad–bed*, and *pick–pig*.

- Consonant clusters – the consonants at the end of words may be omitted in clusters, as in *fact* realized as /fak/ and *left* as /lɛf/, and the deletion of /t/ in *dialect*. The distinction between the following consonants may not be made in the Philippines and Singapore: /tʃ/ and /dʒ/; /f/ and /v/; /s/ and /z/; /s/ and /ʒ/; and /r/ and /l/.
- The vocalization of /l/ – Singaporeans vocalize /l/ as [ʊ] or it is lost altogether, meaning *milk* is pronounced as [miʊk], *well* as [weʊ], and *tall* as [tɔ:].

PROSODIC VARIATION

In general, speech is perceived as syllable-timed, not stress-timed. A Singaporean or Malaysian English speaker may not use lexical stress to signal the difference between a verb (*conduct*) and a noun (*conduct*).

Vocabulary

Lexical variation has been well documented (Jenkins, 2009; Kachru and Nelson, 2006; Low, 2010; Trudgill and Hannah, 2008; Platt *et al.*, 1984; Wee, 1998). Some examples include the following.

- Variety-specific compounds – Singapore: *neighbourhood school* (low-status schools in one's neighbourhood).
- Semantic extension – Singapore: *open* (turn on the light). Also in Singapore: *borrow* and *lend* have the same meaning, stemming from the Mandarin word, 借 (*jiè*), meaning to lend or to borrow (e.g. *can I lend your car?* [can I borrow your car?]). In Singapore and Malaysia: *stay* rather than *live* may be used for permanent or long-term residence. In the Philippines: *stick* (cigarette) and *motel* (a hotel used for premarital or extramarital affairs).
- Blending – Singapore: *distripark* (a distribution park or a warehouse complex).
- Acronyms – Singapore and Malaysia: *MC* (medical certificate).
- Coinages – Singapore: *killer litter* (rubbish discarded from high-rises that may end up killing someone by accident). The Philippines: *ambo* (a Filipino perceived to be too pro-American).
- Borrowing – in Singapore, borrowings from Malay are common. Examples include: *makan* (to eat, food), *tolong* (help), *mee goreng* (spicy fried noodles), *sarong* (skirt), *bomoh* (meaning medicine man with supernatural powers). In the Philippines, items may be borrowed from Spanish, Tagalog, and other indigenous languages, e.g. *as alto* (surprise party), *estafa* (fraud), and *boondock* (mountain).
- Locally coined idioms and word-by-word translations of indigenous phrases – examples include *to shake legs* (coming from the Malay idiom *goyang kaki* (to be idle)).
- Variation in the use of idioms, such as *gift of the gap* in Singapore, instead of the British *gift of the gab* (Jenkins, 2009).

Grammar-syntactic variation

A lot of research has also been conducted with regards to syntactic variation (Ansaldo, 2004, 2010; Lim, 2004; Schneider, 2011; Seargeant, 2012; Trudgill and Hannah, 2008; Platt *et al.*, 1984; Wee, 2004, 2008). Examples include the following.

- Plurality – as with South Asia, English speakers do not always mark nouns for plurality, e.g. *I like to read storybook*. Also, many uncountable nouns often become countable, e.g. *informations, staffs, furnitures, chalks*, at times resulting in phrases such as *sticks of cigarette*.
- Tense and aspect – in present continuous or progressive with stative verbs (the be + verb + -ing) construction is extended. Colloquial Singapore English marks aspect, not tense. Examples include:
  - Perfective instead of the simple past – *I have been in Italy twenty years ago* (I was in Italy twenty years ago);
  - Past perfect instead of present perfect – *he had already left* (he has already left) in the Philippines (Trudgill and Hannah, 2008);
  - Perfective – *oh, they go already ah?* (oh, they have already left?) (Ansaldo, 2010, p. 509);
  - Durative – *they still give my hoping lah* (they still give me hope) (Ansaldo, 2010, p. 509);
  - Habitual – *always seated at the cashier old lady you know* (you know, the old lady [who is] always seated at the cashier) (Ansaldo, 2010, p. 509);
  - Time phrases – *last time got mango trees you know* (there were mango trees in the past, you know) (Lim, 2004, p. 137);
  - *Already* may also act as an aspect marker – *my father already pass away*;
  - *Use to* may be used with present tense, meaning to indicate habitual activity – *I use to go shopping on Mondays* (I usually go shopping on Mondays) (Trudgill and Hannah, 2008, p. 141);
  - Use of *got* – in Singapore *got* is used in many ways. Wee (2008, p. 595–96) gives the following examples:
    - □ Possessive – *you got nice shirt* (you have a nice shirt);
    - □ Perfective – *he got go to Japan* (he has been to Japan);
    - □ Existential – *here got very many people* (there are many people here).
- Conjunctions – may not be used in Singapore and Malaysia, e.g. *I have three dogs* [and] *one cat*.
- Possession – -'s is sometimes dropped, e.g. *I'm going to my mother house*.
- Pronouns – often there is no distinction between he, she, and it. (In Mandarin and Chinese dialects only the written language makes a distinction between the male and female third-person pronouns, not the spoken forms.)
- Question formation – tag questions are often invariant, e.g. *he is going to buy a car, isn't it?*. In Singapore, *can or not* is also common, e.g. *she wants to go, can or not?* (can she go or not?).
- Articles – as with South Asia, there is a tendency to make the specific/non-specific distinction, rather than the definite/indefinite distinction with *a* and *the*. The indefinite article is used less frequently, e.g. *he is teacher*.
- Topic prominence/missing subject – Chinese and Malay are 'pro-drop' languages, prioritizing the topic, not the subject, so the object may be omitted, e.g. *that book got already* (I already have that book) (Ansaldo, 2010, p. 507). Trudgill and Hannah (2008, p. 143) also note that, in the Philippines, verbs that usually have an object may occur without one, e.g. *I don't like*.
- Use of copula verbs – missing copulas are common in Singapore, e.g. *careful, window broken* (be careful, the window is broken).

- Reduplication – in Singapore, citing Ansaldo (2004) and Wee (2004), Ansaldo (2010, p. 514) notes four patterns:
  - N–N for intimacy – *this my girl-girl* (this is my little girl) (affectionate, not very productive);
  - V–V for attenuation – *just eat-eat lah* (eat a little [or pick some]);
  - Pred.Adj–Pred.Adj for 'intensification' – *his face red-red* (his face is really quite red);
  - V–V–V for durative – *we all eat-eat-eat* (keep eating/eat a lot).
- Discourse particles – in Singapore and Malaysia, discourse markers, such as *lah*, are used to add meaning, e.g. at the end of a sentence (*I didn't want go to the party lah*), with imperatives (*drink lah!* [drink!]), and to signal solidarity, emphasis, persuasion, or objection (*please lah come to visit me on Sunday* [please come and visit me]).
- The use of auxiliaries – in Singapore, *would* is often used rather than *will* (e.g. *we hope you would come tomorrow*) to sound more polite.

Status of English in South-East Asia: Singapore's 'Speak Good English Movement'

In Singapore, English has permeated deep into the daily lives of Singaporeans, and has become an integral part of Singaporean society and culture. Many speak English as a first language although, as pointed out in Chapter 3, the increased usage of English has resulted in decreased usage of other languages. Rubdy *et al.* (2008), for example, note the decrease in the use of Tamil in favour of English, heightened by the use of English as a lingua franca among the Indian community. Young Singaporeans today value English, and see it as a language of success and career advancement.

English may be the mother tongue of many Singaporeans, but the use of English that reflects a local or shared identity that differs from 'standard' English is not recognized by the government and is discouraged. This is evident in the public condemnation of colloquial Singaporean English. While the government seems happy that the bilingual policy has helped create an economically prosperous state, the downside has been the development of this home-grown variety.

The 'Speak Good English Movement' (viewable online at www.goodenglish.org.sg) started in 2000 to promote the use of 'standard' English, due to fears that Singlish, which is seen as inferior, is unintelligible to outsiders. This campaign aims to 'encourage Singaporeans to speak grammatically correct English that is universally understood' (SGEM, 2011), and it has workshops, seminars, and games for children to promote 'standard' English usage.

However, many Singaporeans see Singlish as part of their cultural identity and are opposed to this campaign. In addition, Seargeant (2012, p. 110) notes that the 'logic behind the policy is flawed' since Singlish and 'standard' English are both part of the repertoire of speakers, who can switch between them. Singlish is seen by many as being an integral part of their lives and is often preferred in informal situations. As discussed in Chapter 2, code-mixing amongst Singaporean speakers should not, necessarily, be seen as evidence of a lack of proficiency in English, but may be more related to a desire to communicate as effectively as possible, using their bi- or multilingual repertoire, as well as perhaps being a communicative choice.

5c English in Africa

The topic of African Englishes is an immensely wide topic beyond the scope of this book, although, as Mesthrie (2013, p. 518) points out, 'several factors make it a manageable and coherent theme'. This section explores the 'New' Englishes of sub-Saharan Africa. We begin with a history, then look at the role of English today and variation, and end with a brief look at attitudes towards English.

The history of English in Africa

The history of English in both east and west Africa is rooted in colonialism, with the exception of Liberia, a settler colony of free slaves. English contact can be traced to the 1500s, when Africa was used in trading and the slave trade, as discussed in Chapter 1. Formal British colonialism was widespread in west and central Africa, and encompassed almost all of east and southern Africa, resulting in the creation of colonies and protectorates.

Early European contact was through Pidgin Portuguese along the west African coast, but contact with English grew with increased British presence. In addition, many west Africans travelled to Europe to train as interpreters, and Pidgin English was spoken alongside the English spoken by these returnee interpreters. These pidgins served as lingua francas in trade and, as discussed in Chapter 2, pidgins and creoles remain important today although, in northern Nigeria, Hausa functions as a link language for many and Wolof is used in Gambia. Later influence was from the creoles spoken by the repatriated slaves from Britain, North America, and the Caribbean. In the twentieth century, English influence further grew as many African leaders in west Africa adopted English as a symbol of power.

In east Africa, English contact came in the nineteenth century, through trade expansion and missionaries. British and German colonial power was established towards the end of the nineteenth century. However, Kiswahili, the Swahili language, was widely used rather than English or German. British colonial rule regulated official language use differently across the continent, and English was only spoken in elite circles among colonial rulers. A 'trilingual language policy was implemented, with the ethnic "vernacular" for local communication and basic education, Kiswahili in ethnically mixed centers and English for the highest functions in administration, law and education' (Schmied, 2006, p. 189). Thus Swahili was established as the lingua franca, which has given rise to a rather homogeneous localized variety of English. Unlike in west Africa, there is no Pidgin English in east Africa due to the absence of slavery and the use of Kiswahili.

In southern Africa, indigenous languages are important but its closeness to South Africa strengthens the role of English and has also influenced the forms used here (Schneider, 2011).

English contact in South Africa came in 1795 with the arrival of the British. Many British settlers came in 1820 and many teachers were brought over to teach in English, with English soon replacing Dutch as the official language. English has been an official language since 1814. In 1910, with the establishment of the Union of South Africa, English and Dutch (replaced by Afrikaans in 1925) became the official languages. However, there were attempts in the 1940s to strengthen the position of Afrikaans.

Black African opposition led to the Soweto uprising of 1976 and, after this, schools could choose their own medium of instruction for the first four years of primary school. At this time, English gained influence and it is important to point out that it was seen as a language of liberation by black South Africans. In 1961, the Republic of South Africa was established, and Afrikaans and English remained the two official languages. However, in 1994, with the end of apartheid and the establishment of the new South Africa, 11 languages were granted official status.

The role of English today in Africa

Today, English is used as a second language in most of Britain's former possessions, and in some it has been afforded official or co-official status. Since independence, English has been present in the government, education, media, and commerce of many African countries, and is the predominant written language of Anglophone Africa (Table 5.1). However, the functions of English differ throughout the continent, as outlined below.

- West Africa – in Nigeria, Pidgin English is prevalent but, with more than 500 languages, English also acts as a lingua franca. English is the 'official' language of the constitution, but Yoruba, Igbo, and Hausa are also mentioned as national languages. In Ghana, English is an official language and the medium of instruction in most schools, although a local language is often used for younger levels. English is used for government affairs, in the legal system, and for commerce.

Table 5.1 Domains of English use in some eastern and southern African states

	Uganda	Kenya	Tanzania	Zambia	Zimbabwe	Malawi
High court	+	+	+	+	+	+
Local court	*	*	–	*	*	*
Parliament	+	+	–	+	+	+
Civil service	+	+	–	+	+	+
Primary school	+	+	–	+	+	+
Secondary school	+	+	+	+	+	+
Radio	+	+	+	+	+	+
Newspapers	+	+	+	+	+	+
Local novels	+	+	+	+	+	+
Local records	+	+	–	+	+	+
Local plays	+	+	–	+	+	+
Films (not dubbed)	+	+	+	+	+	+
Traffic and vehicle signs	+	+	–	+	+	+
Advertising	+	+	*	+	+	+
Business correspondence	+	+	+	+	+	+
Private correspondence	+	+	–	+	+	+

Key
+ English used
* English sometimes used
– English not used

Source: adapted from Schmied, 1991, p. 41, cited in Schneider, 2011, p. 139

- East Africa – in Kenya and Tanzania, Swahili has official language status. However, English plays a strong role in Kenya, although Kiswahili is spoken by nearly 95 per cent of the population (De Swaan, 2001, p. 119). Tanzania has adopted English as the medium of instruction in secondary schools, although English is not widely used, questioning its categorization as an Outer Circle country.
- Southern Africa – in Namibia, English is the official language but is used by only 7 per cent of the population (*World Fact* book, cited in Kachru and Nelson, 2006, p. 198). In Botswana, the national language is Setswana but English plays an important role, although spoken by about only 2.2 per cent of the population (Ministry of Labour and Home Affairs 2001, cited in Smieja and Mathangwane, 2010, p. 212). English is used for official documents, commerce, and the media. In South Africa (a case which also highlights the problems with Kachru's Three Circle Model), English is used as a first language by those of British descent and by younger generations of those of Indian decent, but as a second language for those who speak African languages and Afrikaans as a first language. According to the 2011 census, English is spoken as a home language by 9.6 per cent of South Africans and language is divided along racial lines, with English being a first language for 86.1 per cent of the Indian-Asian population, 35.9 per cent of the white population, and 2.9 per cent of the Black African population. It is one of 11 official languages in the constitution but has become the de facto working language in the government, and the medium of instruction at the majority of schools and all of the universities.

Features of English in Africa

As in other places, English in Africa has undergone a series of adaptations and innovations at all levels.

Sounds

Despite widespread variation, as well as whether one is speaking the basilectal or acrolectal variety, there are some similarities among the varieties of English, particularly in Englishes that have developed from related substrate languages. A lot of research has been conducted on the systematic description of the phonology of African Englishes (Bamgbose, 1992; Kachru and Nelson, 2006; Kachru and Smith, 2008; Kirkpatrick, 2007; Melchers and Shaw, 2011; Platt *et al.*, 1984; Schmied, 2006; Trudgill and Hannah, 2008; Wolf, 2010). Examples from these sources are given below.

PHONEMIC VARIATION

Many varieties have fewer vowels than other English varieties, particularly those related to the Bantu languages, which have a five to seven vowel system. In general, there are fewer vowels in east African English (Table 5.2) than in west African English (Table 5.3), resulting in distinct features.

- Diphthongs are realized as monophthongs/simple vowels – thus, RP /eɪ/ becomes /e:/ (so *day* becomes /de:/); RP /əʊ/ becomes /o:/ (so *coat* becomes /ko:t/); and

RP /ɪə/ and /ɛə/ vowels become /ia/ and /ea/ in west Africa (so *peer* becomes /pia/ , *pair* becomes /pea/).

- Central vowels replaced by front or back vowels – there is a tendency for the RP central vowels /ʌ/, /ɜː/, and /ə/, as in *but*, *bird*, and *about*, to become more open and less centralized, moving towards sounds like [ɔ], [e], and [a]. The RP /ɜː/ is pronounced as [a] in east Africa, and [ɔ] in west Africa (e.g. *work* becomes [wɔk], *burn* becomes [bɔn]), except for in Ghanaian English. Refer back to Tables 5.2 and 5.3 for vowel contrasts.

CONSONANTS

- Rhoticity – most varieties are non-rhotic, although rhoticity has been described in Kenya due to the influence of American tourists, and in Malawi where Scottish missionaries have influenced variation.
- Retroflex consonants – the alveolars /t/ and /d/ tend to be retroflex [ʈ] and [ɖ].
- Dental fricatives – the phonemes /θ/ and /ð/ may be pronounced as [t] and [d] respectively, as seen in previous examples.
- Postalveolar fricatives and affricates – /tʃ/ and /ʃ/ phonemes are realized as [s] in east Africa, and /dʒ/ and /ʒ/ as [z]. In Gambian English, Wolf (2010, p. 199) notes that *fish* sounds like 'fis' and *measure* like 'meazure'. These forms can be attributed to the fact that /ʃ/ and /ʒ/ are not part of the phonological systems of Mandingo and Wolof, the two dominant languages in Gambia. In east Africa, /s/ is used where the

Table 5.2 West African English vowels

/i/	bid, bee
/e/	bay
/a/	bad, bard, father, butter
/ɔ/	pot, putt, paw, port
/o/	boat
/u/	boot, put
/ai/	buy
/ɔi/	boy
/au/	bout

Source: Trudgill and Hannah, 2008, p. 129

Table 5.3 East African English vowels

/i/	bid, bee
/e/	bed, bay
/a/	bad, bard, bird, putt, father
/o/	pot, boat, paw, port
/u/	boot, put
/ai/	buy
/oi/	boy
/au/	bout

Source: Trudgill and Hannah, 2008, p. 132

background language of the speakers does not use /ʃ/. Dholuo speakers, for example, say 'suga' for *sugar* and 'sat' for *shut*. In Black South African English, the /tʃ/ of *church* is often pronounced /ʃ/ by Zulu speakers although, since southern African languages tend to have a lot of consonants, there is less difference with other Englishes in this aspect (Kachru and Nelson, 2006, p. 206).

- Distinction between /r/ and /l/ may not be made.
- Intrusive nasals – the intrusion of nasals before plosives is common, as some east African languages like Kikuyu have pre-nasalized consonants (Schmied, 2006, p. 193), as in [ᵐb], [ⁿd], and [ᵑg]. In west African Englishes, as a result of this feature words ending in -*mb*, such as *bomb*, *climb*, and *plumb*, are often pronounced with a final /b/ and those ending in -*ng*, such as *ring*, *long*, and *bang*, may be pronounced with a final /g/ (Trudgill and Hannah, 2008, p. 129).
- Voiced consonants may be devoiced. In west Africa, *proud* is pronounced as [praut], and *robe* as [roːp] (Trudgill and Hannah, 2008, p. 129).
- Simplification of consonant clusters – many African languages have a consonant-vowel syllable structure, so consonant clusters are simplified by either inserting a vowel or omitting a consonant, e.g. in west Africa *last* [las] and *passed* [pas].

PROSODIC VARIATION

Like previous examples, English tends not to be stress-timed perceptually, and word stress is not prominent.

Vocabulary

A great deal of work has been conducted documenting lexical variation (Bamgbose, 1992; Bokamba, 1992, cited in Kachru and Nelson, 2006; Gough, 1996, cited in Kachru and Nelson, 2006; Kachru and Nelson, 2006; Kachru and Smith, 2008; Kamwangamalu, 2001; Mesthrie, 2013; Platt *et al.*, 1984; Schmied, 2006; Sebba, 2009; Simo Bodba, 1994, cited in Kachru and Nelson, 2006; Tripathi, 1990; Trudgill and Hannah, 2008; Wolf, 2010). Some popular examples from these sources are illustrated below:

- Same meaning, different words – west Africa: *corner* (a bend in the road). Ghana: *robots* (traffic lights) and *matchbox* (shacks or small dwelling units).
- Conversion – west Africa: *off* (to switch off).
- Semantic extension – Malawi: the verb *to move* has various meanings, e.g. *she has been moving with him for six months* (she has been dating him for six months). West Africa: *to take in* (in addition to the 'standard' meaning it can also mean 'to become pregnant').
- Semantic narrowing – Ghana: *hot drinks* (alcoholic drinks). West Africa: *guy* (an out-going, self-assured young man).
- New meanings given to old words – *brutal American film* (exciting American film) and some older terms that have been lost in 'standard' English may be used (e.g. *can be able*, which dates back to Elizabethan English).
- Compounding/specialized meaning – South Africa: *rainbow x* (see Chapter 2).
- Derivation – Ghana: *enstool* and *destool* (see Chapter 2).
- Blending – *indaba* (a serious meeting involving community leaders) is often used with other words: *indaba bid*, *indaba presentation*, *education indaba*.

- Coinage – *facing a lot of hardcap* (hardship), *been-to* boys (boys who have travelled abroad, specifically to Britain or America) and a *me-and-my-darling* (a small sofa or love seat). Ghana: *scholarize* (have a high rate of school attendance), *guested* (to have a guest). West Africa: *chop bar/canteen* (a restaurant serving local food).
- Borrowing – *kibanda* (black market) in east and west Africa; *matutu* (taxi bus) and *msungu* (white person) in west Africa; *sugali* (the staple food in Kenya and Tanzania), *posho* (the staple food in Uganda) and *draw soup* (okra soup in Nigeria); *kaross* (a cloak worn by the Bushmen in South Africa) and *khansu* (a shirt in east Africa); *lobola* (bride-price) and *bondu/bundu* (a secret society for women).
- Discourse markers – Wolf (2010, p. 204) notes that *na/now* may be used to convey attitudes, *sha* may convey an attitude of impatience, and *finish* may be used to signal the end of an enumeration or the end of the turn itself, e.g. *rice and yam, finish* and *went to visit my friend, finish*.
- Locally coined idioms and word-by-word translations of indigenous phrases – west Africa: *chewing stick* (a twig that is chewed up at one end and used as a brush to clean one's teeth) (Melchers and Shaw, 2011, p. 25).
- New idioms based on native English – east Africa: *to be on the tarmac, I met your absence* (you were not there) (Sebba, 2009, p. 415). South Africa: *I wrote it down in my head* (I made a mental note of it), *snakes started playing mini-soccer in my spine* (I became very excited), *beat someone with a cooking stick* (to feed someone), and *to step with fur* (to tread carefully) (Kamwangamalu, 2001).
- Creativity through a combination of English and indigenous forms – Nigeria: *to put sand in someone's gari* (see Chapter 2).

Grammar-syntactic variation

A lot of research has also focused on the grammatical variation in African Englishes (Alo and Mesthrie 2004; Kirkpatrick, 2007; Mesthrie, 2004, 2006, 2013; Huber and Dako 2004, 2008; Platt *et al.*, 1984; Schmied, 2006; Trudgill and Hannah, 2008; Sebba, 2009; Mbangwana 2004). Examples from some of these sources include the following.

- Plurality – as with previous 'New' Englishes examples, we see both subtractive and additive differences. Speakers do not always mark nouns for plurality and many uncountable nouns often become countable (e.g. *I bought all my furnitures from that shop*).
- Tense and aspect – the following are common:
  - Present continuous or progressive with stative verbs – the be + verb + -ing construction is extended (e.g. *she is not having a university degree* and *I am having a stomache*).
  - Complex tenses (e.g. past perfect and some conditionals) may be avoided (e.g. *it would have been much better if this was done*).
- Articles – the rules for the use of the definite article ('the') and the indefinite article ('a'/'an') are different and tend to make the specific/non-specific distinction, rather than the definite/indefinite distinction.
- Possession – -s is often dropped (e.g. *that is Tom car*).
- Adjectives – e.g. *I find my daughter's behaviour disgracing*.
- Question formation – question tags tend to be invariant (*there we are, isn't it?*).
- Article omission – e.g. *I am going to cinema*.

- Undeletion – in Black South African English, there may be a restoration of elements that usually involve a gap or deletion (e.g. *come what may come* and *he made me to do it*) (Mesthrie, 2006, cited in Mesthrie, 2013, p. 532).
- Pronoun gender conflation – pronouns may be undistinguished by gender (related to the lack of sex distinctions in pronouns in African mother tongues), e.g. *he is called Ann*.
- Resumptive pronouns – east Africa: *there is our glue which we are getting them near* (Schmied 2008, p. 456). Cameroon: *the other teacher that we were teaching English with her went away* (Mbangwana 2004, p. 906). Ghana: *the old woman who I gave her the money …* (Huber and Dako 2008, p. 372). Bokamba (1992, pp. 131–32) also notes that these may occur in non-subject positions, specifically in relative clauses, which is an obligatory structure in various west African languages, e.g. *the guests whom I invited them have arrived*.
- Left dislocation – topics are often isolated and followed with comments. Nigeria: *the students – they are demonstrating again* (Alo and Mesthrie 2004, p. 823). Ghana: *that woman – she cheated me* (Huber and Dako 2008, p. 376). South Africa: *the people – they got nothing to eat* (Mesthrie 1997, p. 127), and Q: *Where did you learn Tswana?* A: *Tswana, I learnt it in Pretoria* (Mesthrie 1997, p. 127).
- Yes/no – in west Africa, *yes* and *no* may be omitted in answering questions, e.g. Q: *Hasn't she done her homework yet?* A: *She hasn't done her homework yet* (meaning 'yes') or *She has done her homework* (meaning 'no').
- Relative pronouns – these are often avoided in African varieties (*the woman sang was my mother*).

Pragmatics

Many discourse features are culture specific. Examples include the following.

- Greetings and address vary – in South Africa, to create a good impression one may ask *how is your family?*, *how is your health?*, or *how was your journey/safari?*
- Formality – in Ghana, Sebba (2009, p. 415) notes that Ghanaians do not eat in the presence of others without offering some food, giving the example of a British visitor on a bus who would be offered food. For some, this may be an invite to participate in a conversation, but it is simply a matter of etiquette.

Attitudes toward English variation in Africa

Due to the large number of languages spoken, the use of English as a lingua franca is favoured by some, although it has also resulted in a number of issues related to educational opportunities and identity due to its role as a gatekeeper in upward social mobility. English usage is widespread but it is not always mastered by the entire population, creating inequalities. For example, in the Botswanan Parliament, all members can speak Setswana but English is often used (Schmied, 1991). Melchers and Shaw (2011) also discuss the English language test for members of parliament in Malawi and note that English is a prerequisite for political activity in Ghana (as in many other countries). The authors also note that many law courts in Africa are carried out in English, meaning that the accused may have to rely on interpreters.

While such issues are alarming, 'the use of English is not seriously challenged at the grass roots level in most cases, and its roles as "modern" and practical is accepted' (Melchers and Shaw, 2011, p. 136). In the case of South Africa, Kamwangamalu (2001) notes that attitudes are more community specific. For example, with a history of apartheid, white Afrikaaners may see English as a threat to their identity and culture, while South African Indians, as well as the black community, may view it positively. Attitudes are complex, and there are those who fear the influence of English on indigenous languages.

Attitudes towards varieties of English also differ. Ghanaians, for example, pride themselves on using RP as a model (Wolf, 2010) and the numerous indigenous languages are seen as inferior (Asante, 2012). In Liberia, connections with the USA, as well as the influence of Anglophone neighbours, have given rise to a mix of American features.

Attitudes towards indigenized varieties are also complex. In Nigeria, for example, English is being popularized in Nollywood, the Nigerian film industry, and in Ghana the distinctiveness of Ghanaian English is generally accepted by its speakers, although grammatical features continue to be viewed as errors (Asante, 2012). However, as in South Asia, Africa has produced a large literature in English and many writers have become successful, such as the Nobel Prize winner Wole Soyinka and Man Booker prize winner Chinua Achebe. The influence of such work on the status of the 'New' Englishes in the African context is further discussed in Section 5d.

5d The status of 'New' Englishes: recognition, invisibility, and acceptability

Invisibility: the case of Hong Kong

When discussing the status of the 'New' Englishes, a useful starting place is Hong Kong. The history of English in Hong Kong is presented in the closing case study, alongside some research that has been conducted documenting its distinctive features. Here, we discuss the current use of English in relation to the recognition of a 'variety' of Hong Kong English.

With a largely monolingual Cantonese background (despite increasing importance attached to Mandarin), Hong Kong has never needed a link language. However, the demand for English has always been high, strengthened after the handover to China when many people resisted attempts to change from English-medium schools to Chinese medium ones. Today, English is afforded a high status and an English education is seen as a valuable asset. Citing Hui (2001), Bolton (2002, p. 9) notes that 134 of the 294 Chinese-medium secondary schools now teach all, or some, Form Four students in English. Cantonese is now used more in the government, the number of 'expatriate' civil servants has been significantly reduced in the civil service, and employees working in other 'English-related' jobs, such as newspapers, have been reduced. Nevertheless, English has continued to be the main language of written documents and is also used for much written communication among Cantonese speakers (Tsui and Bunton, 2002). Bolton (2002, p. 9) adds that Cantonese–English code-mixing is common in government departments, and Evans' (2011) survey-based study of more than 2,000 English users in Hong Kong found that Hong Kong professionals spend a significant proportion of their working lives reading and writing English texts. Immigration is also making Hong Kong more multilingual and multicultural. 'Returnee' children, those who have lived abroad for some time, account for a large proportion of school populations, and many families continue to employ *amahs*, domestic helpers who are mostly from the Philippines.

While research on the distinctive features of Hong Kong English is relatively scarce in comparison with the other contexts discussed in this chapter, it has received attention over proficiency concerns. Many measures have been taken over the years to improve English proficiency, including the recruitment of native English-speaking teachers (discussed further in Chapter 9) and the setting of language benchmarks for English teachers, as well as the introduction of an English test in 2000 for graduate teachers (those already employed as teachers have five years to pass). In addition to these proficiency concerns, there appears to be present in Hong Kong an 'invisibility myth' about the use of English (Bolton, 2002). Debates surrounding the 'New' Englishes often centre on acceptability, but in Hong Kong the debate has more to do with recognition (Evans, 2011). There is a belief that English use is not widespread and, as a result, English cannot develop into a distinct variety, as it has done in the other contexts. This 'non-recognition' suggests that Hong Kong English is in Kachru's (1992a, p. 56) first phase, as discussed in Chapter 2. Luke and Richards (1982, pp. 55–56) note,

> there is no such thing ... as 'Hong Kong English' ... There is no equivalent of the mesolectal or basilectal speech styles found, for example, in Singapore ... since there is no equivalent range of English speech varieties in regular use by Hong Kong Chinese.

They argue that a variety of Hong Kong English does not exist. Similarly, although writing three decades or so ago, Platt (1982) notes that, while certain characteristics do exist, the case for a distinct variety of English is not as strong as it is in Singapore. As the closing case to this chapter demonstrates, interest in documenting such features is on the rise. The case of Hong Kong raises a number of questions. In addition to questions about recognition, we may also ask whether a new variety requires intraethnic communication to establish some kind of legitimacy. Bolton and Kwok (1990, p. 163) suggest that,

> Whether or not one can speak of 'Hong Kong English' as a recognisable 'localised variety' of English remains a matter for further research and investigation. If one can establish that (in addition to identifiable local accent) there are clusters of shared lexical and grammatical items which contribute to a distinctive body of shared linguistic features then this may well legitimise recognition of Hong Kong English as a localised variety.

The development of the 'New' Englishes

While it is important not to forget the increased ELF usage and importance of ELF research (discussed in detail in Section 6d and Chapter 7), the case of Hong Kong raises important questions about variety recognition as well as the status of the 'New' Englishes in general. Is Hong Kong English an exonormative variety, dependent on native English-speaking norms (Bolton, 2000, p. 263)? Has it been 'nativized', as in some of the other contexts discussed in this chapter so far? Evans (2011, p. 309) notes that Hong Kong does, in fact, possess many of the 'essential ingredients needed for the development of a new English', which include a sizeable number of English speakers as well as an international economy. Hong Kong is a hub for international business and English is certainly used.

Chan (2013) discusses Hong Kong English in relation to Schneider's Dynamic Model, introduced in Chapter 2, pointing out that in this model the decisive factor is the transition from Phase 3 (nativization) to Phase 4 (endonormative stabilization). This study revealed that, although an 'Anglophone-centric' attitude may still be found in 'high-stakes English-using situations' (Chan, 2013, p. 71), there is less orientation towards native-speaking norms and fewer reservations about non-nativeness in less formal contexts, leading him to believe that Hong Kong may have, in fact, reached Phase 3. Schneider (2007), however, noted that Hong Kong English has not yet reached Phase 4, primarily due to the attachment to native-speaking norms, particularly for career success.

Kirkpatrick also discusses the case of Hong Kong, but in relation to Butler's (1997, p. 10, cited in Kirkpatrick, 2007, p. 142) five criteria for an emerging variety of English:

1 A standard and recognizable pronunciation handed down from one generation to another.
2 Particular words and phrases that sprang up, usually to express key features of the physical and social environment, and which are regarded as peculiar to the variety.
3 A history – a sense that this variety of English is the way it is because of the history of the language community.
4 A literature written without apology in that variety of English.
5 Reference works – dictionaries and style guides – that show that people in that language community look to themselves, not some outside authority, to decide what is right and wrong in terms of how they speak and write their English.

Kirkpatrick notes that Hong Kong English meets criteria 1, 2, and 3, as is evident from the information we have provided here. In relation to criterion 4, he notes that a distinct literature exists, although this may not be as distinct as the English use by Chinese writers. He notes that it may take some time to meet criterion 5, giving the example of Australian English, which was only codified in a dictionary about 200 years after the country was 'discovered' (Kirkpatrick, 2007, p. 142).

The status of the 'New' Englishes: the Quirk/Kachru debate

While variety recognition is important, most debate surrounding the 'New' Englishes has focused on the battle with acceptance. As Rubdy *et al.* (2008, p. 44) note,

> Thus, while there is a general acknowledgement of the emergence of Singapore English as a nativized variety that has evolved its own autonomous system, there is, at the same time, a reluctance to grant speakers of this variety the recognition and legitimacy they deserve.

As discussed in Section 5b, colloquial Singapore English is viewed by the government as being unintelligible, inferior, and illegitimate. Increased usage of this variety has resulted in governmental fears and an aggressive campaign promoting the use of 'standard' English. It is also clear from this chapter that such concerns are not just limited to Singapore, and many of the 'New' Englishes appear to be stuck in Kachru's (1992a) second stage, viewed as 'inferior'.

In 1984, a conference in London, held to mark the founding of the British Council, ended in an exchange of articles in *English Today*, written by Randolph Quirk (1990) and Kachru (1991), on the status of the 'New' Englishes and whether they should be considered as legitimate varieties in their own right and appropriate models for ELT (a topic that remains contentious today and is returned to in Chapter 9). Quirk questioned whether these varieties were the result of 'the increasing failure of the education system' in Outer Circle countries, which was incapable of teaching students 'correct' English (Quirk, 1990, p. 8). In his view, they are incorrect versions of 'standard' English that should not be used as classroom models. On the other hand, Kachru pointed out that they are, in fact, distinct, rule-bound, and legitimate varieties that need to be classed in their own right, pointing out that Quirk's comments do not reflect the sociolinguistic uses of the language today. Kachru emphasized that speakers' intuitions in such contexts are related to their respective social and cultural contexts, and while they may differ from native English-speakers' intuitions, this does not make them inferior.

This debate may have been 20 years ago, since when a lot of research has been conducted into both the World Englishes and the ELF research paradigms, but today the 'New' Englishes continue to battle for acceptance and legitimacy. Innovations continue to be viewed by some as errors. The media often does not help, where the use of basilectal Singapore English has been ridiculed in the media and also banned from television commercials.

Despite such views, the use of these varieties continues to be an important identity marker for some, a topic first introduced in Chapter 2. Many educated Singaporeans, so-called masters of the acrolectal variety, for example, may still use basilectal features in their colloquial speech as an identity marker. Code-switching even occurs among accomplished bilinguals, and the 'New' Englishes are not failed equivalents, and usage of features that differ from the 'standard' does not mean a lack of proficiency. People code-switch for a number of reasons: a local language may have cultural connotations or a feeling of intimacy, whereas English may have connotations of higher socio-economic status or education. However, while acceptance and legitimacy are important, we must also be wary not to ignore the fact that variation exists within these contexts, and ELF research is highlighting that speech communities are increasingly fluid, a point returned to in Section 6d and Chapter 7.

Discussions surrounding recognition, status, acceptance, and legitimacy also bring us to the native/non-native distinction. As English is deeply ingrained in the culture of the contexts discussed in this chapter and used in a variety of domains, these speakers cannot claim authority to the language. The 'insider/outsider' terminology results in a feeling of alienation and inferiority for the non-native English speaker. Simply put, it belongs to the native speaker, those that were born in a country where the language is spoken as a mother tongue. This is explored in more depth in Chapter 9, in relation to teaching English, but for now it is important to highlight the problems with such a simplistic dichotomy. Davies (1991, 2003) points out that the notion of nativeness in language is a 'myth'. It no longer makes sense to make such a distinction and a number of other terms have been proposed in recent years. Platt *et al.* (1984) (see Figure 5.2) contrast EFL, ESL, and ENL contexts, the difference being in the range of functions that a language has. This is similar to Kachru's *cline of bilingualism*, based on the range of variation in terms of the functions that speakers use English for and their proficiency (Kachru, 1965). However, the arrow suggests that, as a 'New' English expands its functions, it gradually becomes more a native or near-native language. Simplistic categorizations are problematic and, as this chapter has shown, English is already a 'native or near native language'

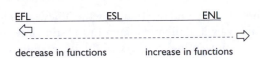

Figure 5.2 The functions of English (source: Platt *et al.*, 1984, p. 23)

for many speakers. Nevertheless, the concept of the arrow is helpful, showing the increased number of functions English has taken on in these contexts. However, as pointed out in Chapter 2, labelling the 'New' Englishes as 'nativized' is problematic, and they develop in very different ways. In Figure 5.2, 'nativeness' appears to be defined by the functions of the language yet, as pointed out in Chapter 2, 'native' varieties are often those that have been around for a long time (Kirkpatrick, 2007) and, as discussed, 'a long time' is vague. Kirkpatrick's (2007, p. 6) third criterion, relating to prejudice and one's image of a 'native speaker', also discussed in Chapter 2, highlights further problems.

Speakers of English in the contexts described in this chapter may, mostly, speak it as a second language, but this does not mean that they should be denied legitimacy and authority. In his article 'The Ownership of English', Widdowson (1994) defined the term ownership as ways in which speakers appropriate language for their own particular use. He argues that native English speakers do not have sole authority over English today, due to the fact that norms of usage are no longer developed in communities where it is spoken as a mother tongue. He describes indigenization as a way of looking at proficiency and criticizes the use of exonormative standards. As he notes, 'You are proficient in a language to the extent that you possess it, make it your own, bend it to your will, assert yourself through it, rather than simply submit to the dictates of its form' (Widdowson, 1994, p. 384). This chapter has shown how speakers in various contexts have made English their own, bringing us back to Widdowson's (1997) distinction between the spread of English and the distribution of English; it has not *spread* as one set of established encoded forms.

Chapter summary

This chapter has outlined variation in countries where English is spoken as a second language, in what is traditionally known as the Outer Circle. We have further examined the historical spread that was introduced in Chapter 1 and returned to the topic of variation, introduced in Chapter 2. We have described the distinct ways in which the English language has adapted as it has come into contact with local languages, and have shown how the long history of English in these countries has led to the nativization of the language. We have also documented World Englishes research that highlights the phonological, lexical, and grammatical variation in the use of English. This chapter has also raised many of the issues discussed in Chapter 3, and it is clear that the spread of English is having both positive and negative impacts on the countries discussed here.

We also revisited the topic of identity, introduced in Chapter 2. Section 5a examined the use of English in South Asia, and it is clear that here, as in other contexts discussed, English has become an integral part of the culture and that writers exploit the language, exemplifying the creative nature of South Asian English. Nevertheless, the 'New' Englishes continue to face a battle for acceptance, and their status has been a central theme here. In Hong Kong, however, the battle appears to be more to do with recognition, returning us to the topic of the development of Englishes. Two decades may have passed since the Quirk/Kachru debate, but the status of the 'New' Englishes continues to be controversial, many still viewing them as inferior. Distinctions between 'native' and 'non-native' do not help, preventing speakers of 'New' Englishes from being classed as legitimate or claiming authority for the language.

Further reading

On the 'New' Englishes:

- Kachru, B., Kachru, Y., and Nelson, C. (eds) (2006). *The Handbook of World Englishes*. Oxford: Blackwell.
- Kirkpatrick, A. (ed.) (2010). The Routledge Handbook of World Englishes. London: Routledge.

On Hong Kong:

- Bolton, K. (ed.) (2002). *Hong Kong English: Autonomy and Creativity*. Hong Kong: Hong Kong University Press.

On the status of 'New' Englishes:

- Quirk, R. (1990). 'Language varieties and standard language.' *English Today*, 6(01), pp. 3–10.
- Kachru, B. B. (1991). 'Liberation linguistics and the Quirk concern.' English Today, 7(01), pp. 3–13.

@ Closing activities

Chapter discussion questions

Section 5a

1 When describing features of Indian English, Verma (1982, p. 180) notes that, 'They are not corrupt, but, rather, different forms of the same language.' Do you agree with this point of view?
2 South Asian writers are very creative in their usage of English. What does this tell us about the 'New' Englishes?
3 Kachru (1994, p. 545) states that, 'English became a vehicle for national unity, and … pan-Indian cultural and political awakening.' In what ways has the spread of English had both positive and negative impacts in South Asia?

Section 5b

1 What are your views on the Speak Good English Movement?
2 There has been a sharp increase in English use in Singaporean homes in the last three decades. What influence do you think this shift has had on interaction between families in these households?
3 What is your opinion on the use of exonormative norms in the classroom in this region?

Section 5c

1 In what ways has linguistic contact influenced the spread of English in Africa?
2 Given the large number of languages spoken, can English function as a neutral lingua franca, or do the negative impacts outweigh the positive ones?
3 This section highlighted some of the distinctive features of African Englishes. Do you know of any others?

Section 5d

1 'The mass of Hong Kong people will not easily accept that a distinctive Hong Kong English exists' (Pang, 2003, p. 17). What is your opinion on this statement?
2 What is your opinion on the Quirk/Kachru debate?
3 Do you think speakers of English discussed in this chapter should be denied legitimacy and authority?

Debate topics

1 We can no longer classify the 'New' Englishes as inferior and illegitimate.
2 Terms such as 'interlanguage' and 'fossilization' are irrelevant today. Language contact is inevitable and language change is natural.
3 English is a gatekeeper in upward social mobility in Africa, thus the spread of English in Africa has a negative effect.

Writing and presentation prompts

Below are ideas for writing and presentation tasks to apply the knowledge learned in Chapter 5.

	Assignment topics
Personal account	Provide an account of English in a 'New' Englishes context that you are familiar with or interested in. As in this chapter, focus on the history, the role of English today, variation, and the status of English.
Research task	Choose a corpus that is relevant to a context you are interested in (e.g. The Asian Corpus of English (ACE) or the ICE-India Corpus). Examine the use of either a word or a grammatical item. Examine its usage and print out a number of lines of relevant text.
Basic academic	'An innovation is seen as an acceptable variant, while an error is simply a mistake or uneducated usage. If innovations are seen as errors, a non-native variety can never receive any recognition' (Bamgbose, 1998, p. 2). Write an essay on the acceptability of the 'New' Englishes.
Advanced academic	In Singapore, English has a two-fold role: a global function as the language of international business and a local function as a marker of cultural identity (Seargeant, 2012, p. 108). Investigate this dual role of English in Singapore, considering issues of identity.

Chapter 6

English in global contexts

Introductory activities

The following introductory activities are designed to encourage the reader to think about the issues raised in this chapter before reading it.

English in the global community

Look at Table 6.1, which shows the age of English-language instruction in Asia.

Discussion questions

1 What is your opinion on the age at which English instruction is introduced in the countries listed in Table 6.1?
2 In what ways do you think English is used in these contexts (and others)? Has this changed over the years?
3 In many of the countries listed in Table 6.1, the internal functions of English are growing. Is it still reasonable to classify them as Expanding Circle, or EFL, contexts?
4 In many of these countries, many parents are enrolling their children in private English lessons before they start elementary school. How effective do you think teaching English at such a young age is?

Case study: East Asia

Read the following quote about English use in Japan, taken from Stanlaw (2004, pp. 1–2).

> We, that is, the Matsumoto family, live in a *manshon* ('mansion') too. At this moment, I am watching *beisu-boru* ('baseball') on *terebi* ('television'). My wife is out shopping at a *depaato* ('department store'), and later she will stop at a *suupa* ('supermarket') to get *pooku choppu* ('pork chops'), *pan* ('bread'), *bataa* ('butter'), *jamu* ('jam') and perhaps some *sooseiji* ('sausage') for breakfast. My daughter has gone to the *byuutii saron* ('beauty salon') to get a *paama* ('permanent'). Oh, the *ter-ehon* ('telephone') is ringing. We cannot live a day in Japan today without these loanwords. Language purists lament the fact. The nationalists would wipe out all foreign-sounding words from our vocabulary. But where will they be without

takushii ('taxi'), *terebi* ('television'), *raijio* ('radio'), *tabako* ('tobacco'), *biiru* ('beer'), *shatsu* ('shirts'), *beruto* ('belt'), and *meetoru* ('meter')?

Discussion

1 It is estimated that loan words comprise about 10 per cent of the Japanese lexicon (MacGregor, 2003). What is the effect of such extensive use of loan words on national languages?
2 Backhaus's (2007) linguistic landscape study in Tokyo looked at signs around the city. He found that, although 14 other languages were identified on the 2,444 signs in the sample, English was contained on almost 93 per cent of all signs. Do you know of any other examples where the internal functions of English are increasing?

Introduction

Chapters 4 and 5 discussed countries where English is spoken as a 'native', 'nativized', 'indigenized', or 'institutionalized' language. As pointed out in the Preface to this book, areas of the world where English has not played a historical role have been relatively under-researched. In a sense, Chapter 6 builds upon this and focuses on the 'rest' of the world, where English is traditionally seen as being a 'foreign' language in the Expanding Circle. However, this chapter will reveal that the role of English is 'expanding' in these nations and becoming much more than a foreign language. We refer to English use in this arena as a 'global context', as it is due to globalization that the role of English, and contexts in which it is used, is changing rapidly.

We begin in Section 6a by looking at Europe, discussing the multilingual policy of the EU and the role that English plays in Europe today. Section 6b focuses on East Asia, specifically Japan, China, Taiwan, and South Korea, while Section 6c describes the current state of English in South-East Asia, specifically Thailand, Vietnam, and Indonesia. In this chapter we focus more on the history and current role of English, how it is taught, and attitudes towards it. Where research has been conducted on variation, this has been

Table 6.1 English language instruction in Asia

Country	English as a compulsory subject	Developments related to English
China	Elementary grade 3 (since 2002), although many start from grade 1	Increased emphasis on content-based instruction
South Korea	Elementary grade 3 (since 1997)	By 2015, South Korean secondary school teachers to teach English in English
Thailand	Elementary grade 1 (since 1996)	In 2010, there was a proposal to make English an official 'second language', although this was rejected
Vietnam	Elementary grade 3	Government initiative Project 2020 means some subjects will be taught in English
Indonesia	Elementary grade 4 or 5	In 2013, English was taken out of the curriculum

presented, but in this chapter we aim to move away from the notion of 'variety' and focus on how English operates as a lingua franca. Thus, we end with Section 6d, which defines the concept of ELF, before ELF research is examined further in Chapter 7.

6a   English as a lingua franca in Europe

In the late 1990s, Graddol (1997, p. 47) contended, 'No other region has been more affected by the rise of English than Europe.' This section opens with a historical overview of English in Europe, followed by an examination of the role it plays today. We then examine debates on the existence of a European variety of English, as well as the use of English as a lingua franca.

English in Europe

With a population of approximately half a billion people, the EU is ethnically, culturally, and linguistically diverse. Before the Second World War, German and French were commonly studied across Europe, with German functioning as the dominant lingua franca. When the war ended, the role of German was downgraded in many countries and was replaced with Russian. However, interest in Russian declined with the collapse of the Soviet Union in 1991 and, despite a revival of German, interest in English grew. The European Community, created in 1958, gave official status to Dutch, French, German, and Italian, being the national languages of the six initial member states (Belgium, France, Germany, Italy, Luxembourg, and the Netherlands). Today, there are 24 official languages of the EU (see Table 6.2), and each time a new member joins, a new language is added to the list.

With such linguistic diversity, the EU promotes a policy of linguistic equality, highlighted in the Maastricht Treaty and the European Charter of Fundamental Rights of the European Union (Article 22).

The policy of multilingualism fosters the idea of a single community with diverse cultures and languages. European citizens are expected to learn two languages in addition to their native language, and documents can be submitted to EU institutions in any of the official languages. Internal documents, as well as EU legislation, can be published in all official languages via the European Parliament's translation services. This multilingual policy may exist in theory, but in practice the situation is different. Not all working

Table 6.2 The official languages of the European Union

Official EU language	Date added
Dutch, French, German, Italian	1958
Danish, English	1973
Greek	1981
Portuguese, Spanish	1986
Finnish, Swedish	1995
Czech, Estonian, Hungarian, Latvian, Lithuanian, Maltese, Polish, Slovak, Slovene	2004
Bulgarian, Irish, Romanian	2007
Croatian	2013

documents are always translated into every language, and the European Commission has adopted English, French, and German as procedural languages. English has become the de facto working language in the EU and the multilingual policy is often discarded, evidence of which is provided below.

- English is a prerequisite for a successful career within the European Commission.
- English is used as a language of communication by many EU employees and delegates.
- English is the main foreign language of business in all member countries.
- English is the main language of translation services – in 2004, 62 per cent of all pages received by the EU-internal translation service for translation were in English (Directorate-General for Translation 2005, p. 6, cited in Mollin, 2006, pp. 175–76);
- English makes up around 88 per cent of the content on the EU websites (see http://euobserver.com/news/25712).
- English is dominant in EU published material – in 1986, 58 per cent of EU documents were initially drafted in French, although today 72 per cent of EU institution texts are drafted in English, and large parts of EU information online is not translated, particularly into minority languages (again see http://euobserver.com/news/25712).

English has emerged as the dominant language of choice for internal communication, and European Parliament members note that the use of a national language, particularly a minor one, means that speeches have limited impact despite the availability of interpretation services. English, then, acts as the de facto working language, which advantages some yet disadvantages others, as discussed in Chapter 3.

Translation and interpretation services have also been criticized for being overly expensive, costing approximately €1.1 billion (approximately one per cent of the budget) each year, and utilizing a tenth of the commission's entire workforce (again see http://euobserver.com/news/25712). In response, the European Parliament plans to cut the translation service budget by approximately €8.6 million per year (see www.euractiv.com/culture/parliament-cuts-translation-budg-news-516201) and the parliament is no longer required to translate parliamentary sessions into all 23 languages. This move brings us back to Robert Phillipson's concept of linguistic imperialism, discussed in Chapter 3, and his concerns about the use of English in Europe and the threat of English to linguistic diversity. In *English-Only Europe?* (Phillipson, 2003), he points out that measures should be put in place to inhibit the spread of English, and he supports the translation and interpretation services.

Outside of the day-to-day business of the EU, the dominance of English is also obvious elsewhere in Europe. English is increasingly being used for wider communication as a lingua franca. Several job websites note English proficiency as a prerequisite for application, and several transnational corporations have started to use English as an in-house company language. The demand for English proficiency is also evident in international diplomacy, where many foreign diplomats are under pressure to learn English. English is used at all levels of education and, with the internationalization of the European student body, the role of English is increasing in the education arena. Many degrees are taught in English, and increasing proficiency levels mean the dominance of English is likely to grow.

English is also taught more than any other foreign language and 90 per cent of all EU pupils now learn English as their first 'foreign' language (Modiano, 2006, p. 223). It is dominant in schools throughout the continent, which, as discussed in Chapter 3, has been at the expense of other European languages. European children are beginning to learn foreign languages earlier, with most beginning between the ages of six and nine. The *Key Data on Teaching Languages at School in Europe 2012* report highlights that English is the most taught foreign language in nearly all European countries (see Figure 6.1). The report also showed that, in 2009–10, 73 per cent of primary school pupils in the EU were learning English (see Figure 6.2), with over 90 per cent learning it in lower secondary and general upper secondary schools.

	English	French	Other*		English	French	Other*
Belgium (N)	✓	✓		**Portugal**			✓
Belgium (F)			✓	**Romania**			✓
Czech R.			✓	**Slovenia**			✓
Denmark	✓			**Slovakia**			✓
Germany	✓			**Finland**			Swedish
Estonia			✓	**Sweden**	✓		
Ireland			✓	**UK**			✗
Greece	✓			**Iceland**	✓		Danish
Spain			✓	**Norway**	✓		
France			✓	**Liechtenstein**	✓	✓	
Croatia			✓	**Luxembourg**	✓	✓	German
Italy	✓			**Hungary**			✓
Cyprus	✓	✓		**Malta**	✓		
Latvia			✓	**Netherlands**	✓		
Lithuania			✓	**Austria**			✓
Bulgaria			✓	**Poland**			✓

* If no language is listed in 'other': ✓ means a non-specified foreign language is compulsory,
✗ means no foreign language is compulsory

Figure 6.1 Specific mandatory foreign languages as specified by central education authorities (at one point during full-time compulsory education), 2010–11 (source: *Key Data on Teaching Languages at School in Europe 2012*)

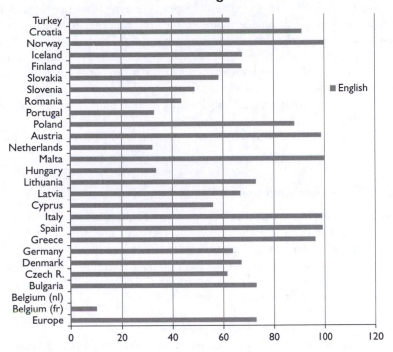

Figure 6.2 Percentage of all students in primary education who are learning English (source: *Key Data on Teaching Languages at School in Europe 2012*)

However, despite such a presence, the role of English does differ across member states. It has a high profile in countries in Scandinavia and in the Netherlands, but a much lower status in places like Italy. Nevertheless, it cannot be denied that 'English impinges on everybody's life in Europe, in many different ways' (Seidlhofer *et al.*, 2006, p. 3). European citizens all over Europe are exposed to English through the media, and some have to use it at work and with tourists, where it is used as a lingua franca. 'In short, English is everywhere, and we cannot avoid it' (Seidlhofer *et al.*, 2006, p. 3).

As a result, English proficiency is viewed as important. The findings from the survey on 'Europeans and their languages', carried out by the European Commission in 2012 and shown below, provide evidence.

- Just over half of Europeans (54 per cent) are able to hold a conversation in at least one additional language, a quarter (25 per cent) are able to speak at least two additional languages, and one in ten (10 per cent) are conversant in at least three.
- The most widely spoken foreign language is English (38 per cent), followed by French (12 per cent), German (11 per cent), Spanish (7 per cent), and Russian (5 per cent), although at national level English is the most widely spoken foreign language in 19 of the 25 member states where it is not an official language (i.e. excluding the UK and Ireland).

- More than four in five (84 per cent) agree that everyone in the EU should be able to speak at least one foreign language, and 72 per cent agree that people should be able to speak more than one language in addition to their mother tongue.
- Eighty-one per cent agree that all EU languages should be treated equally and, even though 69 per cent think that Europeans should be able to speak a common language, this view does not extend to believing that any one language should have priority over others.
- Fifty-three per cent agree that EU institutions should adopt a single language when communicating with citizens.
- Sixty-seven per cent see English as one of the two most useful languages for themselves.

Euro-English/Euro-speak/English as a lingua franca?

English has clearly penetrated into the lives of many Europeans, leading some to suggest that a distinct variety exists alongside a European identity. The question of the existence of a distinct 'variety' of English in Europe has been debated. Kirkpatrick (2007, p. 165) asks, 'Does this mean that a variety or varieties of "Euro-English" will develop, or will English be a lingua franca marked by variation?'. Modiano (2006, p. 233) has also described some of the unique lexical items, which include:

- *Maastricht* (referring to the agreement signed there);
- *Schengen* (a term to encompass those countries that have free borders within the EU);
- *Euro land*, *Euro area*, and *Eurozone* (those countries where the euro has been adopted as the currency);
- *Eurosceptic* (someone sceptical of European integration);
- *four freedoms* (to designate the free movement of goods, money, people, and services across European borders);
- *member state* (member countries of the EU).

Modiano also uses the term 'Euro-speak' to refer to the language of the 'Euro-crats', the vernacular of EU politicians and civil servants. However, he also points out that the existence of a distinct variety of European English is debated among those who work in the EU, echoing the debate on standards. English proficiency has been the subject of great debate and the booklet *How to Write Clearly* (2013), published by the EU in all 23 languages, offers advice for writing in English, including how to avoid using the 'wrong word' which 'can alienate readers' and 'lead to misunderstandings and diplomatic incidents' (European Commission, 2013, p. 11). The Europa website also includes a section called the 'Plain Language Guide to Eurojargon' (see http://europa.eu/abc/eurojargon/index_en.htm), which follows British English. 'Euro-English', then, is viewed rather negatively, reflected in an article in a 2001 issue of the *Finn-Brits Magazine* entitled, 'Euro-English: A problem or a solution?', which discussed 'Euro-waffle' and 'plain bad English' (McArthur, 2002).

However, some scholars, such as Modiano (2006), believe that it does exist and will eventually be codified, bringing us back to the notion of the existence of varieties and ELF. On the other hand, others such as Görlach (2002, p. 151) believe that the concept of 'Euro-English' is 'little more than a catchphrase' and that 'recurrent features' only occur in rather specific contexts.

It is clear from the book thus far that anything distinct from the so-called 'standard' is often viewed suspiciously. The use of ELF in Europe cannot be denied and, as with other contexts, the English language has adapted, and continues to do so, to its surroundings in the European context. It is appropriated by its speakers in different contexts in different ways and, while research has been conducted documenting the features of a so-called 'Euro-English', ELF research, as discussed in Section 6d and Chapter 7, showcases how the usage of English in Europe is not necessarily fixed in any way. That is, ELF is different when used between, say, a Spanish and a French Erasmus student discussing their new course at a Scottish university, compared with a German/Turkish business negotiation in Istanbul. From an ELF perspective, it does not seem appropriate to continue the debate about the existence of a monolithic Euro-English. In fact, a Global Englishes perspective sees the future direction of research as moving away from the varieties depicted by World Englishes (outlined in Chapters 4 and 5) to more fluid constructs. This is explored further in Section 6d and Chapter 7.

6b   English in East Asia: China, Japan, Taiwan, and South Korea

This section focuses on East Asia, including China, Japan, Taiwan, and South Korea. We begin with the history and role of English and a brief overview of some of the descriptive work on variation, and end with an examination of attitudes toward English and the increasing role of English as a lingua franca. We also look at how English is taught in the region, a topic explored in greater depth in Chapter 9.

The history of English in Japan

In Japan, trade links were established with the Dutch in 1608, and an elite group of scholars began to study the language. However, contact was minimal due to isolationist policies. In 1853, with the arrival of the American mission, Japan was 'opened' and scholars began to study English. In 1868, the process of modernization led to an influx of English-speaking foreigners and the widespread study of English in private language academies. After the Second World War, English influence intensified as the USA influenced Japanese modernisation.

English education was further emphasized as Japan's economy grew in the 1960s and 1970s. In the 1980s, a discourse of *kokusaika* or internationalization emerged, with education reforms. Emphasis was placed on communication skills, and native English speakers were invited to teach English as part of the Japan Exchange and Teaching (JET) Programme, which now includes 4,372 participants. As shown in Table 6.3, there is a native English speaking bias (and particularly an American one), a theme returned to in Chapter 9.

English is the only foreign language option in most schools and the only subject tested in all university entrance exams. In 2011 it also became compulsory in primary education. Japanese university undergraduates study English for at least two years, even in unrelated majors. However, despite the high status assigned to English, English education has been promoted alongside a policy of *Wakon-yousai,* or 'Japanese spirit with Western learning', a responsive measure to offset possible Westernization as a result of moves towards internationalization. This intention to preserve Japanese cultural identity and national sovereignty may explain why English has taken on such a distinctive form in Japan, discussed further at the end of this section.

Table 6.3 JET participants by top five countries of origin as at July, 2013

Country	Assistant Language Teacher (ALT)	Co-ordinator for International Relations (CIR)	Sports Exchange Adviser (SEA)	Total
United States	2,268	91	0	2,359
Canada	467	17	0	484
United Kingdom	375	13	0	388
Australia	278	22	0	300
New Zealand	241	14	0	255
Other	371	204	11	586
Total participants from all countries	4,000	361	11	4,372

Source: www.jetprogramme.org/e/introduction/statistics.html

The history of English in China

In China, contact with English can be traced back to 1637, when the first British traders arrived. Chinese Pidgin English developed along the south China coast, used for communication among Chinese and foreigners to conduct trade. However, a ban put on communication with foreigners ceased this development. After the Anglo–Chinese War of 1839–42, Chinese Pidgin English was used again, spreading to other parts of the country. In 1862, further parts of China were opened to foreigners with the Treaty of Tianjin, and missionary schools were established. Contact with Britain increased in the nineteenth century and English education grew due to fears of foreign invasion (Chang, 2006). A modern foreign language training institution was established in 1862 and English was introduced into the national curriculum for middle schools in 1902.

English continued to develop but its role was diminished again with the establishment of the People's Republic of China in 1949. The spread of English accompanied fears of Westernization, as in Japan, and many English departments were closed. This policy was soon revised after China's break with Russia, and English was made the official first foreign language in schools in 1964. Although the Cultural Revolution (1976) resulted in another setback for English, it regained momentum in 1978, leading to an increased demand for English proficiency evident in increasing numbers of university students studying English and increased institutions offering English majors.

Globalization has significantly influenced the spread of English in China. China joined the World Trade Organization in 2001 and this, in addition to the hosting of the 2008 Olympic Games and the 2010 Shanghai World Expo, has resulted in added emphasis on English proficiency. English education is now compulsory in primary schools from age nine (grade 3), although many schools start from the first grade. It is now compulsory in Chinese colleges and universities for two years, and the College English Test (CET) is also becoming increasingly important, with some universities requiring it for graduation. The China Public English Test (PETS) is also increasingly used by Chinese companies to measure English proficiency, just as the Test of English for International Communication (TOEIC) is used in Japan. Since 2000, there has been an increased emphasis placed on content-based instruction in English and the commercial English language teaching market is also rapidly growing, evident in the success of Li Yang's Crazy English enterprise, described in a case study on the accompanying website.

However, as in Japan, the provision of English education has come under scrutiny, as discussed further in Chapter 9, and has also been rather pragmatic, characterized by a fear of Western influence, particularly after the events at Tiananmen Square in 1989. Furthermore, an article in the *South China Morning Post* on 13 September 2013 discussed the debate on the provision of English classes to elementary school education and the need for more classes on *guoxue*, or national study (classes on Chinese traditional culture), concerns that have also been expressed in Japan.

The history of English in Taiwan

Taiwan was isolated before it came to be used for military and trade purposes in the seventeenth century, when European presence grew. Dutch colonialism lasted from 1624 to 1662, after which it fell under Chinese rule. Taiwan was under Japanese rule for a period until 1945, when it was returned to China after the Second World War, although it is important to point out that it has been ruled by a nationalist government since 1949.

English instruction formally began in 1949 in secondary schools, and it was the only required course for first years at tertiary level until 1993 when other foreign languages were introduced (Chern, 2002). As with its East Asian counterparts, the desire for English proficiency has resulted in the lowering of the starting age for English instruction. Before 2001, English was introduced from grade 7 in primary schools. However, in September 2001 the 9-Year Joint Curricula Plan, announced in 2002, stipulated that English education should begin at grades 5 and 6 from 2001. After many urban cities began teaching from grade 1, the Ministry of Education revised this policy in 2003, stipulating that it was to become compulsory from grade 3 starting in 2005. However, local educational bureaus and schools differ throughout the country, and while the majority do introduce English in grade 3, some schools continue to start earlier in grade 1 and 2.

As in other parts of East Asia, there has been increased emphasis on communicative teaching practices. According to the Ministry of Education in 2000, 'The objective of the elementary/junior high school curriculum should be to instil a basic communicative ability, to prepare students to take a global perspective and to give individuals confidence in communicating in the global arena' (cited in Nunan, 2003, p. 603). A new 2014 education policy will also see the eradication of the high school entrance exam, which may have a positive influence on communicative language teaching practices in elementary and junior high schools. However, Taiwanese English education has also been subject to criticism, and with the lowering of the starting age for English education there has been increased concern about the shortage of proficient English teachers, discussed further in Chapter 9. For example, Chang's (2006) survey highlighted that, in 2006, only 51.7 per cent of the teachers teaching English were actually qualified. Measures to address low proficiency include a proficiency test for English teachers, introduced in 1999, and the recruitment of more native English speakers.

The Taiwanese ELT industry is growing. Taiwan has also seen the establishment of 'English-villages' or situational classrooms (e.g. with simulated shopping centres). The high status afforded to English can be seen in the proposal made in the early twenty-first century to make English the second official language in the country. Graddol (2006, p. 89) notes that 80 per cent of respondents in a public opinion survey in 2006 reported that they hoped this would happen.

The history of English in South Korea

In Korea, English education began officially in 1883, when the first English language school was established to train interpreters. Other schools were also opened and English was taught by English and US missionaries, viewed as an important part of modernization. English was downgraded with Japanese occupation but became influential again after the Second World War. By the end of the Korean War (1950–53), English education had become widespread, a time when North Korea came under Russian influence.

Today, English is compulsory from middle school, and in 1997 it was introduced into South Korean primary schools from grade 3. South Korea has also witnessed moves towards communicative teaching practices, and the English test in the national College Scholastic Ability Test (CSAT), necessary to enter South Korean universities, now places more emphasis on communication. As in Japan and Taiwan, there has also been the creation of English-only villages to give people the opportunity to use and improve their English skills. Many universities are also increasingly offering content courses through English and, at one university in Seoul, more than 30 per cent of all classes are conducted in English, a number that is expected to rise (Park, 2009, p. 97). Such moves have been accompanied by the recruitment of native English speakers, as in Japan, through the establishment of government programmes such as the English Program in Korea (EPIK). English-medium instruction is a rather controversial topic and one that will be returned to in Chapter 10.

By 2015, South Korean secondary school teachers will be required to teach English in English, and the national qualifying examination now includes an essay and an oral English interview, as well as a listening exam. However, as with its East Asian neighbours, there are concerns over the availability of proficient teachers. In order to address this, in 2009 the Ministry of Education announced a target of having all English teachers able to teach in English by 2012, and started a Teaching English in English programme. Successful participants who complete the six-months' training, and are tested on their proficiency in speaking, listening, writing, reading, and presenting, get points for promotion and an overseas study programme for one month, as well as other benefits.

English is clearly a prestige language in South Korea, needed today by those wishing to work in the government and many South Korean companies that value English skills in hiring decisions. South Korean parents spend a lot of money on English education and many are also sending their children abroad to study, even at primary school level. Park (2009) refers to 2005 figures, which note that up to 15 trillion Won (nearly $15 billion) was spent on English education, including the taking of English language tests. South Korean parents also spend a lot of money on extra tuition for their children, which mostly goes on *hagwon* (cram schools). Such expenditure, as well as the lowering of the starting age for English education, has sparked controversy. For example, an article in the *Guardian Weekly* (De Lotbinière, 2011) discussed an education pressure group in South Korea called *World Without Worries About Private Education*. Their publication, *What a Waste – Private English Education*, is an attempt to change opinion about early-age English instruction.

Features of English in East Asia

While we acknowledge the problems relating to establishing a 'variety' of East Asian Englishes, it is worthwhile discussing some of the distinct features that have been described in the literature. In China, for example, a number of scholars have argued for the existence of China English, and the *World Englishes Journal* in 2002 had a special issue on China. In Japan, there has also been some scholarly discussion over the existence of a Japanese variety of English. Honna (2003), for example, argues that Japanese learners of English must liberate themselves from native-speakerism and establish *Nihon-Eigo* (Japanese-English), and Morrow (2004, p. 95) points out that it is time for Japanese students to stop regarding themselves as speakers of 'broken English' and see it as a distinct and independent variety. Yano (2001, p. 127), however, contends that there has never been, and never will be, 'a local model of English, established and recognisable as Japanese English, reflecting the Japanese culture and language'. Similarly, in South Korea, Park (2009) notes that Korean English has some distinctive traits in pronunciation, lexicon, syntax, and discourse.

Features of English in East Asia

Sounds

PHONEMIC VARIATION

- In China, less distinction is made between long and short vowels (e.g. *heat* and *hit*).
- In Japan, a very reduced vowel set of English is spoken.
- In Japan and South Korea, speakers often do not distinguish between /r/ and /l/.
- In Japan, /v/ and /b/ are often not distinguished and are realized as [b].
- In China and Japan, the fricatives /θ/ and /ð/ are often replaced by [s] and [z].
- In China, fricative /v/ and approximant /w/ are not distinguished and are realized as [w].
- In China, final consonants in consonant clusters are often omitted.
- In South Korea and Japan, added vowels may be inserted in consonant clusters (e.g. *stop* realized as *sutopu*).

Vocabulary

- Acronyms – Japan: *OL* (office lady); South Korea: *OT* (orientation).
- Conversion – Japan: *furonto* [literally 'front'] (hotel reception), *baikingu* [literally 'Viking'] (buffet); South Korea: *audience* (guests).
- Semantic narrowing – Japan: *mishin* (machine, used only for sewing machine), *rikuesto* (request, used only to ask a band to play a song).
- Abbreviations – Japan: *waa puro* (word processor), *sando* (sandwich); South Korea: *home p* (home page).
- Variety-specific compounds – Japan: *haburashi* (combining Japanese *ha* [tooth] and English *brush*).
- Locally coined idioms and word-by-word translations of indigenous phrases – China: *playing away from home* (having an extramarital affair), *barefoot doctor* (rural untrained doctors).
- New idioms (and collocations) based on native English – South Korea: *eye shopping* (window shopping), *behind story* (background information); Japan: *ofu dei* (off day).

Grammar-syntactic variation

- Plurality: additive differences – often, no distinction is made between countable and uncountable nouns due to the lack of inflectional endings in Japanese and Korean (e.g. *staffs*).
- Plurality: subtractive differences – China: article omission due to the absence of the article system.
- Tense and aspect – South Korea: little distinction between simple present and present progressive or simple past and past perfect.
- Concord with collective noun – for example, *the government is/are* are used interchangeably.

Pragmatics

Gift-giving is an integral part of Japanese culture but givers may downplay their generosity when offering a gift (e.g. *this is something small and inexpensive*). The *yes/no* response can also cause confusion in South Korea and Japan. For example, when responding to a negative question such as *don't you want to go there?* a speaker may answer *yes* to signal agreement with the negative question (meaning 'No, I don't want to go').

Attitudes toward English variation in East Asia

Despite such descriptive work, public opinion towards the English used in these countries appears to be largely negative. In Japan, for instance, there is a multitude of popular books targeted at Japanese English learners that emphasize the need to 'overcome' Japanese-style English. Titles include *Farewell to Japanese English* (Hisama, 1995) and *How your English sounds to Native Speakers* (Thayne and Koike, 2008). Such titles, also found elsewhere in East Asia, fail to see such creativity as innovative. ELF work, described in more detail in Section 6d and Chapter 8, is crucial to show how East Asians are increasingly using ELF.

6c   ASEAN in the Expanding Circle

This section presents the history of English and the role of the language today in those ASEAN countries where it has traditionally been used as a foreign language (see Chapter 5 for Singapore, Brunei, and Malaysia). This section has been largely informed by Kirkpatrick (2010a), a leading scholar of the role of English in ASEAN. As noted in Chapter 5, despite the large number of national languages, as shown in Table 6.4, English was adopted as the official working language in ASEAN in 2010.

Thailand

More than 70 languages are spoken in Thailand and 'standard' Thai is the de facto official language (see www.unescobkk.org). English education began in the reign of the Thai King Rama III (1824–51) through a US missionary. Due to fears of Western colonization, it was actively encouraged by the subsequent King Rama IV (1851–68). In an effort to modernize the nation, English education and Western learning were encouraged,

Table 6.4 The national language and English in education in ASEAN in 2010

Country	Medium of instruction	First foreign language (year of introduction)
Brunei*	Malay and English	English (Primary 1, from Primary 4 as MoI)
Burma	Burmese	English (Primary 1)
Cambodia**	Khmer	English (Primary 5) (French also offered)
Indonesia**	Bahasa Indonesian	English (Secondary 1)
Laos	Lao	English (Primary 3)
Malaysia	Malay and English	English (from Primary 1 as MoI)
Philippines	Filipino and English	English (from Primary 1 as MoI)
Singapore	English	Malay/Mandarin/Tamil (Primary 1)
Thailand	Thai	English (Primary 1)
Vietnam**	Vietnamese	English (Primary 3 in selected schools)

(MoI = medium of instruction)
 * The Arabic script *jawi* is introduced from Primary 3.
** Some bilingual education for minority groups in early primary.
Source: Kirkpatrick, 2010a, p. 63

romanticized in the novel *Anna and the King of Siam* (and the subsequent musical *The King and I*), which documented the story of an English governess, who was invited to teach English in the court (Kirkpatrick, 2010a). English was afforded a high status and became the most prestigious foreign language during the reign of King Rama V (1868–1910) when many foreigners visited the country. A certain level of English proficiency also allowed citizens to be exempt from military service.

King Rama VI (1910–25), educated in the West, introduced English as a compulsory subject in 1913, and more hours were actually devoted to English than to the Thai language. In 1996, English became compulsory for all primary children from grade 1 and became compulsory in universities in 2001. However, as with East Asia (discussed in Section 6b), English education has come under scrutiny. Once again, the lack of qualified teaching staff has been heavily scrutinized, and in 2006 the Thai government advertised for native English speakers to take up teaching positions, although only 11 applications were received due to the low salary (Kirkpatrick, 2010a, p. 49).

English has become an integral part of the daily lives of many Thais. It has become the de facto working language in a number of fields, and in 2010 the Minister of Education announced plans to raise the profile of English, particularly in the teaching of mathematics and science. Greater emphasis has also been placed on English education as Thailand prepares for the ASEAN Economic Community (AEC) in 2015, discussed further at the end of this section.

Indonesia

Indonesia, the largest country in ASEAN, has a population of more than 200 million, comprising some 200 ethnic groups that speak some 400 languages (Kirkpatrick, 2010a, p. 43). It was colonized by the Netherlands for four centuries, during which time Dutch was the medium of instruction. Malay was adopted when Indonesia was fighting for independence and this was furthered by the brief Japanese occupation, which banned the use of Dutch. The decline of Dutch continued after independence was granted in 1945 and Bahasa Indonesia, one form of Malay, was adopted as the national language. English, however, was soon made a compulsory second language at junior and senior high school levels. Today, English is usually taught from primary school (grade 4 or 5), but from July 2013 English was not included in the compulsory primary school curriculum, in favour of an increased emphasis on national language and culture education.

Burma/Myanmar

Burma, renamed as Myanmar in 1989, is ethnically and linguistically diverse, and one of the poorest nations in ASEAN after experiencing years of repressive military rule. After the Anglo-Burmese wars, Burma became a province of British India in 1886. In the 1920s and 1930s opposition to colonial rule began. However, the movement failed as many ethnic minorities favoured British rule, fearing the consequences of majority rule if independence was granted. It became a crown colony in 1937 and, after a brief Japanese occupation (1942–45), Burma became independent in 1948. Burmese then became the official national language and the medium of instruction in schools. English, however, was also taught as a foreign language. Burma is yet another example of a nation that doesn't fit neatly into Kachru's Three Circle Model, being a former British colony but having abandoned English in an official capacity after independence.

The socialist government continued to promote an anti-colonial discourse, but a turning point in English education policy came when one of General U Ne Win's daughters was denied entry to the Royal Medical School in England because of her low English proficiency. At this time, the Burmese-only language policy was re-examined and there was some revival of English, as it was emphasized as the language of modernization. Interest in English education grew and experts, such as Kirkpatrick, were invited in 1984 to advise on English language policy. However, Kirkpatrick (2010a) discusses a number of barriers to developing English proficiency in the country, including one generation of Burmese that had not studied English. The 1988 coup saw schools and universities close and the removal of foreign teachers, and the 1988 State Law and Order Restoration Council (SLORC), later renamed the State Peace and Development Council (SPDC), led to further closures of schools and universities and the departure of many English-speaking educated Burmese, which left few qualified teachers behind to teach English. Although English is taught from kindergarten, there are poor resources available for teaching it. Thus, unfortunately, English education has been restricted to a small elite class and English is only used in a small number of domains today, such as to communicate with aid organizations. Burma was admitted to ASEAN in 1997.

Laos

Laos is one of the most ethnically diverse nations in South-East Asia. It has a population of six million and approximately 84 languages (see www.unescobkk.org) including Tai, Mon-Khmer languages, and Tiberto-Burman languages, but with three dominant languages. Previously a French protectorate, it gained limited independence within the French Union in 1948, and full independence was achieved in 1954. The Lao People's Democratic Republic was established in 1975 after several years of war. A standard Lao was developed by the French, becoming a national language in 1975, and it is the language of instruction at all levels. Laos was admitted to ASEAN in 1997.

Today, English is the first foreign language in schools and has been introduced in elementary school from grade 3. However, once again due to a shortage of teachers and resources, English tends to be confined to a small elite class. Kirkpatrick (2010a) notes that this has meant that those proficient in English, as opposed to those with relevant experience, represent Laos at ASEAN meetings, as discussed in Chapter 3.

Cambodia

Cambodia has had a turbulent history, largely due to the admission of large numbers of North Vietnamese during the Vietnam War, which led to the bombing of the country by the USA. Khmer replaced French as the national language after independence, although French remained as the first foreign language until the time of Pol Pot, who banned all foreign language instruction. During this time (Khmer Rouge rule), 90 per cent of school buildings were destroyed and 75 per cent of teachers, academics, and administrators were murdered (Neau, 2003, cited in Kirkpatrick, 2010a, p. 56). Vietnamese and Russian were taught as the two foreign languages during the ten-year rule, replaced by French and English in 1989. In 1998, Hun Sen came to power and Cambodia has attempted to rejoin the international community. Cambodia joined ASEAN in 1999.

French is increasingly diminishing in favour of English which is the language preferred by the student body, evident in the fact that, when the Royal University of Phnom Penh allowed students to select which foreign language they wanted to study, over 80 per cent chose English (Clayton, 2006 cited in Kirkpatrick, 2010a, p. 56).

Today, English is a prerequisite for a career in foreign agencies and is the language used with non-governmental organizations, even with French aid workers (Kirkpatrick, 2010a). English or French, but mainly English, is taught from grade 5, although the quality of instruction has been criticized, once again, due to the lack of resources and qualified teachers. As in other places discussed in this chapter thus far, Cambodia has witnessed fears in recent years about the spread of English, and a National Language Institute was set up in 2000 to protect Khmer language in education. Chinese is also gaining ground in Cambodia, as in other parts of ASEAN.

Vietnam

In Vietnam, contact with the West can be traced back to 1515 with the arrival of the Portuguese. The missionaries that followed introduced English, before a French colony was established. The Americans brought English in the years leading up to, and during, the Vietnam War. However, after independence English was seen as the language of the enemy and Vietnamese became the medium of instruction. However, a decade or after unification, in an effort to modernize the nation, Vietnam was opened and the Doi Moi policy of economic renovation increased the demand for English.

English is now the dominant foreign language with over 90 per cent of children learning it (Baker and Giacchino-Baker, 2003, cited in Kirkpatrick, 2010a, p. 61). English is compulsory in secondary schools and students are required to pass an English test to graduate. English is a compulsory subject from grade 3 in primary school and English language centres have been established all over the country.

However, a recent government initiative, called Project 2020, is placing pressure on English teachers to improve their proficiency and to pass an English test, as part of a plan to improve school leavers' proficiency. Subjects such as mathematics will be taught through English and English teaching hours will double. However, once again, there is concern over teachers' proficiency and, in order to address this, teachers will be judged against the Common European Framework of Reference (CEFR) and expected to achieve level B2 in English, with school leavers expected to reach B1. Candidates will also be required to provide certificates from tests aligned to the CEFR, such as IELTS, Cambridge ESOL, and TOEFL, tests discussed further in Chapter 9.

ASEAN and the ASEAN Economic Community (AEC)

While English may have had a different history in these ASEAN countries, it is clear that it is playing an increasing role in each, albeit in different ways. This role is likely to increase with the establishment of the ASEAN Economic Community (AEC) in 2015. This brings into question their placement within the Expanding Circle.

The AEC aims to bring together the member nations into a single market that is able to compete in the global economy and aims to transform ASEAN into a region with free movement of goods, services, investment, and skilled labour, and a freer flow of capital. To prepare for this, a lot of emphasis is being placed on English, particularly in Thailand where the Ministry of Education has noted the need to improve Thai students' English skills and attract foreign teachers and students. In Thailand, 2012 was designated as 'English Speaking Year' in an attempt to prepare Thai people for 2015. Britain's former prime minister, Tony Blair, helped to promote this, also acting as an honorary English teacher, stating:

> How happy I am that Thailand decided to take the teaching of English seriously. It makes sense as the world today is more and more one community and English is a universal language. So it is very sensible for the education system in Thailand to do this.
>
> (Quoted in Fernquest, 2012, para. 5)

A target was set for English programmes to cover 150 vocational colleges in 2013; emphasis has been placed on English language education in the government sector, and the Office of the Civil Service Commission has launched an English-language training e-learning project to prepare officials. Branch campuses are also opening in the country, and from 2014 the Office of the Civil Service Commission will require applicants to take an English test. From 2014, Chulalongkorn University will open an English programme for engineering students and Sukhothai Thammathirat Open University will commence their 'Communication Arts for ASEAN' Masters degree. Similar developments can be seen across ASEAN. In Vietnam, for example, the Australian English Language Company (ELC) will provide English-language teacher training, and Brunei and the USA have started a series of English-language courses for teacher trainers and government officials. Courses begin in Brunei and continue in Hawaii, with a four-week course on culture and leadership with the aim of preparing diplomats, officials, and teacher trainers to use English effectively. There is clearly substantial focus on developing English skills and many programmes have emerged, such as the ASEAN English Ready Program, which claims to help people get ready to join the ASEAN English-speaking community, although the website advertises that it is native English-speaking employees who deliver the course.

Thus, despite the fact that Article 2 of the new ASEAN charter aims 'to respect the different cultures and languages of the region', ASEAN countries do not appear to be teaching the languages of their members, and emphasis on English is growing as ASEAN prepares for the AEC in 2015. Kirkpatrick (2008, p. 131) notes, 'This has significant implications for English language learning and teaching in the region. It has implications for language learning goals, for language teachers and for the curriculum.' He proposes that it would be more appropriate to position English as an 'Asian' lingua franca, a language spoken by multilinguals where the learners would be measured against the 'norms' of successful Asian multilinguals. A lot of research has been conducted on ASEAN ELF, discussed in Chapter 7, and its implications for pedagogy will be discussed in Chapter 9.

6d ELF in global contexts: prevalence, issues, and attitudes

It is clear from this chapter that both the number of speakers and the role of English are expanding in emerging global contexts. English is the main lingua franca for communication and functions as more than a mere foreign language. This section introduces the concept of ELF, a research paradigm that focuses on the description of such usage of English. Specific ELF research is examined in Chapter 7, but here we provide a clear definition of this emerging field of study.

More than just a 'foreign language'

The demographics of English speakers around the world have clearly changed. For example, in South Korea 'there is a veritable English language mania' (Park and Abelman, 2004, p. 646) with the English language market estimated to be about $3,300 million a year, $830 million spent on study abroad programmes, and increasing numbers of students enrolling in private after-school English classes, as noted in Section 6b. Similarly, China's Crazy English Enterprise has met with significant success, and an article in the *Jakarta Post*, with the title 'No English, no diplomacy', highlighted the importance of English language skills for foreign diplomats in Indonesia, who risk 'humiliating the country' (Khalik, 2010, para. 1). With an estimated 350 million Chinese English language learners (Xu, 2010, p. 295), the Chinese are the largest group of English learners in the world, as well as being the largest group of international students in the UK. Section 6c has also highlighted that English is taking on an increased role in ASEAN, in preparation for the AEC in 2015.

In addition, although not covered in this chapter, the presence of English is also increasing in South American countries, such as Brazil and Argentina. Rajagopalan (2006), for example, notes that it is the number one foreign language in the continent, Gonzalez (2010) has discussed the increasing presence of and role of English in Columbia, and one of the main aims of the Columbian educational agenda for 2004–19, *Revolucion Educativa* (Educational Revolution), is to make the population bilingual through the mastery of English.

Globalization has had a tremendous impact on the use of English both inside and outside the Expanding Circle and, with increased mobility and interconnectedness, English users now use the language with a wide variety of people across the globe. Research on such usage is clearly essential.

ELF: what exactly is it?

ELF, as a global phenomenon, has grown in intensity, and as a result a new field of study has emerged with a focus on exploring such global usage of the language. World Englishes researchers have done a lot to raise awareness of variation in the English language, yet increased lingua franca usage means that English is used in communities of practice within and across all three of Kachru's circles. Thus, while we have presented different global contexts in this chapter separately, and while we introduce ELF in this chapter alongside Expanding Circle contexts, we want to stress that ELF is used rather differently. It is a contact language, and the interlocutors and location can change, making the concept of national varieties of English somewhat irrelevant. In a nutshell, ELF research examines such global use of English, and showcases how ELF communities are in flux as opposed to being fixed within a strict geographical boundary. ELF researchers are not concerned with identifying core features of national varieties based on geographical boundaries. (See Seidlhofer, 2009a and Cogo and Dewey, 2012 for an overview of the main differences between the World Englishes and the ELF research paradigms.) Instead, they are focused on examining how the use of ELF worldwide not only exhibits a lot of variation, but also adapts and changes in response to the communicative needs of its users in fluid contexts. An ELF exchange between Indian and Thai business colleagues may be different to when the same Thai person communicates with a Spanish colleague. Globalization has resulted in an ever-increasing fluidity of such exchanges, and ELF is not, and cannot be, fixed in that it is both situation-dependent and adaptable to change as speakers appropriate it according to their various situational demands. ELF, then, has further implications for language change and variation.

Descriptive work in the field of World Englishes has been instrumental in raising awareness of the diversity of English around the world. However, ELF challenges the traditional notions of 'variety' and 'community', seeing English as a more flexible and fluid entity. The use of ELF globally makes it rather difficult to identify fixed speech communities, and therefore the very concept of ELF brings into question the relevance of conventional terms such as 'variety' and 'community'. From an ELF perspective, a 'community', then, has more to do with virtual, fluid, and transient interactional networks than geography. For this reason, Seidlhofer (2007) prefers the term '**community of practice**', a term coined by Lave and Wenger (1991). However, despite the differences with World Englishes, Seidlhofer (2006, p. 43), points out that 'it is precisely the work on Outer Circle varieties that has led the way for ELF research'.

It is also important to point out that native English speakers are not excluded from ELF research. As Mauranen (2012, p. 8) notes, 'the prototypical ELF speaker is one who uses English habitually without either being a native speaker or a learner'. Of course, if they are in the majority then the language used may orientate towards native-speaking norms, a point that Mauranen also makes, but this does not mean that they are used as a yardstick of competence, nor are they the focus of ELF research. ELF empirical work does not exclude native English speakers but it does not involve a large proportion of them (Seidlhofer, 2004), and in the ELF research paradigm a native English speaker is not used as a linguistic reference point. Thus, like World Englishes, 'ELF challenges the traditional emphasis on teaching based on the Inner Circle Model' (Kubota, 2012, p. 57). To sum up, ELF:

- embraces a speaker's first language and 'culture';
- is the use of English among speakers of different first languages, who adapt and change according to the communicative needs of their interlocutors in various communities of practice;

- is used in contexts that are changeable, dynamic, and fluid, as opposed to fixed geographical settings;
- is growing as both a phenomenon and a research paradigm;
- focuses on the pluricentric nature of English;
- is not a fixed variety of English, nor a reduced and simplified version of the language;
- includes native English speakers as well as non-native English speakers, but does not use the former as a yardstick of competence;
- has implications for ELT.

ELF or EIL in global contexts: a note on terminology

Before examining ELF research in detail in the following chapter, it is important to revisit our ELF and EIL distinction, which was outlined in the *Preface* to this book. A number of definitions have been posited for ELF in previous publications. Smith discussed EIL as early as 1976, and various other terms have been used to describe the use of English among people from different first-language backgrounds, including:

- World English (Brutt-Griffler, 2002);
- English as a global language (Crystal, 2003; Gnutzmann, 1999);
- English as a world language (Mair, 2003);
- International English (McKay, 2002);
- Global English (Crystal, 1997);
- English as a medium of intercultural communication (Meierkord, 1996).

The large number of terms can cause confusion, and there is also a danger that the multiplicity of terms may cloud some of the important issues and compromise the advancement of research within the field of ELF, and Global Englishes in general. As pointed out in the *Preface*, this is particularly the case with EIL. Sharifian (2009, p. 6) notes that ELF is a theme 'that can broadly be associated with the EIL paradigm', while also noting that 'the ELF movement has only focused on the linguistic code and has failed to engage with the political/ideological dimensions of native/non-native distinction'. Criticisms of the ELF paradigm, and responses to these criticisms, are addressed in Section 7d, but here it is important to point out that, while a lot of ELF research does focus on the linguistic study of ELF communication and the underlying motivations that give rise to certain innovations in the use of the language, ELF research is very much concerned with the political/ideological dimensions of the global spread of English.

In a more recent publication on EIL, Alsagoff (2012b, p. 111) states that,

> A distinguishing feature that characterizes English as a world language is the fact that it is used for communication across linguistic and cultural boundaries. EIL, defined in this broader manner, is a more inclusive definition that includes the use of English as a language of wider communication in both the Outer and Expanding Circles.

Here, the author appears to be describing what we would call ELF, yet she continues to argue that EIL contrasts with ELF, which she considers examines English in the Expanding Circles. Most ELF researchers would disagree that ELF is restricted to this context. We are in agreement with Alsagoff's (2012b) view of English's global role to communicate across (and we would add 'within') linguistic and cultural boundaries, but disagree with where she draws the boundaries of ELF research. ELF does not merely describe the use of English in the Expanding Circle, but involves communication between speakers from all three of Kachru's (1992a) circles. Alsagoff (2012b, p. 111) also fails to acknowledge the discussion of 'communities of practice' by ELF scholars as she continues to define EIL as a 'variety (or sets of varieties) that is (are) spoken by communities of speakers, rather than by isolated pockets of individual learners'. In the same publication, definitions are made further unclear by Gu's (2012) use of the terms EIL and ELF synonymously, and House's (2012, p. 187) assertion that ELF is often used 'in short contact situations, such that fleeting English norms are in operation'. This definition is insufficient given the complex use of ELF in global contexts like the EU and ASEAN, as outlined in this and previous chapters.

At the Centre for Global Englishes (CGE) launch at the University of Southampton in May 2012, Barbara Seidlhofer discussed two kinds of EIL: localized EIL, which includes World Englishes and nation-based varieties, and globalized EIL, involving international communication characterized by hybrid ways of speaking and de-territorialized speech events. Thus, in light of the various contradictory and problematic definitions of EIL discussed above, and as stated in the *Preface*, the term EIL is avoided in this book and 'Global Englishes' is adopted to discuss the way English has spread around the world and its implications on multiple facets of society. Global Englishes includes both localized EIL (which we refer to under the World Englishes paradigm, thus including Englishes out-lined in Chapters 4 and 5, and variety-specific research in Chapter 6) and globalized EIL (which we refer to under the ELF paradigm). As was also pointed out in the *Preface*, our vision of ELF is centred in Global Englishes, and incorporates the complexity of globa-lization and the spread of English. In many ways, ELF can be seen as a translingual practice (see our discussion of Canagarajah, 2013 in the *Preface*), and thus criticisms of ELF as a 'variety' or 'linguistic code' or 'non-inclusive' do not sit well with our posi-tioning (nor with those heavily engaged in ELF research).

We see this anti-ELF rhetoric as a further misunderstanding of ELF, which is discussed in detail in the following chapter. In order to gain ground and acceptance, ELF has to be grounded in empirical research (which will be also covered in the next chapter).

Chapter summary

This chapter has outlined the history and role of English in expanding global contexts, where English is traditionally taught as a foreign language. It is clear that, in Europe, English has assumed a dominant role, irrespective of the multilingual policy of the EU. While arguments for a distinct variety of Euro-English have been put forward, it is clear that ELF is a more relevant construct for English use in Europe. Section 6b examined the historical spread and use of English in East Asia, and it is clear that there is a great emphasis put on English education, as seen by movements lowering the age of English instruction in elementary school. However, while some work has been done on documenting the dis-tinctive features, it is clear that native English ideology remains strong in these countries, which reminds us of points raised in Section 2d. However, it is also clear that, with increasing ELF usage, ideology may be changing. Furthermore, it is clear that English is much more than just a foreign language by becoming an integral part of society. Section 6c returned to ASEAN, looking at the role of English in the 'Expanding Circle' member countries. In these countries, it is clear that English is also more than a foreign language, and ELF is central to international and intranational politics. English is the official working language, reminding us of its power to create and level inequalities, as introduced in Chapter 3. Section 6d returned to ELF, providing a clearer definition and addressing some other definitions, which are further explored in the next chapter. This chapter has also raised pedagogical concerns that will be addressed in Chapter 9.

Further reading

On Europe:

- Modiano, M. (2009). 'Inclusive/exclusive? English as a lingua franca in the European Union.' *World Englishes*, 28(2), pp. 208–23.

On Asia and ASEAN:

- Kirkpatrick, A. (2010a). *English as a Lingua Franca in ASEAN: A Multilingual Model.* Hong Kong: Hong Kong University Press.
- Kirkpatrick, A. (ed.) (2010b). *The Routledge Handbook of World Englishes.* London: Routledge.

On ELF:

- Mauranen, A. (2012). *Exploring ELF: Academic English Shaped by Non-native Speakers.* Cambridge: Cambridge University Press.
- Seidlhofer, B. (2001a). 'Closing a conceptual gap: the case for a description of English as a lingua franca.' *International Journal of Applied Linguistics,* 11(2), pp. 133–58.
- Seidlhofer, B. (2009). 'Common ground and different realities: world Englishes and English as a lingua franca.' *World Englishes*, 28(2), pp. 236–45.

Closing activities

Chapter discussion questions

Section 6a

1 In 2001, Modiano noted that legitimatization, codification, and standardization processes would take place because of the increasing role of English (Modiano, 2001). What is your opinion on this?
2 What do you think of Seargeant's (2012) comparison of the EU and Singapore? Is the regulated language policy at odds with the pragmatic needs of European citizens?
3 What is your opinion on the multilingual policy adopted by the EU?

Section 6b

1 English clearly has a high status in Japan, yet it has been promoted alongside a nationalist agenda. What do you think of these two conflicting stances?
2 What are the arguments for and against categorizing the countries covered in this section as Expanding Circle nations?

3   What do you think about the policy of requiring employees in countries where English has no official status to conduct their day-to-day business in English?

Section 6c

1   Why do you think Asian countries have accepted the pragmatic position of English more readily than Europe?
2   With the start of the AEC in 2015, many countries are placing increased emphasis on English education. Why do you think is important to become 'AEC ready'?
3   What is your opinion on the claim it may be inappropriate to classify these ASEAN countries as being part of the Expanding Circle?

Section 6d

1   In South America, Rajagopalan (2006, p. 153) refers to English as 'a commodity around which a powerful fetish is building up'. In what ways is the role of English changing in the Expanding Circle?
2   Gonzalez (2010) notes that, in Columbia, Inner Circle varieties are the preferred teaching models and other varieties are considered linguistically impure. Why does 'Native' English continue to be held in such high esteem? What influence might ELF research have?
3   What is your opinion on the main misunderstandings of ELF research and Phillipson's (2008; 2009) claim that labels such as 'lingua franca' are misleading?

Writing and presentation prompts

Below are ideas for writing and presentation tasks to apply the knowledge learned in Chapter 6.

	Assignment topics
Personal account	English is now used as a lingua franca by people from very different linguistic and cultural backgrounds. Provide a personal account of your own use of ELF, making reference to some of the issues discussed in this chapter.
Research task	Linguistic landscape studies involve an examination of the use of English in societies around the world. Explore a context you are familiar with and take photos (or collect secondary data) to examine how English is used in a variety of domains (e.g. advertisements, posters, trademarks, shop names, shop products, magazine headings, newspaper headlines). Think about who writes them, who reads them, and how people interact with them.
Basic academic	English has an important role in multilingual Europe. Discuss the commitment of the EU to maintaining and respecting linguistic diversity, and their guarantee of equality and fair treatment for European languages. Also discuss the influence of the use of English on the language and culture of member nations.
Advanced academic	Discuss the promotion of nationalism alongside the promotion of English education in either China or Japan, or elsewhere. Discuss whether this pragmatic approach to English education is feasible, and how ELF research may influence such policies.

Chapter 7

English as a lingua franca

Introductory activities

The following introductory activities are designed to encourage the reader to think about the issues raised in this chapter before reading it.

ELF and EFL

As introduced in Chapter 1, English users in countries where English traditionally has no official status are classed as EFL speakers, who learn the language to use with 'native' English speakers. They learn the language in classroom settings in countries where the language is thought to have no internal purposes. However, as pointed out at the start of this book, the term 'EFL' has become somewhat of a misnomer and such speakers are now often referred to as 'ELF speakers'. Table 7.1 highlights some conceptual differences between EFL and ELF.

Discussion questions

1 In what ways do EFL and ELF differ?
2 Is there a difference between a 'user' and a 'learner'? Are norms different for the two?
3 On their websites, the Longman Learners' Corpus refers to 'mistakes' and the Cambridge Learner Corpus refers to 'problems'. What is your opinion on treating non-native usage of English as mistakes or problems?
4 In what ways are ELF norms *ad hoc* and negotiated?

Case study: ELF examples

Examples of ELF talk

Seidlhofer (2004, p. 220) provides the following list of characteristic features in ELF **lexicogrammar** in the early years of ELF research:
- 'Dropping' the third person present tense -*s*;
- 'Confusing' the relative pronouns *who* and *which*;
- 'Omitting' definite and indefinite articles where they are obligatory in ENL,

and inserting them where they do not occur in ENL;

- 'Failing' to use correct forms in tag questions (e.g. *isn't it?* or *no?* instead of *shouldn't they?*);
- Inserting 'redundant' prepositions (e.g. *We have to study about* …);
- 'Overusing' certain types of verbs of high semantic generality (e.g. *do, have, make, put, take*);
- 'Replacing' infinitive constructions with *that*-clauses (e.g. *I want that* …);
- 'Overdoing' explicitness (e.g. *black colour* rather than just *black*).

Examples of ELF usage

- … *the tourist office provided me with a lot of informations about the city when I arrived.*
- … *in class, we discussed about a lot of interesting topics.*
- … *she is very healthy and swim every day after work.*
- … *he is the one which I used to be attracted to when I was younger.*
- … *my new car is red colour.*

Discussion questions

1 Can you identify the unconventional constructions in the ELF usage examples?
2 Do you think the use of such constructions shows that an ELF user has not reached native-level competence or that ELF users are particularly creative with the language, extending 'native' English constructions?

Introduction

This book thus far has highlighted the global use of ELF. It is a pluricentric concept, growing both as a phenomenon in general and as a field of study. Language acts as a tool in globalization to help people connect, and it is clear from Chapter 3 that the globalization of English has received much attention. However, globalization – and the use of ELF specifically – has also influenced the language itself. ELF as a phenomenon has been described throughout this book, but in this chapter we explore what happens to English when it is used as a lingua franca. In doing so we examine past and current research trends, criticisms and misunderstandings, and the future directions of ELF research.

Table 7.1 Conceptual differences between EFL and ELF

	Foreign language (EFL)	Lingua franca (ELF)
Lingua-cultural norms	Pre-existing, re-affirmed	*Ad hoc*, negotiated
Objectives	Integration, membership in native-speaking community	Intelligibility, communication in a non-native speaker or mixed non-native speaker–native-speaker interaction
Processes	Imitation, adoption	Accommodation, adaptation

Source: Seidlhofer, 2011, p. 18

We begin in Section 7a with a theoretical and descriptive overview of ELF research, focusing on pronunciation and lexicogrammar. Section 7b examines the pragmatics of ELF communication, highlighting the shift in research focus away from the documentation of regularities or common features in early days. ELF research has been conducted in a number of domains; Section 7c provides an overview of the business domain, business English as a lingua franca (BELF). ELF throws a new perspective on language change, and ELF also lets us revisit English and reconceptualize many of the fundamental concepts underpinning language in general. In Section 7d we return to many of the concepts that have been introduced at various points in the book, such as language change and variation, language contact, standardization, language varieties, and ownership. ELF research has become the subject of considerable debate and criticism. We end in Section 7d with an overview of these criticisms and the counterarguments.

7a A growing research paradigm

Chapter 5 showcased some of the work that has been conducted in the World Englishes paradigm, which has been tremendously influential in the development of an ELF field of study, and in Chapter 6 we noted the similarities between the World Englishes and ELF paradigms, with their focus on the pluricentric notion of English. However, while ELF, as a phenomenon, may have become part of the everyday lives of people across the globe, as a field of study, unlike World Englishes, it has had a relatively short life. As Mauranen (2012, p. 1) states,

> what happens to a language when it goes global? We do not really know. It may look like any other language, only bigger. Or scale may do something new to it. What we do know is that when languages get very small, below a certain level they disappear fast, because there is no community to sustain them. When they get very large, they tend to spread themselves thinly and start diversifying. When they get enormous, and a lion's share of the use is as a lingua franca – this is uncharted territory.

This 'uncharted territory' is evident in the lack of attention given to ELF in many publications on the global spread of English and World Englishes (see Table 7.2). Nevertheless, just as the numbers of ELF speakers are growing worldwide, research into the use of ELF has been rapidly growing in the last decade or so. Recent years have seen the publication of a number of entire books on the topic (Cogo and Dewey, 2012; Mauranen, 2012; Seidlhofer, 2011). In 2008, an ELF conference series began. In 2011, the *Journal of English as a Lingua Franca* (JELF) was started, and the University of Southampton established a dedicated Centre for Global Englishes (CGE). In the following subsection, we provide an overview of ELF research, followed by research conducted in the areas of phonology and lexicogrammar.

ELF research overview

Early ELF research can be traced to the 1990s, although it was not until the turn of the millennium that interest in ELF grew, particularly with the publications of Jenkins (2000) and Seidlhofer (2001a) (see Jenkins *et al.*, 2011 for an overview of recent developments).

Table 7.2 Global Englishes materials

Selected books	Audio	Inner Circle	Outer Circle	Expanding Circle	ELF	ELT
		Number of pages covering topic				
Trudgill and Hannah (2008)	Yes	110	17	0	0	0
Jenkins (2009)	No	33	42	14	24	7
Kirkpatrick (2010a)	No	152	82	67	104	50
Kirkpatrick (2007)	Yes	44	54	7	16	14
Melchers and Shaw (2011)	Yes	79	57	21	6	2
Schneider (2011)	Yes	51	54	10	4	5
Matsuda (ed.) (2012)	No	10	5	75	15	200

Jenkins (2000), discussed in detail later in this section, was concerned with the issue of (un)intelligibility and focused on phonology. Her research gained widespread interest in academia, raising questions about the ownership of English as well as the pedagogical implications of the globalization of English (see Chapter 9). One year later, Seidlhofer (2001b, p. 133) called for a large-scale investigation, noting,

> Discussions about 'global English' on the meta-level have not been accompanied by a necessary reorientation in linguistic research: very little empirical work has, so far, been done on the most extensive contemporary use of English worldwide, namely English as a lingua franca.

She argued for the need for empirical research to fill what she called a '**conceptual gap**' (p. 134) and announced the compilation of the Vienna–Oxford International Corpus of English (VOICE), the first corpus showcasing over one million words of transcribed real-life ELF usage. Since then, interest in ELF has flourished.

What exactly is ELF 'research'?

Recent ELF studies may have different foci, but what they have in common is that they highlight that ELF speakers, who are mostly bi- or multilingual speakers, do not just adhere to a fixed set of ENL norms but exploit the language in rather creative ways to negotiate communication. In brief, ELF researchers showcase how:

- ELF has a global ownership;
- ELF users exploit the language in different ways to suit their own needs;
- ELF is a very different phenomenon to ENL or ELF (refer back to Table 7.1);
- ELF usage, and the use of 'non-standard forms', are more than mere 'errors' caused by the different first languages of users who are somewhere on a cline towards native English competence – there is a degree of systematicity to ELF usage;
- ELF users in their negotiations orientate towards content as well as their interlocutors, as opposed to 'native' English norms, and exploit their linguistic and plurilingual resources to achieve communicative success.

In sum, ELF research highlights what ELF speakers 'do' with the language, how they appropriate it, and what strategies they use to achieve successful communication. The next subsection provides an overview of research in phonology and lexicogrammar.

Phonology

ELF research into phonology began with Jenkins (2000), who examined which pronunciation features impede mutual intelligibility in non-native English-speaking interactions, and also how these speakers accommodate each other by adjusting phonological features to improve intelligibility. The study was based on the increased awareness of the irrelevance of native English-speaker norms for ELF speakers, and highlighted that some of the phonological and lexicogrammatical features that have been conventionally emphasized in ELT do not affect intelligibility (Jenkins, 2000, 2009). When intelligibility was necessary, participants replaced some 'non-standard' features with a more 'standard form', but questionnaires and interviews revealed that this was not the case when intelligibility was not crucial. The study led to the development of a 'pedagogical core of phonological intelligibility for speakers of EIL', which focuses attention on those items that are essential for intelligibility thus representing a more relevant, and perhaps achievable, goal for students. Some of these 'core features' include:

- all consonant sounds, except [θ ð];
- vowel quality/length contrasts (e.g. between lax/short and tense/long vowels) to distinguish between such pairs of words as *sit* and *seat*, i.e. [sɪt] and [siːt];
- initial and medial consonant clusters (not deleting sounds at the beginning and middle of words), e.g. *stay* as [steɪ], but not [teɪ] or [seɪ];
- nuclear (or tonic) stress production/placement – *THIS belongs to me* compared with *this belongs to ME*.

The many features that were found not to be necessary for intelligible pronunciation (the 'non-core' features) in ELF include:

- consonant phonemes /θ ð/, e.g. the initial phoneme in *think* and *they* is also intelligible as [t d], [f v], or [s z];
- the final phoneme in *pool*, as [ɫ] is also intelligible as [l];
- vowel quality (except for the vowel sound /ɜː/ in RP *fur*);
- addition of vowels to consonant clusters, e.g. *stay* [steɪ] as [ɪsteɪ] or [səteɪ];
- features of connected speech, such as elision, assimilation, and weak forms;
- word stress placement, e.g. *aPARTment* compared with *apartMENT;*
- pitch movement/patterns.

The 'core' features are, then, important for mutual intelligibility, and Jenkins argued that in the non-core areas speakers engaged in ELF communication should not have to strive to sound like native English speakers or be seen as making pronunciation errors. She wrote, 'There is really no justification for doggedly persisting in referring to an item as "an error" if the vast majority of the world's second language (L2) English speakers produce and understand it' (Jenkins, 2000, p. 160). However, despite the implications for ELT, the aim was not to devise a pronunciation-teaching model and she called for further research. Her research also showcases the importance of accommodation in ELF talk, suggesting that ELF speakers need to be able to adjust their speech to accommodate their interlocutors, who can come from a variety of language backgrounds. Deterding and Kirkpatrick (2006) also point out that the ability to accommodate one's pronunciation is one of the most important skills in ELF talk. This topic is returned to in Section 7b.

Research on pronunciation in ELF is scarce, but there have been some replications of Jenkins' (2000) study. Pickering (2009) found that pitch movement (tone choice) and relative pitch level (key choice) are also important in successful ELF interactions, although the study was conducted in experimental conditions. However, Pickering and Litzenberg's (2011) follow-up study of naturally occurring ELF talk demonstrated that ELF users employ intonational signals as a resource, to negotiate and maintain successful interaction. Pitzl (2005) also found that, in business settings, a combination of tonic stress placement and rising intonation was used by participants to signal feedback. This indicator was recognized by interlocutors, suggesting that stress and intonation are meaningful prosodic cues in ELF interaction. These latter studies are also evidence of the changing trend in ELF research, from the identification of surface-level features to an understanding of the underlying processes that give rise to such features.

Lexicogrammar

Research into ELF lexicogrammar shows how ELF users utilize their linguistic resources in creative and systematic ways, and highlights new uses of lexis and grammar. Such research began with Seidlhofer's (2004) initial observations, shown in the chapter-opening case study. The compilation of ELF corpora, which captures naturally occurring ELF interactions and shows how ELF users actually use the language, has enabled a number of ELF researchers to look at how ELF speakers interact in ELF settings, just as native English corpora, discussed in Chapter 4, allowed researchers to look at how native English speakers use the language. Their findings are summarized in a case study on the companion website. Such corpora aid ELF research in numerous ways and, since Seidlhofer (2004), more work has been conducted on lexicogrammar, with many studies focusing on one or more of her findings. We provide an overview of some of this work in the following subsections.

Zero marking

Chapter 5 highlighted that present singular verbs in third-person singular often occur with zero marking in place of the -s morpheme in many of the 'New' Englishes. This is also a well-documented feature of ELF. However, Cogo and Dewey (2006) note that this is more than just a case of 'dropping' the -s morpheme, since it is used with a degree of systematicity and frequency, and argue that the third-person -s and third-person zero are, in fact, 'competing variants in ELF interactions' (Cogo and Dewey, 2012, p. 49). Examples from their data include where it is used for a variety of verbs

Table 7.3 Cases of third-person singular zero

Example	Source
and er the stage **involve** er working and also studying. erm, it's a good job.	LI Italian
because if some…if one woman **have** a very ugly appearance so…erm she hm…she **have** hm… she **have** some complex	LI Korean
No no no(,) I mean if somebody **do** a very severe …crime.	LI Mandarin

Source: adapted from Cogo and Dewey, 2012, p. 50

(more than third-person –s) by people from different first language (L1) backgrounds. (See Table 7.3.)

Article usage

Article usage has also received considerable attention. Mauranen (2012, p. 124) argues that it 'is the most widely reported non-standard feature in ELF'. Articles are:

- often dropped (*I always walk to shop as it's so close*);
- redundant (*I went to the home after work*);
- different from 'native' English usage (*Can you pass a salt please?*).

Once again, we can see similarities with the 'New' Englishes presented in Chapter 5. Article usage in ELF has also been compared with native English usage. Comparing the MICASE (Chapter 4) ENL corpora with ELFA (a corpus of ELF used in academic settings – see ELFA, 2008), Mauranen (2012, p. 125) found that *the* ranks high in ELFA, while *a* ranks low and is among the differentiators of MICASE from ELFA, concluding that,

> Since there is this relationship, non-standard article use may not be best seen as a collection of random errors, but may reflect an ongoing shuffle of article functions.

However, despite often being dropped, this does not mean that they are not important in ELF talk. Cogo and Dewey (2012, p. 62) note that this is more than just a simplification of native English and that their frequency is similar to native English usage. Also comparing their corpus data with an ENL corpus (BNC Baby), they found that *the* was the most frequent item in both sets of data, which also accounts for 4.2 per cent of the total text in VOICE (Cogo and Dewey, 2012, p. 62), similar to BNC Baby and their own corpus. Thus, articles are not unimportant in ELF, they are just used differently.

Relative pronouns

Cogo and Dewey (2012) found that pronoun use in relative clauses often differs from established norms, and their comparison with BNC data highlighted that *who* (with 1,020 tokens) is more frequent than *which* (with 956 tokens). However, in their own ELF corpora, *which* (with 77 tokens) occurred more frequently than *who* (with 57 tokens). Their data shows that *which* is used differently than in native English (sometimes in place of *who*), and may account for the increased frequency.

Use of 'which'

Source: Cogo and Dewey, 2012, p. 74.

1   two months ago and I research **Bush, which** is the father Bush, hm, hm, not the
2   family, but there are a lot of **children which** need a family and so many Italian
3   of identity in a bilingual **community which** will be the second generation of
4   the United States, they do **everything which** they want yeah they … a bit bossy
5   aliens but: the second **generation which** is actually born and raised in
6 London, I live in North East of **London which** is Southgate. And you? I'm living
7   learners, in English resemble **those which** are the most frequent ones in

Prepositions

Both Chapters 4 and 5 highlighted that the use of prepositions exhibits variation. Cogo and Dewey (2012, p. 53) discuss the example of the adjective *different*, which occurs as *different from*, *different to*, or *different than* in native English. They show how dependent prepositions that follow certain verbs and nouns are often omitted completely in ELF, particularly with verb plus preposition combinations, another example from their data, showing that variation in the use of prepositions happens with a wide range of speakers from different backgrounds and does not cause a breakdown in communication. In addition to omitting prepositions, different ones are also used. (For an overview of such usage see Cogo and Dewey, 2012, pp. 55–56.)

ELF research also highlights the extension of already existing patterns in prepositional usage. Cogo and Dewey (2012), for example, provide the example of the verb *influence* used with the preposition *on*, a combination that is a feature of ENL when *influence* is used as a noun (e.g. have an *influence on* somebody). An ELF speaker may, for example, say something like *I would like to influence on her decision*, unlike a 'standard' English speaker, who may say, *I would like to influence her decision*. ELF speakers are, then, extending the pattern to include another word class, exemplifying how they are particularly accomplished at exploiting the meaning potential of the language to suit their own purposes, and also that there is a degree of systematicity in ELF interactions.

Regularization and coinage

ELF research has also shown how verb forms are often regularized. Seidlhofer (2011), for example, gives evidence from the VOICE corpus, including: *conspirate*, *examinate*, *financiate*, and *pronunciate*. (See Pitzl *et al.*, 2008 for an overview of such processes of lexical innovation.)

This can also happen with nouns, and Seidlhofer (2011) gives the example of *increase* and the coining of the word *increasment*, resulting in unambiguous marking for 'noun-ness' (in native English, if we disregard word stress, *increase* can be either a verb or a noun).

Other examples include *bigness, clearness, mutualness, forbiddedness,* and *unitedness* (Seidlhofer, 2011, p. 108), formed with the familiar word formation process of combining an adjective or past participle with the suffix -ness, e.g. *playfulness/cheerfulness.* Despite being viewed as 'errors' by some, such examples are evidence of how ELF speakers are particularly creative with the language, and Seidlhofer (2011, p. 103) emphasizes the 'complementary relationship between creativity and conformity with ELF users exploiting the alternative encoding possibilities inherent in the language'.

Creativity has also been examined in the area of lexical patterns. Pitzl (2009), for example, looked at idiomaticity and how it is used differently in ELF to native English. Using examples from the VOICE corpus, she looked at the use of idioms in ELF and their metaphorical function. Her example *we should not wake up any dogs,* used by some ELF speakers instead of *let sleeping dogs lie* by natives (Pitzl, 2009), was presented in the opening activity of Chapter 2, to exemplify variation in the use of English or, more specifically, variation in the use of idioms today. This example shows how idioms are coined in ELF and, once again, that they are not adhering to a fixed code or 'standard' native English version of the language – the idioms go through a process of 're-metaphorization' (Seidlhofer and Widdowson, 2009).

Underlying processes of ELF talk

As will be highlighted in Section 7b, ELF research has begun to take a more process-oriented approach, exploring the underlying reasons behind descriptions of forms and developing an understanding of what motivates speakers to use them when they communicate. Many ELF researchers go beyond identifying surface-level features and investigate the underlying processes and motivating forces involved in ELF communication, highlighting how ELF communication is not fluid in so far as it is context-dependent, and meaning and performance driven. Many features of ELF are related to increasing clarity but they may also be a result of the desire to do the following.

- Exploit redundancy – e.g. ELF speakers may omit non-essential items and exploit the redundancy in English by dropping the third-person -s when they extend the regular present tense form to third-person singular verbs. Seidlhofer (2011, p. 106) notes that this can 'be regarded as contributing to *economy* of expression for speakers', and the third-person zero has long been recognized as a 'typological oddity' (Trudgill 2002, p. 98, cited in Seidlhofer, 2011, p. 106). The interchangeable nature of *who* and *which,* discussed earlier, is another example, given that the distinction is equally redundant. ELF speakers, then, may simply not feel that it is necessary to make a distinction, if the pronoun is a relative one.
- Regularize patterns – e.g. in the examples cited earlier where ELF speakers may extend word formation processes, as in the combination of an adjective, or past participle, with the suffix -ness.
- Enhance prominence – e.g. the use of the definite article in front of uncountable nouns, for example *she is very adventurous and enjoys being around the nature,* may also be a result of enhancing prominence to highlight the importance of the noun. The level of importance attached to a noun or noun phrase is important; 'If an item is deemed particularly

important it is often preceded by the definite article, while if the item is relatively unimportant the zero article is often used' (Dewey, 2007, p. 341). This highlights the importance of context and meaning in ELF communication compared with in ENL.

- Accommodate interlocutors – e.g. adjust one's speech by converging towards or diverging away from an interlocutor, discussed in more depth in the following section.

These motivating forces, along with others, result in innovative forms in ELF communication, although it should be pointed out that they can occur together and do not necessarily occur alone. A lot of research has been conducted on the identification of surface-level features, but a shift towards more of an understanding of why such features occur is evident. This topic is returned to in the next section, which provides an overview of research in ELF pragmatics and also discusses the expression of culture and identity.

7b Understanding and ELF: pragmatics

As this chapter has highlighted, ELF is by its very nature as a worldwide lingua franca unstable, fluid, and dynamic. It is characterized by situationality in that it is context-dependent and meaning-driven and is different from 'standard' English in many respects. It is not spoken by a homogeneous group of people (although it is clear from Chapter 4 that native English is not either), and speakers do not have a shared linguistic or cultural history but differing ones. In this section, we further explore the use of ELF by examining how successful communication is achieved through the use of a variety of pragmatic strategies. Of course, the study of pragmatics is not something unique to ELF. Pragmatic variation was first introduced in Chapter 2 and people have studied the transmission of meaning in language for a long time, looking at pragmatic competence (the ability to understand someone's intended meaning).

Research has also been conducted on cross-cultural pragmatics, which looks at the use of language in different lingua-cultural contexts, often assuming the existence of fixed cultural norms. There is a focus on the different pragmatic uses of language in different contexts, and often a focus on how this results in cross-cultural pragmatic failure. Similarly, research on intercultural pragmatics, which looks at what happens when speakers from diverse lingua-cultural backgrounds communicate with different pragmatic conventions, also generalizes sociopragmatic conventions to some extent. ELF users do bring different pragmatic knowledge to ELF encounters, resulting in pragmatic transfer, but this section will showcase how this transfer does not necessarily result in communicative failure. Instead, ELF users are rather accomplished at employing a range of pragmatic strategies to negotiate meaning on the spot and overcome miscommunications when they do arise.

Overview of research

In 2010 the *Journal of Pragmatics* published a special issue on the pragmatics of ELF in the international university. Early research focused on the importance of achieving mutual understanding when communicating. Firth's (1990, 1996) examination of telephone conversations between Danish export managers and clients revealed how ELF speakers focus on communicative effectiveness, employing various strategies including letting unclear utterances pass (the 'let it pass' strategy). House (1999) found that misunderstandings were rare in her examination of simulated conversations of international students. Many later studies have focused on miscommunication and how ELF speakers signal non-understanding. While they highlight that misunderstanding is in fact rare, such studies showcase the various strategies that ELF speakers use to negotiate, or avoid, such miscommunications and non-understandings in their content-oriented talk.

Chapter 2, for example, introduced the notion of accommodation theory, which involves the adaptation of one's speech to help communication; that is, speakers may either converge towards or diverge away from their interlocutor. As stated, accommodation theory provides a good framework for analysing ELF talk, although most of the work in the field of communicative accommodation theory (CAT) has looked at native English speaking–native English speaking interactions, and particularly phonology. However, within the field of ELF, it has been identified as one of the most important strategies in ELF communication. It was first discussed in relation to ELF by Jenkins (2000) (see Section 7a) and has since become a major topic of study. As Cogo (2009, p. 270) notes, 'successful ELF communication relies on crucial adaptive accommodation skills along with appreciation and acceptance of diversity'. The growing number of studies into the pragmatics of ELF are showing how speakers use a variety of accommodation strategies that 'allow their exchanges to be more intelligible than if they had referred to standard native-speakers' norms' (Cogo, 2009, p. 257).

Pragmatic strategies

There are various strategies associated with accommodation, including:

- repetition (Cogo, 2009; Lichtkoppler, 2007);
- clarification and self-repair (and repetition) (Mauranen, 2006);
- rephrasing, topic negotiation, and discourse reflexivity (Mauranen, 2007);
- paraphrasing (and repetition) (Cogo, 2009; Kaur, 2009);
- silences (Böhringer, 2007);
- pre-empting strategies (Kaur, 2009).

Of course, native English speakers employ similar strategies in communication and the strategies above are not unique to ELF use. Chapter 4, for example, highlighted the importance of accommodation in native English usage. However, ELF users, as speakers of one or more languages, also utilize their plurilingual resources, such as code-switching (Cogo, 2009) and shared non-nativeness (Hülmbauer, 2009). Such strategies are employed to increase clarity and explicitness, e.g. an ELF speaker may rephrase something to make sure the interlocutor understands, or code-switch, or repeat something to effectively co-operate and ensure smooth co-operation, or signal affiliation as a member of a particular community and mark identity. ELF communication is a joint endeavour and speakers may also pre-empt problems of misunderstanding before they even occur, and they may repair misunderstandings by repeating or paraphrasing something.

An example from the ELFA corpus is illustrated below, where Mauranen (2012, p. 50) shows how, in this seminar conversation about same-sex marriage, ELF speakers accommodate and then converge on one of the words. Example A shows where the topic starts, and Example B shows snippets of all turns in the discussion where the term surfaces. ELF speakers then converge on a 'non-standard' form, which would be treated as an error in an EFL context, but clearly does not hinder ELF communication.

Seminar conversation from ELFA corpus

Source: Mauranen, 2012, p. 50.

Example A

< S$_1$ > [yeah] from time to time I think, er, it kind of, er, first this law for that. You can *registrate* your, er, how you say, you (S$_5$: sort of partnership) partnership, er, I think, er, you cannot argue for too much in, in, in Finland, you have to, go li-by [steps] (S$_5$: [(it was)]) yeah (S$_5$: yes) with small steps so [that you can]

< S$_5$ > [was it] in this, er

< S$_1$ > it was [together]

< S$_5$ > [this spring], spring 2002, was it 2001 (S$_1$: mhm) that it became possible in Finland that you can *register* you can't [get] (NS$_2$: [ah]) married and you can't, you can *register* yourself, to be partners [with]

Example B

< S$_1$ > … you can *registrate* your, er, how you say, your …

< S$_5$ > … you can *register*, you can't get married and you can't, you can *register* yourself …

< S$_5$ > … very much against this, er, *registration* thing because …

< S$_3$ > … between *registration* and marriage so …

< S$_5$ > … got the right to *registrate* so I suppose in another ten years …

< S$_1$ > … er, getting re-*registrated* was, were kept together but then …

Another form of accommodation is collaboration and an example from the ELFA corpus is provided in the following box. In this example of a seminar discussion, S6 is speaking, although S1, S3, and SU interrupt (there were six people in total); S1 offers a different expression (*pull it down*) instead of S6's *tear away*. S3 then joins with a collaborative completion (*saved it*), anticipating what S6 wants to say next. An unidentified student (SU) then demonstrates back-channelling (*mhm-hm*) to demonstrate that they are listening. Mauranen (2012) points out that such co-operation in ELF talk does not, however, necessarily result in consensus or agreement, and that co-operation is also required in arguments or when different views are expressed.

An example of accommodation from the ELFA corpus

Source: Mauranen, 2012, p. 52.

< S$_6$ > about stalin i heard i heard that er during the 70's they had a vote in the city council that should they tear this old toompea castle, @away@ and build

< S₁ > [pull it down] < /S₁ >
    [a new] new techno city and it was like one or two votes that @@
< S₃ > saved it < /S₃ >
    that saved it so it was
< SU > mhm–hm < /SU >
    pretty close that that @@ those castles wouldn't be there anymore < /S₆ >

ELF speakers as agents of change: the virtual language

The notion of a virtual language helps us understand not only the dynamic and fluid nature of ELF, but also the 'underlying encoding possibilities that speakers make use of' (Seidlhofer, 2011, p. 111). This chapter has exemplified how ELF is different to native English in many ways. Figure 7.1 shows how the virtual language acts as a third point of reference for both ELF and native English speakers. It is reference to this virtual English that enables the coinage of many new words, such as those described above in Section 7a. Adding an 's' suffix to an uncountable noun such as *furniture*, for example, may not conform to native English-speaker norms, but it does conform to morphological rules of the language. Thus, the concept of the virtual language refers to how speakers explore the theoretical possibilities for the language, which have not been coded. In this way, language can be seen as a dynamic system, and ELF speakers draw on ELF as a **complex adaptive system**, which is recurrently transformed by use (Larsen–Freeman and Cameron, 2008). Native English speakers are also capable of being agents of change, of course, but ELF speakers, coming from a range of backgrounds, create even more possibilities for change as they draw on their plurilingual repertoires. They have access to another language(s) (Hülmbauer, 2013), and this section has shown how this additional language can be a useful resource to achieve communicative success.

Culture and identity

ELF research has also been done on the language–culture relationship. The dynamic nature of lingua franca communication means that speakers join and depart various communities of practice, bringing into question the relevance of native English-speaker cultural norms, as well as traditional theories about the relationship between language and culture. Baker's (2009) study in Thailand, for example, revealed that in ELF communication, cultural frames of reference need to be viewed as more fluid and emergent

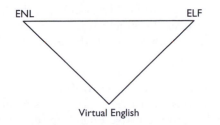

ENL   ELF

Virtual English

Figure 7.1 A schematic representation of 'virtual' English (source: Seidlhofer, 2011, p. 111)

resources. In his study, participants used ELF to construct and express individual, local, national, and global cultures in dynamic and hybrid ways. Thus, just as language itself has to be viewed as a more dynamic and changeable construct, the same can be said of culture and identity in ELF. As Baker (2012, p. 38) notes,

> ELF communication is no longer tied to the cultures of the 'inner circle' English-speaking countries. Instead the language and culture relationship is created in each instance of communication, depending on the speakers, setting and subject.

ELF users need to be trained to negotiate and mediate English and cultural references, as opposed to learning about a fixed, minority native English-speaking 'culture', which is in itself a slightly essentialist view. Successful ELF communication does not require knowledge of native English cultures. More accurately, culture is constructed in discourse, and thus is not something that can be learned, acquired, or known. Identity is also a negotiated and fluid construct, and it is irrelevant for learners of English to 'give up' their identify in order to take on a native English-speaker identity. Traditional assumptions about the links between language and culture and language and identity have changed, and, as with culture, a speaker's identity in relation to using ELF may vary depending on the context of use. Chapter 10 will further explore the concept of 'culture' and identity in an increasingly globalized world.

7c English in the workplace

The use of English in the business field has come to be known as BELF (Louhiala-Salminen *et al.*, 2005). Globalization means that international business people now work across borders, engaging in meetings, negotiations, and telephone conversations with people from diverse linguistic and cultural backgrounds. English has come to be adopted as an official working language of many international companies, even in those places where it has no official status, as discussed in Chapters 1 and 6. It has become the dominant language in the international business arena and English, or rather ELF, is a fact of life for many people working in international business. Kankaanranta and Planken's (2010) study in European multinational companies, for example, highlighted that 70 per cent of the English used by international business professionals could be characterized as BELF, taking place between non-native English speakers. BELF communication also dominated their interviews, with interactions with non-native English speakers ranging from 70–100 per cent of the total of their English language interactions.

BELF: a definition

As Nickerson (2005, p. 354) points out, 'the realities of the business context are often considerably more complex than the simple label of English as a lingua franca would imply'. However, BELF research complements the ELF research described in this chapter. Both BELF and ELF:

- share an acknowledgement that they differ to native English in many ways;
- acknowledge that the norms of native English speakers are not relevant, and that ownership does not belong to the native English speaker but is a shared concept;
- see users in their own right, as opposed to comparing them to native English speakers.

The difference lies in BELF's focus on the business domain, a specific community of practice where there may be a common business culture, domain-specific knowledge, and vocabulary. However, research into BELF, with the focus on the 'B', 'will eventually contribute to a better understanding of the overall lingua franca phenomenon' (Ehrenreich, 2010, p. 427).

Research overview

BELF has become a growing field of interest. In 2005, there was a special issue on BELF in the *English for Specific Purposes* journal. As with ELF usage in general, many researchers have highlighted the role of other languages, as well as the utilization of various pragmatic strategies. Research also showcases how communication is a collaborative process and some researchers have focused on co-operation. Pullin (2013), for example, explored the role of stance markers, particularly hedges (e.g. *perhaps*, *might*, and *sort of*) and boosters (e.g. *clearly* and *excellent*) in authentic audio-recorded BELF interactions, finding that they contributed to the achievement of comity when BELF users are negotiating tasks, handling disagreements, or trying to clarify understanding.

In their studies of the discourse of business professionals, Poncini (2002, 2007) and Louhiala-Salminen (2002a) have also examined the use of pragmatic strategies and the strategic use of ELF alongside other languages. Ehrenreich's (2010) study of the role of English and other languages in a German multinational corporation found that while English is important – an 'indispensable "must"' (Ehrenreich, 2010, p. 408) – other languages, particularly German, are also important. Conformity with native English-speaker norms was also seen as fairly irrelevant and it is communicative effectiveness in BELF, not conformance to native English norms, that is needed. Such studies complement the ELF research discussed in this chapter thus far, highlighting the role of other languages as a useful resource.

Other work in the field of BELF includes Cogo (2012a), who looked at the link between ELF and superdiversity in the multilingual business context of a small IT company. Cogo found that the company's practices were multilingual. ELF interactions were collaborative, and participants used various multilingual resources to negotiate meaning, including code-switching, translation for strategic purposes such as concluding, and making themselves sound more precise, as opposed to just explaining the meaning of unknown words. Cogo (2012a, p. 308) concluded that these BELF users were,

> skilled languagers that cross, mix and play with their resources, which assume different meanings in the contexts in which they are used and with the interlocutors with whom they are negotiated.

However, while this study highlighted the use of multilingual practices, Cogo also emphasized that the participants were flexible and responsive to certain contexts; that is, strategies may be context and speaker dependent.

Pedagogical implications

The use of English in international business is also a popular topic outside academia. *The Economist*, for example, reported that, 'In Brussels, native English-speakers are notoriously hard for colleagues to understand: they talk too fast, or use obscure idioms' (*The Economist*, 12 February 2009), and it was reported in *Newsweek* (5 May 2008) that native English speakers are often at a disadvantage when brokering deals in their mother tongue and that foreign clients often prefer to work with other non-native English speakers. Consequently, companies such as London's Canning School have been set up to teach 'Offshore English', which consists of roughly 1,500 of the most common English words and excludes idioms, and is a similar concept to 'Globish', a reduced and simplified variety of English. Such reports appear to acknowledge that adherence to native English is insufficient in the field of international business, and that the onus is not merely on non-native English speakers to 'perform' but that native English speakers may also have to 'learn' to communicate more effectively in international business settings.

However, while articles in places like the *Harvard Business Review* acknowledge that, 'You don't have to reach native fluency to be effective at work' (*Harvard Business Review*, May 2012, p. 119), suggestions that '3,000 to 5,000 will do it' (p. 119) and that non-native English speakers who are 'less proficient' may require coaching by native English-speaking colleagues and should 'refrain from reverting to their mother tongue', which may 'ostracize native speakers' (p. 121), are clearly not reflective of the BELF research described above, which highlights that knowledge of another language is a useful resource.

The use of English in international business clearly attracts considerable attention and concern. Rogerson-Revell (2008) cites the Groupe Consultatif Actuariel Européen (GCAE, now the Actuarial Association of Europe), a consultative and advisory organization facilitating discussion with European Union institutions on existing and proposed EU legislation, which forms part of a larger international actuarial body, the International Actuarial Association (IAA). An internal report of an IAA task force on 'How to encourage more active participation of non-English speakers' made some recommendations to improve participation in meetings, including recommending that native English speakers speak slowly, use simple words, and write a summary of what they intend to say before meetings. Non-native English speakers are recommended to rehearse, bring a dictionary, and to ask for clarification when they don't understand something. Chairs of such meetings are encouraged to actively help non-native English speakers with their vocabulary.

Many BELF researchers have discussed the pedagogical implications of their research. Louhiala-Salminen, *et al.* (2005, p. 419), in their study of the communicative practices of two international firms, for example, noted that in,

> BELF teaching, learners should be trained to see themselves as communicators, with real jobs to perform and needs to fulfill; it is these jobs and needs that should be emphasized, not the language they use to carry them out.

The authors emphasized listening skills, and making future BELF users aware of their own and their interlocutors' discourse practices, conventions, and cultural preferences to help them appreciate the need to be flexible, a skill needed in the 'rapidly changing business community of today' (Louhiala-Salminen, *et al.* (2005, p. 419). This study revealed that forms that differed to native English rarely hindered communication.

BELF research also has implications for native English-speaker training. Louhiala-Salminen and Rogerson-Revell (2010), for example, note the need for native English-speaker training in BELF, which includes techniques to simplify idiomatic expressions as well as to increase knowledge of the role of other languages. Kankaanranta and Planken (2010) also note that native English speakers require such training. They note that while in business textbooks the native English-speaker model is often used, for the participants in their study the model was a business professional. Participants in this study reported the importance of real-life practice to learn BELF. Ehrenreich (2010) likewise notes that BELF skills can be developed through exposure to BELF communities of practice.

Bjørge's (2012) study also indicated a mismatch in the advice concerning ways to express disagreement that is provided to English learners in business English textbooks and in ELF usage. Much ELF research has explored the cooperative aspect of ELF interactions, yet in business disagreement is common. Corpus analysis of 25 simulated negotiations by international business students showed that the ELF speakers did not make a lot of use of the recommended one-sentence examples and expressions of disagreement suggested by the textbooks. However, they did use the mitigation strategies that were implicit in the textbook examples. Bjørge concludes by noting that those involved in business communication coaching need to raise their students' awareness of the use of mitigation strategies, but also that stating their position clearly is an important ELF communication strategy.

BELF is a growing field of study, highlighting how ELF is used in the international business area. While English may be the language of international business, this does not necessarily mean it is the English spoken by native English speakers. BELF, as with ELF, is characterized by collaboration, and communication is a co-operative process.

7d   ELF: future directions

ELF may be a flourishing field of study but unlike World Englishes, which has gained much respect over the years, ELF continues to face a number of challenges. As Seidlhofer (2009a, p. 237) points out,

> currently, there is a very considerable gap between the extent of the spread of ELF and the extent to which efforts have been made to describe it. This lag is likely to be due to what elsewhere I have termed a conceptual gap ... the difficulty that seems to be inherent in accepting a language that is not anybody's native tongue as a legitimate object of investigation and descriptive research.

Ten years on from her first statement about the 'conceptual gap', the problem of engaging with the concept of ELF, something that differs from 'standard' English, continues. Many ELF scholars argue that resistance to the concept of ELF stems from deep-rooted attachments to 'standard' English, first discussed in Chapter 2. ELF scholars have found themselves having to continually define what it is and what it is not. Thus, in our discussion that follows of the main criticisms of ELF research, we also find ourselves having to revisit some of the definitions that have already been put forward in this book.

ELF misunderstandings/criticisms

Seidlhofer (2006) identifies five misunderstandings of ELF and Jenkins (2007) adds a further three (see Jenkins, 2009, pp. 14–15 for a discussion of the main criticisms of her lingua franca core research). Here, we have grouped the criticisms of ELF into the following headings:

1 language hierarchization and denial of diversity;
2 the invisibility myth;
3 imposition of a single variety of English or English 'rules';
4 promotion of a reduced, simplified version of English – an 'anything goes' policy;
5 that it is unrepresentative of ELF usage;
6 that ELF is linked with pedagogy and promotes a teachable model.

1 Language hierarchization and denial of diversity

Phillipson (2008; 2009) claims that labels such as 'lingua franca' are misleading, lead to the belief that the language is culturally and ideologically neutral, and substantiate the processes of language hierarchization. He believes that 'English is frequently legitimated in this way by its native speakers' (Phillipson, 2008, p. 260), a point also raised by Holliday (2005, p. 9) who criticizes the concept of ELF as 'yet another "centre-led" definition of what English should be'. O'Regan (2014, p. 8) has also noted that 'although the ELF movement wishes to pretend that "ELF" is ideology and culture free, in fact it is very much neoliberal-bound as well as geoculturally Eurocentric', and calls it an 'ideologically conservative project' that fails to mention capitalism or neoliberalism.

It is clear from this book thus far that English is already the 'default language' in a number of fields. ELF research does not 'ignore' other languages, but seeks to empower non-native English speakers and embrace their various first languages. Seidlhofer (2006) also pointed out that the field is criticised for ignoring the polymorphous nature of English and denying tolerance for diversity. However, ELF research recognizes the problems associated with the spread of Inner Circle English and ELF minimizes the aspects of linguistic and cultural imperialism, seeing the first language and culture of its users as a resource, not a hindrance. The widespread use of ELF is not a threat to other languages, to multilingualism, or to multiculturalism and, as House (2012, p. 174) states,

> ELF and multilingualism are not 'either – or' matters, and the use of ELF need not damage linguistic–cultural diversity. The vast majority of ELF speakers are per se bilingual or multilingual speakers, which means that transfer from other languages and code-mixing are common in ELF interactions.

ELF research seeks to remove ownership of the language from native English speakers and to enable ELF speakers to construct their own norms, and unlike Inner Circle English it is not a 'lingua frankensteina' (Phillipson, 2008): it does not destroy other languages but embraces them. ELF research may have begun in Europe, and a lot of research has been conducted there, but this cannot be a legitimate criticism of ELF. The underlying ideals of ELF are not Eurocentric and research is now taking place around the world, which will shed new light on how English is used.

2 The invisibility myth

Jenkins (2007, p. 19) points out that many criticisms of ELF stem from misunderstanding, and that an 'invisibility myth' appears to exist. Trudgill (2005), for example, dismisses the claims that non-native English speakers use English more than native English speakers, and Quirk (1985) argues that, since speakers in the European Community use English for mainly external purposes, a single standard form is appropriate. Nevertheless, as Jenkins (2007) notes, Quirk fails to recognize that no such thing exists, except ideologically (for a detailed overview of these misconceptions and responses see Jenkins, 2007; Seidlhofer, 2006). As Chapter 4 has shown, native English speakers use English in varied forms, and a monochrome standard form, even within a small geographical location, does not exist.

3 A single variety of English or English 'rules'

Seidlhofer (2006) notes that ELF research has been criticized for aiming at an accurate application of a prescribed set of rules and that ELF researchers are suggesting that there should be one monolithic variety. ELF researchers are often criticized for attempting to codify a single variety of English, and many of these comments have been made by World Englishes and EIL scholars who, despite preferring approaches to viewing language use that see it as a pluricentric construct, see ELF as ignoring the diversity associated with its global spread. Some examples of such criticism include:

- Rubdy and Saraceni (2006, pp. 10–11), who call it a 'monomodel' and raise the question, 'once the core features are established, are these likely to assume the character and force of a new dogma?';
- Matsuda and Friedrich (2012, p. 18), who critique the ELF paradigm on the basis that 'one or a limited set of specialized varieties of English' does not reflect the reality of international communication and the use of EIL. However, since this time Matsuda (2014, personal communication) has clarified that she no longer sees her former claims as relevant to the evolving field of ELF. In fact her view of World Englishes incorporates many of the shared endeavours of ELF, and is thus defined in much broader terms than we have used in this book.

In her response to some of these misconceptions, Seidlhofer (2006) highlights the fact that ELF corpora work is in fact contributing to the diversity of Englishes. ELF offers alternatives to strict native English rules and stresses local variation, not a single ELF norm. Like EIL, ELF exchanges also involve speakers from diverse backgrounds and also employ a variety of communication strategies.

Unlike 'standard' English, ELF is not a 'monomodel' but a description of how English is used by people from different linguistic and cultural backgrounds. Globish, or Offshore English, discussed briefly in Section 7c, assumes a monolithic variety, ELF research describes the dynamic and fluid nature of ELF communication and how ELF users are creative and innovative, adapting the language to suit their needs. ELF communities of practice are transient in nature and 'what is certain is that ELF is not monolithic or a single variety, because cultural and linguistic resources are inevitably transformed as they are locally appropriated' (Cogo, 2011, p. 98). This chapter has also highlighted the shift in ELF research from the identification of surface-level features of ELF to an understanding of the underlying processes resulting in such forms.

4 A reduced, simplified version of English – an 'anything goes' policy

Jenkins (2007) notes that ELF has been criticised for promoting an 'anything goes' policy. It is claimed that ELF allows 'errors' and lacks standards in its acceptance of deviations from 'standard' English. Criticisms along these lines include:

- Sobkowiak (2005, p. 141), who notes that, in relation to pronunciation, ELF will 'bring the ideal down into the gutter with no checkpoint along the way';
- Prodromou (2006, p. 412), who has described ELF as 'a broken weapon', with ELF speakers 'stuttering onto the world stage'.

These criticisms are reminiscent of the historical criticisms by prescriptionists, who lacked an understanding that language change is not only normal but unstoppable. Such critics as Jonathan Swift in 1712 (see Chapter 2) are noted in history as being ignorant of this fact, and critics today will no doubt be noted in the future as being the same. Such criticisms are clearly linked to attachments to 'standard' English, yet it is clear from the opening activity to this chapter that EFL and ELF are two different constructs. The idea of learners being at an '**interlanguage**' stage was first introduced by Selinker (1972). However, this chapter has highlighted that ELF features are more than mere errors; many occur repeatedly and ELF displays an element of systematicity. As Mauranen (2012, p. 123) notes,

> We cannot dismiss repeated findings of non-standard forms as arbitrary mistakes. Some, of course, are just passing slips of the tongue or idiosyncrasies, but even among hapaxes (words that occur only once) it is possible to discern patterns of instances that are similar, such as regularised past tenses, even if each individual case concerns a different verb.

ELF is very different to EFL and involves language contact. In ELF, code-switching, code-mixing, and translating are all used as useful strategies to help achieve successful communication. They are not seen as signs of deficiency or that a learner is not quite 'there yet'.

5 Unrepresentative of ELF usage

Criticisms include:

- Modiano (2009), who accuses ELF research of excluding native English speakers;
- O'Regan (2014, p. 8), who criticizes VOICE and ELFA for only including 'the usage of a narrow range of bilingual elites in globally rarefied international business, education, research and leisure domains'. He adds that such speakers have been educated in the language at school and that many of these 'learners' will not become 'users'.

However, it is clear from this chapter that ELF empirical work does not exclude native English speakers, although it does not involve a large proportion of them. VOICE does limit the number of native English speakers, only permitting up to 10 per cent to be present in any interaction, but this is related to a concern that any more would result in too many ENL forms, as well as pressure to conform. Similarly, native English speakers account for 5 per cent of the data in ELFA and, as with the VOICE corpus, they are only included when ELF speakers are in the majority. It is true that both these corpora have a limited scope of language interactions and interlocutors that they contain and thus, as with any empirical research, the findings of these studies should be treated within the boundaries the study has drawn around its data collection. Therefore, rather than criticise these corpus studies based on the interactions they do not include, it would be better to draw attention to the need for building larger corpora of ELF interactions in order to generalize findings to a more global context.

Furthermore, much ELF research has specifically been done on the role of native English speakers in ELF interactions. Carey (2010, p. 88), for example, looked at native English-speakers' accommodation in ELF speech events, with a focus on self-rephrasing and unsolicited co-constructions, and notes that, 'As a NS [native speaker] involved in ELF research, my base assumption is that native English speakers could improve their communication skills at home and abroad through an active under-standing of ELF interaction'. He also refers to 'the immense grey area between two extreme myths: that of the "perfect" English speaker and the non-accommodating, ethnocentric dullard' (Ibid).

Many BELF researchers have also discussed the implications of their studies in relation to native English speakers. As noted in Section 7c, for example, Louhiala-Salminen and Rogerson-Revell (2010) and Kankaanranta and Planken (2010) dis-cussed the need for native speaker training in BELF. Native English speakers are not ignored, but they are not seen as providing a linguistic reference point. As with the World Englishes paradigm, ELF challenges native English norms and models of competence.

6 ELF is linked with pedagogy: a teachable model

Both Seidlhofer (2006) and Jenkins (2007) discussed the criticism that ELF research involves the creation of a teachable model that should be taught to all non-native speakers. Such criticism includes:

- Kuo (2006, p. 216), who fears that 'ungrammatical but unproblematic' features may become 'standardised' if they occur frequently and certain grammatical features (such as the past perfect progressive) may be left out of ELT if they are found to be rare. She adds that ELF and lingua franca core descriptions do not address reading and writing, and concludes that the native-speaker model represents a 'complete and convenient starting point, particularly with its socio-cultural richness' (Kuo, 2006, p. 220), although the choice should be made by the TESOL professionals and the learners;
- Matsuda and Friedrich (2012, p. 18) who, as noted above, felt that ELF research is an attempt to codify a single variety of English, which is 'likely to serve as the basis for the establishment of a "teachable" international English variety to be used in classrooms in the future', although this claim has since changed.

However, while ENL corpora, such as those introduced in Chapter 4, has often been directly transferred into teaching materials, ELF researchers have been much more cautious. That description should not lead to prescription was pointed out in Section 7a: the intention of the lingua franca core research was not to create a teaching model, but simply to highlight a core of pronunciation features that occur in successful non-native and native-speaker interactions to achieve mutual intelligibility. The purpose of ELF research is not to establish a teachable model and prescribe what should be taught in English classrooms around the world but, as this chapter has pointed out, is simply about examining and showcasing how English is used as a global lingua franca. Such research does have pedagogical implications, discussed further in Chapter 9 where we explore the various proposals that have been suggested for change to ELT practice. Here, it is important to summarize some of these implications briefly. In relation to pedagogy, ELF research is important because it:

- raises awareness of the changing sociolinguistic uses of the language, which is often different to what is 'taught' in the classroom;
- enables teachers and learners to reconsider what is relevant and useful for their specific contexts;
- increases choice and enables teachers and learners to make better-informed decisions about the content of their lessons and the appropriateness of the norms that are often expected – a native speaker model may well be the most appropriate but alternatives should be provided, so ELF increases the options available;
- raises awareness that the many features that are traditionally categorized as 'errors' are actually common and do not impede mutual intelligibility;
- prompts us to consider the very notion of 'competence and its connection with performance' (Widdowson, 2012, p. 8). Non-native speakers are often referred to as being incompetent if they do not 'perform' as a native speaker would and 'non-conformity is equated with incompetence'. ELF research highlights that this 'incompetence' does not prevent ELF users from being able to communicate rather successfully. They simply use the language in a different way to native English speakers.

ELF research is clearly highly relevant to ELT and, as the opening case illustrates, EFL and ELF are very different constructs. In the latter, deviations from the 'standard' are not seen as inferior and the use of the first language is a help, not a hindrance. Non-native English speakers are not seen as 'failed natives' but as legitimate users of the language, and it is clear from this chapter that they are skilled communicators despite not always adhering to fixed native English speaker norms. Swan (2012, p. 388) criticizes the division between EFL and ELF, referring to a 'false opposition between "ELF" and "EFL"'. He criticizes attempts to see ELF as 'more systematic than it actually is', notes that it is not a language in opposition to EFL, and points out that the many 'uncodifiable Englishes of non-native speakers have not turned into a current or emergent variety with its own norms, capable of being taught as an alternative to NS English, and of influencing the development of NS varieties in important ways' (p. 388).

Conclusions: the future of ELF research

The ELF movement clearly brings into question established modes of thinking about English. As noted above, part of the struggle is related to the conceptual transition that ELF requires. Nevertheless, while ELF appears to be accepted as a phenomenon in the recognition of the global spread of English, its legitimacy as both a communication tool and a field of study still needs time. While the development of ELF corpora is promising, it is still far behind the large body of native English corpora. In addition, ELF research continues to face a lot of criticism, much of which stems from attachments to 'standard' English. This conceptual gap needs to be addressed since, as Seidlhofer (2011, p. 23) notes, 'as long as "English" is kept in the conceptual straightjacket of ENL, it is difficult to see how change can be proactively brought about'.

World Englishes went through a similar struggle, and continued research into ELF will help to provide a strong base for further understanding of how the language is used today. More research is needed and, as Seidlhofer (2009b, p. 239) notes,

> acceptance of the very concept of ELF as a legitimate alternative to the concept of ENL will be furthered when it is clearer just what it is that is waiting to be accepted – that is, when documentation and analyses of a wide range of speech events carried out through ELF become available.

Thus, just as World Englishes had a long history of research, ELF needs more work too. With more research and larger corpora, ELF researchers will be able to undertake more descriptive work, to showcase how lingua franca communication takes place today, and to enable us to theorize about the nature of language. Research on attitudes to Global Englishes is presented in Chapter 8 and the pedagogical implications are further discussed in Chapter 9. However, more research is also needed in the area of written ELF (Flowerdew, 2008; Lillis and Curry, 2010) and English language testing, discussed in Chapter 9.

Chapter summary

This chapter has expanded the definition of ELF that was given in Chapter 6 and has given an overview of related research. While World Englishes and ELF have been treated as separate entities in this book, there are some similarities, and it is these similarities that the field of Global Englishes aims to unite. Both focus on the use of English by non-native English speakers and both focus on the pluricentric notion of English. However, ELF research is concerned with the ongoing process of linguistic accommodation and the use of English across and between all three of Kachru's circles. ELF research has gained momentum over the years. Section 7a provided an overview of research, with a focus on phonology and lexicogrammar, and it is clear that the development of ELF corpora has enabled a number of researchers to investigate the use of ELF. Section 7b looked at pragmatics and culture, showing how communicative success is achieved through the use of a number of pragmatic strategies. There has been a shift in ELF research from the identification of surface-level features to an exploration of the processes giving rise to such features, emphasizing the flexibility and hybridity inherent in ELF talk. With growing interest in ELF research, the domains are also increasing and Section 7c examined research in the field of BELF. English has become part of the daily lives of many involved in international business, and BELF researchers have shown how these speakers use ELF in their 'business' communities of practice. BELF research complements ELF research and also has clear pedagogical implications.

However, just as we saw in Chapter 5 with the World Englishes paradigm, Section 6d highlighted that ELF faces a battle and many criticisms, suggesting that Seidlhofer's 'conceptual gap' may still be present. Our discussion of the many criticisms of ELF returned us to the deep-rooted attachments to 'standard' English first presented in Chapter 2. This chapter also raised issues about the nature of some fundamental concepts, such as language and variety, first introduced in Chapter 2 and further discussed in Chapter 10.

To sum up, ELF research is showing how being a non-native English speaker does not make someone 'incompetent' but, in fact, when it comes to ELF communication, being a non-native English speaker can be a useful resource. ELF speakers draw on numerous resources and exploit the malleable nature of the language, being rather creative and innovative in the process.

Further reading

Overview of ELF research:

- Jenkins, J., Cogo, A., and Dewey, M. (2011). 'Review of developments in research into English as a lingua franca.' *Language Teaching,* 44(3), pp. 281–315.
- Seidlhofer, B. (2011). *Understanding English as a Lingua Franca.* Oxford: Oxford University Press.

On lexicogrammar and pragmatics:

- Cogo, A. and Dewey, M. (2012). *Analysing English as a Lingua Franca: A Corpus-driven Investigation.* London: Continuum.
- Seidlhofer, B. (2004). 'Research perspectives on Teaching English as a Lingua Franca.' *Annual Review of Applied Linguistics,* 24, pp. 209–39.

On BELF:

- Ehrenreich, S. (2010). 'English as a Business Lingua Franca in a German Multinational Corporation: Meeting the Challenge.' *Journal of Business Communication,* 47(4), pp. 408–31.
- Kankaanranta, A. and Planken, A. (2010). 'BELF Competence as Business Knowledge of Internationally Operating Business Professionals.' *Journal of Business Communication,* 47(4), pp. 380–407.

Closing activities

Chapter discussion questions

Section 7a

1 What have been the main developments in ELF research in the past decade or so?
2 What are the possible implications of Jenkins' (2000) research for the teaching of phonology?

3 ELF research is showcasing how ELF speakers are creative with the language, extending patterns found in 'standard' English. For example, coinage of the verb *examinate* is related to an underlying pattern, e.g. *communication–communicate* is like *examination–examinate* (Seidlhofer, 2011, p. 108). Are you familiar with any other innovations?

Section 7b

1 To what extent does ELF research show that proficient ELF speakers are very skilled users of English, exploiting the language in flexible and resourceful ways rather than relying on one rigid code?
2 What do you think Jenkins (2009, p. 201) means by the statement, 'ELF involves both common ground and local variation'?
3 What is your opinion in the change in focus from the identification of linguistic features to a more process-oriented view of ELF?

Section 7c

1 In what ways is BELF content-focused and what is the role of other languages in BELF talk?
2 What implications does BELF research have for the teaching of business English?
3 How do you think ELF researchers would react to the IAA task force recommendations?

Section 7d

1 Mortensen (2013, p. 26) has noted that 'defining ELF as an object of study has been – and continues to be – a troublesome affair'. What are the major criticisms of ELF research, and why are there problems associated with definitions?
2 What does Jenkins (2007, p. 19) mean when she notes that many criticisms of ELF stem from misunderstanding, and that an 'invisibility myth' appears to exist?
3 'For the most part, the still ongoing argument around teaching and ELF generates yet more debate rather than serious research' (Mauranen, 2012, p. 9). Why is ELF research often criticized in relation to ELT?

Debate topics

1 'ELF has major implications for language learning and teaching' (Dewey, 2012, p. 142).
2 ELF users should be regarded as users in their own right and not as deficient interlanguage users.
3 '[T]here are fundamental problems, both practical and theoretical, with the ELF project' (Sowden, 2012, p. 91).

Writing and presentation prompts

Below are ideas for writing and presentation tasks to apply the knowledge learned in Chapter 7.

	Assignment topics
Personal account	VOICE showcases ELF interactions in a range of speech events in terms of domain, function, and different speech event types. Prepare a presentation showcasing your community of practice(s) to exemplify your past, present, and future use of English.
Research task	Seidlhofer (2011, p. 20), notes that some of the large-scale ENL corpora 'make it possible to conduct extremely revealing, fine-grained analyses of native-speaker usage and are a very impressive descriptive achievement'. However, she notes that they may enhance the prestige and authority of ENL. Choose one ENL corpus and compare it with VOICE. Critically evaluate both and make recommendations for change.
Basic academic	Discuss the World Englishes and ELF research paradigms, noting their similarities and differences, and the questions they raise for pedagogy.
Advanced academic	'ELF is a controversial topic. Both as a phenomenon and as an area of study, it has aroused a good deal of animated debate and animosity' (Seidlhofer, 2011, p. xiii). Examine both the criticisms of ELF research and the responses of ELF researchers to such criticism. In doing so, examine the dominant ideologies and possibilities for challenging the status quo.

Chapter 8

Attitudes to English varieties and English as a lingua franca

Introductory activities

The following introductory activities are designed to encourage the reader to think about the issues raised in this chapter before reading it.

Look at quotes in the box, which are taken from McArthur (1998, p. 3).

> 'Yes, he speaks English, but it's *American* English. And *New York*.'
>
> 'Well, yes, she speaks English, but if *that's* what they do in Scotland ... '
>
> 'Sometimes I'm not sure they *really* speak English in London – the ordinary people, I mean. I can't make head nor tail of them. I think they do it *deliberately*.'
>
> 'You know, his Irish (or Yorkshire or Ozark or Newfoundland) dialect is impenetrable. I don't understand *a word he says*.'
>
> 'Well, Jamaican isn't English at all, is it?'

Discussion questions

1 While we may not always be consciously aware of them, 'Language attitudes permeate our daily lives' (Garrett, 2010, p. 2). To what extent is this true? Are you familiar with any negative language attitudes expressed through the media?

2 The attitudes expressed in the box may make some speakers feel that their English is inferior.

  a How do you think Scottish or Jamaican speakers would react to these comments?

  b Have you heard similar remarks in your own context?

Case study: UK teacher criticized because of accent

In an article titled, 'Teacher "told to sound less northern" after southern Ofsted inspection' (Garner, 2013), *The Independent* reported that Ofsted (the Office for Standards in Education, Children's Services and Skills, a UK governmental organization responsible for inspecting schools) told one teacher to tone down her northern English accent. After this inspection, the school established this as one of the teacher's 'targets' to improve her performance, sparking criticism from language societies. A week earlier, another school was reported to have distributed a list of ten banned regional phrases, including *ya cor* (you can't) and *ay?* (pardon?). These phrases were seen as a threat to students' future prospects.

Discussion

1   What is your opinion on the teacher being told she sounded 'too northern'?
2   What does this article tell us about attitudes towards dialects in the UK?
3   Do you think that having a regional accent can hinder one's future prospects?

Introduction

This chapter is devoted to relevant research in the field of English language attitudes. Section 8a begins with a definition of 'attitude', followed by an explanation of why language attitude studies are important. This section also discusses what influences the way in which people perceive languages and accents. Due to the high vitality of the English language and the role it plays in the world today, it is not surprising that many studies have been conducted on attitudes towards English; these are examined in Section 8b. Section 8c examines attitude studies related to the pedagogical context of ELT, and Section 8d looks at attitude studies related to Global Englishes.

8a   The importance of language attitudes and factors influencing attitudes

Defining 'attitudes'

Attitudes are often said to be one of the most distinctive and indispensable concepts in social psychology. However, no single definition is used, with many having been put forward. Sarnoff (1970, p. 279) describes an attitude as 'a disposition to react favourably or unfavourably to a class of objects'. Attitudes have been said to be composites of cognitive, affective, and behavioural components. Attitudes are cognitive due to the fact that they involve beliefs about the world, such as believing that English is useful or may lead to job promotion. They are affective because they often involve an emotional response, such as anxiety of speaking English in public, or even in front of a native English speaker. They are behavioural because they are determinants of behaviour, such as in the employment of native English speakers over non-native English speakers in many contexts. Attitudes are also mental constructs acquired through a variety of factors, including positive and negative experiences.

Attitudes toward language in society

People make inferences about others on a daily basis based on their language use. It is not uncommon, for example, to wonder where a person is from based on their accent.

It is also not uncommon to condemn accents we feel are 'inappropriate' in certain contexts, or to praise those that we feel are more prestigious or 'correct', as has been highlighted at various points throughout this book. Attitudes can be positive or negative, leading to inferences and, because they can bias social interaction, 'language attitudes represent important communicative phenomena worth understanding' (Cargile *et al.*, 2006, p. 443).

The media is full of stories about how accents influence life opportunities. For example, a Pakistani immigrant, discussing his experiences moving to Seattle, advocates that other immigrants to the USA try to imitate American English through adapting intonation, mastering the American accent, studying American idioms, and separating themselves from members of their own cultural community. In his article he is critical of immigrants who do not make these changes and writes, 'There are immigrants I met who have been here for ten years or so and they still speak like they just got off the plane because they have never taken it seriously' (Ismail, 2012). Cases like this are not uncommon and illustrate negative attitudes toward Englishes that do not conform to stereotypes of 'standard' English. Many enrol in accent reduction classes and, like the case above, feel that their own first language and cultural background is a hindrance to integrating into the target culture. This is unfortunate, considering ELF usage does not require a native English-speaker accent or integration into this 'target' culture.

Similarly, there are reports in the media of people losing their jobs for accent-related reasons. *The Insurance Journal* (2012) reported that more people in the workforce are claiming discrimination over their English-speaking ability or foreign accents. Garrett (2010) reports a number of cases of attitudes that had an impact on employment, including an Indian-born customer adviser from the UK working in New Delhi who was dismissed for his Indian accent, which wasn't 'English enough'.

Language attitudes can also impinge at a political level in terms of what languages receive institutional support, and some accents are seen as being more prestigious. It is clear from this book so far that General American English has high 'objective' vitality in a number of contexts. This high status leads to institutional support due to the economic power of the USA, as well as the greater numbers of speakers of American English compared with British English (Ladegaard and Sachdev, 2006). Various chapters in this book have highlighted the use of ELF, and a shift in attitudes towards English being the language of both non-native English speakers and native English speakers, a movement that fights against these attitudes of legitimacy and ownership.

Factors influencing attitudes

A number of factors serve to influence the way people judge accents and therefore varieties of English, or even the language itself, in ways illustrated in the case study at the beginning of this chapter. These are discussed in the following paragraphs.

Cultural and social groups develop norms that imply what is 'correct' and 'incorrect', often based on history, politics, and prevailing stereotypes. As is clear from this book so far, some languages, varieties, dialects, and their speakers are valued within a culture as high in vitality, while others are stigmatized as non-standard. Thus people often evaluate language variation – and Englishes – in a hierarchical manner.

The issue of standard language ideology was raised in Chapter 2, which showed that many speakers of English challenge the legitimacy of 'New' Englishes, and many are stuck in Kachru's (1992a) first stage, where prejudice exists towards the local variety by those who are attached to native English. Even native English speakers whose dialect is different from the 'standard' can face discrimination. It is important to point out, however, that regional native English-speaker accents are evaluated more positively than non-native English varieties (Derwing, 2003), as will become clear in this chapter. Elsewhere, English is seen as a prestigious language and the concept of a 'standard' language has continued in non-native English-speaking countries, where stereotypes are perpetuated through the use of native English in educational models.

Attitudes towards language, especially English, are often influenced by the process of standardization, and therefore standard language ideology, which has taken place over a long period of time. Thus, the difficulty in defining 'standard' English (given the fact that language is an unstable construct, as we have shown in preceding chapters) is even more problematic given its global use. Such powerful ideological positions, based on the 'supposed existence of this standard form' (Milroy, 2007, p. 133), influence people's attitudes. Galloway (2011) also suggested that attitudes towards English may be influenced by notions of standard language ideology towards speakers' first language, and suggests that, in countries such as Japan, a monolithic view of linguistic diversity exists, thus making it difficult to recognize and accept variation in English.

Stereotypes are also important and can help to sustain inequalities, and, as discussed in Chapter 4, attitudes towards British regional varieties can be very varied. A survey reported on the BBC News website ('Regional Accents "Bad for Trade"', BBC, 2005) noted that some regional accents were bad for trade, particularly Liverpool, Birmingham, Cockney (London working class), Geordie (Newcastle), and the West Country accents. This was in contrast to Home Counties, Scots, American, European, Indian, and Asian accents, which were viewed as a sign of success. An article in *The Scotsman* (2006) was given the title 'Is Scotland turning into a call centre nation?' and referred to the 'trust' callers have in a 'friendly' Scottish accent. This is juxtaposed with proposals that advocate the creation of a new post in the BBC to scrutinize the syntax, vocabulary, and style of thousands of staff heard on the air (Anushka and Thorpe, 2007). These attitudes echo throughout history in calls to preserve the English language (as seen in Chapter 2) and the very people who criticize ELF today (as seen in Chapter 7), all of whom cling to the notion that a 'standard' exists.

Familiarity with certain Englishes, or familiarity with using ELF in specific situations or with ELF speakers from specific contexts, may influence attitudes towards them and also towards English in general. Lippi-Green's (1997) study, for example, revealed that accent attitudes in the USA are closely related to patterns of immigration; over time, the groups whose English has been most criticized have corresponded to the largest recent immigrant groups. There was a positive correlation between listening comprehension scores and the amount of classes students had taken that were taught by teaching assistants in Rubin and Smith's (1990) study, and therefore they conclude that 'North American undergraduate students need to be trained to listen to accented English' (Rubin and Smith, 1990, p. 350). Dörnyei *et al.* (2006) add that, in EFL environments, learners do not have the opportunity to establish contact-based attitudes towards 'New' Englishes. However, indirect contact can also influence attitudes through exposure to cultural products, such as films, videos, books, magazines, and music. In addition, we have highlighted in this book that the term 'EFL' may be a rather unrepresentative view of English in the Expanding Circle given the increased role English has taken on over the years, which has resulted in increased ELF usage. In such contexts, the dominance of native English clearly increases familiarity with it, which in turn may lead to more favourable attitudes.

People also tend to favourably or unfavourably judge particular vocal qualities, such as pitch and loudness, and thus language attitudes may also be person specific (Bradac *et al.*, 2001). A speaker's physical features can also influence attitudes and many studies have highlighted the influence of race on language attitudes. In fact, people may 'hear' an accent that may not exist, which may lead to lower comprehension rates. In addition, Amin (1999) found that ESL students perceived Canadian and native speaker identities as being analogous to whiteness, and Lippi-Green (1997, pp. 238–39) has argued that, in terms of non-native English in the USA, it is 'not all foreign accents, but only accent linked to skin that isn't white … which evokes such negative reactions'. Thus, some speakers and teachers may be evaluated, and comprehended, in relation to their racial or geographical origin.

Levels of expertise are also important and, while this area has rarely been investigated, the available research indicates that ability in a language and attitude towards it are linked (Baker, 1992). The higher the achievement, proficiency, and ability in a language, the more favourable is the attitude (Gardner, 1985). Jenkins (2007), who provides an extensive overview of attitude studies of English in relation to ELF, also expresses a concern with previous attitudinal studies on perceptions of non-native English-speakers' speech because of the low language level of some of the participants, although it should be pointed out that it is difficult to measure proficiency using the current prevailing native English-speaker norms, a topic further explored in Chapter 9.

Language attitudes can serve various functions for those who hold them (Bradac *et al.*, 2001), and it is also important to research non-native English speakers' current and future use of the language, as well as their motivation for learning. If the person that a learner would like to become is proficient in English, the learner can be described in Gardner's (1985) terminology as having an integrative disposition. As mentioned previously, traditional theories of integrativeness are being revised in light of the spread of English. Dörnyei (2009) looks at this from a 'self' perspective, in that motivation is integrated with the identity of the speaker. Attitudes towards members of the L2 (second language) community are related to an ideal language self-image and, in this sense, students are unlikely to have a vivid and attractive ideal L2 self if the L2 is spoken by a community that they despise. The L2 Motivational Self System also stresses the importance of the learning environment, and thus previous experiences with the learning process (e.g. successful engagement) may also motivate a student to learn, as with the type of experiences they have had communicating in English. This 'linguistic self confidence' (Dörnyei *et al.*, 2006, p. 15) has important implications for Global Englishes since a speaker's past experiences naturally shape their attitudes toward language.

Attitude change

Attitudes are not static and are subject to change. Languages are shaped by their use and it is possible that attitudes towards them change as contact opportunities increase, too. It is clear from previous chapters that attitudes towards prestige accents have changed over the years. In fact, Morrish (1999, cited in Garrett, 2010, p.14) points out that RP is much more popular with the 1.5 billion English speakers outside Britain than it is within its own borders, where RP has moved from a place of prestige value to negative value in the last half-century. An example of this is the sacking of Zenab Ahmed, a BBC news presenter, who was 'sacked ... for sounding too posh' (*Daily Telegraph*, 30 October 2003, cited in Garrett, 2010, p. 14). A similar case was reported on the BBC News website (BBC, 1999), where Boris Johnson claimed he was sacked as a presenter on BBC Radio 4 because his accent was 'too posh'. On the other hand, a news video on the BBC website (BBC, 2011) reports how British pop star Cheryl Cole was sacked from the judging panel of the US version of *The X Factor*, a popular talent show, because of her strong Geordie (Newcastle) accent, which was difficult for the US audience to understand. Beal (2010, p.1) points out the public interest in regional dialects, discussing the BBC Voices project which invited listeners and readers of their website (www.bbc.co.uk/voices) to contribute their word for certain concepts, and to take part in activities such as an accent recognition test.

Thus, attitudes are complex constructs made up of a number of factors. They are underpinned by many factors, including cultural and social norms, which are based on history, politics, prevailing stereotypes, standard language ideology, familiarity, pedagogical beliefs, language proficiency, person-specific factors, current use, experience, and motivation. However, attitudes are also clearly subject to change and, with the increased use of ELF worldwide, attitudes towards English may also be subject to change.

8b Attitudes: methods and studies investigating attitudes towards native and non-native English

Research methods used to investigate attitudes

Language attitude studies have a long history and can be grouped under three broad headings according to their research approach: **societal treatment**, indirect measures, and direct measures.

Societal treatment

This approach is designed to gain insights into the relative status of language varieties, involving an analysis of the 'treatment' given to them and to their speakers through content analysis, observation, and ethnography, and by analysis of government policies, job advertisements, and media output. It can be an important first step in understanding language attitudes, looking at the treatment of languages in the public domain (e.g. official language policies, such as those introduced in Chapter 3). Research into **linguistic landscapes** is also important; this has been defined by Landry and Bourhis (1997, p. 25) as how the 'language of public road signs, advertising billboards, street names, place names, commercial shop signs and public signs on government buildings combine to form the linguistic landscape of a given territory, region or urban agglomeration'. Linguistic landscape studies also examine artefacts like newspapers and even tattoos, and this type of research has flourished with digital photography and globalization. Linguistic landscape studies shed light on the treatment of language in society and, according to Backhaus (2007, p. 11), who provides an overview of research in the field and an analysis of linguistic landscape data in Tokyo, they can also provide insights into a range of issues, such as official language policies and language attitudes, as well as power relations between linguistic groups within a society.

Indirect measures

The indirect approach is generally seen as synonymous with the **matched guise technique** (MGT). Here, participants are asked to evaluate audio-taped speakers and are told that they are listening to a number of different speakers, although it is one speaker in different 'guises'. An attitude-rating scale is used to evaluate the speakers on factors like friendliness, sociability, intelligence, and so forth. Because other linguistic factors are supposedly controlled (e.g. voice quality interference), evaluations of the speakers are thought to better reflect their underlying attitudes. Thus, it involves the use of a more subtle approach, and may even be viewed as a slightly deceptive way of conducting research, as opposed to simply asking people about their attitudes.

MGT was developed by Lambert and his colleagues in the 1960s (Lambert *et al.* 1960; Lambert 1967). Despite the popularity of this approach, it has been criticized for deceiving respondents, for problems with the ability to keep vocal characteristics constant across experimental conditions, the inability to measure other important variables, and for being 'acontextual' due to the fact that nothing is said to the respondents about the context. This latter point is important, especially when results are used to make pedagogical recommendations for ELT.

Modified versions have been developed in response to the various criticisms, and in the **verbal guise technique** (VGT), for example, it is an authentic speaker of each variety who is recorded. Nevertheless, participants still think they are rating people, rather than language. However, when this method is not contextualized or supported with other more qualitative methods, it is difficult to see how rating language varieties based on adjectives such as 'intelligent' can really tell us what people think in relation to ELT, including their opinions on models, policy, and communication.

Direct measures

The direct approach involves asking direct questions about language evaluation, preference, and so forth through questionnaires, interviews, and/or focus groups. This method has been very common in recent years, as will be demonstrated in the next section. One technique is **perceptual dialectology**, a relatively recent approach employed to measure language attitudes directly. A branch of folk linguistics, it involves rating languages without having any exposure to them and thus examines 'people's (more conscious) beliefs about language use' (Jenkins, 2007, p. 75) and their perceptions in depth. Various studies include drawing speech zones on a blank (or minimally detailed) map, ranking accents according to criteria such as 'correct' and 'pleasant', and interviewing respondents about the tasks and discussing the varieties. This method is very useful in explaining attitudes and is particularly useful in the context of Global Englishes, where it is necessary to investigate attitudes towards often-unfamiliar varieties of English, or unfamiliar ELF contexts.

There are, then, clearly a number of different approaches available to study language attitudes, and researchers in the field have chosen to use them alone or together, as the next section will demonstrate.

Attitudes of native English speakers towards native English

A common thread of many studies into attitudes towards native English is that RP and General American still reign supreme in attributions of social status and/or attractiveness. In New Zealand, Huygens and Vaughan's (1983) verbal guise study, involving 120 Pakeha (white New Zealand) university students, investigated attitudes towards English (both British and Pakeha), Dutch, and Maori speech samples (from three status groups). Participants rated the speakers on social and personal scales, and described the type of accent heard. Maori speakers were the least successfully identified by ethnic group; prestige ratings were as follows: English, Dutch, and then Maori.

In the USA, Stewart *et al.*'s (1985) verbal guise study explored 60 university students' attitudes to standard British and General American English (two male speakers read a text for each variety and were presented as either lower class or middle class). The results show that British speakers were rated more highly than American English speakers on status, but the opposite was the case for solidarity. The study also found that RP was rated higher than the students' own accent for social status, but as less intelligible.

Using 400 students in New Zealand, Australia, and the USA, Bayard *et al.*'s (2001) verbal guise study involved evaluations of New Zealand, Australian, American, and 'RP-type' English. Overall, American English was the most highly evaluated, Australian students ranked their own accents in third or fourth place on most traits, the New Zealand group ranked their own accent below American, Australian, and RP but the Australians did not, and the New Zealanders and Australians did not give their own accents top ratings in solidarity. The authors concluded that American English is on its way to equalling or replacing RP as the prestige accent and discussed the power of the USA and the influence of globalization, factors highlighted in Chapter 1.

These attitude studies reveal much about how English is viewed in the Inner Circle. Despite assertions in Chapters 2 and 4 that people were moving away from standard language ideology, attitude studies show that RP and General American are still held in high regard. There is also evidence from the Bayard *et al.* (2001) study that, in Australia and New Zealand, there is a movement away from British English toward American English as the prestige English of the world. Huygens and Vaughan's (1983) and Bayard *et al.*'s (2001) studies also suggest that speakers value international 'standard' Englishes more highly than their own locally spoken Englishes, raising serious issues for language and identity. The fact that in not one study did New Zealanders rate their own English highly, and negatively rated Maori English in the other, may be an alarming finding for some researchers who have aimed at positively connecting national identity and language.

Attitudes of non-native English speakers to native English

Many studies have examined the attitudes of non-native English speakers to native English, some of which will be outlined in this section, in order to illustrate attitudes in the Expanding Circle. Ladegaard and Sachdev's (2006) verbal guise study explored 96 Danish EFL learners' attitudes to a range of native-speaker English accents: RP, American, Australian, Scottish, and Cockney. Despite the recognition of the high vitality of American culture, there was a preference for RP on important dimensions (status, competence, and linguistic superiority) but not on the perceived social attractiveness of the accent. The Scottish speaker was the most favourably evaluated on friendliness and helpfulness, the Australian speaker was the most reliable, and the American speaker was the most humorous. There was no desire to adopt an American accent and RP remained the favourite model of pronunciation. The authors noted the possible influence of the teachers' own preferences for RP, although the majority did not emphasize this in the classroom, further highlighting the complexity of attitudes. They conclude that a 'high level of "objective" vitality may not be a sufficient factor in determining the attractiveness of a language to out-group members, at least not in this EFL context' (Ladegaard and Sachdev, 2006, p. 19). This study highlights the language–culture discrepancy hypothesis; that is, it is possible to have positive attitudes towards members of another ethnolinguistic group, and preferences for certain elements, without wanting to adopt every element, including their language. Students may feel more culturally similar and geographically closer to the British, supporting Morrish's (1999) assertion that RP is much more popular with speakers outside England than it is within its own borders.

A survey in Malaysia showed that over 90 per cent of 439 university students believed that the use of British English, American English, or Australian English is essential for Malaysians to be understood internationally (Crismore et al., 1996). Similarly, in China over 64 percent of the 171 university students agreed that Chinese people need English in order for them to communicate with native English speakers and non-native English speakers (Kirkpatrick and Xu, 2002) and, while one third had no preference, many preferred American English to British English. No reasons, however, are provided. A Japanese student-teacher in Jenkins' (2007) study, which made use of an open and closed questionnaire, a map labelling exercise, and interviews, also mentioned a preference for General American English, because '[Japanese people] are so accustomed to American English that any other accents sound "unfamiliar" or "not mainstream"' (Jenkins, 2007, p. 182), which highlights the importance that familiarity and the influence that the prevalence of American English, which is widely familiar due to it being a favoured educational model, can have on attitudes towards English.

A limitation of the above studies, however, is a lack of acknowledgement of varieties of English within the USA and Britain. There have been a few notable studies that have looked at learners studying in the Inner Circle and their attitudes to local dialects of English that exist within national borders. McKenzie's (2008a; 2008b) verbal guise study, which also incorporated techniques from perceptual dialectology, revealed that Japanese learners who were studying in Scotland were more positive towards Scottish standard English speech than Glaswegian vernacular speech. Cargile et al.'s (2006) study found Japanese students rated African American Vernacular English less positively in terms of status, but more favourably in terms of social attractiveness than Midwest American English. These studies are important and interesting due to the fact that they did not group Inner Circle English as one single variety but recognized the presence of regional varieties, something often ignored. They also highlight the tendency to judge language varieties hierarchically. McKenzie's (2008a; 2008b) studies were also two of the few that involved non-native English speakers' perceptions of regional varieties.

The studies discussed thus far have used multiple guise and verbal guise techniques. However, these methods tell us little about attitudes or what factors serve to explain these attitudes. A longitudinal study was conducted by Adolphs (2005), who followed a group of 24 international students on a pre-sessional English language course through their first year at a British university. Interviews conducted at two-monthly intervals suggest that many learners have a simplistic notion of the native English speaker, and familiarity led to more negative attitudes. This finding is interesting, suggesting that students do not always hear what they expect to when they move to a native English-speaking country. The students in this study did not encounter the 'standard' variety that they had been exposed to in their previous classroom, highlighting the importance of familiarity and pedagogical beliefs. Students also became increasingly aware of the need to understand English in international communication as they communicated with each other, which may have been another reason for their progressively more negative attitudes towards native English speakers, although this was not investigated in any depth. Such findings have clear implications for universities' eagerness to accommodate and attract the expanding and lucrative international student market, a major issue further explored in Chapter 10.

In summary, attitude studies that have investigated non-native English speakers' attitudes towards native English have shown a tendency for students to gravitate toward a 'standard' English, although it is clear from Chapter 2 that this is rather difficult to define. In Ladegaard and Sachdev's (2006) and Taylor's (2000) studies, the dominance of RP in non-native English-speaking countries was clear, even for students who had received education in the American English medium. The Jenkins (2007) and Kirkpatrick and Xu (2002) studies, however, highlighted the importance of American English in countries like China and Japan, who perhaps favour American English due to strong economic ties with the USA, as discussed in Chapter 6. The McKenzie (2008a; 2008b), Cargile *et al.* (2006), and Adolphs (2005) studies also show a clear attachment of status to a 'standard' English when comparing perceived minority Englishes (such as African American or Glaswegian) with others that fit more into preconceived notions of a standard. Furthermore, when students encounter Englishes that do fit these preconceived notions, it can lead to negative evaluations of them and their speakers, as shown in the Adolphs (2005) study. This once again points to the powerful influence that standard language ideology has on the creation of attitudes and stereotypes.

Attitudes of non-native English speakers to non-native and native Englishes

While the evaluation of non-native English to native English was an indirect focus of some of the above studies, other studies have sought to compare them more directly. Two notable studies are Matsuura *et al.*'s (1994) and Chiba *et al.*'s (1995) studies in Japan. The second verbal guise study was a follow-up to the former. 169 Japanese university students rated nine male speakers (three Japanese, two Americans, one British, one Sri Lankan, one Hong Kongese, and one Malaysian) based on items like 'clear/ unclear' and 'friendly/unfriendly'. Unlike other verbal guise studies, the second part of the questionnaire included 21 statements about foreign languages and language learning. Students responded more positively to the native English speakers and were influenced by familiarity, although familiarity did not improve attitudes towards Japanese English. As discussed in Chapter 6, the Japanese English accent is often viewed negatively in Japan, where standard language ideology is strong. Nevertheless, this was not investigated with more qualitative methods or the wider social context and the attitudes were not explored in depth. The authors also concluded that educators in Japan must advocate the existence of Global Englishes, but this was not explored and no practical proposals were made.

In a study of Japanese students studying in New Zealand, Starks and Paltridge (1994) found that students rated American English and British English much more favourably than New Zealand English. The second highest preference (after American English) was for learning English with a Japanese accent. This was different to the results of Matsuura *et al.*'s (2004) investigation of 50 university EFL teachers and 660 students, who viewed the term 'Japanese English' negatively. This study, however, utilized a closed questionnaire. Speakers of English are often heavily critical of the variety of English spoken in their own country. However, such attitudes are influenced by a number of factors and it is important to examine respondents' uses of English, as well as their goals, given the influence that familiarity and motivation can have on attitudes, as discussed in Section 8a. This also relates to Dörnyei's (2009) notion of the 'ideal self', also discussed in Section 8a.

In summary, the majority of studies reveal a preference for native English accents, although this may be related to the use of the native English-speaker model in ELT and the high vitality of native English, explored further in Chapter 9. The studies also show a negative attitude towards speakers' own first language group's accent, as can be seen in three of the above studies. Even though some of the studies show a higher ability for speakers to comprehend their own accents, this is very different from the prestige value attached to the accent. Intelligibility, therefore, does not always equate with acceptance.

8c Attitude studies related to the pedagogical context of English language teaching

Several researchers have related their research of attitudes towards English to the pedagogical context of ELT. (Please note that a full exploration of attitudes towards native English-speaking teachers and **non-native English-speaking teachers** can be found in Section 9b.) Studies related to ELT are important. Awareness of learners' beliefs, for example, can make both the learners and their teachers aware of their needs, which may result in increased autonomy and self-awareness. Friedrich's (2000) study of attitudes towards English in Brazil highlighted that awareness of such attitudes can raise students' awareness and help them evaluate their own stereotypes and prejudices, in addition to linguistic features. Moreover, improved teacher knowledge of students' attitudes can lead to more effective lesson planning and course implementation, and improved satisfaction, particularly important today as traditional approaches to ELT are no longer meeting the needs of many students, particularly those who will use ELF (see Section 9c for an in-depth discussion of this point). El-Dash and Busnardo (2001) add research on attitudes to English can contribute towards curriculum development. Furthermore, positive attitudes towards the target language group are linked with successful language learning (Dörnyei *et al.*, 2006) although, as discussed in Chapter 7, for those learning English for lingua franca communication this group is not necessarily always the native English speaker. The next section (Section 8d) will explore this notion further, examining in particular attitudes towards ELF. Attitudes vary greatly according to context and thus studies in this section are presented according to geographic location.

Greece

In Greece, Prodromou's (1992) survey-based study investigated 300 English students' attitudes on the content of language teaching, including attitudes towards bilingual and bicultural teachers, native English-speaking models, and the cultural content of lessons.

Just over half thought that native English-speaking teachers should know the learners' mother tongue and the local culture. The popularity of British English compared to American English is related to the 'bad-press' (Prodromou, 1992, p. 44) that the Americans have had in post-war Greece (the presence of US bases on Greek soil, a history of interference in internal affairs, etc.), as well as the widespread feeling amongst Greeks that British English is a 'purer', more 'refined' form of English (Prodromou, 1992, pp. 44–45). Overall, 62 per cent of students said they would like to speak English like a native speaker, and a strong interest in British life and institutions (60 per cent) was found. The authors also discuss the predominance of British-based Cambridge examinations in Greece. However, this rather descriptive study only utilized questionnaires and the attitudes of these Greek students are not explored in any depth.

Austria

Dalton-Puffer et al. (1997) conducted an Austrian-based modified MGT study involving 132 students of EFL (two-thirds planned to become English teachers) in a provided context (listeners thought the purpose of the study was to choose voices for an upcoming audio-book). The Austrian accent received the most negative response and the majority favoured RP as a model of pronunciation, with familiarity listed as a reason. In this study, personal experience was found to be much more important in choosing General American English over RP. Almost half of the respondents had not experienced English in a native English-speaking country and, of those who chose RP as a model, even more students (55 per cent) had not spent more than one month in a native English-speaking country. However, of those who preferred an American model, only 34 per cent had not been on an extended stay abroad.

The USA

In Rubin and Smith's (1990) matched guise study, two native speakers of Cantonese recorded highly accented and moderately accented versions of simulated classroom lectures. Undergraduate students listened to the speakers with a photograph of either a European or an Asian instructor. Perceptions of accent were the strongest predictors of teacher ratings, and when students believed an instructor's accent to be 'foreign' they also viewed them to be a poor teacher. As discussed earlier, the number of courses students had taken that were taught by non-native English-speaking instructors was also found to be the best predictor of listening comprehension scores. In a follow-up study, Rubin (1992) focused solely on ethnicity and asked participants to rate General American English instructors of varying ethnicity using verbal guide technique. Sixty-two undergraduate students listened to a speech sample (a lecture) and again saw a photograph, one of a Caucasian and one of an Asian (Chinese) woman. Students perceived the accents differently and this influenced their comprehension, highlighting the importance of race on attitudes. It is possible that students had a stereotypical image of what an English speaker should look like, which affected their comprehension. This finding also echoes Milroy's (2001) assertion that, in the USA, a discriminating attitude toward a speaker has more to do with race than in the UK, where linguistic cues are used to discriminate a speaker's social background. This also has serious implications for those who advocate the employment of more non-native English-speaking teachers to teach outside of their home countries, discussed in Chapter 9, and it also has implications for those in contexts where they are exposed to native English but are more likely to use ELF in their futures.

Kelch and Santana-Williamson's (2002) study asked 56 ESL students to listen to and rate three native English speakers and three non-native English speakers of different varieties, who read the same script. The native English speakers and non-native English speakers were only correctly identified in 45 per cent of the occasions, and perceptions of nativeness strongly influenced attitudes. Additionally, teachers perceived as native English speakers were seen as more likeable, educated, experienced, and overall better teachers, especially for speaking/listening skills. The dominance of the native English speaker in traditional ELT clearly influences attitudes and may be a major reason for positive attitudes towards these speakers. However, students were also aware of the fact that non-native speaking English teachers can act as good role models, sources of motivation, and fellow language learners who understand students' learning difficulties, although this study, as with many others, failed to distinguish between non-native English-speaking teachers of the same nationality as the students and those working in countries other than their own. This issue will be raised again in Chapter 9.

South Korea

Butler's (2007) matched guise study, which looked at the effects of South Korean elementary teachers' oral proficiencies and pronunciation on 312 grade 6 students' listening comprehension, examined students' attitudes towards teachers with American-accented English and Korean-accented English. The results failed to find any difference in comprehension, although students who thought the American English guise had better pronunciation, was more confident in using the language, would focus more on fluency, and also use less Korean when teaching. This attitude, however, may change in the future, as Korean English teachers have since been encouraged to use English in the classroom through the new Teaching English Through English (TETE) policy, discussed in Chapter 9. The students also preferred the American-accented guise as their teacher.

Japan

A further verbal guise project that related the findings to the pedagogical context of ELT was McKenzie's 2008 study of 558 Japanese university students' attitudes towards six varieties of English. Once more, the results suggest a favourable attitude towards standard and non-standard varieties of British and American English in regards to status. However, greater solidarity was expressed with the 'heavily-accented' Japanese English speaker. This study, which also investigated the influence of background factors on attitude formation, also found that gender, self-perceived proficiency in English, exposure to the language and attitudes towards English and evaluations of varieties of Japanese all influenced their attitudes significantly. McKenzie points out the need for those involved in language planning and curriculum development to understand the general complexity of learners' attitudes in relation to curriculum design, teacher recruitment, and linguistic model(s), and that 'it seems unreasonable to impose a single, or, indeed, a restricted range of pedagogical models for English language classrooms' (McKenzie, 2008a, p. 79).

Nevertheless, how far his results are transferable to the classroom context is questionable, since MGT and VGT studies reveal just a little about attitudes.

China

He and Li's (2009) study in China with 795 students and 189 teachers involved a questionnaire, a matched guise survey, and also interviews for one-tenth of the sample. Despite the adoption of multiple methods, no information is provided on whether the reader's text in the matched guise part of the study was related to ELT. Rankings based on words such as 'friendly, intelligent and sincere' say little about attitudes in relation to ELT. A further problem is with asking students whether they had heard of World Englishes, despite not offering them a clear definition.

It is no surprise that General American received higher ratings on the positive traits. 81.9 per cent wanted to sound like a native English speaker but 62.6 per cent advocated incorporating select features of 'China English' into the existing teaching model, though only 26.6 per cent believed it could replace the present model. No further information was given on these 'select features', however. In the interviews, 78.6 per cent also expressed a preference for American English as the teaching model, although the question was ambiguous. 'Lingua franca English' was translated into Chinese but it is unclear how far students were aware of it. Students were asked, 'If you can choose the pedagogic model for teaching of college English in China, which one(s) would you choose: China English, standard British/American English or the Lingua Franca English? Why?' (He and Li, 2009, p. 78). Thus, the fact that students may have been unfamiliar with the concept of ELF may explain why nobody chose it. This study would have benefited from a fuller investigation of students' uses of English although, despite its pitfalls, it is important in that it directly relates English language attitudes to both Global Englishes and the ELT context, something that is rather rare.

In summary, the above studies show that positive attitudes towards native English are also present in the ELT context. They advocate for curriculum and educational change in order to shift attitudes of students in the Expanding Circle. Section 8b showed a tendency for speakers in the Expanding Circle to hold an attitude that perceived 'standard' Englishes, such as British RP or General American, as having more prestige than other varieties, including non-native English-speaking ones. The studies in Section 8b also showed belief in the Outer and Expanding circles that standard varieties were superior and more attractive than regional varieties within the USA and Britain. This section has shown that studies conducted in relation to the pedagogical context of ELT highlight a strong attachment to native English-speaking norms. However, there is also a suggestion that many factors influence these attitudes, including the predominance of the native English-speaker **episteme** in ELT, familiarity, stereotypes, proficiency, and gender, as introduced in Section 8a.

8d Attitudes towards English as a lingua franca

With increasing awareness of the use of ELF worldwide, a number of researchers have begun to look at teachers' and students' attitudes towards ELF. Jenkins (2007) provides an extensive review of studies in this field and many of these are also discussed in this section.

Teachers' attitudes towards ELF

Mixed countries

Jenkins' (2007) questionnaire-based study of 326 English teachers (300 were non-native English speakers) in 12 countries used perceptual dialectology techniques. Respondents were asked to select, label, and rank (on a map) the five English accents they considered to be the best, and to rate ten specified accents for correctness, pleasantness, and international acceptability. US and British accents were ranked first and second 'best'. However, while the majority did not consider their own accents to be 'best', some did nominate their own group and Jenkins (2007) notes that it marks a possible trend that many will soon 'resist the pressure to "aspire" to NS English accents, and instead will demand recognition for their own accents as a sort of act of resistance' (Jenkins, 2007, p. 161).

This study also highlighted the issue of familiarity. American English was more familiar than British English but also perceived as less correct and pleasant. On the other hand, Swedish English was rated more unfamiliar than all the non-native English accents except Brazilian and Indian English, and yet more correct, acceptable, and pleasant than any other non-native English-speaker accent. Increased familiarity did not lead to greater acceptance, and some respondents clearly had preconceived stereotypes of this variety and perhaps had heard that it is 'native like' (Jenkins, 2007, p. 166). Furthermore, Brazilian English was rated the most unfamiliar but not the most incorrect, unacceptable, or unpleasant, while the opposite was true of Japanese English. While attitudes were not followed up with interviews, due to the dispersion of respondents in 12 different countries, they were asked to provide written comments.

Greece

Sifakis and Sougari's (2005) questionnaire-based study of 421 Greek teachers revealed that their attitudes are still norm bound and there was a lack of awareness of English as an international language. More than 70 per cent felt English belongs to native English speakers or to people with **native English-speaker competence**. Interestingly, primary school teachers in particular valued the native English-speaker model; while this was not researched, it may relate to a belief that the native English-speaker model is required for lower-level learners, highlighting the importance of language proficiency on attitudes. However, for their own pronunciation teaching practices, they revealed a need to focus more on communication, as opposed to rules and standards, when considering non-native English speaker–non-native English speaker communication. Thus, as Jenkins (2007) notes, while they can conceive of ELF and the importance of intelligibility, they do not consider it when teaching, preferring a native English-speaker model.

Germany

In Decke-Cornill's (2002) study of the attitudes towards Global Englishes of teachers in two different types of German schools, which used two group interviews, the non-selective school teachers were more relaxed than the selective school teachers with the concept of ELF. In addition, the teachers overall still felt compelled to teach their classes 'proper English'. Thus, once again, pedagogical beliefs may influence attitudes towards language. English teachers appear to have a firm belief in how English should be taught and, as will become clear in Section 9d, this has serious implications for the introduction of a more Global Englishes-oriented approach in the ELT classroom.

Switzerland

Murray's (2003) study surveyed 253 Swiss teachers from private and state schools on their attitudes to 'Euro-English' (54.6 per cent were native English-speaking teachers, 41.1 per cent non-native English-speaking teachers, and 4.3 per cent bilingual). Questionnaire results revealed that 67.6 per cent agreed that they felt non-native English deserved more respect, but a significant difference was found between native English-speaking teachers and non-native English-speaking teachers, with the former agreeing with the statement much more strongly. When asked to judge whether 11 typical Euro-English sentences were acceptable or unacceptable, the study again found differences between the two types of teachers. A higher percentage of non-native English-speaking teachers felt they were unacceptable, and this group was found to be less tolerant of errors. The author concluded that the non-native English-speaking teachers tend to 'cling to the status quo when it comes to concrete changes in the direction of Euro-English' (Murray, 2003, p. 160). A possible reason suggested for this is the investment of non-native English-speaking teachers in developing their own competence in native English, and that English teachers not only have strong beliefs about how English should be taught but their own stereotypes, and investment in adhering to native English-speaker norms, can also influence their attitude. Thus, it highlights the importance of Global Englishes awareness in teacher training courses.

Likewise, Sasaki (2004, cited in Yoshikawa, 2005) notes that 80 per cent of 97 Japanese high school English teachers surveyed recognized the necessity of touching on the English varieties in their classes, but only 7.8 per cent of them actually do so, and those who do introduce varieties of English only focus on Inner Circle differences. The reasons were, once more, stated to be lack of time and knowledge about World Englishes, highlighting the need for resources and teacher education, another barrier to adopting a more Global Englishes-oriented approach in the classroom (discussed in depth in Sections 9c and 9d).

Austria

Seidlhofer and Widdowson's (2003) study of the attitudes towards ELF of 48 third- and fourth-year students taking the teacher education option at the University of Vienna used essay responses to an article by House (2002) that challenged native English-speaker norms in ELT. Word frequency lists created using WordSmith Tools' key word program, used to identify dominant topics, revealed that the respondents' primary concern was with teaching, and specifically with cultural aspects and pronunciation. Zacharias's (2005) investigation of 100 tertiary level teachers' (94 non-native English speaking) beliefs about the use of teaching materials produced locally and in English-speaking countries ('internationally published') also highlights the need for more locally produced materials and Global Englishes-related materials. Using questionnaires, interviews, and classroom observations, there was a preference (86 and 87 per cent) for materials produced in native English-speaking countries. Thus, not only are teachers unsure of adopting a more Global Englishes approach, they also remain attached to materials produced in the Inner Circle.

Mixed countries

In Jenkins's (2007) interview study of 17 non-native English-speaking teachers, participants were asked about their attitudes towards ELF, and several claimed to support ELF pronunciation but aimed at native English themselves, and most referred to non-native English as 'incorrect'. However, only two were entirely against the notion of ELF and many reasons were offered for these attitudes, including pressure from government, schools, and parents to teach native English, a lack of ELF pronunciation materials, and teachers' traditional attachment to native English. Furthermore, several also thought that teachers need ELF experience to appreciate the irrelevance of the native English-speaker model for international communication. This study reveals important insights into teachers' attitudes and highlights that attitudes are not simple constructs. It is not sufficient to simply state that teachers or students prefer native English, and to use this to justify the status quo.

It is clear from these studies that a **theory/practice divide** exists. ELF is often accepted in the abstract by teachers but rejected in the classroom. While the main and often-stated obstacle appears to be the lack of materials and research available, it is also possible that it is related to teachers' own investments in achieving native English-speaker competence, as well as a fear of replacing the status quo with something that appears to be a radical departure from the norm. However, as pointed out at the start of this section, teachers can learn a lot from studies of students' attitudes. Attitudes are clearly not fixed and they are subject to change, just as the English language itself is, and it is possible that research studies on students' needs, and uses of and attitudes towards English, may influence teachers' attitudes towards changing their classroom approach.

Students' attitudes towards the role of Global Englishes

There is a lack of research investigating students' attitudes, which is surprising given that, as the main receivers of English education, their attitudes are invaluable to teachers, language planners, and others alike.

Mixed countries

Timmis's (2002) study utilized questionnaires (180 teachers from 45 countries and 400 students in 14 countries) to explore attitudes towards English as an international language. Both groups revealed an overall preference for native English, although the teachers, particularly the native English speakers, seemed less attached than the students. Sixty-seven per cent of students wanted listeners to think they were native English speakers, and a further 68 per cent also wanted to sound like a native English speaker (Timmis, 2002), leading Timmis to conclude that, 'while it is clearly inappropriate to foist native-speaker norms on students who neither want nor need them, it is scarcely more appropriate to offer students a target which manifestly does not meet their aspirations' (Timmis, 2002, p. 249). Furthermore, while this study highlights the differences between teachers' and students' attitudes, he notes that the results may be different in ten years' time, with increased awareness of the issues involved. Students have clearly been influenced by the dominance of native English and the native English speaker in language teaching, and it is unsurprising that their ultimate goal is to sound like one.

Further studies are needed which investigate the effect of raising ELF awareness, for example through a Global Englishes course, discussed in the next chapter.

The UK

Kuo (2006) used data from her own learners at a British university. No information is given on the number of respondents but, not surprisingly given the fact that they have travelled to the UK to study English, her informants express a preference for native English over non-native English because of the latter's 'phonological and grammatical inaccuracy' (Kuo, 2006, p. 218). This, the author argues, supports Timmis's (2002) finding that students still desire to conform to native English-speaker norms. However, Kuo does not fully investigate these attitudes and the factors that might explain them (including, possibly, the perspective that she presented as a teacher and an interviewer). Furthermore, mention is made of the students who, worried about their IELTS score, prefer a native English-speaker model. Thus, assessment and the success of commercial tests such as IELTS and TOEFL, which are developed in native-English countries, represent an obstacle for a more Global Englishes-related approach to learning English. Furthermore, their continued use also perpetuates existing stereotypes about English speakers and the ownership of the language, discussed in full in Section 9d.

Germany

Grau's (2005) Germany-based study of 231 first-year university students used a questionnaire and a follow-up discussion that focused on varieties to be taught and to be included in teaching materials and pronunciation objectives (including Jenkins' own 2002 lingua franca core). It is a welcome attempt to link language attitude studies with both ELT and Global Englishes. Once more, 'Grau's results reveal the same "abstract/ concrete" divide' (Jenkins, 2007, p. 102). There was a general openness towards the position that Global Englishes should have in ELT. A considerable number of students favoured introducing learners to a variety of Englishes and the majority agreed on the priority of intelligibility, although British English and American English were still considered to be a sound basis for learners (Grau, 2005). Nevertheless, students were only given the choice of 'America', 'British', 'both', or 'other', suggesting that there are only two models or that these are the two most common choices. Furthermore, while 65 per cent opted for intelligibility as a pronunciation objective, when specific examples of substitutions were given the position was almost the reverse. As Jenkins (2007) points out, however, 'perhaps there would have been fewer objections to the two specific linguistic examples ... had she not referred to them as a "problem" ... and a "mistake"' (Jenkins, 2007, p. 102). These students were also training to be teachers and were taking a course that involved current issues in the field of ELT, and more information is required about the possible influence this had.

The influence of previous experience on attitudes, previously discussed in Section 8a, is also relevant here. A positive experience speaking with a non-native English speaker may, for example, lead to more positive attitudes towards that variety, and thus help to explain perceptions. In Erling's (2005) study involving 101 questionnaires, analysis of essays on the role of English in students' lives, and interviews with five at a university in Berlin, over half preferred native English and 34 per cent expressed interest in a neutral, non-cultural variety, labelled a 'lingua franca cluster' (although this is not explained in any depth). However, in the interviews students appeared to want to be accepted by native English speakers and not to be perceived as German. The interview comments are descriptive and no detailed coding was conducted, nor was the influence of background factors investigated. There is also no information on students' previous experiences with native English speakers and non-native English speakers, and whether these were positive or negative. Moreover, the questions used – such as, 'Whom do you like the best, the Americans or the British?' and 'Which model of English do you try to imitate when you speak English?' – are also asking very different things. Also, 'What do you like the best, British English or American English?' is as problematic as Grau's (2005) study. Therefore, while Erling (2005) concludes that university-level ELT should accommodate students' global needs for the language and teach English as a world possession, it is clear that researchers must also be cautious with their research design.

Japan

Matsuda's (2003) study of 33 Japanese high school students also concluded with calls for more sociolinguistic instruction. Utilizing questionnaires, in-depth interviews (four teachers of English and ten students), and classroom observations, the results showed that, while students saw English as an international language, they considered the owners to be Inner Circle speakers (Americans and British), wanted a native English-speaker model, and lacked an awareness of other varieties, which is unsurprising, given the image of English portrayed in Japan. Matsuda concluded that it is vital to increase the exposure to, and to raise the awareness of, different varieties of English among both students and teachers of English.

Galloway (2011, 2013) studied Japanese university students' attitudes towards English and English teachers in relation to the use of ELF. Galloway (2011) used questionnaires (120), interviews (20), and focus groups (48). The findings suggest that students believe English is a language belonging to native English speakers, students want to sound like native English speakers, that native English speakers are the target interlocutors, that native English is the most attractive, and that a native English accent is the same as being proficient in English, giving students confidence. There was an awareness of regional varieties of native English, but American English was the most familiar variety, seen as the 'standard' and 'boss' English. However, there was also an awareness of Global Englishes, and many discussed potential future ELF usage, feeling more comfortable speaking English with non-native English speakers and being aware of non-native English. Nevertheless, attitudes were largely negative towards non-native English, which is seen as 'imperfect' and 'wrong'. Students were also very critical of Japanese English.

In relation to ELT, the findings were similar: Students had positive attitudes towards native English and native English speakers; felt native English speakers were more useful for learning English; and wanted English teachers and ELT materials from the Inner Circle, since native English was seen to be more authentic. American English was, once again, the most-discussed variety. On the other hand, several students were interested in non-native English-speaking teachers, and Japanese teachers were seen as beneficial for teaching grammar, teaching in the students' first language, and for their experience as language learners. Once again, students noted that they are more comfortable with non-native English speakers. However, students' attitudes towards non-native English were largely negative, particularly with regards to ELT, and many negative comments related to pronunciation. However, the results of this study highlighted that a number of factors influence students' attitudes, including:

- students' images of English, including their beliefs about 'standard' English, their belief that native English is best for international communication, and that native English is the most spoken variety;
- students' familiarity with varieties of English, including their current use of English, the nationalities of their native English-speaking teachers, and the use of the native English-speaker model in their education system;
- students' experiences abroad and their experiences using ELF;
- their perceived future use of English;
- their ideas about identity as English users;
- their pedagogical beliefs about the way the language should be learned.

This study also investigated the influence of Global Englishes instruction on attitudes, which is discussed in the next chapter.

There have, therefore, only been a few studies conducted in the field that have investigated students' attitudes towards Global Englishes. The main conclusions to be drawn are that, while students continue to favour native English, more research is required to support proposals for Global Englishes, outlined in the next chapter. However, Galloway's (2011) study presented a thorough examination of attitude formation, particularly the influence of native English-speaker norms in ELT. It also investigated the possible influence of new approaches to ELT on attitudes towards English. With limited experience with and exposure to non-native English speakers, as well as a lack of awareness of the role of English today and the changing representations of speakers of the language, students are not making decisions based on the availability of sound information.

Chapter summary

This chapter has provided a detailed discussion on the nature of language attitudes and outlined the main studies that have been conducted. It has also shown that attitudes are not straightforward and are influenced by a number of factors including culture, familiarity, vitality and prestige, pedagogical context, race, proficiency, and motivation. Language attitudes are also subject to change, and there is a need for both short- and long-term studies. Research into the attitudes of learners towards the target language in the ELT context can provide teachers with an awareness of their learners' beliefs and help inform curriculum development. It can also increase self-awareness among the learners and foster autonomous learning. Furthermore, the findings of attitudinal research can help learners reflect on their own stereotypes.

Methodologically speaking, however, many of these studies have limitations and very few investigate the possible reasons for attitudes. Furthermore, these results should not be used as evidence for the continued dominance of native English and the native English speaker. Learners need more choice and 'the choice needs to be made in full knowledge of the sociolinguistic facts and without pressure from the dominant NS community' (Jenkins, 2006, p. 155). More studies are needed that discuss the possible influence that awareness raising of Global Englishes may have on students' attitudes. Chapter 9 builds on these studies, and it also introduces some studies that have investigated the influence of Global Englishes instruction on attitudes.

Further reading

Language and attitudes:

- Garrett, P. (2010). *Attitudes to Language: Key Topics in Sociolinguistics*. Cambridge: Cambridge University Press.
- Giles, H. and Billings, A. C. (2004). 'Assessing language attitudes: Speaker evaluation studies.' In A. Davies and C. Elder (eds), *The Handbook of Applied Linguistics*. Oxford: Blackwell.

Attitudes towards ELF:

- Jenkins, J. (2007). *English as a Lingua Franca: Attitude and Identity*. Oxford: Oxford University Press.

Closing activities

Chapter discussion questions

Section 8a

1 'Language attitudes represent important communicative phenomena worth understanding' (Cargile *et al.*, 2006, p. 443). Why are language attitudes important to study?
2 'Positive attitudes towards the target language group are linked with successful language learning' (Dörnyei *et al.*, 2006). Who is the 'target language group' for English learners in your context?
3 What languages and accents have high vitality and prestige in a context you are familiar with? Is there any evidence of attitudinal change? If so, what factors are contributing to this?

Section 8b

1 Matched guise studies require participants to evaluate audio-taped speakers on things like friendliness, intelligence, etc. What adjectives would you use to describe the English spoken in your region/country?
2 Adolphs' (2005) study suggested that many learners have a simplistic notion of the native English speaker, and familiarity led to more negative attitudes. Why do you think participants' attitudes became more negative?
3 If you were designing a language attitude study, what method would you use and why?

Section 8c

1 What is your opinion on Rubin's (1992) findings? Is race an important factor in understanding attitudes toward English?

2 Several studies have been conducted on attitudes towards English teachers. What skills do you think are important for an English teacher?

3 Kubota (2001) concluded that her study is evidence of the need for commencing education about cultural–linguistic diversity at earlier stages of life. How is English taught to young learners in a context you are familiar with? Do you think a more Global Englishes approach would be useful for such young learners?

Section 8d

1 In Jenkins' (2007) study, attitudes toward Swedish English suggest that people may have preconceived stereotypes about certain English varieties. What varieties are commonly believed to be more 'native like' than others?

2 Seidlhofer and Widdowson's (2003) participants were concerned with teaching and, specifically, with cultural aspects and pronunciation. Why do you think English teachers have such concerns?

3 Do you think that Timmis's (2002) findings support the use of the native English-speaker model?

Debate topics

1 In general, non-native English speakers should try to emulate standard varieties of English.

2 Just because ELF speakers are the majority doesn't mean it is acceptable. Research shows that students prefer native English.

3 Non-native English speakers would benefit from exposure to a wide variety of Englishes from the beginning of their language studies.

Writing and presentation prompts

Below are ideas for writing and presentation tasks to apply the knowledge learned in Chapter 8.

	Assignment topics
Personal account	Write about your own attitudes to English and discuss how they have changed over time. Discuss stereotypes you have about varieties of language, and evaluate why these exist.
Research task	Collect data from English-language learners on their attitudes to English. Write a short report analysing the findings of your research. Comment on how your data compares to that of the studies described in Chapter 8. (Please adapt the questions provided on the companion website.)
Basic academic	Friedrich (2000) notes that information on learners' own attitudes can raise awareness of their own stereotypes, prejudices, and expectations, as well as the linguistic features of the language. In a context you are familiar with, what stereotypes, prejudices, and expectations do you think students have about language? Why do they exist and what can be done to challenge them?
Advanced academic	In this chapter, the authors argue that a theory/practice divide appears to exist because ELF is often accepted in the abstract but rejected in the classroom. Write an essay that examines this paradox and explains why it exists.

Chapter 9

English language teaching

Introductory activities

The following introductory activities are designed to encourage the reader to think about the issues raised in this chapter before reading it.

The English language teacher

The box below shows two advertisements for English language teaching (ELT) jobs in Japan.

> ENGLISH TEACHER. Full-time, 40 working hours/week. Native English speaker required. '**University degree not required** if applicant has visa.'
>
> ENGLISH TEACHER. Full-time, 40 working hours/week. Follow an English language curriculum which contains detailed lesson plans for every class. Teaching experience preferred. 'Applicants from countries where English is not the native language must have a total of at least **10 years of education** from schools where English is the primary mode of education, including a **Bachelor's degree** from an English speaking country.'

Source: ohayosensei.com, February 2009

Discussion questions

1 What is your reaction to the job advertisements? Why do some institutions value the nativeness of a teacher's English over formal qualifications?
2 Think of English language teachers in a context you are familiar with.
   a What qualifications are needed to teach in this context?
   b Is there a divide between native English-speaking teachers and non-native English-speaking teachers? If so, why does this divide exist?
3 In what other ways does the English language teaching profession in non-native English-speaking countries promote a standard language ideology?

Case study: The value of 'native' in English language teachers

Pacek (2005) conducted a study in the UK with students at the University of Birmingham. The results show that, while a non-native English-speaking teacher is often the norm in the students' own countries (particularly in the Far East), they expect a native English-speaking teacher when studying in an English-speaking country. However, when these students were asked to rank the qualities they viewed as important to a teacher, the nativeness of the teacher's English did not rank as highly as other characteristics. Students viewed a teacher's sensitivity to their needs and problems as the most important characteristic, followed by clear explanations and pronunciation. Professional qualities were more important than nationality.

Discussion

1 Why do you think many students expect to be taught by a native English-speaking teacher when they go to study abroad?
2 Do you think sensitivity to students' needs and problems are qualities that only non-native English-speaking teachers have?
3 What are the most important qualities for an English teacher? If you were the manager of a language institution, what type of teacher would you employ?

Introduction

The internationalization of English has precipitated a need to understand the new global role of the language, and it is becoming increasingly clear that a critical evaluation of ELT practice worldwide is needed. This chapter examines ELT in relation to the globalization of English. Section 9a focuses on the dominance of the native English speaker. Section 9b focuses on the use of native English-speaking teachers, followed by a discussion on the diminishing importance of the native-English speaker in light of the internationalization of English. Section 9c further explores proposals suggested for change and the need for alternative approaches to ELT, particularly those that include greater emphasis on raising awareness of Global Englishes. This approach, termed a **Global Englishes language teaching** (GELT) approach, challenges the monolithic, static view of English and, although it is recognized that curriculum changes should not be made prematurely, it examines this approach in depth, based on the previous critical examination of ELT. This chapter concludes with Section 9d, which examines the various barriers to making changes to traditional ELT.

9a Striving to become a 'native' English speaker

Job advertisements like those in the introductory activity are common in the ELT profession, where the native English-speaker episteme prevails. All over the world, students learning English strive to imitate native English speakers, and it is clear from Chapter 8 that both teachers and students hold positive attitudes towards native English in relation to ELT. However, it is also clear from the chapters thus far that English has become a global language and such sociolinguistic changes in the use of English have led many to question the relevance of the traditional native English-speaker model in ELT. The issue of expecting near-native proficiency has been widely discussed in the last two decades, and many now believe that it is not necessary to sound like a native English speaker and that new goals are needed, particularly for those students who wish to use English in ELF contexts. This section explores the dominance of the native English-speaker episteme in ELT and also the various criticisms of this model.

The native English speaker

Traditionally, theories about language learning have typically posited the native English speaker as the goal and it has been used as a yardstick of competence for a long time all over the globe. As with 'many hegemonic practices, there has been a tendency to accept it without question' (Phillipson, 1992b, p. 15). The historic importance placed on the native English speaker, such as Chomsky's (1965) use of the expression 'native speaker' as the 'ideal speaker–listener', has resulted in the native English-speaker ideal remaining a central part of the ELT profession and, as Chapter 8 highlighted, this influences attitudes towards the language. Furthermore, even when the focus shifted from the Chomsky-inspired idea of 'linguistic competence' to Hymes' (1966) notion of 'communicative competence', the native English speaker continued to serve as the yardstick for comparison, even if that was not the original intention. The attitudinal loading of terms such as 'native' and 'non-native' appears to translate into a preference for native English and native English speakers in ELT, as evidenced in Chapter 8, and in the ELT industry the native English speaker's status as 'the uncrowned king of linguistics' (Mey, 1981, p. 73) is upheld.

Native English speakers dominate ELT materials and English-language examinations, discussed further in Section 9d and again in Chapter 10, and as Jenkins (2007, p. 48) states, 'NNS English countries emerge as places where NSs of English go to teach, NS countries as places that NNSs go to learn, and where experts and authoritative publications originate.' According to the British Council, the UK continues to attract over 600,000 international students every year who come 'to use the language in its natural home' (www.britishcouncil.org/learn_english_in_the_uk-2.pdf, accessed 2 January 2014). Universities claim to be offering an 'international' education yet this is questionable, considering the focus on native English norms. Students are required to pass tests that use the native English speaker as a yardstick, are often recommended to use native proofreaders for assignments, and are also encouraged to get accustomed to the Western style of education. In effect, these students are not receiving the advertised 'international' education but a native English-speaker-oriented education, a topic discussed fully in Chapter 10. The dominance of native English-speaker norms is also clear in ELT reference materials. Examples include:

- *The Cambridge Grammar of English* (Carter and McCarthy, 2006), which has 'error warning symbols';
- *The Oxford Advanced Learner's Dictionary*, which notes that, 'You cannot say "discuss about something"';
- *Practical English Usage*, which has a section called 'Don't say it', which outlines 130 common mistakes (Swan, 2005, pp. xxvi–xxix).

While some students may desire to learn native English (e.g. those who plan to go there to study/work), more awareness needs to be raised of the global uses of English today.

This book has highlighted the immense variation that exists, and Chapter 7 highlighted the increasing use of ELF.

Language attitudes mean that prejudice for native English speakers is also evident in hiring practices, as the introductory activity of this chapter shows. In countries such as Japan (where ELF usage is on the rise, as discussed in Chapter 6), obtaining a teaching position for a non-native English-speaking teacher is almost impossible, although, for a native English speaker, this requirement is also waived if the applicant already has a visa. As discussed in Chapter 8, these advertisements serve to perpetuate stereotypes that native English is 'correct' and that English should be learned from a native English speaker. Native English-speaking teachers still continue to be employed in large numbers in many countries, and Caucasian foreigners feature on the websites of popular English schools such as Aeon (www.aeonet.co.jp) and ECC (http://recruiting.ecc.co.jp/about/index.html), and the latter even has links on its recruitment page for people to apply directly from the USA, Canada, the UK, Australia, or New Zealand. Some examples of such employment bias around the world are shown in Figure 9.1. 'On a global level, the ELT profession is perhaps the world's only occupation in which the majority faces discrimination' (Ali, 2009, p. 37) and it is clear that, while non-standard accents may lead to the loss of jobs, as discussed in Chapter 8, beliefs in the existence of a standard form of English result in favouritism in the workplace towards native English speakers.

However, Chapter 8 also raised the importance of exploring attitudes and stereotypes in depth. As Cook (1999, p. 196) points out, 'this acceptance of the native speaker model does not mean these attitudes are right'. Attitudes, which often result in biased actions, are the consequence of a number of factors. Studies have shown that 72 per cent of administrators responsible for hiring teachers judge the 'native speaker criterion' to be either moderately or very important (Clark and Paran, 2007). Recruitment of native English speakers is often driven by economic factors: they are not necessarily employed because they are 'superior' teachers but because they attract students, 'fit' the stereotypical image of an English speaker, and therefore make money. However, accommodating such demands is questionable and it is uncertain how far students' preferences would be provided for if, for instance, they requested male or white teachers (Holliday, 2008). Race is clearly another important factor and, as highlighted in Chapter 8, the image of a native English speaker may not only be an Inner Circle speaker but a Caucasian Inner Circle speaker. The prevalence of native English-speaker norms is evidently complex, yet this complexity should not act as a deterrent for a critical examination of current ELT practice.

As introduced in Chapter 2 and discussed in Chapter 5, despite the spread of English and the use of ELF, indigenized 'new' varieties are still viewed as 'deficient' or 'fossilized' versions. It is native English that remains seen as the legitimate and 'correct' variety. This was raised again in the previous chapter, and Bamgbose's (1998) points are worth reiterating: that while native English-speaker language change is often seen as a sign of creativity and innovation, non-native English-speaker-led change is labelled as an error. The dominance of native English and the native English speaker is clearly related to the prevalence of standard language ideology in general, with serious implications for ELT.

However, the idealistic notion of the native English speaker has been called into question in recent years. This decline in importance of the native English speaker is evident in three main areas, as shown in Figure 9.2. Each of these will be discussed in the following paragraphs.

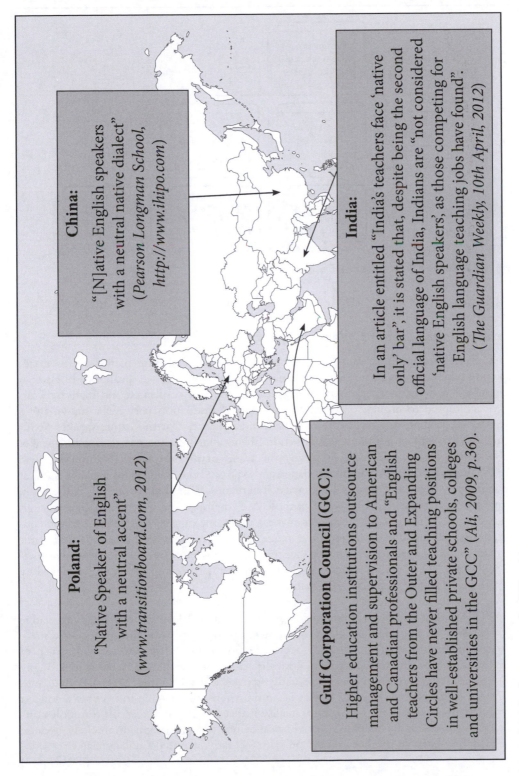

China:

"[N]ative English speakers with a neutral native dialect" (*Pearson Longman School, http://www.ihipo.com*)

Poland:

"Native Speaker of English with a neutral accent" (*www.transitionboard.com, 2012*)

India:

In an article entitled "India's teachers face 'native only' bar", it is stated that, despite being the second official language of India, Indians are "not considered 'native English speakers', as those competing for English language teaching jobs have found". (*The Guardian Weekly, 10th April, 2012*)

Gulf Corporation Council (GCC):

Higher education institutions outsource management and supervision to American and Canadian professionals and "English teachers from the Outer and Expanding Circles have never filled teaching positions in well-established private schools, colleges and universities in the GCC" (*Ali, 2009, p.36*).

Figure 9.1 Job advertisements for ELT positions

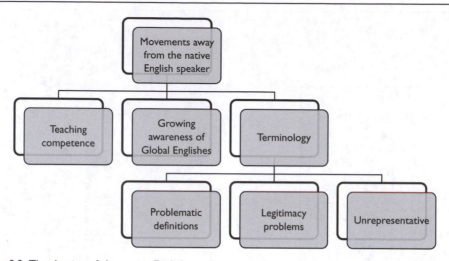

Figure 9.2 The demise of the native English speaker

Terminology

Problems defining the terms 'native' and 'non-native'

It is clear from the book thus far that the terms 'native' and 'non-native' are used frequently when discussing the English language, but who is a 'native' speaker of English? A substantial body of literature exists on what defines a native speaker, and many scholars have attempted to provide a workable and rational distinction between a native and a non-native English speaker. Paikeday (1985, p. 25) argues that the native speaker 'exists only as a figment of a linguist's imagination' in his attack on the native English speaker (*The Native Speaker is Dead!*), preferring the term **'proficient user'**. Rampton (1990, 1995) proposed that, in addition to language expertise, the concept of a native speaker includes language affiliation and language inheritance, although 'expertise' is the main criterion. Davies (2003, 2013) also proposed six defining features of a native speaker, including childhood acquisition, grammatical intuition, capacity for fluent spontaneous discourse, and creative communicative range. However, these are neither necessary nor present in all average native English speakers, hence his more recent use of 'native user' (Davies, 2013), and all but childhood acquisition of a native language can be achieved by non-native English speakers. As he states,

> The answer to the question of L2 [second language] learners evolving into native speakers of the target language must therefore be 'Yes': but the practice required, given the model of the child L1-acquirer who for five or six years spends much of his/her time learning language alone, is so great that it is not likely that many second-language learners become native speakers of their target language. The analogy that occurs to me here is that of music where it is possible to become a concert performer after a late start but the reality is that few do. It is difficult for adult non-native speakers to become a native speaker of a second language precisely because I define a native speaker as a person who has early acquired the language.
>
> (Davies, 2013, p. 4)

Thus, there is no exact definition of a native speaker to which everyone subscribes. If we cannot define a native speaker, then can we define a non-native speaker? The distinction is clearly blurred, even more so as it becomes increasingly difficult to categorize English speakers neatly, as discussed in Chapter 1. This is further complicated by the fact that many non-native English speakers are often mistaken for native English speakers by both interlocutors and students.

Legitimacy of the terms 'native' and 'non-native'

In addition to problems with definitions, use of the terms 'native' and 'non-native' has also been criticized for being judgemental, ascribing power to native English-speaking teachers while presenting the non-native English-speaking teachers as 'lacking' something (Holliday, 2005). It is clear from Chapter 8 that the recruitment of native English speakers for teaching positions and the use of native English speakers in ELT materials perpetuates the stereotype that this is right. However, the native English-speaker goal has been viewed as 'a skewed perspective' (Firth and Wagner, 1997), and this life-long apprenticeship for non-native English speakers (Tollefson, 1995) undoubtedly has negative effects on the confidence of non-native English-speaking teachers and hinders acquisition of the language. Therefore we may ask, is it right to label someone as a 'non' something? Cook (1999) refers to Labov's (1969) point that it is unfair to judge one group against the norm of another. People cannot be expected to conform to the norm of a group to which they do not belong, regardless of whether groups are defined by race, class, sex, or any other feature. Furthermore, it is clear from this book that it the native/non-native dichotomy is irrelevant, and people should not concern themselves with the differences. They may be different, yes, but this is irrelevant. ELF research, discussed in Chapter 7, for example, is showing the irrelevance of native-speaker norms today, and that there is no need for them to drop their own language and culture which should, in fact, be viewed as a valuable resource.

Unrepresentative

The terms 'native' and 'non-native' are also problematic because they imply homogeneity, and it is clear from Chapter 4 that most native English speakers do not speak a 'standardized' version and from Chapter 1 that monolingualism is no longer the norm. As discussed in Chapter 1, it is not so simple to categorize English speakers into the Inner, Outer, or Expanding circles. ELF research, discussed in Chapter 7, has also highlighted the increased use of English within and across these circles, and the relevance of the notion of a 'community of practice'. It is clear from Chapter 2 that it becomes problematic when we try to label English speakers based on their mother tongue. Once again, the division is not clear cut and 'the concepts "native speaker" and "mother tongue speaker" make little sense in multilingual societies, where it may be difficult to single out someone's mother tongue' (Kirkpatrick, 2007, p. 9).

Nevertheless, despite such criticisms, the terms 'native English speaker' and 'non-native English speaker' have become the reality, and the former continues to be used as a yardstick of competence in the language. These terms are commonly used and have been used in this book. However, the criticisms are acknowledged, and it is hoped that more importance will continue to be placed on multilingual users and that alternative terms will soon become the norm.

Teaching competence: native English-speaking teachers as the 'ideal' teacher

The suitability of the native English speaker as a norm has been questioned. Phillipson (1992a, p. 185) discussed the '**native speaker fallacy**', referring to the belief that native English speakers make the best teachers. Phillipson challenged this, stating that native speaker abilities could be acquired by non-native speakers, and that non-native speakers have first-hand experience learning the language, which is a beneficial attribute for teaching. As discussed in Chapter 8, Dörnyei and Csizér (2002) have also revisited the notion of integrative motivation, and it is clear that the target English-speaking community is now difficult to define.

Growing awareness of Global Englishes

The native English-speaker model has also been criticized in terms of its impossibility, and research carried out from the 1970s to the 1990s involving both native and non-native English speakers has demonstrated that native English accents are by no means the most intelligible to non-native ears (Jenkins, 2006). This was highlighted in Chapter 7. This realization is occurring not only at the academic level but also in real practice, with reports in *The Economist* and *Newsweek* about the problems native English speakers have when communicating in international business settings. The concept of 'Offshore English' was discussed in Section 7c, and it is clear that a market is emerging that recognizes that BELF training is not something that is only reserved for non-native English speakers.

As introduced in Chapter 7, the issue of expecting near-native proficiency has also been heavily discussed in relation to the World Englishes and ELF research paradigms. With the rise in the diversity of English speakers, as discussed in Chapter 1, it is becoming increasingly clear that new competencies are required to make English more relevant for ELF usage. The native English-speaker model fails to equip students for the real-world uses of English, at least for those who do not require English for native English-speaking contexts. As discussed in Chapter 3, many believe that English now belongs to all speakers of the language and thus the very notion of striving to become a native speaker is flawed because 'it is nobody's mother tongue' (Rajagopalan, 2004, p. 111). Leung and Street (2012, p. 88) point out that, 'The unquestioned assumption that the language norms and practices associated with native-speaker varieties should be regarded as automatically relevant and legitimate has been considerably lessened.' However, it is also clear from Chapter 8 and Section 9a that the arguments put forward by ELF researchers about the irrelevance of native English-speaker norms do not necessarily resonate in the ELT industry itself, in terms of student and teacher attitudes toward native English and the native English speaker. Since the emergence of World Englishes and ELF as fields of study, a number of proposals have been suggested for change in the ELT profession. This warrants detailed attention and thus an overview is given in the following section (Section 9b).

9b Global Englishes language teaching

With the changes in the use of English outlined in this book, there has been an increased interest in the pedagogical implications of the spread of English. There is growing literature on the topic, including:

- a large number of World Englishes, Global Englishes, and ELF book sections and chapters devoted to the topic of ELT (e.g. Jenkins, 2009; Kachru and Nelson, 2006; Kirkpatrick, 2007, 2010a, 2010c; Melchers and Shaw, 2011; Seidlhofer, 2011);
- entire books on the topic (e.g. Alsagoff *et al.*, 2012; Dogancay-Aktuna and Hardman, 2008; McKay, 2002; Matsuda, 2012a; Sharifian, 2009; Walker, 2010);
- ELF-related articles in language teaching journals (e.g. Baker, 2012; Cogo, 2012b; Jenkins, 2012; Jenkins *et al.*, 2011; Sowden, 2012; Suzuki, 2011; Kirkpatrick, 2011).

Several proposals have also been put forward for a change in ELT. We have grouped these into six key themes:

1 increasing World Englishes and ELF exposure in language curriculums;
2 emphasizing respect for multilingualism in ELT;
3 raising awareness of Global Englishes in ELT;
4 raising awareness of ELF strategies in language curriculums;
5 emphasizing respect for diverse cultures and identities in ELT;
6 changing English teacher hiring practices in the ELT industry.

These themes are examined in the following subsections.

Increasing World Englishes and ELF exposure in language curriculums

As this book has highlighted, World Englishes and ELF research has been instrumental in highlighting the diversity of English in use around the world, and has clear pedagogical implications. English learners will most likely use English with other non-native English speakers in ELF interactions. Thus, teaching learners that English conforms to a singular 'standard' will ill-prepare them to use the language. McKay (2012) argues that it is the responsibility of English language teachers to prepare learners to use English in these international contexts, with speakers who speak and use English very differently from prescribed standards. Exposing students 'to as many varieties of English as possible would do more to ensure intelligibility than trying to impose a single standard on everyone' (D'Souza, 1999, p. 273). Within the World Englishes paradigm, there are suggestions that students should be exposed to World Englishes and that these should be viewed as legitimate models of communication, and that such countries should utilize endormative nativized models as opposed to exonormative native-speaker models. To be able to communicate successfully with people all over the globe, students need to comprehend different varieties 'so that they are better prepared to deal with English interactions in international contexts' (McKay, 2012, p. 73).

However, classroom models are complex and we recognize that it is both impossible and unnecessary to expose students to all of the varieties of English in the world. Learners have differing needs in their respective communities of practice and a one-size-fits-all approach cannot meet the needs of all students in such diverse contexts. However, ELT classrooms should expose students to Englishes or ELF contexts that are salient to them, and thus analysis of learners' needs is essential. With regards to classroom models, Seargeant (2012, p. 66) discusses two sets of dichotomies: practical concerns and ideological concerns; and those relating to what happens in the classroom. He points out that American and British English varieties have been codified, and therefore reference texts already exist, whereas it will become clear in Section 9d that the lack of materials for incorporating Global Englishes into the classroom is problematic. With regards to ideological issues, he suggests that native English varieties also have prestige and legitimacy in many parts of the globe, which can lead to a motivation to learn them. It is clear from Chapter 8 that Inner Circle varieties of English have international currency, a factor which certainly influences their status and institutional support as well as attitudes towards them. It cannot, however, continue to be used as a reason for the ongoing dominance of the native English-speaker episteme.

Matsuda and Friedrich (2012) discuss three possible options: teaching a particular variety of English; using the speakers' own variety of English; or using an established variety of English while introducing other varieties as part of common classroom practice. However, as discussed in Section 7d, there is a slight misunderstanding of ELF research, suggesting that it attempts to establish a variety and a 'teachable' model, with established varieties said to be those that have been codified, which does not leave a lot of choice. Notwithstanding the problems with the notion of a 'variety' of English highlighted in Chapter 7, variety choice is also clearly problematic and the authors themselves point to the need for needs analysis. Autonomous approaches may be useful here, especially when students have diverse needs, allowing opportunity for students to tailor the curriculum to the Englishes and ELF contexts most salient to them. An example of such an approach is Galloway and Rose (2014), where students were encouraged to reflect on real-life ELF exchanges and exposure to different Englishes through the use of listening journals. Galloway and Rose (2013) was another attempt to provide students with indirect exposure to variation in English, with the use of international exchange students in business-content courses as classroom assistants to provide ELF opportunities for local students.

These proposals do not suggest abolishing all teaching practices centred on native English, but suggest that ELT practitioners re-examine their practice in relation to Global Englishes to ensure that they are meeting the needs of students today. It might be prudent in the case of many traditional EFL settings, for example, to follow a General American English model, such as would be the case with an English for academic purposes (EAP) preparatory course for study in North America, although many of these students may still find themselves in ELF situations with other international students. However, such a model might not serve the needs of students who are likely to go on to use it to converse with business counterparts, the majority of which is made up of ASEAN and Indian nationals.

Emphasizing respect for multilingualism in ELT

Another suggestion involves having more respect for multilingualism in the language classroom, which also includes a reconceptualization of English models and norms. Traditional ELT tends to view the students' first language as a hindrance and the cause of error transfer and interference. A Global Englishes approach to ELT views the first language as a resource and, 'It is important that we, as language educators, recognize this fact and work to preserve and promote all languages that an individual has access to' (McKay, 2012, p. 36). Chapter 7 has highlighted that, in international communication, transactions often occur bi- and multilingually, and it is often the monolingual English speaker that is at a disadvantage. Nevertheless, traditional approaches to ELT, modelled on the native English-speaker episteme, often take an 'English-only' policy, rejecting the opportunity to use other shared languages and placing the onus on the non-native speaker to conform to the needs of the monolingual native English speaker. This policy has also been furthered through the promotion and spread of communicative language teaching (CLT) as a popular ELT methodology. Kim and Elder (2009), for example, point out that in South Korea there is a Teaching English Through English (TETE) policy, which encourages an 'English-only' policy in the classroom, and there are numerous similar cases across the globe. A GELT approach includes more respect for the learners' first language in framing the curriculum, including an understanding that English learners' future interlocutors will rarely be the monolingual native English speaker. In this respect, code-switching and code-mixing may be the norm, and the use of one's first language is not viewed as a hindrance but rather as a useful resource.

McKay (2012) notes that learners need to be trained to make use of their multilingualism in advantageous ways. Recognizing the multilingual nature of ASEAN, as discussed in Chapters 5 and 6, Kirkpatrick (2012) proposes that English could be presented as an 'Asian' lingua franca, spoken by multilinguals, and that students be measured against the 'norms' of successful Asian multilinguals. He also suggests adapting the Common European Framework of Reference (CEFR) to Asian contexts, since at present it does not distinguish between English and other foreign languages and uses the native English speaker as a benchmark. As Friedrich (2012, p. 50) points out, 'If the only constant in lingua franca situations is diversity, then we should anchor our practices in that assumption and educate students to encounter such diversity with respect, curiosity and wisdom.' Learners need to be trained to make use of their multilingualism as **'multicompetent language users'** (Cook, 1999, p. 190). Unlike an EFL classroom, where the goal is to imitate native English speakers, those likely to use ELF in their future should be encouraged to see themselves as successful, multilingual speakers, discarding native English-speaker benchmarks and having confidence in their own strength as multicompetent language users. Multicompetence, then, is favoured over native-like competence.

Raising awareness of Global Englishes in ELT

A further proposal involves the direct teaching of issues surrounding Global Englishes in order to raise learners' awareness of the global spread of and use of English, and to encourage them to think critically about the language. With the increase in content and language integrated learning around the world, Global Englishes-related subject matter can become the object of learning itself. As discussed in the next section, for example, studies (Galloway, 2011, 2013) reveal that Global Englishes instruction can raise students' awareness of how they will most likely use English in the future and increase their confidence as speakers of an international language. Of course, not all teachers have the luxury of being able to create a Global Englishes course, in which case content can be integrated in more creative ways, as in the aforementioned study by Galloway and Rose (2013) where it was incorporated into existing class materials in an English for academic purposes programme.

Raising awareness of ELF strategies in language curriculums

Both World Englishes and ELF research have been instrumental in raising our awareness of how English is used globally, and such research has implications for ELT benchmarks of competence. In ELF, emphasis is on successful communication and negotiation of meaning across communities of practice. Students need to acquire various strategies to help them '**shuttle between communities**' (Canagarajah, 2005, p. xxv), and between the local and the global, where a variety of norms and a repertoire of codes are to be expected. This advocates a move away from native English-speaker expertise to a focus on multilingual and multicultural – or translingual and transcultural if you prefer – communicative practices, and on negotiation and communicative strategies. In fact, Seidlhofer (2004) has proposed language awareness classes which would focus on the fluid nature of ELF. It has also been suggested that learners learn to develop interaction strategies (McKay, 2002) and be exposed to ELF interactions in order to raise their awareness of how ELF is used (House, 2012). However, House also points out that they would need appropriate meta-language (language to talk about language) in order to do this, so an introduction to interaction and intercultural pragmatics may also be needed. Such awareness of successful strategy usage, however, does not exclude native English speakers and, as highlighted in Section 7c, many BELF researchers also highlight the need for native English speakers to undertake some training.

The centrality of communication strategies to a Global Englishes approach to ELT is not out of sync with current literature in the field of TESOL, in which communication is a core focus. For example, **strategic competence** and communication strategies are central to the concept of communicative language teaching, albeit with reference to native English-speaker norms. If communication and the teaching of strategies such as those outlined above are further integrated into ELT classroom practices, it will better equip students to negotiate meaning when using English in international contexts.

Emphasizing respect for diverse cultures and identities in ELT

Many ELT materials and curriculums are built on notions that students are engaged in English language learning in order to participate in a foreign culture. Reference to culture is prevalent in textbooks, where the EFL user is usually depicted as a novice first language learner and the interlocutor is depicted as an Anglo-Saxon native English speaker. The goal of learning is usually depicted as a means to join the native English-speaking language culture, as outlined in the quote from the British Council in Section 9a that students come to the UK 'to use the language in its natural home'. However, as discussed in Chapter 7, recent research into culture and identity in ELF communication has illustrated that culture is a fluid concept, and that culture emerges from communities of practice and changes as speakers join and depart the community or as the community evolves. This highlights the need to move away from monocultural and monolingual norms, and the need to 'look at the communicative practices of multilingual and multicultural speakers to understand ELF communication' (Baker, 2012, p. 46). Chapter 10 sheds further light on this increased hybridity in communication around the world, where cultures are hybrid, diffuse, and de-territorialized (Canagarajah, 2005). The importance of developing students' **intercultural competence** has been stressed and this is a subject area that is rapidly growing in prominence, with House (2012, p. 200) suggesting that a pragmatics-oriented approach be given preference in order to heighten 'linguistic and cultural awareness'. Of course, knowledge of specific cultures may still be important but it is essential that it is framed in the diverse intercultural interactions that learners will encounter, and also to combine this with raising learners' awareness that culture in intercultural communication is a fluid and emergent concept. Accordingly, needs analysis is crucial.

Changing English teacher hiring practices in the ELT industry

A final proposal is a change in hiring policies within the ELT industry. Calls for the employment of more non-native English-speaking teachers are not new and many native English-speaking teachers' qualifications have been under scrutiny for many years. Changes to the sociolinguistic use of English have led many to question how far 'foreign' expertise and methods are exportable to different cultures, and since the early 1990s there has been an ever-increasing importance attached to non-native English-speaking teachers with their merits having been well documented (Braine, 1999, 2010; Cook, 1999; Medgyes, 1994, 2001; Thomas, 1999). These merits often include good teaching qualifications, English learning experience, knowledge of students' first language and cultural backgrounds, experience as an English language learner, knowledge of students' needs, and shared expectations of teacher/student roles in the classroom. However, it should not be forgotten that many native English-speaking teachers also possess these qualities. Both groups of teachers have benefits and contribute something to the classroom, as evidenced in Chapter 8. Nevertheless, with further changes in the global use of English, proposals for changes in hiring practices have gathered momentum in recent years.

As McKay (2012) argues, there is a need to re-examine the concept of qualified teachers. A non-native English-speaking teacher of a different first language, where English plays the role of a true lingua franca in the classroom, might have a lot to offer learners. Indeed, Kirkpatrick (2009, 2012) calls for an increase in the hiring of **multilingual English teachers** (METs), especially in multilingual societies such as ASEAN. It is clear from Chapter 7 that, to prepare students for future ELF usage, a teacher should be able to develop students' intercultural communicative skills and a multilingual teacher may be better able to do this. ELF researchers have also argued that competent ELF users serve as better role models than the traditional native English speaker. Such proposals do not exclude the native English speaker but place more value on expertise in using ELF.

However, hiring practices continue to favour the native English speaker, as pointed out in Section 9a. It is also clear from Chapter 8 that stereotypes and standard language ideology influence attitudes towards native English. It is vital that advertisements use more representative images of English speakers. Section 9a also highlighted the difficulty in defining a native speaker, and such advertisements may also benefit from changed terminology including 'expert' or 'global' user of English. However, whether we call them **'expert ELF users'**, 'expert users', or 'multilingual English teachers', it is suggested that students be informed and engage critically with the notion that monolinguals from a minority group of English users do not necessarily make the best English teachers. There is already a large talent pool and about 80 per cent of the English teachers worldwide are non-native English-speaking teachers (Braine, 2010, p. x). Two 'position statements' by the International Association Teachers of English to Speakers of Other Languages (TESOL, 1992, 2006), opposing employment discrimination based on the native/non-native distinction, suggest that things are changing and the TESOL organization's Non-Native

English Speakers in TESOL Interest Section (see http://nnest.asu.edu/), which stemmed from a caucus started in 1998, shows increasing attention to these issues at the scholarly level. 'However, the tenet that the ideal teacher is the native speaker remains resilient, even in multilingual settings, where the major role of English is as a lingua franca' (Kirkpatrick, 2012, p. 133).

Summary of proposals

The arguments put forward here reflect a very different concept to traditional ELT. The proposed changes are summarized in Table 9.1, where traditional ELT is contrasted with GELT, a more Global Englishes approach to language teaching. GELT focuses on diversity and the function of English as an international lingua franca, rather than traditional approaches to ELT which aim to teach people to speak with native English speakers. A GELT approach acknowledges that the 'owners' are ELF users and the target interlocutors are other ELF speakers, as well as native English speakers. As a reflection of this, a GELT approach would promote the recruitment of teachers from around the world, with a focus on multilinguals with ELF experience rather than monolinguals with no ELF experience. Likewise, 'norms' would centre on diversity and flexibility, and on the development of strategies to interact with people from many different backgrounds. Similar to Canagarajah's (2005) description of shifts in pedagogical practice, the GELT model would view a learner's first language and own culture as a resource, and not a hindrance or object of interference in the learning of the second language. GELT would also need to be represented in the materials used in classes, which should focus on Global Englishes as opposed to the English used by native English speakers.

The movement from ELT to GELT requires the **epistemic break** (Foucault, 1970, 1972) that was called for by Kumaravadivelu (2012, p. 14), who defined it as a 'thorough

Table 9.1 Differences between ELT and GELT

	ELT	GELT
Target interlocutor	Native English speakers	Native English speakers and non-native English speakers
Owners	Native English speakers	Native English speakers and non-native English speakers
Target culture	Fixed native English culture	Fluid cultures
Teachers	Non-native English-speaking teachers (same first language) and native English-speaking teachers	Non-native English-speaking teachers (same and different first language), native English-speaking teachers
Norms	Native English and concept of standard English	Diversity, flexibility, and multiple forms of competence
Role model	Native English speakers	Successful ELF users
Materials	Native English and native English speakers	Native English, non-native English, ELF, and ELF communities and contexts
First language and own culture	Seen as a hindrance and source of interference	Seen as a resource
Ideology	Underpinned by an exclusive and ethnocentric view of English	Underpinned by an inclusive Global Englishes perspective

reconceptualization and a thorough re-organization of knowledge systems'. An epistemic break occurs when new epistemological orientations appear with a considerable degree of regularity and is different to a **paradigm shift** (Kuhn, 1962), which is confined to scientific-world views and practices. Kachru (1992b, p. 250) called for a 'paradigm shift', given that World Englishes requires such a thing. However, as pointed out by Kumaravadivelu (2012, p. 15), a paradigm shift would require a 'near total replacement of one paradigm with another', and it might have been better for Kachru to call for an epistemic break. Native English has been an enduring episteme in ELT for many years, despite the problems in defining both a native English speaker and native English competence, as pointed out in Section 9a. Kumaravadivelu notes that,

> the native-speaker episteme has not loosened its grip over theoretical principles, classroom practices, the publication industry or the job market. What is surely and sorely needed is a meaningful break from this epistemic dependency, if we are serious about sanitizing our discipline from its corrosive effect and sensitizing the field to the demands of globalism and its impact on identity formation. How and where do we start?
>
> (Kumaravadivelu, 2012, p. 15)

This epistemic break, then, requires a shift in materials design, views on ownership, cultures, norms, and role models, as well as a change in those who teach English. However, this approach does not necessarily mean that teaching methods have to be changed, rather that the assumptions about the English language are changed and permeate into ELT materials, language assessment, cultural ideology, language ideology, and recruitment practices. In addition, such proposals are not suggesting 'that we abolish all teaching of discrete linguistic items, nor that we ignore the pull that nativeness still has over learners and users' (Friedrich, 2012, p. 50). Instead, it simply involves a re-examination of current ELT practices in light of the changes in the use of English highlighted in this book thus far.

9c Studies on attitudes towards English teachers and the influence of Global Englishes instruction

A number of research studies have been conducted on attitudes towards English teachers and the influence of Global Englishes instruction. These are discussed in turn below.

Attitudes towards teachers of English

There is a body of research on the respective capacities of non-native English-speaking teachers and native English-speaking teachers and attitudes towards them. These are examined below.

Studies that involve attitudes when non-native English-speaking teachers share the same first language

Barratt and Kontra's (2000) studies in Hungary (116 students and 58 teachers) and China (100 students and 54 teachers) required students to free-write about their experiences with native English speaking teachers. Almost identical factors were pinpointed in favour of and against native English-speaking teachers, including authenticity as the most valuable characteristic, along with pronunciation, a wide vocabulary, and cultural information, although the native English-speaking teachers were not noted to be keen on grammar, and lack the linguistic and cultural awareness that non-native English-speaking teachers have.

Similar results were yielded from questionnaires in Benke and Medgyes's (2005) study in Hungary of 422 students, where the advantages of non-native English-speaking teachers were given as exam preparation, grammar explanations, and a familiarity with the students' background. The advantages of native English-speaking teachers were seen as speaking skills, cultural information, friendliness, and good pronunciation. However, this survey also elicited preferences and nationality was compared with level of professionalism. Non-native English-speaking teachers were seen as helpful for beginners and native English-speaking teachers for more advanced students, although it should be pointed out that this is assuming that native English is the goal. Over 50 per cent of the students in the study thought that ability to teach was more important than nationality, and only 22.3 per cent would be happy to trade a non-native English-speaking teacher for a native English-speaking one, although students' definition of 'ability to teach' is unclear. Hence, while native English-speaking teachers are often recruited to satisfy student demand, this study highlights that many students actually prefer teaching ability over nationality.

Preference for a native English-speaking teacher was also related to higher proficiency in Lasagabaster and Sierra's (2005) study, which utilized open and closed questionnaires with 76 undergraduate students from the University of the Basque Country. There was a clear preference for a native English-speaking teacher in the areas of pronunciation (81.5 per cent), culture and civilisation (71.1 per cent), and speaking (64.5 per cent), although vocabulary only yielded 46 per cent and listening 44.7 per cent. The open-ended results also revealed 46 positive statements for native English-speaking teachers compared with 29 for non-native English-speaking teachers. However, these results must be treated carefully because some of the attitudinal statements were somewhat vague. For example, 'I would have more positive attitudes towards English speaking countries and their speakers if I had a native teacher' does not clarify what an 'English speaking country' is. The open-ended part also simply asked students to list the pros and cons of both types of teachers, and students were not given the opportunity to expand on their answers in interviews.

Catalan non-native English-speaking teachers also preferred native English-speaking teachers in Llurda and Huguet's (2003) study, when they were asked how many non-native English-speaking teachers and native English-speaking teachers they would hire if they owned a language school. In addition, Cook's (2005) survey of younger students (aged 14 on average) and adults in six countries revealed that 72 per cent of children in England, 33 per cent of children in Belgium, 82 per cent of adults in England, and 51 per cent of adults in Taiwan preferred a native English-speaking teacher. Thus, in this study there was not an overwhelming preference for native English-speaking teachers with the exception of in England, where English was being learned in an Inner Circle country. With regards to non-native English-speaking teachers, who once again are lumped into one group, students noted that they provide a good model of a language learner, and often have more appropriate training and background, although they have worse fluency. 'Fluency', however, is not defined. Nevertheless, it should be remembered that native English-speaking teachers and non-native English-speaking teachers are often employed to do very different jobs, the former often being employed to teach oral skills.

Studies that involve attitudes toward non-native English-speaking teachers with a different first language

The majority of studies have grouped non-native English-speaking teachers together and provide no information on students' attitudes towards non-native English-speaking teachers from different countries, where the often-stated benefits of a shared first language are unlikely to hold strong. Moussu and Llurda (2008) point out the importance of recognizing that non-native English-speaking teachers are not one single group, and that their approaches may differ depending on the level they are teaching, their English proficiency, and their teaching style. It is also clear that researchers should consider the fact that many non-native English-speaking teachers teach in countries other than their own. Given the number of studies that have compared attitudes towards native and non-native English speakers, it is surprising that very few studies have extended this comparison to the language classroom.

Kirsty Liang's 2002 investigation of students' attitudes towards non-native English-speaking teachers at California State University (cited in Braine, 2005, 2010) involved the opinions of 20 ESL students towards six ESL teachers (five non-native English speakers from different language backgrounds and one native English speaker) after listening to audio recordings. Although the students rated pronunciation/accent as very important, this did not affect their attitudes towards their previous non-native English-speaking teachers in their home countries, about whom they held positive attitudes. Thus, while it was not discussed in this study, there is a possibility that students have different opinions towards non-native English-speaking teachers of nationalities other than their own, and that other factors, such as a shared first language and culture, may be important when choosing an English teacher. This study also suggests the influence of familiarity on accent, which was discussed in Chapter 8, and it would be interesting to replicate the study after students had been exposed to more non-native English speech. Furthermore, personal and professional features derived from the teachers' speech, such as 'being interesting', 'being prepared', 'being qualified', and 'being professional', played a role in the students' preference for teachers, although it is difficult to determine how far students can judge these aspects of a teacher's professionalism based on taped recordings.

A further US-based study by Mahboob (2004) elicited written responses from 32 students with diverse language backgrounds and varying proficiency levels who were enrolled on an intensive English programme. Opinion essays on native English-speaking teachers and non-native English-speaking teachers were coded by four readers. Results were similar to previous studies. Both received positive and negative comments related to oral skills. Positive comments about native English-speaking teachers related to vocabulary and culture, and negative comments related to grammar, experience as an ESL learner, ability to answer questions, etc. Non-native English-speaking teachers, on the other hand, were positively evaluated with regards to things like experience as learners, knowledge of grammar, etc., while negative comments related to oral skills and culture, although it is unclear whose 'culture' the author is referring to.

The ideal English teacher

In addition to simply comparing the attributes of both types of teachers, several studies have investigated students' opinions of what makes a good language teacher. Once more, while students may appear to favour native English and native English speakers, it is important to remember the important role that the dominance of native English ideology plays in the formation of such perceptions, as discussed in Chapter 8.

Pacek's (2005) UK-based study used informal interviews with students at the University of Birmingham, who studied with a non-native English-speaking teacher from an Eastern European country with 20 years' experience teaching English, linguistics, and ELT methodology. Two questionnaires were sent out, one week apart to make them seem unconnected, to two groups of students: those taking a vocabulary class (n = 43; n = 38) and those taking a teacher training course for Japanese teachers (n = 68; n = 46). The results show that, while a non-native English-speaking teacher is often the norm in students' own countries (particularly in the Far East), they expect a native English-speaking teacher when studying in an English-speaking country, highlighting the influence of pedagogical beliefs on attitudes, as discussed in the previous chapter. However, students see sensitivity to their needs and problems as the most important characteristic of a foreign-language teacher, followed by clear explanations and pronunciation. Gender and age do not appear to be important, which is interesting, considering many institutions in places like Japan advertise for 'young' native English-speaking teachers. In this study, teachers' professional qualities were more important than nationality, although this study only involved one non-native English-speaking teacher and there is a possibility that comments may have been teacher-specific.

In Hong Kong, Cheung (2002, cited in Braine, 2005, 2010) used questionnaires (n = 420) and interviews (n = 10) with students, and classroom observations. The opinions of 22 teachers, 60 per cent of whom were native-English speaking teachers, were also sought. A high proficiency in English, the ability to use English functionally, and awareness of the cultures of English-speaking countries were noted as native English-speaking teachers' strengths. In this study, for non-native English-speaking teachers, empathy as a second language learner, a shared cultural background, and a grammar focus were noted as strengths. However, Cheung also elicited important teacher qualities, and both groups referred to knowledge of English, ability to design relevant and enjoyable lessons and motivate students, and sensitivity to their needs. However, this study reveals little about what they actually prefer.

In Galloway and Rose (2013), Japanese university students in a bilingual business programme rated the qualities they viewed as important in a language teaching assistant. Qualities such as having 'knowledge of the content area', being 'approachable', and having the 'ability to explain concepts clearly' were rated much higher than those linked with native-speaker norms, such as 'pronunciation' and 'grammatical accuracy of speech'. The ELF-oriented opinions of these students toward their teachers cannot fully be attributed to the ELF-oriented curriculum. However, focus groups with these lecturers and teaching assistants indicated that the curriculum and the existence of expert ELF users as role models in the programme played a large role in attitude formation.

Despite not being covered in this book due to space constraints, language planners, curriculum developers, and educators alike can learn a lot from the various studies that have concentrated on the self-perceptions of teachers (e.g. Árva and Medgyes, 2000; Medgyes, 1992; Reves and Medgyes, 1994; Samimy and Brutt-Griffler, 1999) due to the influence this has on teaching.

Conclusion of studies

Studies that have examined attitudes toward native English-speaking teachers and non-native English-speaking teachers have yielded varied results. Nevertheless, they indicate a trend that students do not focus on the nativeness of their teachers as much as literature and societal beliefs may suggest. In the ELT industry, there is an ideology that students are drawn toward the native English speaker, which manifests in teacher recruitment of native English speakers over non-native English speakers and the perpetuation of native English speaker norms in ELT teaching materials and assessment. However, these perceived attitudes are not supported by research, which overwhelmingly indicates that students rank the personal and professional qualities of a teacher over the nativeness of their English language proficiency. Such studies provide a huge platform for change in the ELT industry in terms of movements toward GELT. In fact, some studies have also directly investigated the influence of Global Englishes instruction on students' attitudes, and these are discussed next.

The influence on language attitudes of Global Englishes instruction

Research on GELT, and the influence of such instruction on attitudes, is scarce. However, a few notable studies are discussed here.

South Korea

In South Korea, Shim (2002) investigated the attitudes of both teachers (24 enrolled on a TESOL Masters degree in Seoul) and students learning about World Englishes, through surveys and interviews from 1995 to 2000. The first, in 1995, involved 57 intermediate level students, who listened to tape recordings of five different female native English-speaking teachers and non-native English-speaking teachers reading portions of *Cinderella*. The majority favoured American English as the teaching model, 49 per cent wanted Australian English, and no-one wanted to learn Pakistani or Korean English. The study was repeated two years later with 24 TESOL graduate students who were reported to be familiar with World Englishes theories and Kachru's model, although no further information is given. Out of these participants, 22 preferred American English and only two stated that 'ideally' South Koreans should be exposed to other varieties, although it is 'practically impossible'. Shim conducted a third study in 1998, after World Englishes exposure through TV (a programme called *Crossroads Café*), and, of the 27 in the researcher's own class, 23 wanted an internationally accepted teaching model (although this is not explained), 27 felt a need to understand non-native English speakers, and all 27 would be willing to participate in an ELT programme that introduced non-native English speakers. While there is a clear change in attitudes, Shim fails to discuss the influence that he, as both researcher and teacher, may have had, and gives little account of the content of the course and the students' backgrounds, motivations, and goals. The last group of students may simply have had more positive experiences with non-native English speakers, more experience using English as a lingua franca, or different goals for their future use of the language.

Canada

Derwing *et al.*'s (2002) study involved native English speaker respondents' attitudes towards the comprehension of foreign-accented Vietnamese English before and after a period of cross-cultural awareness training and explicit linguistic instruction, which lasted for eight weeks. Attitude questionnaires conducted with full-time first-year Canadian social work students indicated increased empathy for immigrants. However, those who learned about Vietnamese accented English showed improved confidence that they could communicate with non-native English speakers, highlighting the need for Global Englishes programmes to better prepare students. It also shows the importance of familiarity and brings attention to the fact that it is not only non-native English speakers that need training.

The USA

Kubota's (2001) study investigated the change in attitudes of 17 US high school native English speakers taking a course in World Englishes, which included eight lessons focusing on the varieties of English used in the USA and worldwide, the history of English, the difficulty of acquiring native English-speaker proficiency, ways to communicate with World English speakers, and an investigation of the implications of the spread of English. The questionnaire asked about speech samples (six US-based speakers from Australia, China, India, Ecuador, Nigeria, and France who spoke about education in their home country for one minute), and classroom observations and interviews were also held. However, only some of the students showed positive reactions, and some biased views towards non-native English speakers were reinforced. Kubota concludes that this indicates a need to start education about cultural linguistic diversity at earlier stages of life (Kubota, 2001).

Japan

As discussed in Chapter 8, two studies conducted by Galloway (2011, 2013) investigated the influence of Global Englishes instruction. In both studies the students were split into an experimental group and a control group, the experimental group receiving 13 weeks of Global Englishes instruction twice a week and the control group receiving traditional content-based lessons on the topic of tourism. The Global Englishes course included raising students' awareness of Global Englishes and also exposing them to the diversity of English through weekly listening journals, classroom debates, and weekly readings on the topic. The aim was to bridge the gap between theory and practice and to examine how to address the various proposals for change that have been put forward in the literature, as discussed in Section 9b. A pre- and post-course questionnaire was administered to measure attitudinal change. Interviews and focus groups were also conducted at the end of the course in Galloway (2011), and interviews were used in Galloway (2013). Both studies demonstrated that Global Englishes instruction clearly influenced students' attitudes in a number of ways, including their motivation for learning English, attitudes towards varieties of English, and attitudes towards English teachers. It encouraged them to question notions of 'standard' English, was helpful for future ELF communication, and raised their confidence as English speakers. In sum, it was concluded that the findings provide an empirical basis for a re-evaluation of ELT and suggest that GELT is something that should be further investigated.

In a more recent attempt to apply theory to practice and address the proposals discussed in Section 9b in an Expanding Circle context, Galloway and Rose (2013) redesigned the academic English element in an English-medium bilingual business degree programme to include a Global Englishes focus. Students not only engaged in a four-week module on ELF, but the school also actively sought good ELF role models in the hiring of non-native English-speaking business lecturers, language teaching assistants, and guest speakers. As noted, while it was difficult to attribute the ELF-oriented opinions of these students toward their teachers to the ELF-oriented curriculum, focus groups with these lecturers and teaching assistants indicated that the curriculum, and the existence of expert ELF users as role models in the programme, played a large role in shaping the opinions of the students in the programme. The students adopted a global perspective of language in later years, often displaying a more ELF-oriented view of English use than even their language and business-content teachers.

Galloway and Rose (2014) conducted a further study to re-assess this gap, which investigated ways of making the curriculum salient to the needs of the students. In this study, listening journals were introduced into an English curriculum as both a pedagogical and research tool in order to raise student awareness of the diversity of English and to encourage ELF usage and reflection. The study analysed 108 listening journals, consisting of 1,092 reflections on ELF usage or exposure to speakers from different countries. The results highlighted students' current use of English, the impetus behind the selection of material for the listening journal, and their reflections on this exposure. The results highlight a benefit in using listening journals to raise awareness of Global Englishes but also highlight the limitations, including the reinforcement of stereotypes for some students and a tendency for students to reflect more on attitudes toward Englishes, rather than the development of an awareness of the specific features of successful ELF communication.

9d Barriers to innovations in English language teaching

Despite calls for an epistemic break as outlined in Section 9b, it may not be easy for ELT practitioners to implement. As Chapter 8 highlighted, there appears to be a theory/practice divide in terms of current teaching practices and 'the volume of such academic attention does not seem to have had a tangible impact on actual classroom reality' (Saraceni, 2009, p. 177). GELT may be a very foreign concept to teachers in some parts of the world, and it is unsurprising that many have ambivalent attitudes towards the kind of change outlined in Section 9c. This section explores five possible barriers to innovation in ELT that have caused this theory/practice divide:

1 lack of materials;
2 language assessment;
3 teacher education;
4 attachment to 'standard' English;
5 teacher recruitment practices.

Lack of materials

As Matsuda (2012b, p. 169) notes, few teachers,

> have a rich enough knowledge of and personal experience with all of the varieties and functions of Englishes that exist today, and, thus, they need to rely on

teaching materials in order to introduce students to the linguistic and cultural diversity of English.

It is clear from Chapter 8 that the lack of materials influences teachers' reluctance to change. Some ground has been gained in recent years and the ELT industry has seen the inclusion of sections on the global spread of English in teacher training manuals. For example:

- Harmer (2007) has a section on World Englishes in the opening chapter, although there is only a brief mention of ELF, which is introduced as a 'newly-observed phenomenon' (Harmer, 2007, p. 10);
- the recent English course book series *Global Textbook* has excerpts from David Crystal, and audio material called 'Global Voices', but the course book continues to focus on native English-speaker norms.

This may indicate that the ELT publishing industry is beginning to make slow headway into bridging the theory/practice divide, yet the majority continue to focus on native English-speaker norms. Nevertheless, recent years have seen the publication of a number of books that introduce students to the history of English, the sociolinguistic uses of the language, and descriptions of different varieties and the issues surrounding them, as was shown in Table 7.2. However, as the table shows, only four of these texts include audio material, they are aimed at a relatively advanced audience, several have limited coverage of ELF, and very few include practical activities. Further points include:

- Kirkpatrick's (2007) accompanying CD includes 31 tracks on Inner Circle usage (seven speakers), 16 tracks on Outer Circle usage (ten speakers), and four ELF exchanges, although these ELF encounters do not include native English speakers;
- Melchers and Shaw (2011) includes 17 speakers in total, including 11 Inner Circle, three Outer Circle, and two (perhaps three) Expanding Circle speakers;
- Jenkins (2009) includes discussion questions and activities, but may be challenging for lower level students – nevertheless, this book has been instrumental in facilitating the incorporation of Global Englishes into classrooms worldwide;
- Alsagoff *et al.* (2012) is another useful resource which includes many chapters that include example syllabi from an EIL perspective and the chapter (Matsuda, 2012) on evaluating teaching materials with an EIL focus is useful, but few practical suggestions are made;
- despite its aim 'to guide critical and informed practice and reflection in teaching' in relation to EIL, Alsagoff *et al.* (2012a), which covers topics such as curriculum, assessment, learning strategies, etc., does not provide teachers with any practical suggestions for incorporating a Global Englishes perspective in their classroom and it is overly theoretical.

Overall, materials are scarce. Until the publication of more materials, Kirkpatrick (2007, p. 195) points out that English language teachers who wish to work in Outer and Expanding Circle countries should 'be able to evaluate ELT materials critically to ensure that tests do not, either explicitly or implicitly, promote a particular variety of English or culture at the expense of others'. Questions such as those shown in the box, for example, may be useful when conducting such an evaluation.

Questions teachers should ask when evaluating textbooks

Models

- Which variety/varieties of English or ELF communities of practice are my students familiar with (and why)? Which of these are relevant to my students and which are included in our classroom materials?
- What image of English is portrayed in these materials?

Culture

- What foreign cultures are my students familiar with (and why)? Which are relevant to my students and which are included in our classroom materials?
- Is there any consideration of the role of culture in ELF communication, and how can I provide ways for students to practice mediating and negotiating culture in ELF contexts?
- Does the book raise awareness of Global Englishes (e.g. diversity/global use of English)?
- Does the book help prepare my students to use ELF in the future?

Language assessment

Language testing represents another barrier to these suggestions for an epistemic break, due to the popularity of tests such as Test of English for International Communication (TOEIC), TOEFL, IELTS, and the Certificate of Proficiency in English (CPE). Proficiency scales and language tests use native English and native-like proficiency as yardsticks for assessing non-native English, despite its irrelevance for many test-takers. Two examples follow.

- On their website, Pearson (www.pearsonpte.com) note that 'the ability to communicate effectively in English is crucial to international success', suggesting that communicative success, not native English-speaker proficiency, is important, yet in their scoring guide the Pearson Test of English General scores are related to the CEFR, which focuses on native English-speaker norms. Measuring students on their ability to use 'assimilations and deletions comparable to native-like speech' or the ability to make 'regular interaction with native speakers quite possible without strain for either party' is clearly inappropriate.
- Large-scale tests like TOEFL and IELTS that continue to require students to defer to native English-speaker academic norms.

These large-scale proficiency tests have huge consequences for English language learners and users, and 'the fundamentally changed landscape of EIL requires a critical examination of the established assessment practices' (Hu, 2012, p. 123). Some proposals for change include the following.

- Despite a lack of practical suggestions, Hu (2012) points out that linguistic norms for a test should be determined according to its intended use and that a 'standard variety' is acceptable if more than one variety is adequate for the intended use in a society. This is a valid point since the native English speaker is sometimes the intended audience. He also advocates that candidates be exposed to multiple native and non-native varieties of English, that the construct of EIL tests should incorporate intercultural strategic competence, and that allowances should be made for individual aspirations to Inner Circle norms.

- Canagarajah (2007) notes the importance of measuring the ability to employ strategies for interpreting the behaviours and expectations of English users from various backgrounds, given the heterogeneous nature of norms today. Thus there should be a move away from tests of formal grammatical competence to tests that 'focus on one's strategies of negotiation, situated performance, communicative repertoire and language awareness' (Canagarajah, 2007, p. 936).

- Jenkins (2007) suggests prioritizing accommodation skills and not penalizing students for forms that ELF researchers show are common and intelligible among ELF speakers.

- Khan (2009, p. 203) notes that, 'To promote English as an international language, English language tests should cater to international speakers and societies, and should aim to foster communication amongst linguistically diverse groups of people.'

- Widdowson (2012) discusses the need to define communicative competence, pointing out that the focus should be on how people know the language, not how much they know. As discussed in Chapter 7, 'Learners construct their own version of the language they are being taught and this gets carried over and developed further when they escape from the classroom and become ELF users' (Widdowson, 2012, p. 23). He highlights the importance of ELF research, which showcases how the language is actually used.

- McNamara (2012) notes the need to determine how achievement is defined, noting that the use of ELF brings into question the relevance of constructs based on native English-speaker norms.

Thus there is an emphasis placed on strategic competence, ability to use ELF in international situations, and ability to demonstrate accommodation skills. Such arguments are based on the premise that it is questionable to penalize test-takers for using forms that Chapter 7 has shown are common and intelligible among ELF speakers around the globe. As discussed in Chapter 7, EFL and ELF are two very different constructs and concepts such as interlanguage and **fossilization** are irrelevant. Nevertheless, assessing a student's strategic competence is far more difficult (and expensive) to do, and thus high-stake tests still focus on prescribed English grammar. As McNamara (2012, p. 202) notes in relation to such changes, 'The consequences are likely to be as revolutionary as the advent of communicative language teaching some forty years ago.' Change may not be easy but, since assessment has a washback effect on the objectives of many language classes, it remains a formidable barrier of innovation in ELT and one that needs to be addressed.

Teacher education

A third barrier is teacher education and teacher ambivalence to change. However, this is one area where massive change has begun to occur in recent years. Global

Englishes-related subject matter is being increasingly integrated into teacher training programmes and postgraduate courses in language education and applied linguistics. In addition, as discussed in Chapter 7, the University of Southampton has established a Centre for Global Englishes, attracting a number of students wishing to pursue doctoral study in the subject. In the Expanding Circle, Matsuda's (2009) study of teacher education programmes found that, although the majority noted that they expose students to American and British English, more than half offer courses that include topics on the spread of English, World Englishes, and social and regional dialects of English, 12 offered a course on the role of English as an international language, and four offered courses on the linguistic and functional diversity of English. The author concluded, however, that there is a lack of practical suggestions for teachers to implement change, contributing to the abstract/theory divide highlighted in Chapter 8.

In the process of making changes in teacher education, it is important not to tell teachers that their current methods are irrelevant and outdated, and Jenkins (2012, p. 492) does not believe 'it is our place to tell teachers what to do'. As she points out, change must come from teachers themselves, and students should be provided with choice based on the teaching and learning of sociolinguistic aspects related to the spread of English around the world.

Teacher education is important yet, as Chapter 8 highlighted, many teachers are ambivalent towards ELF because of their own investment in learning native English, and the concept of ELF, for example, may be a very foreign concept to those who have fixed notions of what is 'right' and 'wrong'. Dewey (2012) has suggested change must come from working with teachers themselves, but much of what is taught in teacher training programmes is at odds with ELF research – language is often characterized by norms of 'standard' varieties rather than the diversity and plurality of ELF interaction. Both Dewey (2012) and Widdowson (2012) note the need for teachers to reconceptualize the notion of language, the very subject they teach. 'The first step is to raise the awareness of teachers that there is an alternative way of thinking about the subject they teach, based on an understanding of English as a lingua franca' (Widdowson, 2012, p. 24).

Attachment to 'standard' English

A fourth barrier is attachment to 'standard' English. Teachers have often spent a lot of their lives striving to meet such standards in their own studies, and thus adhere to them in their own practices despite the fact that its existence is questionable, as discussed in Chapter 2. As this book has highlighted, language change is both a normal and natural phenomenon, and the many languages that the English language comes into contact with have resulted in tremendous variation. Widdowson (2003) argues that English is not transported around the world like a product. Instead, it is unstable and cannot travel without being transformed. Thus standard language ideology is often grounded in fundamentally flawed notions. It is clear from Section 9a that both the construct of a native English speaker and native English competence are rather difficult to define.

Nevertheless, English standards, which are usually based in the grammatical, lexical, and syntactical choices in written English, dictate the type of English that is taught in classrooms and learned by learners – and this deeply ingrained ideology is perhaps the largest barrier to bridging the gap between theory and practice in the fields of Global Englishes and ELT. As discussed in Chapter 5, despite being over 20 years old, the

Quirk/Kachru debate is still relevant and many teachers may continue to view teaching anything other than the native English norm to be a 'cheat' (Quirk, 1990, p. 6). As with Quirk, many English language teachers assume the role of guardian of 'standard' English, believing that they should adhere to native English-speaking norms that can empower learners to be successful in education and careers. As discussed in Chapter 7, when ELF research is discussed in relation to ELT it has been heavily criticised. Jenkins (2012) notes a paradox in criticism toward ELF, where some researchers and practitioners criticize ELF because they see the field as trying to establish a single global ELF 'variety', and others criticize the field as adopting an 'anything goes' policy. Jenkins (2012, p. 492) views this paradox of opinion as 'amusing' because 'none of these accusations is true, as those who make them would discover, were they to read the copious ELF literature in this dynamic, fast-moving field'. In order to make progress towards changing traditional ELT, one must stop looking upon English as this static thing that cannot and should not be changed. It is clear from Chapter 8 that such a view of English perpetuates the stereotype that native English is the only 'correct' form.

Teacher recruitment practices

A fifth barrier to innovation is English teacher recruitment, which centres on the notion that the ideal English language teacher is a native English speaker, or a non-native English speaker who shares a common first language with their learners. Phillipson (2009, p. 22) notes, 'One wonders how it can be that monolinguals are seen as experts in second language acquisition.' However, hiring native English speakers is often driven by economic factors and thus, as long as learners demand native English speakers, practices are unlikely to change as native English speakers do attract business in the commercial ELT market. Maley (2009, p. 194) insists that such a change will be difficult for 'very compelling practical and financial reasons' since 'neither ELT publishers nor examination boards can see any profit' in replacing something that makes money with something that people are unsure of. Thus it may be difficult to convince such money-making institutions to change their recruitment policies since they tend to focus on sales, as opposed to ethical and pedagogical factors. In Japan, for example, 'foreign language schools represent a 670 billion yen industry' (Seargeant, 2009, p. 95). Such institutions occupy a prominent position in society and the image that they portray of how English should be learnt successfully influences the public attitude. Therefore, 'this commercial popularism means that they are the propagators of stereotype' (Seargeant, 2009, p. 95). Clearly, such socially ingrained ideology of native English in recruitment and advertising in the ELT industry is not an easy entry point for the instigation of change, and perhaps accounts for the biggest barrier to innovation in ELT.

However, both Moussu and Llurda's (2008) and Galloway and Rose's (2013) studies indicate that the attitudes of learners are changing quickly. Learners in the latter study, for example, valued skills in a teacher that related to communication, personality, teaching ability, and experience more highly than those qualities associated solely with native English.

Chapter summary

It is clear that recent years have seen a number of proposals for ELT change in relation to the globalization of English. Traditionally, ELT has posited native English as the main goal of English learning, and the native English speaker has been placed on a pedestal and hired around the world, regardless of their qualifications. This perpetuates stereotypes that English is only spoken by native speakers and that learning English from someone from this group is the best way to learn.

Nevertheless, this model has been challenged from a number of angles, and today it is increasingly recognized that students have different uses of English, which the native English-speaker model doesn't prepare them for. GELT is very different from traditional ELT. There is a focus on exposure to non-native English and ELF, including: students' own varieties of English; Global Englishes awareness raising in both the language class-room and teacher training programmes; alternative 'models' or 'norms'; ELF contexts and communities; Global Englishes culture and identity; and teacher recruitment. In this new approach, the native English speaker and the non-native English speaker are placed on equal footing, and the aim is to emancipate non-native English speakers from the norms of a minority group of English users. The ELT industry needs to go beyond viewing English as a static, monolithic entity, and a discourse favourable to Global Englishes needs to replace the native English-speaker episteme.

However, a number of barriers exist. While it is imperative to break away from this epistemic dependency on native English and the native English speaker, it may not be such an easy task. As Matsuda and Friedrich (2012, p. 25) note, this change cannot simply be made by,

> adding a new lesson or component on EIL to an existing program. What is needed is a complete revision of the entire program, using one's understanding of the use of English in international contexts as a foundation that influences every single aspect of the curriculum. It entails a major overhaul, but a much-needed one.

Despite the fact that Galloway (2011, 2013) and Galloway and Rose (2013, 2014) showcase how Global Englishes can be incorporated into the curriculum in different ways, much more is needed. While literature on Global Englishes may be diverse, it is united in the joint desire to move ELT forward and instigate innovation and change.

Further reading

Native speakerism in ELT:

- Phillipson, R. (1992). *Linguistic Imperialism*. Oxford: Oxford University Press.

Non-native English-speaking teachers:

- Braine, G. (2010). *Non-native Speaker English Teachers. Research, Pedagogy, and Professional Growth*. New York: Routledge.

Global Englishes language teaching and barriers to ELT innovation:

- McKay, S. L. (2002). *Teaching English as an International Language: Rethinking Goals and Approaches*. Oxford: Oxford University Press.

- Kumaravadivelu, B. (2012). 'Individual identity, cultural globalization and teaching English as an international language: The case for an epistemic break.' In L. Alsagoff, S. L. McKay, G. Hu and W. A. Renandya. (eds), *Teaching English as an International Language: Principles and Practices* (pp. 9–27). New York: Routledge.

Closing activities

Discussion questions

Section 9a

1 Does the 'native speaker criterion' influence English teaching recruitment practices in a context you are familiar with?
2 What is your opinion of Holliday's (2008) statement that it is doubtful how far students' preferences would be provided for if, for instance, they requested male or white teachers?
3 What is your opinion on the definitions of native English speakers that have been put forward?

Section 9b

1 Native English-speaking teachers are often hired for their perceived authenticity. What is your experience, if any, of non-native English-speaking teachers and native English-speaking teachers?
2 There is a lack of research on students' attitudes towards non-native English-speaking teachers from diverse linguistic backgrounds. Do you think such studies would yield different results to those outlined in this chapter?
3 Do you think English learners in a context you are familiar with may have similar opinions to those in Pacek's (2005) study?

Section 9c

1 To what extent is it important for English learners to sound 'native-like'?
2 What are the main differences between ELT and GELT? To what extent would a GELT approach be possible in a context you are familiar with?
3 GELT advocates that the aim should be to achieve mutual intelligibility and mutual understanding in a wide range of contexts and communities. What, in your opinion, can English teachers do to encourage this?

Section 9d

1 The majority of ELT textbooks continue to be filled with Inner Circle culture. To what extent is this true in a context you are familiar with?
2 In regard to testing and assessment, Kim (2006, p. 37) states, 'Rating criteria and the practices of raters should be re-considered and re-established, so as to acknowledge the evolution of World Englishes.' To what extent does testing reflect the current uses of English in a context you are familiar with?

3   With regards to English teacher recruitment, Seargeant (2009, p. 95) notes, 'If the image of academic excellence appeals and is believable, it is probably of little concern how orthodox or effective it is.' How accurately is this opinion reflected in the institutions you know where English is taught?

Debate topics

1   For English conversation teachers, being a native English speaker is more important than a teaching qualification.
2   All other factors being equal, an 'expert in ELF use' is a more desirable quality in a teacher than being a native English speaker.
3   Quirk (1990, p. 6) is correct in his opinion that teaching learners non-native varieties of English is a 'cheat' because they mark out learners as having acquired a local 'deviant' English.

Writing and presentation prompts

Below are ideas for writing and presentation tasks to apply the knowledge learned in Chapter 9.

	Assignment topics
Personal account	Present your own views of the native English-speaking teacher and non-native English-speaking teacher division in institutions you are familiar with where English is taught.
Research task	Collect data from English language learners on their attitudes to native English-speaking teachers and non-native English-speaking teachers. Present the findings of your research. (Please adapt the questions in the questionnaire on the website.)
Basic academic	Write a paper outlining the main differences between ELT and GELT, and discuss the feasibility of the changes proposed in the GELT framework, in a chosen context.
Advanced academic	Critically examine approaches to ELT in a context you are familiar with in relation to Global Englishes. Draw on relevant studies in the field and examine the pedagogical implications of such research for your chosen context.

Chapter 10

The future of English as a global language

 Introductory activities

The following introductory activities are designed to encourage the reader to think about the issues raised in this chapter before reading it.

The current and future position of English as a global language

Look at Figure 10.1, reproduced from Graddol's (1997) **World Language Hierarchy**.

Discussion questions

1 Do you agree with the placement of the different languages?
2 Graddol (1997, p. 13) notes, 'English and French are at the apex, with the position of French declining and English becoming more clearly the lingua franca.' Do you agree with the other 'big languages' that he predicts to replace French by 2050?
3 What do you believe is the future of English? Will it remain at the apex of this hierarchy or will it eventually fall out of favour?

Case study: the power of Sesame Street

Sesame Street first aired on television in the USA in 1971 and has since been exported to over 140 different countries. In the 1970s it was seen as entertaining and educational, with each episode focusing on various letters of the alphabet and numbers. With the introduction of *Sesame Street* in places like Australia, Canada, the UK, and New Zealand, it became apparent that the show was influencing the language that children used, particularly apparent with the adoption of the pronunciation of *zee* instead of *zed* when naming the last letter of the alphabet. Evidence as far-flung as Canada and Australia shows that a high frequency of children born in the 1970s used *zee* as the preferred term during much of their childhood, but by adulthood many had reverted to *zed* or used either interchangeably. The influence was stronger in this generation than in subsequent generations because television did not have strong competition in the earlier era, and thus there was more national conformity with the shows that children were exposed to.

Other famous examples of popular media affecting change in language include the spread of the Australian high-rising tone (discussed in Chapter 4) to UK teens via popular Australian TV soaps, and the popularization of the expression *D'oh!* around the

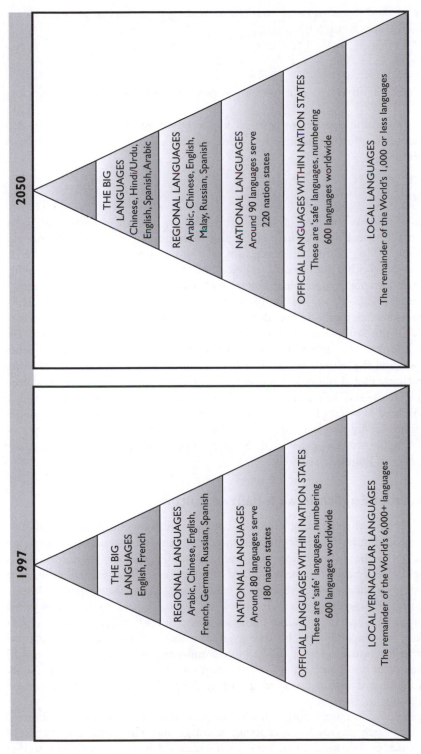

Figure 10.1 The World Language Hierarchy (source: Graddol, 1997, p. 13 and p. 59)

world courtesy of the US animated sitcom *The Simpsons*, prompting its inclusion in the *Oxford English Dictionary* from 2001.

Discussion

1 Can you think of other examples where popular media has influenced the way people speak?
2 What do you see as the negative or positive sides to exposure through popular media?
3 With distances being further bridged by online communication, consider the impact of this on English.

Introduction

This final chapter widens the lens of Global Englishes to examine current and likely future trends in the spread (or decline) of English in important domains. Section 10a examines the topic of English in the globalization of a more interconnected world. With the rise of social networking sites like Facebook (with over 800 million active monthly users), video over Internet protocol like Skype (with over 600 million registered users), and user-generated media like YouTube (with over one billion unique monthly users), people communicate differently and in different communities of practice. This section will examine what this will mean for language use in geographically defined boundaries. Section 10b will look at the **internationalization of higher education** in universities around the world and the role that English will continue to play in this process as more universities develop a global outlook. This section will also examine the issue of written ELF in academic settings and English as a global lingua franca for scientific publications. Section 10c will look at what globalization and a shift in world economic power might mean for the future of English language use. Following this, the future convergence or divergence of English will be debated in Section 10d, drawing into question many notions at the core of linguistic research.

10a The future of English in a globalized culture

The spread of English through globalization, coupled with the introduction of new online forms of communication over the past three decades, has had a huge impact on English exposure. As the introductory case study illustrated, *Sesame Street* spawned a generation that no longer called the letter 'z' *zed* or who were at least acutely aware that *zee* was the American alternative. This event is unsurprising given the numerous historical and current examples throughout this book of what happens to language when speakers of various linguistic backgrounds come together. But what about when a child's social network is no longer bound by the geography that defines language variation? What happens in the future when a child's local community becomes a fluid concept? A global culture of online communities, of shared YouTube videos, a global network of Facebook friends, and instant access to global media will surely have an impact on English language use.

Indeed, changes in communication technologies have spawned new uses of language in new mediums, such as instant messaging, texting, and emailing. The types of online English, such as 'textspeak', that have been examined in recent linguistic studies have fallen out of use as quickly as they emerged as new technology, like predictive text, rendered them obsolete. Thus we will avoid the pitfall of examining language itself for fear that the world will change faster than the publishing process. Instead, this section will examine the impact on language use of the increasing interconnectedness of global culture, driven by technology and globalization.

Technology and Global Englishes

Language spread through developments in communication technology is not merely a hypothetical argument but one that is historically traceable. Chapters 1 and 2 showed how technologies, such as the printing press, radio, and television, not only had an effect on a society but also on the language it spoke. While print showed an ability to transport written English, more modern communication has caused the spread of spoken language, with all of its phonological and prosodic features. Now, in the digital age, language is being transmitted in a much more accessible, immediate, and unedited fashion. This, together with globalization, has meant a realignment of communities from the physical to the virtual, allowing speakers to engage in a wide range of communities of practice without having to leave their homes.

In the past decade, we have seen leaps in technology that have changed the way the world communicates: in 2002, mobile phones outnumbered fixed lines for the first time (Graddol, 2006), and these phones are increasingly more internet integrated. The ELF research presented in Chapter 7 has shown what innovations occur when speakers from different communities meet. Thus, we are likely to see further innovation and usage of ELF as technology brings speakers together in new domains. We are entering a new era of communication, driven by rapidly emerging new technologies. Thus, it is difficult to predict how uses of English in these new mediums are likely to shape or change it. Crystal (2006, p. 401) notes,

> A new technology always has significant effect on the character and use of a language, but, when a technology produces a medium that is so different from anything experienced hitherto, the linguistic consequences are likely to be dramatic, involving all areas of English structure and use.

Ironically, as this technology has grown, the world has seen an explosion in spontaneous *written* communication, blurring the lines between written and spoken language, and even challenging previous definitions of language itself. Little more than eight years ago, Connor-Linton (2006, p. 403) explained a fundamental difference between spoken and written language:

> People speaking to each other can use facial expressions, gestures and eye gaze (and other paralinguistic cues) to express more than what they actually say. Writers must rely almost exclusively on their language; they can't wink to show they are being ironic, for example.

A person today would find such a comment absurd due to the recent explosion of smileys and emoticons (graphic representations of emotions, actions, and objects) in electronic communication. While there is evidence that the still popularly used emoticon for a wink ;-) dates back to as early as 1982, its use was, apparently, not widespread enough, even in 2006, for Connor-Linton to see the shortcomings of his example. As technology continues, we are likely to see new innovations with how language is used online.

Localization, globalization, and glocalization

Despite arguments that globalization is bringing the world closer together, current and future trends actually indicate that popular media is fragmenting global audiences, and businesses are returning to **localization** strategies (adjusting products to meet local needs), causing more diversity in what is on offer. As a result, television today is having less of an impact on global culture and language due to this fragmentation of audiences. Compared with the days of *Sesame Street*, when there were few alternative channels, TV shows no longer have the same level of national impact. As Graddol (1997, p. 47) states, 'when there are 500 channels to choose from – some showing the same film, but at different starting times, others showing the same film, but in different languages – national viewers will no longer have a shared experience'. We are unlikely to see the national viewership of shows such as *M*A*S*H* in the US, *EastEnders* in the UK, *Roque Santeiro* in Brazil, or *Friends* globally (through TV syndication) in the fragmented TV viewing experiences of tomorrow.

Moreover, even within individual channels we are seeing more localization. MTV are producing more local content, news channels are branching out into local languages, and movies are often made available in dubbed languages at the press of a button. Similar trends can be seen in online media, where localization of content and use of other languages is eating into the market share held by English language content (see Chapter 3), although ELF still remains the preferred medium for online discussions (Danet and Herring, 2007).

This synchronicity between localization of products and globalization of markets has been termed **glocalization**, which Block (2012, pp. 59–60) has defined as follows.

> In the social sciences, glocalisation is associated with the cultural theorist Roland Robertson and it is used to capture the idea that the global does not merely overwhelm or swallow the local; rather, syntheses emerge from contacts between the global and the local … Importantly, glocalisation entails a synergetic relationship between the global and the local as opposed to the dominance of the former over the latter and the homogenisation which would result from such dominance.

Block (2012) goes on to warn that glocalization might oversimplify the processes involved, and warns against an idealized view that localized forces shape globalization rather than the other way around. Indeed, there is much indication that local cultures are homogenizing across markets in certain domains despite maintaining local identities, and that we are witnessing the emergence of new demographic groups that transcend national borders. Many business experts point to the fact that there is a **global youth culture** emerging that constitutes the world's largest truly global market segment – that is, a clearly defined demographic in the world population that is not bounded by geography. The global youth segment has meant that similar demands for popular media and consumer products exist across the world, even though the demands are localized.

While the global youth culture is considered the biggest global market segment, it is clearly not the only one. Pennycook's (2007) theories on language and culture – which propose that global languages and cultures offer alternative identities and forms of expression while at the same time being reshaped to meet local needs in what he terms transcultural flows – are of relevance here. Transcultural flows describe the movement and adaptation of cultural forms to create new identities in a globalized world. Moreover, these transcultural flows are not moving from America to the world, as some pundits once feared when coining the term 'Americanization' (see Chapter 3). YouTube, for example, reports that as of 2013 the site was localized in 61 languages, and that over 80 per cent of user traffic came from outside the USA. Because of the interconnected interests of these global segments, we can see how a South Korean pop song (*Gangnam Style*), a Japanese animated TV show (*Naruto*), or a Norwegian comedy duo (*Ylvis*) can transcend national borders and obtain an instant global following.

Global Englishes are bound up with these transcultural flows, as are other languages and cultures (Pennycook, 2007). Young people are great experimenters, and new coinages and creative usages of language catch on quickly in the globalized segments (e.g. the proliferation of the word *selfie* to describe taking your own photo and posting it to social networking sites). It is also not unusual, for example, for varieties of American English to find their way into youth vocabulary worldwide, particularly if it is packaged to represent an identity of music, fashion, or sport (Graddol, 1997). Moreover, popular media delivered over the internet provides opportunities to use English in briefly emerging and disappearing virtual cultures, which was impossible with previous technologies. These new cultures emphasize the hybridity, fluidity, and the emergent nature of Global Englishes communication as speakers construct new communicative possibilities that are not tied to a specific culture or language, nor is it viewed as deficient in any way.

Moreover, these transcultural flows are not resulting in the spread of English into youth pop culture, as once predicted – at least not in the traditional sense. The global and local are mixing together, causing a seamless use of ELF which includes other languages. In Hong Kong, for example, Cantonese pop music has seen the integration of Cantonese, Mandarin, and English over the years, and there is a 'virtual absence of "monolingual" singers' (Chik, 2010, p. 514). Pennycook's (2007) study into language and hip hop also shows how the use of English in hip hop is not just imitative of its American origin, but brings Global Englishes and a global culture into the local subcultures, with the English used representing both a global and a local identity.

There are many ways to view the relationship between language and culture in relation to Global Englishes. There have been a number of studies that examine the construction of culture in communication (e.g. Meierkord, 2002; Baker, 2009) and argue that all languages, particularly one like English that is used as a lingua franca, can take on new cultural meanings or **languacultures** (Risager, 2006, p. 110). It is argued that language and culture are created in each instance of communication, and are fluid and unfixed. Canagarajah (2005) refers to cultures as hybrid, diffuse, and de-territorialized, pointing out that English learners today are not learning the language in order to join a single language community, but are 'shuttling between communities', between the local and the global, where a variety of norms and a repertoire of codes are to be expected. World Englishes and ELF research clearly has implications for how we view the relationship between language and culture, suggesting that it cannot be viewed as a fixed homogeneous entity. As with the language itself, in the Global Englishes paradigm culture is viewed as hybrid and fluid, with cultural references negotiated in situ.

In a more recent publication, Canagarajah (2013, pp. 7–8) draws into question terms, such as 'multilingual', as being poor descriptions of language use in many of these communities, positing the term 'translingual'.

> The term multilingual typically conceives of the relationship between languages in an additive manner. This gives the picture of whole languages added one on top of the other to form multilingual competence … What should be clear is that the term multilingual doesn't accommodate the dynamic interactions between languages and communities envisioned by translingual. In other words, the multilingual orientation to language relationships is still somewhat influenced by the monolingual paradigm … The term translingual conceives of language relationships in more dynamic terms.

While it is clear that globalization and new communication technology are changing the ways English is being used, it would be foolish to make any long-term predictions of what this will mean for future English usage. Instead, we will conclude by stating that technology – that makes the world smaller, creates geographically unbound virtual communities, and creates innovative uses for language – has the power to change language dramatically. There is strong indication that notions such as the drawing of national boundaries around varieties of English, as popularized by World Englishes research, may be an exercise of the past, as geographic boundaries will no longer be an indicator of language exposure, linguistic choices, or communities of practice. Future users of ELF will likely need to negotiate language use as they shuttle between local, global, monolingual, multilingual, translingual, physical, and virtual communities of practice.

10b The future of English in 'international' education

The spread of English around the world has seen an increase in importance placed on English language education throughout the world – a concept that has been explored thoroughly in previous chapters while looking at national language policies and pedagogies. This section will build on this foundation through a focus on the internationalization of higher education. Internationalization can be described as 'the process of integrating an international, intercultural or global dimension into the purpose, functions or delivery of postsecondary education' (Knight 2003, p. 2). Overall, internationalization has been shown to positively influence a university's reputation, research quality, teaching quality, and graduate employability (Delgado-Márquez et al., 2013). Thus, as a result, many higher educational institutions are seeking to internationalize through a policy that enables:

- an increase in the international student population;
- an increase in the internationalization of faculties;
- an increase in the reputation and presence of the institution in the global market;
- an increase in student mobility options.

Despite criticisms of commercialization (e.g. Phillipson, 2008), internationalization of higher education remains a priority for universities worldwide, and movements are inextricably linked with increasing the role of the English in the university setting. While

English has a firm foothold in the domain of education and scientific research, this section will argue that in the future we will likely see a more Global Englishes model of language use in this important domain.

A Western perspective of international education

Many institutions in ENL nations view international students as '"empty vessels" to be filled with Euro–American knowledge' (Singh 2005, p. 10). In these institutions, internationalization is seen as a business transaction where the international students are consumers and the universities provide the product (education). As a result of these financial gains, a number of ENL nations are in fierce competition to attract international student numbers. In Australia, for example, international education is considered the nation's third most important export industry (Forbes-Mewett and Nyland, 2012) and is treated as a commodity. In the UK, international students account for 13 per cent of the student body but one-third of the income from tuition fees – an estimated £5 billion in 2006, in addition to another £5 billion in living expenses to the UK economy (Brown and Holloway, 2008).

The dangers of such a business- and Western-centric model of internationalization can be seen in the case of Australia, where there is very little thought as to what the international student brings to the university. Forbes-Mewett and Nyland (2012, p. 191) note that Australia's attractiveness to international students has diminished in recent years:

> The implications of compromising international student support are short-term gain at the cost of long-term reputational damage. Australian education exporters' and regulators' decision to embrace a 'no frills' highly commercial approach to international students and their welfare has almost certainly contributed to the major slump in the number of international students studying in Australia in recent years.

In the UK as well it has been observed that the amount of energy expended on the drive to increase international student numbers has not been matched with spending on understanding the challenges faced by international students, who are learning in a new culture and, often, in a second language (Dean, 2010). Much research has also shown that many who attend universities that market themselves as 'international' find they are in fact very nation-oriented, with language expectations bound by local language and cultural norms. These norms include native English language expectations when evaluating the quality of academic work, and nationally bound expectations of classroom culture. As Jenkins (2011, p. 927) notes, 'while many universities claim to be deeply international, they are, in essence, deeply national at the linguistic level. And, given that language is such a key component of academic life, their claim to internationalism rings somewhat hollow.'

Although many universities appreciate the cultural diversity added to the university campus by international students, sudden internationalization has led many faculty members to draw stereotypical distinctions between native and non-native students, whether or not it is warranted (Tange and Jensen, 2012).

Western models of internationalization are also spreading to the non-Western Expanding Circle nations. In response to the internationalization of education, the Chinese government opened up the education market in recent years and allowed Western universities to offer programmes in China (Mok and Xu, 2009). Accordingly, a number of Western universities have set up campuses, such as Nottingham University in Ningbo. Such movements are not new, as Teacher's College of Columbia University and Temple University also set up programmes, or campuses, in Tokyo during the height of the Japanese economic boom in the 1980s. In more recent years, we have seen the internationalization of universities extend throughout the Expanding Circle, with the expansion of English-medium programmes in higher education around the world, as illustrated in Chapters 3 and 6. Jenkins (2013) has noted a trend for internationalization to be equated with 'English' in many of the 60 institutions in her study, with little evidence of internationalization in other facets of the university.

A global and Global Englishes perspective of international education

Tange and Jensen (2012) note that there is a difference between postcolonial views of internationalization, typical of ENL-based institutions, and those of more globally oriented institutions emerging in the Expanding Circle. They argue that in other parts of Europe institutions have a more global perspective of internationalization, seen as a means to develop a more international knowledge economy. In fact, it has been observed that Chinese students perceive a difference between British universities and French, German, and Danish universities, in that the UK views internationalization as a source of income but European universities see internationalization as a means of 'attracting and keeping the best brains from around the world to help develop their own economies' (Shen, 2008, p. 223). This statement is supported by research in Norwegian universities which concluded that the rationale for internationalization in higher education was deeply embedded in academic, rather than financial, incentives (Frølich, 2006).

Because of this key difference, the future of international education might, indeed, lie in the Expanding Circle. Chapter 3 has already shown a 1,000 per cent increase in the past ten years of English programmes catering for international mobility in Europe. Table 10.1 shows such increases in greater detail. Although the Netherlands and Germany lead the way in the number of English-taught Masters programmes in Europe, this can be somewhat misleading considering that many Scandinavian countries have switched most of their postgraduate taught courses to English, leaving little room for further growth (Brenn-White and Faethe, 2013).

According to the same report, the leading disciplines in taught Masters programmes in English are business and economics (28 per cent) and engineering and technology (21 per cent). However, recent research into nations that made the early switch to English education, like Sweden, have indicated a return to first language use in higher education, particularly with parallel language use. Such movements are not out of sync with how ELF is used in a fluid nature across the region. A similar trend is occurring in Asia, where domestic universities are integrating English language into domestic programmes not only for the purpose of allowing international student mobility but also to meet domestic demand for an '**internationalization at home**' experience. For example, many of the leading universities in Japan, China, South Korea, and ASEAN nations have seen increases in English-taught undergraduate and postgraduate courses in recent years, but where other languages play an important role in everyday university discourse. In other parts of Asia, the internationalization movement is forcing smaller nations to compete, causing a knock-on effect. In Taiwan, for example, 'rising investment in top universities in other countries (particularly Taiwan's neighbours) has alarmed the government as a

Table 10.1 Number and percentage of recent increases in English-medium taught Masters programmes in major European countries

	Number of programmes in June 2013	Percentage increase 2011–2013	Ranking in total number of courses
Denmark	327	74%	6
Sweden	708	73%	3
Italy	304	60%	7
Finland	261	52%	9
France	494	43%	4
Switzerland	281	19%	8
Belgium	253	18%	10
Netherlands	946	16%	1
Spain	373	14%	5
Germany	733	13%	2
Europe (total)	6,407	38%	

Source: Brenn-White and Faethe, 2013, p. 6

potential threat to the country's competitiveness in the long run' (Song and Tai, 2007, pp. 326–27). Thus, Taiwan is also aggressively pursuing an internationalization policy, which is indicative of a growing trend throughout Asia in the future.

In Latin America, Berry and Taylor (2013) argue that less attention has been given to the internationalization of higher education when compared with other parts of the globe, but this is beginning to change:

> The international imperatives observed elsewhere, often based upon fierce market-isation of higher education and driven by rankings and comparative measures, are less apparent; nor do institutions in Latin America seem as aware of the financial opportunities arising from internationalisation. The perceived benefits of the international campus and the desire of academic staff to work with international students, not for financial motives, but to enhance the educational and pedagogic experience, are also less established.

Although there is some indication that the focus on the internationalization of universities in this region is changing, the movement is not as large as in the USA, Europe, Asia, and Australasia. This finding is also apparent in Jenkins' (2013) study, where she found that Latin American universities do not make the same link with internationalization and English.

Finally, there is evidence that a Western-oriented view of international education may erode in ENL nations in the future. Many scholars are pointing to the fact that Western universities will need to move away from a nation-centric model in the future in order to compete with institutions that offer a more 'international' student experience. Svensson and Wihlborg (2010, p. 608), for example, state that they 'believe that intercultural experiences and knowledge must become a part of teaching and learning, if higher education is to become internationalised.' In the UK, there is more emphasis on catering to international students' needs, including the emergence of higher education courses for dealing with the language issues of non-native English-speaking international students. In Australia, there is growing awareness of 'a dissonance between policy makers and implementers, and the students themselves, on "what a truly international higher education organisation" in fact is' (Kondakci, Broeck and Yildirim, 2008, p. 448). There is also speculation that the internationalization of Western universities is largely the result of an unregulated international student market, and that in the future these universities might return to the domestic market if it becomes more economically viable:

> Internationalisation observed to date is *primarily* a product of distortionary government policy and, as higher education sectors around the world are inevitably liberalised and deregulated over time, the last 15 years may prove to have been a transitory but rather dramatic 'blip' around a much more modest underlying trend.
>
> (Healey, 2007, p. 354)

One large barrier will need to be addressed if ENL nations are truly to continue even a modest trend of internationalization: the resistance of those adhering to academic language norms.

The remainder of this section will examine the issue of written academic English, in an attempt to look for future trends in this formidable barrier to true internationalization.

Internationalization and academic written ELF

Chapter 3 touched on the bottom-up forces that caused many researchers to switch to English as the primary medium of scientific publication, one simplified reason being that writing in English meant a wider readership and therefore a larger impact. Figure 10.2 shows the percentage of academic publications by language over the past 100 years, of which the percentage in English has skyrocketed. Now English holds a near monopoly of published research with German, French, and Russian publications hardly visible, a situation unlikely to change in the future.

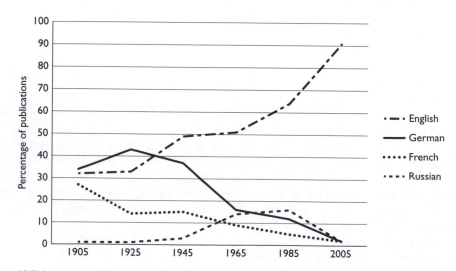

Figure 10.2 Language shares in total academic publications over the past 100 years (adapted from Montgomery, 2013, p. 90)

What this shift means is that academics are coming under increasing pressure to publish in English, but 'despite pressure from the university to increase international publication, where ENL writing standards seem to be the only accepted norm, no official writing support is offered' (Ingvarsdóttir and Arnbjörnsdóttir, 2013, p. 123). This fact indicates that non-native English-speaking academics are at a disadvantage in publishing, hurting their institutions' internationalization. Conventions in academic writing are highly standardized and safeguarded by publishers of scholarly work, and this seems one domain that is resistant to change. Many journal guidelines still state that non-native English speakers should have their work checked by a native English speaker. Jenkins (2011) argues that international journals have an international, rather than an ENL, audience, and thus such practices are not only unjustified but serve to disadvantage academics based on language alone.

On a more positive note, in recent years some journals are beginning to respond to changes in English ownership. The *Journal of English as a Lingua Franca* (JELF), for example, aims to respect the linguistic choices of the author and edits language for clarity only. This journal also advises the abstract to be submitted in a language other than English in order to respect the diversity of its readership. Moreover, acceptances of variations in language are being made outside of ELF-oriented disciplines. For example, in the author guidelines of Cambridge's *Journal of Cardiology in the Young*, the editors explicitly state that manuscripts are evaluated on scientific rather than grammatical content, and they support publication from non-native English-speaking academics. Such statements offer a glimpse of a future where the safeguarding of academic English is being wrestled from the hands of purveyors of academic publishing norms, aiming to be more inclusive of research that might previously have been dismissed on language grounds alone.

The future might also see a shift in focus away from native-speaker norms in academic writing as more and more non-native English-speaking writers publish in academic journals. The total number of scientific papers in English written by Chinese researchers increased by 174 per cent from 2002 to 2008 alone (Montgomery, 2013, p. 84), and it has been noted that,

> Given recent trends, the Chinese could even match the US levels in peer-reviewed English-language 'output' by about 2025, perhaps sooner … However, interpreted in political terms, its fortifying impact on scientific English would be beyond question. Aside from America, China may well be the most powerful force behind the spread of English in science.

China, while leading English-language scientific publications in terms of growth, is not alone in this wave of scientific research emerging from non-native English-speaking countries. According to the same report, nations such as India have also seen tremendous growth in English-language publications in recent years.

Just as we have seen ELF research shift perceptions of non-native English-speaker language to view innovation rather than error, the future may see a loosening of native-speaker norms in academic writing. Recent years have seen research into ELF usage in academic settings, and the use of the ELFA (Academic ELF) corpus has shown that in spoken academic settings speakers use the language in innovative ways, often improving on superfluous forms found in ENL corpora (as discussed in Chapter 7). Further research into written ELF, such as through the WrELFA (Written Academic ELF) corpus under development at the University of Helsinki, may in the future shed light on similar developments in written academic English. History has shown that written (published) language often plays catch up with changes in vernacular uses of the language, and usually requires a shift in language ideology. Thus, for the future of academic writing, 'cultivating tolerance in the academic community for these types of ELF textual characteristics may be less of a hurdle than calling for acceptance of salient surface errors' (Ingvarsdóttir and Arnbjörnsdóttir, 2013, p.124). Just as World Englishes research helps legitimize notions of variation in acceptable forms of language, here ELF research is pertinent to show that surface 'errors' are, in fact, characteristic of a language that is being used to share academic knowledge within this global community of practice.

10c The future of English: spread, recession, or reconceptualization?

Globalization has marked a new era for English language use and leads us to ask the question: what will happen to the English language in the future? While the historical, economical, political, and social prestige associated with English resulted in its rise, if the global power structure shifts as the world moves away from the postcolonial influence of the UK and the economic influence of the USA, many believe so too will attachment to English. Also, as geographical distances and national boundaries are bridged in our increasingly mobile society, new arenas of ELF usage emerge, bringing into question concepts of 'variety' and 'language'. In addition, ownership of English is shifting to the Expanding Circle, which is where the growing majority of future English speakers can now be found. Will the changes in the way English is used by this critical mass of language users affect the future of the language itself? Based on differing understandings of the above issues, linguists are in disagreement on the future of English language.

Possible 'black and white' directions for the future use of English

The following two subsections will explore two key dimensions linked to the future of English (see Figure 10.3), before offering a Global Englishes-oriented view of the future.

The first key dimension of concern is whether English will spread or recede in its global presence in the future. This dimension is represented by the vertical axis in the figure, and will be discussed in the remainder of this section. The second key dimension is the question of whether English will converge or diverge, which is represented by the horizontal axis and is discussed further in Section 10d. Obviously, this view is a simplification of the future of English as it looks at the scenarios in extreme terms and ignores the research on ELF, which shows language use is not occurring in such contained terms. Nevertheless, exploring the arguments behind each of these 'black and white' arguments can help us to better understand the 'grey' area, in which the fate of English will likely fall.

How tenuous or temporary is English's position as the global lingua franca?

Before we discuss the potential strengthening or weakening of the English language, it is first important to understand its current position in relation to its future competitors. In Figure 10.1 in the introduction to this chapter, Graddol (1997) places English (with French) at the top of his World Language Hierarchy, but acknowledges other languages, such as Arabic, Chinese, Russian, and Spanish, as unifying regional lingua francas of numerous national languages. These, in turn, are unifying languages for thousands of

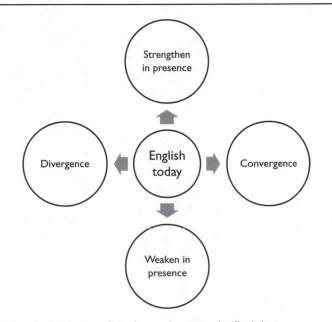

Figure 10.3 A 'black and white' view of the future directions for English

local vernacular languages. Graddol's World Language Hierarchy somewhat mirrors De Swaan's (2001) **Global Language System**, which places English in the centre and relegates French to the second tier, alongside a more exhaustive list of supercentral languages (see Figure 10.4).

In De Swaan's Global Language System, the relationships between lingua franca languages are explored. That is, in the world there are *central* languages that usually play a pivotal role in unifying a nation or large community of speakers. When speakers of mutually unintelligible central (or peripheral) languages come together, they usually use a supercentral language to communicate. For example, speakers of a number of languages in east Africa may use English, whereas those in Francophone west African nations may use French. Likewise, speakers of eastern European languages may gravitate towards Russian; those in the Middle East may use Arabic; and a Tibetan and a Cantonese speaker may use Mandarin Chinese. In the centre of the diagram, the *hypercentral* language (English) is what speakers of mutually unintelligible *supercentral* languages use. For example, Arabic, Chinese, and German businesspeople would most likely conduct communication in English. De Swaan states that it is also possible that higher-tier languages are taking over the role of those below them, and this is a likely scenario for the future. For example, speakers of the central languages of Danish and Dutch may forgo historical use of the supercentral German language in favour of the hypercentral language of English in more modern times.

If the connection between English and economic power, prestige, and personal advantage shifts, we might also see a shift in the preferred language of a newly structured global community. As Graddol (1997, p. 2) warns,

The global popularity of English is in no immediate danger, but it would be foolhardy to imagine that its pre-eminent position as a world language will not be

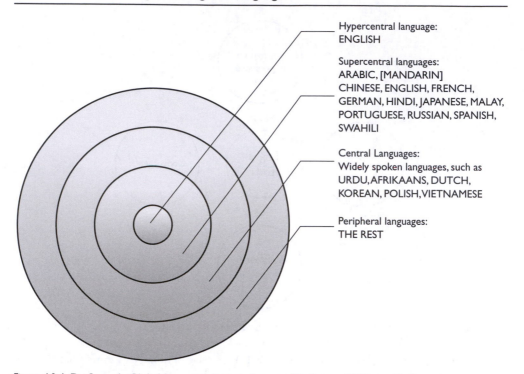

Hypercentral language:
ENGLISH

Supercentral languages:
ARABIC, [MANDARIN]
CHINESE, ENGLISH, FRENCH,
GERMAN, HINDI, JAPANESE, MALAY,
PORTUGUESE, RUSSIAN, SPANISH,
SWAHILI

Central Languages:
Widely spoken languages, such as
URDU, AFRIKAANS, DUTCH,
KOREAN, POLISH, VIETNAMESE

Peripheral languages:
THE REST

Figure 10.4 De Swaan's Global Language System (source: De Swaan, 2001, pp. 5–6)

challenged in some world regions and domains of use, as the economic, demographic and political shape of the world is transformed.

Such shifts in world power have caused predictions of changes to the current world
language hierarchy, with many scholars downgrading the future importance of languages
like German, Japanese, and French in lieu of increasingly important languages like
Chinese, Hindi, and Arabic. Based on statistics of world economic trends, such as
those that show Asia will hold 60 per cent of the world's wealth in 2050 as opposed to
21 per cent in 1990 (Graddol, 1997, p. 29), growing economies in China and India are
likely to spur the study and use of the unifying languages of Hindi/Urdu and Mandarin
Chinese in these areas, in addition to the current use of English. Moreover, the recent
global financial crisis, which put major English-hub economies such as the USA and
Europe into deep recession, has likely hastened the shift towards Asia as the new world
economic centre (Pennycook, 2010). There is some evidence of this shift in markets like
Japan, where more and more youth are reportedly opting to study Chinese and Korean
as their second foreign language, instead of the historically important French or German
(Kobayashi, 2013). The use of Spanish as the lingua franca for the Americas is also
becoming more prevalent, with the added advantage of serving as a lingua franca for
growing economies in South America (with the assumption that Brazil will turn to
Spanish as the unifying lingua franca for the region).

Such movements position other languages as possibly rising to a similar position as
English as alternative global lingua francas in the near future, which does not necessarily

indicate English's demise. In the distant future, whether English will fall from its perch is impossible to predict, as Crystal (1997, p. 139) rightly argues that there are 'no precedents to help us see what happens to a language when it achieves genuine world status'. In response to this claim, some scholars point to Latin, arguing that it is a historical example of a powerful language that receded from use. The simple answer to this claim is that Latin is not a good barometer of the future fate of English, for the reasons discussed next.

The demise of English (the Latin analogy)

The predicted demise of English is often discussed with a Latin analogy (McArthur, 1987). Wilton (2012, p. 342) argues that 'the history of Latin makes an attractive backcloth against which the present state of English can be assessed and its fate – or, more neutrally, its future – predicted.' Latin was a pervasive language across much of Europe during and after Roman times, and its fall from widespread usage sparks many to predict a similar future fate for the English language.

One comparison often made with Latin is that the future will see the fragmentation of English into a number of Englishes, and the use of a standard form will recede from use as the political and economic influence of ENL nations recedes. This book has shown English to be an adaptable language, and thus some linguists question whether the nature of variation and change in the English language will cause Global Englishes to eventually diversify so much that they will become separate languages, through contact with other rising and more important languages. Some linguists predict that English used in Asia alongside Chinese or Urdu will develop a separate set of norms than the English used in the Americas alongside Spanish, and that used in western Africa alongside French. As other languages overtake English in the global arena, will these differences fail to be reconciled due to a lack of use across speech communities? This is a notion entertained by Crystal (2003) but dismissed by others (e.g. Pennycook, 2007).

Wilton (2012, pp. 243–44) argues that three problems can be identified with the analogous comparison of English to Latin:

1 Modern linguists draw comparisons with Latin without a thorough understanding of the historical development of Latin. Likewise, Latin experts draw comparisons with English despite a lack of knowledge of ELF and World Englishes research.
2 The historical study of Latin's development over a long period of time cannot be compared with the relatively shorter rise of English. While superficial comparisons can be used – such as both languages' use in education, science, and as a second language – this is where comparisons end. One glaring difference is the lack of access to any 'standard' form of classical Latin for large parts of society, compared with the access to English today.
3 The largely written record of Latin only gives glimpses into its oral uses as a lingua franca, as opposed to spoken English which has been recorded and codified in much more detail. Any comparison of English and Latin as a spoken lingua franca is only speculative, and thus conclusions that English will fragment into separate vernacular languages like Latin did are tenuous.

In addition to the above arguments, the demise of Latin has been largely attributed to the distance between its rigid written form and the ever-changing spoken language. While we can see similar divisions between written English and spoken English, such comparisons are very suspect. Isolated language communities brought about rapid changes in vernacular languages across post-Roman era communities, which were not reconciled in the written form of Latin. As written language among the elite minority and spoken languages among the illiterate majority grew, the varieties diverged and new vernacular languages were born. With the highly literate and interconnected world of today, a repeat of history is entirely improbable. This book has shown the world is getting smaller and linguistic boundaries are becoming more blurred. Thus, the largely literate and highly connected world of modern times is vastly different from the fragmented Europe that saw the demise of Latin. Such evidence appears to suggest that the Latin analogy is fundamentally flawed.

The 'grey' area: a Global Englishes-oriented view of the future

History has shown that languages attached to power, wealth, and prestige have spread at the expense of those viewed less favourably. Therefore, as the power attached to Mandarin Chinese or Hindi/Urdu grows, so too will the use of these languages in the global arena. While we do not deny a future shift in world power, it is unlikely that these languages will 'replace' English. The idea of 'replacing' seems at odds with ELF research on how language is used in language-contact situations, where multilingualism is the norm. As Pennycook (2010) argues, the growth of other languages will not necessarily be at the expense of English because the trade-off between the languages is not a zero-sum game.

The era of globalization has been well underway for the better part of 60 years, built on a foundation of centuries of colonialism before it. Block (2012) argues that many applied linguists mistakenly take on a 'presentist' view of the social implications of globalization. In fact, globalization is not *occurring*, it *has already occurred*. As stated in Chapter 1, the rise of English as the first global lingua franca was almost entirely due to it being in the right place at the right time in the processes of colonization and globalization, and these times and places are long past. Even though the power of the USA and the UK has been declining in recent decades, the spread of English has not halted, with its growth spurred on by the developing world which has embraced it as its global language. Countries like China and India are highly invested in English language development, so the role of English is likely to be maintained even after ENL economic juggernauts, like the USA, are toppled from the world economic hierarchy. As De Swaan (2010, p. 73) notes,

> Even if the hegemonic position of the US was to decline, English would continue to be the hub language of the world language system for quite some time, if only because so many millions of people have invested so much effort in learning it and, for that very reason, expect so many millions of other speakers to continue to use it.

A Global Englishes-oriented view would argue that we need to reconceptualize what we understand by 'language' and 'lingua franca'. The question of whether English will weaken or strengthen in the future is flawed from the outset because it imagines language to be a static and monolithic entity with clearly defined parameters, so that growth and recession can be accurately measured. Our argument is supported by Canagarajah's (2013) positioning of translingual practice, where he shows text and talk involve the meshing of diverse codes and languages, even if not superficially evident. He argues that the separation of language with different labels is problematic as 'languages' are always in contact and under mutual influence.

What this book has shown is that English when used as a lingua franca is a fluid, hybrid entity used for the purposes of speakers for each separately constructed culture. If other languages are integrated into these cultures in the future it will not be at the expense of English, but as a naturally occurring process of translingual speakers in contact. In the long term, the future of English is harder to predict; certainly the immovable position of English as the world's first true lingua franca is dependent on unforeseeable forces of a political, economic, health, social, and technological nature, and any world-changing occurrence in any one of these fields could dislodge English from its current position. However, if the world continues to develop as expected, the dislodgement of English as a world language seems improbable.

10d The future of English: convergence, divergence, or adaptation?

The previous section examined the key question of whether the English language will strengthen or weaken as a global lingua franca. It concluded by arguing that, rather than measuring language spread and growth in concrete terms, we need to reconceptualize the notion that English is a stable or measurable entity, a notion explored throughout this book. This conclusion leads us to another question: considering English is a fluid and changeable entity, what will become of this entity in the future? Now that English is being used alongside more languages and in more diverse contexts than any other language that has come before it, how will this affect its future development as a language? Will the plurality of Englishes be further exaggerated as the language adapts to its surroundings, or will the globalized and connected world community mean that variation in the language will reduce and we will see emerge a semblance of a global standard form of English? While Chapter 7 has shown ELF to be a fluid entity, many linguists view this as a necessary process to stabilization, and not as indicative of its global use. This final section will examine arguments for possible future convergence and divergence, before offering an alternative possibility that it will do neither.

The convergence of a Global English

One future scenario looks at the standardization of a Global English (Crystal, 1997; 2006; McIntyre, 2009) as the world becomes a more interconnected place. Indeed, there is evidence of standardization on a domestic and international scale in many studies of variation in English within the Inner Circle. For example, phonological levelling is rapidly occurring, such as the *Mary–merry–marry* vowel merger in the youth segment in North America (see Chapter 4). Similarly, in the UK the fronting of dental fricatives (resulting in *think* and *with* being pronounced like *fink* and *wif*) is spreading rather than retreating in youth accents. Prosodic features, such as high rising tone, can be found transnationally in regions as far-flung as Australia, the USA, and the UK. A levelling of grammatical variation is also occurring, such as the deletion of the adverbial -ly in the speech of many younger generations around the world, in addition to a global levelling of tenses in irregular verbs. There is considerable evidence that lexical levelling might also be occurring, with avoidance of local terms and the adoption of 'foreign' ones.

Jenkins (2009) uses evidence from Trudgill (1998) to highlight lexical and grammatical standardization between British and American English, including:

- the spread of the American usage of sentence adverbial *hopefully* in British English;
- the spread of the American usage of *have to* contexts where it was not used in British Englishes;
- the spread of the British *do* where Americans would have traditionally omitted it, such as in the sentence *I shouldn't go to work tomorrow, but I might [do]*;
- the spread of American lexis, such as *briefcase, sweater, radio,* and *dessert.*

With increases in population mobility, it is seen as a possibility that the same processes of koineization, which formed many native varieties of accents, might also result in a more levelled international English, particularly in major global cities where a mix of immigrant accents is already shown to be taking effect. Might, then, an idealized future contain a more standardized English that is influenced and shaped over time by those with populous and prestige attached? This is a view of the future of English popularized by linguists (e.g. Crystal, 2006), who predict a world standard English to emerge. Such levelling does not necessarily mean converging to existing models of native speaker language use, and could involve a global community of native and non-native speakers. McIntyre (2009, p. 33) writes,

> World Standard English might avoid the use of idioms (expressions that are common only to some varieties of English) and colloquialisms, and it might utilise particular pronunciations. The important point here is that it is not likely to be an Anglo-centric standard. The notion that English belongs to Britain and America is simply no longer true (if, indeed, it ever was) and we can fully expect to see other communities world-wide exerting an influence on the development of any new standard.

ELF research, on the other hand, has showcased how the changing sociolinguistic uses of the language are resulting in a lot of variation. These uses of English bring into question concepts of 'variety' and 'language', throwing a new perspective on language change and variation that was first introduced in Chapter 2, and explored in Chapters 4, 5, and 6.

The divergence of Global Englishes

If a case can be built for the convergence of a Global English, then one can equally be made for the divergence of many Global Englishes. A running theme throughout this book has been that prestige and speaker quantity shape the languages we speak, the lexical choices we make, and the accents we imitate. Such prestige is likely to differ according to social and political alliances, and the mix of Englishes found in each region. In Europe, a more European English than that used in the USA might emerge. The same might be said for the Middle East, Africa, and South Asia. Depending on where future prestige and power is to be placed, many nations where English is spoken as a foreign language might gravitate towards one or the other, or continue to develop their own variety with its unique characteristics.

This is a future seen by Crystal (2003), who discusses the possibility of a family of Englishes in which a central variety, called Standard World Spoken English, might be used to unite them all. If such diversification occurred, the question arises as to what extent these Englishes will continue to diversify in parallel – and sometimes in opposition – to one another. Obviously, the points raised in Section 10c, of a more globalized and interlinked community, render the fragmentation of English into a number of dialects an unlikely outcome, and is not the right way to think of language at all.

So we are left with the conclusion that English will not diversify into a number of Englishes, nor will it converge into a single language. What, then, is the prediction for the future? It can be argued that notions of identity are a central part of communication, thus individual identity is constructed in the diversity that exists in language. For this reason, forces of diversity will always pull at the seams of convergence, and divergence will always be met by convergence, to meet the demands for an intelligible lingua franca. It might be true that linguistic boundaries may not be geographically defined in the future, due to the globalization forces that are bringing the world together, but language will continue to flow and adapt accordingly to various communities of practice on both the global and local scale.

The 'grey' area: viewing language as a complex adaptive system

When trying to think of an apt illustration of the elastic nature of language and the future of English, we found it difficult to come up with an explanation of how the English language might both diverge and converge. At first, we imagined an ongoing tug-of-war with an elastic bungee cord, with one team representing divergence and the other representing convergence. This metaphor did not seem right, however, as it indicates that one would end up a victor and that a pull in one direction was at the expense of the other. It did not seem to represent the fact that language *is* diversifying in many facets; globalization *is* also causing convergence in others; but at the same time, each force is not working in opposition to the other. Directionality ebbs and flows in a somewhat synchronized, fluid way – not the image represented by a tug-of-war, where movement occurs in fixed and predictable directions.

Larsen-Freeman and Cameron (2008, p. 79) prefer to view language as a complex adaptive system. They argue that, while linguists 'treat language as a stable, even static system', applied linguists need a very different theory of language: 'complex systems are at one and the same time both stable and variable'. Viewing the English language as a complex adaptive system frees applied linguists from historically limited research perspectives because,

> Change is inherent to most of our concerns as applied linguists, and yet in our theories we, everywhere, find processes converted to objects. A post-modern response to over-simplification of the world through a focus on entities is to fragment and disperse, to deny wholeness by making it multiple, hybrid and difficult to grasp. Complexity theory, in contrast, embraces complexity, interconnectedness and dynamism, and makes change central to theory and method.
>
> (Larsen-Freeman and Cameron, 2008, p. 1)

Thus, our answer to the fundamental question of whether English will converge or diverge is that it will do both, and this diversification and standardization will always move the language forward in creative and unexpected ways. English, in its written form and spoken form, will never be static and thus will not fall the way of Latin, which disappeared due to a failure to contain and preserve that which could not be contained.

English's position will unlikely be compromised in the foreseeable future, although other languages will certainly join it in certain domains of society and business as powerful alternative lingua francas, but English will adapt accordingly to its new environment. Originally, linguists such as Crystal (1997) proposed that such a future English might mirror General American or RP English, and later hinted that a more Asian English might emerge (Crystal, 2006). However, the central notion here is not *what type* of English will emerge, but that the language will *adapt* according to the changes occurring in the complex systems within which it is situated.

Throughout this book, and especially in those chapters connected to ELF research, we have tried to show that the nature of language itself may need to be rethought. Our description of ELF in Chapter 7 has shown how speakers are manipulating the language to suit their varied purposes. Thus, in this respect, we can never expect a global lingua franca to stabilize entirely in any given direction. Schneider (2007) notes that codification can only take place when endonormative stabilization occurs, but this is not true in the case of ELF and is certainly not true of any complex adaptive system. In Chapters 4, 5, and 6 we showed that the purpose of a lot of World Englishes work was to codify national varieties as part of a nativization process. But codification also presents a false notion that language is stable and static, and is reminiscent of the type of thinking that applied linguists need to be distancing themselves from. In fact, Chapter 7 has shown that ELF communities are unstable and fluid, and thus the codification of ELF, despite the misunderstandings of critics, is not the focus of researchers in this field simply because it does not mirror the true nature of language in use.

However, just as World Englishes has a long history of research, ELF needs more work, too. More analytical studies are needed to showcase how lingua franca communication takes place today and enable us to theorize about the nature of 'language'. Outside the ELF paradigm, researchers are drawing similar conclusions. Pennycook (2007, 2010) has questioned whether English as a language, or Englishes as many languages, exists at all, as the very idea of language constrains us to draw boundaries around forms and variation.

> To argue for a monolithic version of English is clearly both an empirical and political absurdity, but we need to choose carefully between the available models of pluricentric Englishes, avoiding the pitfalls of states-centric pluralities that reproduce the very linguistics they need to escape, in order to deal with globalized linguascapes. This can help us avoid the national circles and boxes that have constrained World Englishes and, indeed, linguists more generally. In pedagogical terms, this means treating English less as a discreet object – even with its variations – that can be taught only in its own presence, and rather deal with English as multilingual, as a language always in transition, as a language always under negotiation.
>
> (Pennycook, 2010, p. 685)

Thus the title of our book may, in the end, have been somewhat misleading because, in our attempt to show the plurality of Englishes used around the world, we may inadvertently be encouraging people to think that Englishes are countable and codifiable entities, which has never been the case and will certainly not be the case for the future of English. Once again, complexity theory seems to work hand-in-hand with a Global Englishes perspective, where drawing lines around complex systems like language is entirely problematic (Larsen-Freeman and Cameron, 2008). This view is, once again, supported in Canagarajah's (2013, p. 7) positioning of the translingual orientation, in that treating language as 'a tightly knit system' and 'a self-standing product' that is detached from its environment distorts the real practices underlying how meaning is created in communication.

We encourage the reader to end this chapter with the view of language as a moving, breathing, and unpredictable organism – much in line with Larsen-Freeman and Cameron's (2008, p. 79) call for an 'ecological metaphor applied to language use in context'. English, like any organic system, is capable of changing and adapting to its surroundings; it is made up of many distinct parts that give it its whole interconnected form, but is entirely dependent on the systems which surround it. It is capable of morphing to such a degree that it is entirely possible that, in the future, it will adapt and change into a completely different-looking organism in response to its ever-changing environment.

Chapter summary

This chapter has examined issues surrounding the future growth and use of English, based on current and predicted trends. Section 10a examined issues surrounding the emergence of global culture, where new opportunities to use English have emerged. We saw that new technologies have not only changed the way that English is used but have also caused a re-examination of how we define language. Issues of globalization, localization, and glocalization were explored, which have created a geographically fragmented but globally interconnected community that has brought into question linguistic boundaries defined by national borders. In Section 10b, the use of English in education was discussed in order to analyse how English will be used in the future. In particular, we saw a dramatic trend of English monopolizing academic publications at the expense of the other big languages that had been prominent in the twentieth century. Unlike online and popular media content, which is becoming more multilingual, education is one area where English has placed a firm foothold, particularly true in the internationalization of higher education. The danger of equating internationalization with native-English norms in such programmes was discussed at length. However, we concluded with a somewhat optimistic view that the formidable barrier of a standard academic English, based on native-speaker norms, might be showing signs of cracking as internationalization moves away from its Western centre.

The final two sections of the chapter examined the future, or fate, of English, according to key questions posed throughout the book. The questions of English's future expansion or recession, and its future convergence or divergence, were discussed. Some bleak 'black and white' scenarios were explored in order to understand the 'grey' area in which the future of English will most probably lie. In the end, we predict a future where English will remain a global language but we do not see this as a zero-sum game; thus other viable, alternative lingua francas might grow in certain domains. We also concluded that the emergence of a standard global English was as equally improbable as the fragmentation and stabilization of many Englishes. Such a view ignores ELF research that suggests a third alternative. We considered the out-of-date and futile linguistic practice of drawing boundaries around something that is as fluid and ever changing as language.

In our view, the English language will continue being moulded and adapted by its users to fulfil immediate purposes; it will always be influenced by exposure to alternative, creative uses of language. English, or Englishes – plural, though uncountable – has a definite place in the world's future as a global lingua franca, even if its future form is less predictable.

Further reading

Globalization and Global Englishes:

- Pennycook, A. (2007). *Global Englishes and Transcultural Flows*. Abingdon and New York: Routledge.

On English in international education:

- Jenkins, J. (2013). *English as a Lingua Franca in the International University: The Politics of Academic English Language Policy*. Abingdon: Routledge.
- Jenkins, J. (2011). 'Accommodating (to) ELF in the international university.' *The Journal of Pragmatics*, 43(4), 926–36.

On the future of English:

- Pennycook, A. (2010). 'The future of Englishes: one, many, or none?' In A. Kirkpatrick (ed.), *The Routledge Handbook of World Englishes*. Abingdon and New York: Routledge.
- Crystal, D. (2006). 'Into the 21st century.' In L. Mugglestone (ed.), *The Oxford History of English*. Oxford: Oxford University Press.

Closing activities

Chapter discussion questions

Section 10a

1 Current trends indicate the use of English on the Internet and in popular media is decreasing, in terms of its share of content. What do you think is driving this trend?
2 Do you think online communications are changing the definition of language? Are the already-fuzzy lines between spoken and written language being blurred further?
3 Can virtual communities really have the same influence over language as physical ones?

Section 10b

1 What do you see as the advantages and disadvantages of having English as a unifying language for academic scholarship?

2   What do you think of Jenkins' (2011) advice to international students that they educate their lecturers about ELF?

3   Some people are worried about the decline of academic writing standards. What is your opinion on this?

Section 10c

1   Ignoring the conclusions drawn in the section, which of the 'black and white' futures of English do you perceive as most convincing?

2   Compare Graddol's 1997 and 2050 World Hierarchy (Figure 10.1). Using De Swaan's Global Language System (Figure 10.4), what adjustments would you make to the model to represent the year 2050?

3   Do you agree that English is unlikely to topple from its apex position, but might be joined by other global lingua francas in certain domains?

Section 10d

1   In the distant future, do you think a kind of global koineization would be theoretically possible?

2   Schneider (2007) notes that codification can only take place when endornormative stabilization occurs, but this is not true in the case of ELF. Crystal (2003) sees a family of Englishes emerging (of which a standard spoken form is one branch). Are the authors in disagreement?

3   Pennycook (2010) argues that drawing circles and boxes around Englishes has constrained linguists, thus criticizing linguistic practices of codifying varieties of the English language. Do you think there is no longer worth in such study?

Debate topics

1   With a more connected global community, the emergence of a World Standard Spoken English, as outlined by Crystal (2003), is a real possibility.

2   Within 50 years, the use of English in academic publications grew from 50 per cent to over 90 per cent. In the next 50 years, this trend can just as easily reverse, as other languages take over in importance in research and publication.

3   Jenkins (2011, p. 934) is right in her assertion that 'it is a contradiction for any university anywhere that considers itself *international* to insist on *national* English language norms'.

Writing and presentation prompts

Below are ideas for writing and presentation tasks to apply the knowledge learned in Chapter 10.

	Assignment topics
Personal account	How has the role of English in education and popular media been changing in a context you are familiar with? How will it likely change in the future?
Research task	Copy a sample of online English (e.g. blog posts, messenger chats, comments on videos, twitter feeds). Analyse your sample in terms of grammatical and lexical complexity. (See the companion website for ideas.)
Basic academic	Conduct secondary research on an emerging national economy. Using this information, propose the impact of this emerging market on the language used as a lingua franca with its close trading partners.
Advanced academic	Explore the arguments for the future convergence or divergence of the English language. Examine competing theories of historical linguists with those engaged in ELF research.

Phonetic symbols

The subset of phonetic symbols used in this book

The corresponding word items represent the sounds found in most RP accents, unless otherwise indicated. Please note these are illustrative examples only for reference, because variation also exists within these accents. Use of RP here is as a convenient illustration rather than as a norm. The example word is the initial sound, unless otherwise indicated by an underline.

For a list of all phonetic symbols, see the IPA website at www.langsci.ucl.ac.uk/ipa/

Vowels

Table 11.1 Vowels

ɪ	pin
ɛ	bed
æ	cat
ə	the
ʊ	look
ɒ	cot
ɑ	cot (General American)
ʌ	cut
ɜː	girl
ɑː	car
ɔː	or
oː	or (Australian English)
iː	sea
uː	too
i	happy

Diphthongs

Table 11.2 Diphthongs

eɪ	day
aɪ	five
ɔɪ	boy
əʊ	road

Table 11.2 (continued)

eɪ	day
oʊ	road (General American)
aʊ	round
ɪə	here
eə	bear
ʊə	cure

Consonants (examples show the initial sound unless otherwise indicated)

Table 11.3 Consonants

p	cup
b	pub
t	net
pʰ	put
tʰ	tack
kʰ	cup
d	dad
k	tick
g	got
f	food
v	vet
θ	thin
ð	they
s	sit
z	zoo
ʃ	she
ʒ	genre, measure
h	hat
m	man
n	not
ŋ	long
tʃ	chair
dʒ	just
l	like
ɹ	red
j	yes
w	way
r	girl (Scottish English)
ɫ	pool
ɻ	red (Indian English)
ʈ	ten (Indian English)
ɖ	dog (Indian English)
t̪	think (Irish English)
d̪	they (Irish English)
x	loch (Scottish English)
ᵐb	comb (Kikuyu English)

Glossary

This glossary provides definitions of many of the terms used throughout this book (highlighted in bold for first usage). The definitions were developed by the authors.

accent A form of language that relates to pronunciation (the sounds speakers produce and other prosodic variation that accompanies sound), marked by geographic or social phonological features.

accommodation Adapting language features (e.g. syntax, accent, lexis) to enhance intelligibility. A speaker may, for example, wish to converge towards, or diverge away from, their *interlocutor*.

acrolect The variety of language that is considered the most prestigious form, especially in an area where a creole is spoken.

additive differences Relates to variation in grammar (or syntax) involving things like turning uncountable nouns into countable ones (e.g. *informations*, *staffs*) in some varieties of English and ELF usage.

affricates Sounds, such as [tʃ] and [dʒ], produced by the stopping of airflow followed by the immediate release of air through a narrow opening.

alveolar plosives Sounds that are articulated with the tongue against or near the roof of the mouth, including the phones /n/, /t/, /d/, /s/, and /z/.

article omission Relates to variation in grammar where articles are often deleted (sometimes because they are used differently) in some varieties of English and ELF usage.

ASEAN A political and economic association consisting of 10 countries in south-east Asia.

attitudes (towards language) The way people think or feel about other languages and variation in linguistic features.

auxiliaries, use of Relates to variation in the use of auxiliaries in some varieties of English and ELF usage, which may differ to 'standard' English and also includes the creation of new auxiliaries.

basilect The variety of language that is most remote from the prestige variety, especially in an area where a creole is spoken.

Bilingual Education Act A series of influential language policies in the USA that were in place from 1968 to 2002.

blending Where parts of words are combined, such as *distripark* (a distribution park or a warehouse complex) in Singapore.

borrowing The transference of words, sounds, and structures from one language to another.

bottom-up perspective A view that language policy is influenced by society and its people.

business English as a lingua franca (BELF) Lingua franca English in business contexts.

Canadian rising A term used to describe the phonological distinction in some diphthongs of Canadian English, which makes it distinctive from General American English.

Chancery English A form of middle English used by clerics and in the courts.

Chancery Standard See *Chancery English*.

code-mixing When multilingual speakers switch between different languages or varieties during a conversation.

code-switching The transfer of linguistic items from one language into another in multilingual speech, usually within the phrase level.

codification The process of standardization and making a norm for a language through recording linguistic features.

coinages New word creations such as *killer litter* (rubbish discarded from high-rises which may end up killing someone by accident) in Singapore.

communicative competence A term coined by Dell Hymes to describe a user's ability to use a language based on grammatical and phonological knowledge, but also the social appropriateness of language use.

community of practice A term coined by Lave and Wenger (1991) to describe a group of people sharing common interests and purposes, using in-group linguistic practices. It is a common term used within ELF due to the problems associated with identifying fixed speech communities. In ELF communication, a 'community' has more to do with virtual, fluid, and transient interactional networks than geography.

complex adaptive system A notion based on complexity theory that embraces interconnectedness and dynamism, and views language as a part of its environment.

compounding/specialized meaning Where new words are formed by compounding or giving a specialized meaning to a combination of words (e.g. in South Africa, the end of apartheid in South Africa led to the creation of compound *rainbow x*).

conceptual gap A term associated with Barbara Seidlhofer, relating to the need for empirical research within linguistics on the widespread use of ELF.

concord with collective nouns Relates to variation in language use where group terms (e.g. *flock, government*) are treated as a grammatically singular or plural entity.

consonant clusters When two or more consonant sounds appear without a vowel between them, such as the initial sounds in *string* and the final sound in *dialects*.

contact language The language used to communicate when speakers of mutually unintelligible languages come into contact with each other.

conversion A shift of a word class with retention of meaning, such as *off* meaning *to switch off* in West Africa.

corpus A collection of language examples used in linguistics to study the features of a language in use.

creole A mother tongue formed from the contact of two languages, usually occurring when a pidgin is passed on to a generation who then use it as their first language.

creolization The development of a contact language into a creole.

de-creolization The process where the features that make a creole distinct from a parent language are lost, usually due to policy that emphasizes the most formal form of the language.

dental fricatives Sounds that are produced with the tongue and the teeth, for example /θ/ and /ð/.

derivation When new words are created by adding prefixes or suffixes to an old one, such as *prepone* (to bring forward in time) in India.

dialects A form of a language that denotes a geographical subdivision of a language form, and is usually associated with a region or a class or group. It can also be influenced by a number of factors including class, ethnic group, age group, and gender. Unlike *accent*, which relates to pronunciation, a dialect includes its grammar and vocabulary.

diphthongs A sound formed by the joining of two vowel sounds.

endogenous See *internally driven changes*.

endonormative Looking inward to local bodies to establish norms and customs. In terms of ELT, an endonormative model would be the use of a locally grown variety of English.

English as a foreign language (EFL) The use of English in a context where it has no official status and is not widely used in the local community, and thus is limited to special contexts like the classroom.

English as a native language (ENL) The use of English in a context where it is the mother tongue of the majority of the population, and is used in an official capacity.

English as a second language (ESL) The use of English in a context where it is an official second language spoken alongside other mother tongue languages.

English-medium instruction The use of English as the medium of education.

English-only policy Language policy that restricts the use of languages other than English.

Englishes A term used to emphasize the plurality of English.

episteme Beliefs and theories that determine the certainty of knowledge at a particular time.

epistemic break A movement away from ideas that many believe to be true at a particular time.

exogenous See *externally driven changes*.

exonormative Looking outward to foreign bodies to establish norms and customs. An exonormative native speaker model is used in many ELT contexts.

Expanding Circle Geographical contexts where English doesn't play an official or historical role.

expert ELF users Speakers who are particularly accomplished at using ELF successfully; can include both native and non-native English speakers.

extended pidgin A pidgin language that has stabilized in its development but lacks the features of a creole (e.g. it is not yet used widely as a mother tongue).

externally driven changes Changes to a language from external forces, such as the arrival of another language or a change in national language policy. Also known as *exogenous* changes.

first diaspora The spread of English to new settlements, which caused the emergence of new native English-speaking nations.

fort creoles Creoles that were formed due to contact situations in trading and military posts, and exploitation colonies.

fossilization A term closely associated with *interlanguage*, used to describe the stage in second language acquisition when a learner plateaus and their target language ceases to develop further.

gendered pronouns The assignment of gender to an inanimate object, e.g. *she's a nice car*.

General American A form of American English that is lacking in any marked features that would cause people to associate it with a particular geographic region or social group.

Global Englishes A paradigm that includes concepts of World Englishes, ELF, and EIL. It examines the global consequences of English's use as a world language. In many ways, the scope of Global Englishes extends the lens of World Englishes and ELF to incorporate many peripheral issues associated with the global use of English, such as globalization, linguistic imperialism, education, language policy, and planning.

Global Englishes language teaching An approach to English language education that addresses the implications of Global Englishes.

Global Language System De Swaan's model of world languages, organized according to their influence as locally, regionally, nationally, internationally, or globally unifying languages.

global youth culture A term used to describe a global market segment of people of a similar age who share similar interests.

globalization The process in which the world has become increasingly interconnected as business and other organizations start operating on an international scale.

globalization (fourth channel) The spread of English due to the forces of globalization.

glocalization The process of incorporating both local and global needs into international integration.

hybrid forms A combination of English and borrowed terms, such as *lathi-charge* (a charge by the police with batons) in India.

Inner Circle Geographical contexts where English is spoken as the majority, native language.

innovations Creative, non-standard uses of language that are thought to be creative.

intelligible/unintelligible Adjectives used to describe whether communication is understandable to an interlocutor (intelligible) or not understandable (unintelligible).

intercultural competence The ability to communicate effectively with people from different cultural backgrounds.

interlanguage A term often attributed to Larry Selinker describing the output of a non-native English speaker at any stage before full acquisition of the target language. It assumes the learner to be on a cline of development towards native English-speaker competence.

interlocutor A participant in a conversation.

internally driven changes In a linguistic context, changes to a language from internal forces, such as the simplification of superfluous language features. Also known as *endogenous* changes.

internationalization of higher education The process of integrating a global perspective into the purpose, functions, or delivery of tertiary education.

internationalization at home The process of integrating a global perspective into local education in Expanding Circle countries that have traditionally looked to foreign countries to provide such a dimension.

koineization The process of the levelling of differences in dialects, usually found in communities of speakers of mutually intelligible languages.

labiodental fricatives Sounds that are produced with the lips and the teeth, for example [f] and [v].

languacultures A term used to present languages as constituting linguistic features such as grammar and lexis, but also cultural aspects such as customs, behaviours, and knowledge.

language contact A situation where two or more languages come into contact with each other, usually as the result of mobile populations.

language ideology A system of beliefs about a language.

language maintenance The protection of a heritage language in an individual or social group, particularly with reference to policies that protect minority languages.

language policy Official measures to restrict, maintain, or promote the use of certain languages, usually in the context of recognition in domains such as education, business, and politics.

language revitalization The process of reviving or increasing the use of a language that had been falling out of use.

language standardization The development of language-community consensus on a perceived set of language norms regarding features such as phonology, grammar, and vocabulary.

levelling The erosion of irregularities or differences in language.

levelling of irregular verb forms Relates to variation in grammar, for example in America *spoiled* is used for the past tense instead of *spoilt*.

lexicogrammar Features pertaining to the lexis (vocabulary) and grammar of a language.

lingua franca A language used for communication between speakers of two mutually unintelligible languages.

linguicism Discrimination based on language that unfairly treats certain linguistic communities, or unfairly advantages some languages over others.

linguistic diversity A term that denotes the multiplicity of living languages or dialects of languages that exist in a geographic region or social group.

linguistic imperialism Phillipson's term used to define an intention to impose one nation's language on another, usually at the expense of local languages.

linguistic landscapes The visibility and prominence of languages in public spheres.

localization The process of incorporating local needs into international integration.

locally coined idioms Word-by-word translations of indigenous phrases and variation in the use of native English idioms. New idioms are also created in many contexts through a combination of English and indigenous forms.

matched guise technique A research method used to measure attitudes, where participants are asked to evaluate audio-taped speakers and are told that they are listening to a number of different speakers, although it is one speaker in different 'guises'.

mercantilism An economic theory and practice of the sixteenth to eighteenth centuries in Europe, where it was believed to be economically advantageous to increase the wealth of a nation through unequal trade with other nations.

mesolect The variety of language that is between the most prestigious variety (*acrolect*) and the most colloquial (*basilect*), especially in an area where a creole is spoken.

Middle English The English language from the twelfth to the mid-fifteenth centuries, which was marked by substantial Norman-French influence.

multicomponent language users A term proposed by Vivian Cook as an alternative to the deficiency perspectives of terms like 'non-native speakers' or 'non-native language'. This book uses this term to replace the 'native speaker' as the goal of language learning.

multilingual English teachers A term proposed by Andy Kirkpatrick as an alternative to the deficiency perspectives of terms like 'non-native English-speaking teachers', with the multilingual repertoires of teachers viewed as an asset.

mutual intelligibility The ability of two speakers of different languages or dialects to understand each other.

'Native' Englishes A problematic term used to describe the English used by speakers of English as a first language.

native English speaker A problematic term used to describe a speaker for whom English is a first language, usually acquired from birth.

native English-speaker competence A view that uses the problematic term 'native English speaker' as the yardstick to measure non-native English-speaker proficiency.

native English-speaking teacher A problematic term used to define teachers for whom English is a 'native' language.

native speaker A problematic term used to describe a speaker's use of their first language.

native speaker fallacy A term coined by Robert Phillipson to challenge notions that a native English-speaking teacher is an ideal teacher.

native-speaker yardstick A benchmark of competence for non-native speaker performance that takes a deficit view of language ability.

nativized A problematic term referring to the influence of local language and culture on English in contexts where it has become ingrained in a community. The 'New' Englishes are often described as being nativized, unlike 'native' Inner Circle varieties which are not seen to have been influenced in such ways. Kirkpatrick prefers to classify all varieties as 'nativized'.

negation Making a clause negative, usually through use of a word with negative force (e.g. *no, not, never, nothing*).

'New' Englishes A term used to describe varieties of English that have emerged in former colonies or territories of English-speaking nations.

non-native English speaker A problematic term used to describe a speaker for whom English is not a first language.

non-native English-speaking teacher A problematic term used to define teachers for whom English is not a first or 'native' language.

No Child Left Behind Act A United States Act of Congress that was passed in 2001, and provides funding to programmes especially aimed at disadvantaged children and 'English language learners'.

norms (language) A group-held belief about the expectations of behaviours in a social context. In ELT, the 'native-speaker norm' refers to the superiority of the native English speaker, used as a target of competence.

Northern Subject Rule A grammatical pattern in northern English and Scottish spoken dialects where present tense verbs can take an -s in certain grammatical constructions, such as *the birds sings*.

Old English The English language spoken in Britain until about 1100.

Outer Circle Geographical contexts where English is spoken as a second language in an official capacity alongside other prominent national languages.

paradigm A set of theories and practices that underpin a discipline of scientific research.

paradigm shift A term coined by Thomas Kuhn to define a change in the established assumptions that underpin a discipline of scientific research.

perceptual dialectology A method used to analyse the explicit opinions that respondents hold about different language varieties based on beliefs rather than providing exposure to them, as the *verbal guise technique* does.

phonemes The smallest contrastive linguistic unit that is perceived to be distinct from other linguistic units. For example, English speakers always distinguish between vowel phonemes in words like *bet* and *bit*.

pidgin A contact language formed from two or more mutually unintelligible languages, and emerging from the need of the two communities to communicate.

plantation creoles Creoles that were formed due to contact situations in the plantation colonies, usually associated with the slave trade.

plosives A sound that is articulated by blocking airflow with the tongue (e.g. /t/ or /k/), lips (e.g. /p/ or /b/), or throat (e.g. /ʔ/), and building up pressure before releasing the air and realizing a sound.

pluricentric Having a quality of numerous accepted norms or forms. Within the Global Englishes paradigm, English is seen as being pluricentric due to the variation that exists. Such pluricentricity has grown as English has become a global lingua franca.

postalveolars Sounds that are articulated with the tongue against or near the back section of the roof of the mouth, including the *phones* /ʃ/, /tʃ/, /dʒ/, and /ʒ/.

pragmatics The linguistic study of how context influences meaning.

prestige A value attached to language which indicates a level of respect in relation to other languages.

proficient user An alternative term proposed by Thomas Paikeday to replace the problematic definition of a 'native' speaker.

prosodic Features of sound that describe intonation, stress, and rhythm of speech.

question formation Relates to variation in grammar where question patterns may be used differently in some varieties of English and ELF usage.

re-metaphorization A term used by Marie-Louise Pitzl to show how idioms are expressed rather differently in ELF communication and how speakers coin idiomatic language.

Received Pronunciation (RP) An accent of English associated with a social class rather than a geographical region. The accent is often assigned a prestige value.

reduced vowel system A set of fewer vowel phonemes compared to other languages or dialects.

register A variety of language used for a specific context or situation. For example, a speaker will use a different register when conversing with their friend at home than with their employer at work. It can be used to refer to a spoken or written register.

retroflex Sounds that are produced with the tip of the tongue curled up against the hard palate.

rhotic/rhoticity A rhotic accent is one where the /ɹ/ is pronounced in all positions of a word (e.g. in *rat*, *tar*, and *tartan*), and a non-rhotic accent is one where /ɹ/ is pronounced only when it precedes a vowel (e.g. in *rat*, but not in *tar* or *tartan*).

rising tone A phonological characteristic of an increase in pitch towards the end of a declarative sentence, resulting in statement rising in intonation like questions.

same meaning, different words Used to refer to variation in vocabulary usage with regards to different words being used for the same meaning, such as *jumper* in the UK and *sweater* in North America.

second diaspora The spread of English to new territories, which caused the emergence of nations where English was used alongside other languages.

semantic extension Where terms are assigned new meanings in addition to their original one. For example, in Malawi the verb *to move* takes on various meanings, e.g. *Suzagao is moving with my cousin* (dating).

semantic narrowing Where words take on a more restricted meaning, such as in Middle English where a *girl* was a young person of either sex.

settler colonization A channel of English spread due to the movement of English-speaking populations to new territories to establish new British colonies.

shuttle/shuttling between communities A term coined by Suresh Canagarajah to describe the practice of moving between speech communities and adjusting language accordingly.

sibilants The manner in which a sound is produced by directing air towards the teeth with the tongue, such as with the sounds /s, z, ʃ, ʒ, tʃ, dʒ/.

slavery The third channel of the spread of English which involved the establishment of new uses of English in displaced African communities, especially in plantation colonies.

societal treatment A research method that aims to investigate the relative status of language varieties. It involves an analysis of the 'treatment' given to them and to their speakers through content analysis, observation, and ethnography, and analysis of government policies, job advertisements, and media output.

split When a distinction is made between two phonemes that is not made in other varieties, or was not historically made, e.g. the historic *lad–bad* split from the same vowel phoneme (/æ/) to a long vowel sound for the latter (/æː/), or the *foot–strut* vowel split that occurred in some English accents but not in others.

standard Norms that are thought to be consistent and widely accepted as 'correct'.

'standard' English A variety of spoken English that is perceived to represent the accepted norms of grammatical, lexical, and phonological features that are thought to be 'correct'.

standardization The levelling of irregularities and variation in a language or a dialect through prescriptive ideas of what is acceptable or 'correct'.

strategic competence The ability of a user to adjust and use language to facilitate successful communication.

submersion An alternative term used to criticize language immersion practices that offer no language support to students.

substrate language The parent language of a creole that is considered to be the 'local' language, such as the West African languages spoken in trading settlements established by many European countries.

subtractive differences Relates to variation in grammar (or syntax) involving the omission of -*s* endings in some varieties of English and ELF usage.

superstrate language The parent language of a creole that is considered to be the 'imposed' language, such as the English language for the pidgins spoken along coastal trading routes of West Africa, or plantations in the Caribbean.

tense and aspect Relates to the grammatical system where speakers may use different forms to indicate a location in time (tense), and the quality of action in time (aspect), e.g. whether the action was completed or continuous.

theory/practice divide An incongruence between what experts claim is the case (or prescribe should be the case) and actual practices. It also denotes an incongruence between theoretical-level discussions and a lack of practical, empirical research at the classroom level in relation to ELT.

top-down perspective A view that language policy is prescribed by those with the power to instigate change.

trade and exploitation A channel of the spread of English due to the establishment of colonies for economic purposes which were not accompanied by mass migration of native English-speaking populations.

transcultural flows A term associated with Alastair Pennycook to describe the movement and adaptation of cultural forms to create new identities in a globalized world.

two diaspora A model that categorizes the spread of English, but which is problematic due to its focus on time and geographic factors.

unintelligible See *intelligible*.

varieties Group-specific, nation-based language forms. It is a problematic term in the ELF paradigm due to the difficulty in defining boundaries around something as fluid as language.

variety-specific compounds Relates to variation in vocabulary whereby new compounds are created for specific contexts, such as *salary man* (company employee) in Japan.

verbal guise technique A research method used to measure attitudes, where participants are asked to evaluate audio-taped speakers. This is a modified version of the *matched guise technique*; it was developed in response to the various criticisms of participant deception.

vowel merger The convergence of two previously distinct vowel sounds to form the same sound, e.g. the vowels in *cot* and *caught*, which have merged in many North American Englishes.

World Englishes A field of study that examines varieties of English that have developed in regions that were especially influenced by the United Kingdom and the United States of America.

World Language Hierarchy David Graddol's model of world languages in which they are organized according to their influence as locally, regionally, nationally, internationally, or globally unifying languages.

World Standard English A variety of spoken English that is perceived to conform to globally accepted norms of grammatical, lexical, and phonological features.

References

Adolphs, S. (2005). 'I don't think I should learn all this – A longitudinal view of attitudes towards "native speaker" English.' In C. Gnutzmann and F. Intemann (eds), *The Globalisation of English and the English Language Classroom* (pp. 115–27). Tübingen: Gunter Narr Verlag.

Ali, S. (2009). 'Teaching English as an international language (EIL) in the Gulf Corporation Council [sic] (GCC) countries: the brown man's burden.' In F. Sharifian (ed.), *English as an International Language: Perspectives and Pedagogical Issues* (pp. 34–57). Bristol: Multilingual Matters.

Alo, M. A. and Mesthrie, R. (2004). 'Nigerian English: morphology and syntax.' In E. W. Schneider, K. Burridge, B. Kortmann, R. Mesthrie and C. Upton (eds), *A Handbook of Varieties of English Volume 2: Morphology and Syntax* (pp. 813–27). Berlin: Mouton de Gruyter.

Alsagoff, L. (2012a). 'Another book on EIL? Heralding the need for new ways of thinking, doing, and being.' In L. Alsagoff, S. L. McKay, G. Hu and W. A. Renandya (eds), *Principles and Practices for Teaching English as an International Language* (p. 5). New York: Routledge.

——(2012b). 'Identity and the EIL learner.' In L. Alsagoff, S. L. Mckay, G. Hu and W. A. Renandya (eds), *Principles and Practices for Teaching English as an International Language* (pp. 104–22). New York: Routledge.

Alsagoff, L., McKay, S. L., Hu, G. and Renandya, W. A. (eds). (2012). *Principles and Practices of Teaching English as an International Language.* Bristol: Routledge.

Amin, N. (1999). 'Minority Women Teachers of ESL: Negotiating White English.' In G. Braine (ed.), *Non-native Educators in English Language Teaching* (pp. 77–92). Mahwah, New Jersey: Lawrence Erlbaum Associates.

Anderwald, L. (2008). 'The varieties of English spoken in the Southeast of England: morphology and syntax.' In B. Kortmann and C. Upton (eds), *Varieties of English 1: The British Isles* (pp. 440–62). Berlin: Mouton de Gruyter.

Ansaldo, U. (2004). 'The evolution of Singapore English: Finding the matrix.' In L. Lim (ed.), *Singapore English: A Grammatical Description* (pp. 127–49). Amsterdam: John Benjamins Publishing.

——(2010). 'Contact in Asian Varieties of English.' In R. Hickey (ed.), *The Handbook of Language Contact* (pp. 498–517). Malden, MA: Blackwell.

Anushka, A. and Thorpe, V. (2007, 28 October). 'Mind your language, critics warn BBC.' *The Observer.* Retrieved 5 September 2014 from www.theguardian.com/media/2007/oct/28/bbc.television

Apelman, V. (2010). *English at Work. The Communicative Situation of Engineers.* University of Gothenburg.

Árva, V. and Medgyes, P. (2000). 'Native and non-native teachers in the classroom.' *System,* 28(3), pp. 355–72. doi:http://dx.doi.org/10.1016/S0346–251X(00)00017–18

Asante, M. Y. (2012). 'Variation in subject–verb concord in Ghanaian English.' *World Englishes,* 31(2), pp. 208–25. doi:10.1111/j.1467–1971X.2012.01751.x

Australian Bureau of Statistics. (2012). *Census of Population and Housing: Characteristics of Aboriginal and Torres Strait Islander Australians, 2011.* Retrieved 5 September 2014 from www.abs.gov.au/AUSSTATS/abs@.nsf/DetailsPage/2076.02011?OpenDocument

Backhaus, P. (2007). *Linguistic Landscapes: A Comparative Study of Urban Multilingualism in Tokyo*. Clevedon: Multilingual Matters.

Baker, C. (1992). *Attitudes and Language*. Clevedon: Multilingual Matters.

Baker, F. J. and Giacchino-Baker, R. (2003). 'Lower secondary school curriculum development in Vietnam.' *California State Polytechnic, Pomona Journal of Interdisciplinary Studies*, 16(2003), pp. 1–11.

Baker, W. (2009). 'The cultures of English as a lingua franca.' *TESOL Quarterly*, 43(4), pp. 567–92. doi:10.1002/j.1545–7249.2009.tb00187.x

——(2012). 'From cultural awareness to intercultural awareness: culture in ELT.' *ELT Journal*, 66(1), pp. 62–70. doi:10.1093/elt/ccr017

Bamgbose, A. (1992). 'Standard Nigerian English: issues of identification.' In B. B. Kachru (ed.), *The other Tongue: English Across Cultures* (pp. 140–61). Urbana, IL: University of Illinois Press.

——(1998). 'Torn between the norms?: innovations in world Englishes.' *World Englishes*, 17(1), pp. 1–14. doi:10.1111/1467–1971X.00078

Barratt, L. and Kontra, E. H. (2000). 'Native-English-speaking teachers in cultures other than their own.' *TESOL Journal*, 9(3), pp. 19–23. doi:10.1002/j.1949–3533.2000.tb00263.x

Bauer, L. and Warren, P. (2008). 'Maori English: phonology.' In K. Burridge and B. Kortmann (eds), *Varieties of English 3: The Pacific and Australasia* (pp. 77–88). Berlin: Mouton de Gruyter.

Baumgardner, R. J. (1987). 'Utilising Pakistani English newspaper to teach grammar.' *World Englishes*, 6 (3), pp. 241–53.

Bautista, M. L. S. and Gonzalez, A. (2006). 'English in Southeast Asia.' In B. Kachru, Y. Kachru and C. Nelson (eds), *The Handbook of World Englishes* (pp. 130–44). Oxford: Blackwell.

Bayard, D., Weatherall, A., Gallois, C. and Pittam, J. (2001). 'Pax Americana? Accent attitudinal evaluations in New Zealand, Australia and America.' *Journal of Sociolinguistics*, 5(1), pp. 22–49. doi:10.1111/1467–9481.00136

BBC. (1999). 'Radio 4 dumps "plummy" Boris.' *BBC News*. Retrieved 18 April 2014, from http://news.bbc.co.uk/2/hi/uk_news/468895.stm

——(2005, 29 December). 'Regional accents "bad for trade"'. *BBC News*. London. Retrieved from http://news.bbc.co.uk/2/hi/uk_news/england/4566028.stm

——(2011). 'Cheryl Cole: US *X Factor* accent snub offends Geordies.' *BBC News Video*. Retrieved 18 April 2014 from www.bbc.co.uk/news/uk-england-tyne-13559526

——(2013, 27 June). 'Japan's NHK sued over use of English words.' *BBC News*. Retrieved 12 September 2014 from www.bbc.co.uk/news/world-asia-23079067

Beal, J. (2008a). 'English dialects in the North of England: phonology.' In B. Kortmann and C. Upton (eds), *Varieties of English 1: The British Isles* (pp. 122–44). Berlin: Mouton de Gruyter.

——(2008b). 'English dialects in the North of England: morphology and syntax.' In B. Kortmann and C. Upton (eds), *Varieties of English 1: The British Isles* (pp. 373–403). Berlin: Mouton de Gruyter.

——(2010). *An Introduction to Regional Englishes: Dialect Variation in England*. Edinburgh: Edinburgh University Press.

Benke, E. and Medgyes, P. (2005). 'Differences in teaching behaviour between native and non-native speaker teachers: as seen by the learners.' In E. Llurda (ed.), *Non-Native Language Teachers. Perceptions, Challenges and Contributions to the Profession* (Vol. 5, pp. 195–215). New York: Springer US. doi:10.1007/0-387-24565-0_11

Berry, C. and Taylor, J. (2013). 'Internationalisation in higher education in Latin America: policies and practice in Colombia and Mexico.' *Higher Education*, 67(5), pp. 585–601. doi:10.1007/s10734-013-9667-z

Bjørge, A. K. (2012). 'Expressing disagreement in ELF business negotiations: theory and practice.' *Applied Linguistics*, 33(4), pp. 406–27. doi:10.1093/applin/ams015

Blake, R. (2008). 'Bajan: phonology.' In E. W. Schneider (ed.), *Varieties of English 2: The Americas and the Caribbean* (pp. 312–19). Berlin: Mouton de Gruyter.

Block, D. (2012). 'Economising globalisation and identity in applied linguistics in neoliberal times.' In D. Block, J. Gray and M. Holborow (eds), *Neoliberalism and Applied Linguistics* (pp. 56–85). London: Routledge.

Blommaert, J. M. E. (2010). *The Sociolinguistics of Globalization*. Cambridge: Cambridge University Press.

Blommaert, J. M. E. and Dong, J. (2010). *Ethnographic Fieldwork*. Bristol: Multilingual Matters.

Böhringer, H. (2007). *The Sound of Silence: Silent and Filled Pauses in English as a Lingua Franca Business Interaction*. Unpublished MA thesis: University of Vienna.

Bokamba, E. G. (1992). 'The Africanization of English.' In B. B. Kachru (ed.), *The Other Tongue: English across Cultures* (2nd ed., pp. 125–47). Urbana, IL: University of Illinois Press.

Bolton, K. (2000). 'Introduction.' *World Englishes*, 19(3), pp. 265–285. doi:10.1111/1467–1971X.00178

——(2002). *Hong Kong English: Autonomy and Creativity* (p. 332). Hong Kong: Hong Kong University Press.

Bolton, K. and Kwok, H. (1990). 'The dynamics of the Hong Kong accent: social identity and sociolinguistic description.' *Journal of Asian Pacific Communication*, (1), pp. 147–172.

Bowerman, S. (2008). 'White South African English: phonology.' In *Varieties of English 4: Africa, South and Southeast Asia* (pp. 164–76). Berlin: Mouton de Gruyter.

Bradac, J., Cargile, A. C. and Hallett, J. S. (2001). 'Language attitudes: respect, conspect and prospect.' In W. P. Robinson and H. Giles (eds), *The New Handbook of Language and Social Psychology* (pp. 137–55). Chichester: Wiley.

Bradley, D. (2008). 'Regional characteristics of Australian English: phonology.' In K. Burridge and B. Kortmann (eds), *Varieties of English 3: The Pacific and Australasia* (pp. 77–88). Berlin: Mouton de Gruyter.

Braine, G. (1999). *Non-native Educators in English Language Teaching*. Mahwah, NJ: Lawrence Erlbaum Associates.

——(2005). 'A history of research on non-native speaker English teachers.' In E. Llurda (ed.), *Non-Native Language Teachers: Perceptions, Challenges and Contributions to the Profession* (pp. 13–23). New York: Springer.

——(2010). *Non-native Speaker English Teachers. Research, Pedagogy, and Professional Growth*. New York: Routledge.

Brenn-White, P. M. and Faethe, E. (2013). *English-Taught Master's Programs in Europe?: A 2013 Update* (pp. 1–12). New York: Institute of International Education (IIE).

British Council. (2014). 'Frequently asked questions, the English Language.' Retrieved 5 September 2014 from www.britishcouncil.org/learning-faq-the-english-language.htm

Brock-Utne, B. (2012). 'Language and inequality: global challenges to education.' *Compare: A Journal of Comparative and International Education*, 42(5), pp. 773–93. doi:10.1080/03057925.2012.706453

Brown, L. and Holloway, I. (2008). 'The adjustment journey of international postgraduate students at an English university: An ethnographic study.' *Journal of Research in International Education*, 7(2), pp. 232–49. doi:10.1177/1475240908091306

Bruthiaux, P. (2003). 'Squaring the circles: issues in modeling English worldwide.' *International Journal of Applied Linguistics*, 13(2), pp. 159–78. doi:10.1111/1473–4192.00042

Brutt-Griffler, J. (2002). *World English: A Study of its Development*. Clevedon: Multilingual Matters.

Burridge, K. (2010). 'English in Australia.' In A. Kirkpatrick (ed.), *The Routledge Handbook of World Englishes* (pp. 132–51). London: Routledge.

Butler, S. (1997). 'Corpus of English in Southeast Asia: implications for a regional dictionary.' In M. L. S. Bautista (ed.), *English is an Asian Language: The Philippine Context* (pp. 103–24). Sydney, NSW: Macquarie Library.

Butler, Y. G. (2007). 'How are nonnative-English-speaking teachers perceived by young learners?' *TESOL Quarterly*, 41(4), pp. 731–55.

Canagarajah, A. S. (1999a). 'Interrogating the "native speaker fallacy": non–linguistics roots, non–pedagogical results.' In G. Braine (ed.), *Non-native Educators in English Language Teaching* (pp. 77–92). Mahwah, NJ: Lawrence Erlbaum Associates.

——(1999b). *Resisting Linguistic Imperialism in English Teaching*. Oxford: Oxford University Press.

——(2005). 'Introduction.' In A. S. Canagarajah (ed.), *Reclaiming the Local in Language Policy and Practice*. Mahwah, NJ: Lawrence Erlbaum Associates.

——(2006a). 'The Place of World Englishes in Composition.' *College Composition and Communication*, 57(4), pp. 586–619.

——(2006b). 'Negotiating the local in English as a lingua franca.' *Annual Review of Applied Linguistics*, 26, pp. 197–218.

——(2007). 'Lingua Franca English, Multilingual Communities, and Language Acquisition.' *The Modern Language Journal*, 91, pp. 923–39. doi:10.1111/j.1540–4781.2007.00678.x

——(2013). *Translingual Practice: Global Englishes and Cosmopolitan Relations* (p. 216). London: Routledge.

Carey, R. (2010). 'Hard to ignore: English native speakers in ELF research.' *Journal of English as a Lingua Franca*, 6, pp. 88–101.

Cargile, A. C., Takai, J. and Rodríguez, J. I. (2006). 'Attitudes Toward African–American Vernacular English: A US Export to Japan?' *Journal of Multilingual and Multicultural Development*, 27(6), pp. 443–56. doi:10.2167/jmmd472.1

Carter, R. and McCarthy, M. (2006). *Cambridge Grammar of English*. Cambridge: Cambridge University Press.

Caxton, W. H. (1490). *Boke of Eneydos (Prologue of the Aeneid)*. Westminster: William Caxton.

Chan, J. Y. H. (2013). 'Contextual variation and Hong Kong English.' *World Englishes*, 32(1), pp. 54–74. doi:10.1111/weng.12004

Chang, J. (2006). 'Globalization and English in Chinese higher education.' *World Englishes*, 25(3–4), pp. 513–25. doi:10.1111/j.1467–1971X.2006.00484.x

Chern, C. (2002). 'English Language Teaching in Taiwan Today.' *Asia Pacific Journal of Education*, 22(2), pp. 97–105. doi:10.1080/0218879020220209

Chiba, R., Matsuura, H. and Yamamoto, A. (1995) 'Japanese attitudes toward English accents.' *World Englishes*, 14(1), pp. 77–86.

Chik, A. (2010). 'Creative multilingualism in Hong Kong popular music.' *World Englishes*, 29(4), pp. 508–22.

Childs, B. and Wolfram, W. (2008). 'Bahamian English: phonology.' In E. W. Schneider (ed.), *Varieties of English 2: The Americas and the Caribbean* (pp. 239–55). Berlin: Mouton de Gruyter.

Chomsky, N. (1965). *Aspects of the Theory of Syntax*. Cambridge, MA: MIT Press.

Clark, E. and Paran, A. (2007). 'The employability of non-native-speaker teachers of EFL: A UK survey.' *System*, 35(4), pp. 407–30. doi:http://dx.doi.org/10.1016/j.system.2007.05.002

Clayton, T. (2006). *Language choice in a Nation under Transition: English Language Spread in Cambodia*. Boston, MA: Springer.

Cogo, A. (2009). 'Accommodating difference in ELF conversations: a study of pragmatic strategies.' In A. Mauranen and E. Ranta (eds), *English as a Lingua Franca: Studies and Findings* (pp. 254–73). Cambridge: Cambridge Scholars.

——(2011). 'English as a Lingua Franca: concepts, use, and implications.' *ELT Journal*, 66(1), pp. 97–105. doi:10.1093/elt/ccr069

——(2012a). 'ELF and super-diversity: a case study of ELF multilingual practices from a business context.' *Journal of English as a Lingua Franca*, 1(2), pp. 287–313. doi:10.1515/jelf-2012-0020

——(2012b). 'English as a Lingua Franca: concepts, use, and implications.' *ELT Journal*, 66(1), pp. 97–105. doi:10.1093/elt/ccr069

Cogo, A. and Dewey, M. (2006). 'Efficiency in ELF Communication: From Pragmatic Motives to Lexico-grammatical Innovation.' *Nordic Journal of English Studies*, 5(2), pp. 59–93.

——(2012). *Analysing English as a Lingua Franca: A Corpus-driven Investigation*. London: Continuum.

Collins, P. and Peters, P. (2008). 'Australian English: morphology and syntax.' In B. Kortmann, K. Burridge, R. Mesthrie, E. W. Schneider and C. Upton (eds), *Varieties of English 3: The Pacific and Australasia* (pp. 593–610). Berlin: Mouton de Gruyter.

Connor-Linton, J. (2006). 'Writing.' In R. W. Fasold and J. Connor-Linton (eds), *An Introduction to Language and Linguistics*, pp. 401–433. Cambridge: Cambridge University Press.

Cook, V. (1999). 'Going Beyond the Native Speaker in Language Teaching.' *TESOL Quarterly*, 33(2), pp. 185–209. doi:10.2307/3587717

——(2005). 'Basing teaching on the L2 user.' In E. Llurda (ed.), *Non-Native Language Teachers SE – 4* (Vol. 5, pp. 47–61). New York: Springer US. doi:10.1007/0-387-24565-0_4

Cooke, D. (1988). 'Ties that constrict: English as a Trojan horse.' In A. Cumming, A. Gagne and J. Dawson (eds), *Awarenesses: Proceeding of the 1987 TESL Ontario Conference* (pp. 55–62). Ontario: TESL Ontario.

Coulmas, F. (2005). *Sociolinguistics: The Study of Speakers' Choices* (p. 263). Cambridge: Cambridge University Press.

Cowie, C. (2007). 'The accents of outsourcing: the meanings of "neutral" in the Indian call centre industry.' *World Englishes*, 26(3), pp. 316–30. doi:10.1111/j.1467–1971X.2007.00511.x

Crismore, A., Ngeow, K. Y.-H. and Soo, K.-S. (1996). 'Attitudes toward English in Malaysia.' *World Englishes*, 15(3), pp. 319–35. doi:10.1111/j.1467–1971X.1996.tb00118.x

Crystal, D. (1995). *The Cambridge Encyclopedia of the English Language*. Cambridge: Cambridge University Press.

——(1997). *English as a Global Language*. Cambridge: Cambridge University Press.

——(2002). *Language Death*. Cambridge: Cambridge University Press.

——(2003). *English as a Global Language*. Cambridge: Cambridge University Press.

——(2006). 'Into the 21st century.' In L. Mugglestone (ed.), *The Oxford History of English*. Oxford: Oxford University Press.

——(2008). 'Two thousand million?' *English Today*, 24(01), pp. 3–6.

D'Souza, J. (1999). 'Afterword.' *World Englishes*, 18(2), pp. 271–74. doi:10.1111/1467–1971X.00139

Dalton-Puffer, C., Kaltenboeck, G. and Smit, U. (1997). 'Learner attitudes and L2 pronunciation in Austria.' *World Englishes*, 16(1), pp. 115–28. doi:10.1111/1467–1971X.00052

Danet, B. and Herring, S. C. (eds). (2007). *The Multilingual Internet: Language, Culture, and Communication Online* (Vol. 50, p. 464). Oxford: Oxford University Press.

Dauenhauer, N. M. and Dauenhauer, R. (1998). 'Technical, emotional, and ideological issues in reversing language shift: examples from Southeast Alaska.' In L. A. Grenoble and L. J. Whaley (eds), *Endangered Languages: Language Loss and Community Response* (pp. 57–98). Cambridge: Cambridge University Press.

Davies, A. (1991). *The Native Speaker in Applied Linguistics*. Edinburgh: Edinburgh University Press.

——(2003). *The Native Speaker Myth and Reality*. Clevedon: Multilingual Matters.

——(2013). *Native Speakers and Native Users: Loss and Gain* (p. 186). Cambridge: Cambridge University Press.

De Lotbinière, M. (2011, November). 'South Korean parents told: pre-school English "harmful."' *The Guardian Weekly*. London. Retrieved 5 September 2014 from www.theguardian.com/education/2011/nov/08/south-korea-english-teaching-fears

De Swaan, A. (2001). *Words of the World: The Global Language System* (p. 253). Malden, MA: Polity Press.

——(2010). 'Language systems.' In N. Coupland (ed.), *The Handbook of Language and Globalization* (pp. 56–76). Malden, MA: Blackwell.

Dean, A. (2010). 'Improving the learning experience for international students.' *International Journal of Management Cases*, 14(4), pp. 207–23.

Decke-Cornill, H. (2002). '"We would have to invent the language we are supposed to teach": the issue of English as lingua franca in language education in Germany.' *Language, Culture and Curriculum*, 15(3), pp. 251–63. doi:10.1080/07908310208666649

Delgado-Márquez, B. L., Escudero-Torres, M. Á. and Hurtado-Torres, N. E. (2013). 'Being highly internationalised strengthens your reputation: an empirical investigation of top higher education institutions.' *Higher Education*, 66(5), pp. 619–33. doi:10.1007/s10734-013-9626-8

Derwing, T. (2003). 'What do ESL students say about their accents?' *Canadian Modern Language Review/La Revue Canadienne Des Langues Vivantes*, 59(4), pp. 547–67. doi:10.3138/cmlr.59.4.547

Derwing, T. M., Rossiter, M. J. and Munro, M. J. (2002). 'Teaching native speakers to listen to foreign-accented speech.' *Journal of Multilingual and Multicultural Development*, 23(4), pp. 245–59. doi:10.1080/01434630208666468

Deterding, D. and Kirkpatrick, A. (2006). 'Emerging South-East Asian Englishes and intelligibility.' *World Englishes*, 25(3–4), pp. 391–409. doi:10.1111/j.1467–1971X.2006.00478.x

Devonish, H. and Harry, O. G. (2008). 'Jamaican Creole and Jamaican English: phonology.' In E. W. Schneider (ed.), *Varieties of English 2: The Americas and the Caribbean* (pp. 256–89). Berlin: Mouton de Gruyter.

Dewey, M. (2007). *English as a Lingua Franca: An Empirical Study of Innovation in Lexis and Grammar.* London: University of London.

——(2012). 'Towards a post-normative approach: learning the pedagogy of ELF.' *Journal of English as a Lingua Franca*, 1(1), pp. 141–70. doi:10.1515/jelf-2012-0007

Dogancay-Aktuna, S. and Hardman, J. (2008). *Global English Teaching and Teacher Education*. Virginia: Teachers of English to Speakers of Other Languages.

Dorian, N. (1998). 'Western language ideologies and small-language prospects.' In L. A. Grenoble and L. J. Whaley (eds), *Endangered Languages: Language Loss and Community Response* (pp. 3–26). Cambridge: Cambridge University Press.

Dörnyei, Z. (2009). 'Motivation, language identity and the L2 self.' In Z. Dörnyei and E. Ushioda (eds), *Motivation, Language Identity and the L2 Self* (pp. 9–42). Bristol: Multilingual Matters.

Dörnyei, Z. and Csizér, K. (2002). 'Some dynamics of language attitudes and motivation: Results of a longitudinal nationwide survey.' *Applied Linguistics*, 23(4), pp. 423–62.

Dörnyei, Z., Csizér, K. and Németh, N. (2006) *Motivation, Language Attitudes and Globalisation.* Clevedon: Multilingual Matters.

'English is Coming: The adverse side-effects of the growing dominance of English.' *The Economist.* Retrieved 5 September 2014 from www.economist.com/node/13103967

Education Counts (2014). 'Ministry of Education – education counts.' Ministry of Education. Retrieved 17 January 2014, from www.educationcounts.govt.nz/publications/91416/maori-medium-and-english-medium/5851

Ehrenreich, S. (2010). 'English as a business lingua franca in a German multinational corporation: meeting the challenge.' *Journal of Business Communication*, 47(4), pp. 408–31. doi:10.1177/0021943610377303

El-Dash, L. G. and Busnardo, J. (2001). 'Brazilian attitudes toward English: dimensions of status and solidarity.' *International Journal of Applied Linguistics*, 11(1), pp. 57–74. doi:10.1111/1473–4192.00004

ELCat (Catalogue of Endangered Languages). (2014). 'Endangered languages.' Retrieved from www.endangeredlanguages.com/

ELFA. (2008). 'English as a lingua franca in academic settings (ELFA).' Retrieved 5 September 2014 from www.helsinki.fi/englanti/elfa/

Erling, E. J. (2005). 'Who is the global English speaker? A profile of students of English at the Freie Universität Berlin.' In C. Gnutzmann and F. Intemann (eds), *The Globalisation of English and the English Language Classroom* (pp. 215–30). Tübingen: Gunter Narr Verlag.

European Commission. (2013). 'How to write clearly.' Brussels: The European Commission.

Evans, S. (2011). 'Hong Kong English and the professional world.' *World Englishes*, 30(3), pp. 293–316. doi:10.1111/j.1467–1971X.2011.01655.x

Farr, M. (2013, 19 February). 'Abbott: "We always speak with a strong Australian accent".' news.com.au. Retrieved 12 September 2014 from www.news.com.au/national/abbott-attacks-labors-imported-politics/story-fncynjr2-1226581145008

Fasold, R. W. and Connor-Linton, J. (eds). (2006). *An Introduction to Language and Linguistics.* Cambridge: Cambridge University Press.

Fennell, B. (2001). *A History of English: A Sociolinguistic Approach.* Malden, MA: Wiley.

Ferguson, G. (2006). *Language Planning and Education.* Edinburgh: Edinburgh University Press.

——(2012). 'The practice of ELF'. *Journal of English as a Lingua Franca*, 1(1), pp. 177–80.

Fernquest, J. (2012, 17 January). 'Tony Blair teaches English to Thais.' *Bangkok Post.* Retrieved 12 September 2014 from www.bangkokpost.com/learning/learning-from-news/275567/tony-blair-teaches-english-to-thais

Filppula, M. (2008). 'Irish English: morphology and syntax.' In B. Kortmann and C. Upton (eds), *Varieties of English 1: The British Isles* (pp. 328–59). Berlin: Mouton de Gruyter.

Firth, A. (1990). '"Lingua franca" negotiations: towards an interactional approach.' *World Englishes*, 9(3), pp. 269–80. doi:10.1111/j.1467–1971X.1990.tb00265.x

——(1996). 'The discursive accomplishment of normality: On "lingua franca" English and conversation analysis.' *Journal of Pragmatics*, 26(2), pp. 237–59. doi:http://dx.doi.org/10.1016/0378–2166(96) 00014–18

Firth, A. and Wagner, J. (1997). 'On discourse, communication, and (some) fundamental concepts in SLA research.' *The Modern Language Journal*, 81(3), pp. 285–300. doi:10.1111/j.1540–4781.1997. tb05480.x

Flowerdew, J. (2008). 'Scholarly writers who use English as an additional language: what can Goffman's "Stigma" tell us?' *Journal of English for Academic Purposes*, 7(2), pp. 77–86. doi:http://dx.doi.org/ 10.1016/j.jeap.2008.03.002

Forbes-Mewett, H. and Nyland, C. (2012). 'Funding international student support services: tension and power in the university.' *Higher Education*, 65(2), 181–92. doi:10.1007/s10734-012-9537-0

Foucault, M. (1970). *The Order of Things*. London: Tavistock.

——(1972). *The Archaeology of Knowledge*. London: Tavistock.

Friedrich, P. (2000). 'English in Brazil: functions and attitudes.' *World Englishes*, 19(2), 215–23. doi:10.1111/1467–1971X.00170

——(2012). 'ELF, intercultural communication and the strategic aspect of communicative competence.' In A. Matsuda (ed.), *Principles and Practices for Teaching English as an International Language* (pp. 44–54). Bristol: Multilingual Matters.

Friginal, E. (2007). 'Outsourced call centers and English in the Philippines.' *World Englishes*, 26(3), pp. 331–45. doi:10.1111/j.1467–1971X.2007.00512.x

Frølich, N. (2006). 'Still academic and national – internationalisation in Norwegian research and higher education.' *Higher Education*, 52(3), pp. 405–20. doi:10.1007/s10734-005-3080-1

Galloway, N. (2011). *An Investigation of Japanese Students' Attitudes towards English*. PhD dissertation. University of Southampton.

——(2013). 'Global Englishes and English Language Teaching (ELT) – Bridging the gap between theory and practice in a Japanese context.' *System*, 41(3), pp. 786–803. doi:10.1016/j.system.2013.07.019

Galloway, N. and Rose, H. (2013). '"They envision going to New York, not Jakarta": the differing attitudes toward ELF of students, teaching assistants, and instructors in an English-medium business program in Japan.' *Journal of English as a Lingua Franca*, 2(2), pp. 229–53. doi:10.1515/jelf-2013-0014

——(2014). 'Using listening journals to raise awareness of Global Englishes in ELT.' *ELT Journal*, 68(4), pp. 386–96. Retrieved 12 September 2014 from http://eltj.oxfordjournals.org/content/early/2014/ 05/26/elt.ccu021.abstract

Gardner, R. C. (1985). *Social Psychology and Second Language Learning: The Role of Attitudes and Motivation*. London: Arnold.

Gargesh, R. (2006). 'South Asian Englishes.' In B. Kachru, Y. Kachru and C. L. Nelson (eds), *The Handbook of World Englishes*. Oxford: Wiley-Blackwell.

Garner, R. (2008, 19 August). 'Dramatic decline in foreign languages studied at university.' *The Independent*. London. Retrieved from www.independent.co.uk/news/education/dramatic-decline-in-foreign-languages-studied-at-university-901855.html

——(2013, 18 November). 'Teacher "told to sound less northern" after southern Ofsted inspection.' *The Independent*. London. Retrieved from www.independent.co.uk/news/uk/home-news/teacher-told-to-sound-less-northern-after-southern-ofsted-inspection-8947332.html

Garrett, P. (2010). *Attitudes to Language: Key Topics in Sociolinguistics*. Cambridge: Cambridge University Press.

Gil, J. (2010). 'The double danger of English as a global language.' *English Today 101*, 26(1), 51–56. doi:10.1017/502660784099905

Giles, H. and Coupland, N. (1991). *Language Contexts and Consequences*. Milton Keynes: Open University Press.

Giles, H. and Powesland, P. F. (1975). *Speech Style and Social Evaluation*. London: Academic Press/ European Association of Experimental Social Psychology.

Gnutzmann, C. (ed.). (1999). *Teaching and Learning English as a Global Language: Native and Non-native Perspectives*. Tübingen: Stauffenburg.

Gonzalez, A. (2010). 'English and English teaching in Colombia: tensions and possibilities in the expanding circle.' In *The Routledge Handbook of World Englishes*. New York: Routledge.

Gordon, E. and Maclagan, M. (2008). 'Regional and social differences in New Zealand: phonology.' In K. Burridge and B. Kortmann (eds), *Varieties of English 3: The Pacific and Australasia* (pp. 64–76). Berlin: Mouton de Gruyter.

Görlach, M. (1988). *Even More Englishes: Studies 1996–1997*. Amsterdam: John Benjamins.

——(1990). *Studies in the History of the English Language*. Heidelberg: Carl Winter.

——(2002). *Still more Englishes*. Amsterdam: John Benjamins.

Gough, D. (1996). 'Black English in South Africa.' In V. de Klerk (ed.), *Focus on South Africa* (pp. 53–77). Amsterdam: John Benjamins.

Graddol, D. (1997). *The Future of English? A Guide to Forecasting the Popularity of the English Language in the 21st Century*. London: British Council.

——(2006). *English Next*. London: British Council.

Gramley, S. (2012). *The History of English: An Introduction*. London: Routledge.

Grau, M. (2005). 'English as a global language: what do future teachers have to say?' In C. Gnutzmann and F. Intemann (eds), *The Globalisation of English and the English Language Classroom* (pp. 261–74). Tübingen: Gunter Narr Verlag.

Grenoble, L. A. and Whaley, L. J. (1998). 'Preface.' In L. A. Grenoble and L. J. Whaley (eds), *Endangered Languages: Language Loss and Community Response* (pp. vii–xvi). Cambridge: Cambridge University Press.

Gu, Y. (2012). 'Learning strategies: prototypical core and dimensions of variation.' *Studies in Self-Access Learning Journal*, 3(4), pp. 330–56.

Hale, K. (1998). 'On endangered languages and the importance of linguistic diversity.' In L. A. Grenoble and L. J. Whaley (eds), *Endangered Languages: Language Loss and Community Response* (pp. 192–216). Cambridge: Cambridge University Press.

Harmer, J. (2007). *The Practice of English Language Teaching* (4th ed.). Harlow: Longman.

He, D. and Li, D. (2009). 'Language attitudes and linguistic features in the "China English" debate.' *World Englishes*, 28(1), pp. 70–89.

Healey, N. M. (2007). 'Is higher education in really "internationalising"?' *Higher Education*, 55(3), pp. 333–55. doi:10.1007/s10734-007-9058-4

Hickey, R. (2010). 'The Englishes of Ireland: emergence and transportation.' In A. Kirkpatrick (ed.), *The Routledge Handbook of World Englishes* (pp. 76–95). London: Routledge.

Hisama, T. (1995). *Sayonnara Nihonin-Eigo [Farewell to Japanese English]*. Tokyo: Taishukan.

Hogg, R. and Denison, D. (2006). 'Overview.' In R. Hogg and D. Denison (eds), *A History of the English Language*. Cambridge: Cambridge University Press.

Holliday, A. (2005). *The Struggle to Teach English as an International Language*. Oxford: Oxford University Press.

——(2009). 'English as a lingua franca: "non-native speakers" and cosmopolitan realities.' In F. Sharifian (ed.), *English as an International Language: Perspectives and Pedagogical Issues* (pp. 21–33). Bristol: Multilingual Matters.

Holliday, A. S. (2008). 'Standards of English and politics of inclusion.' *Language Teaching*, (41), pp. 119–30.

Honna, N. (2003). *Sekai no Eigo wo aruku [Walking through World Englishes]*. Tokyo: Shueisha.

Horvath, B. M. (2008). 'Australian English: phonology.' In K. Burridge and B. Kortmann (eds), *Varieties of English 3: The Pacific and Australasia* (pp. 89–110). Berlin: Mouton de Gruyter.

House, J. (1999). 'Misunderstanding in intercultural communication: interactions in English as lingua franca and the myth of mutual intelligibility.' In C. Gnutzmann (ed.), *Teaching and Learning English as a Global Language: Native and Non-native Perspectives* (pp. 73–89). Tübingen: Stauffenburg.

——(2002). 'Developing pragmatic competence in English as a lingua franca.' In K. Knapp and C. Meierkord (eds), *Lingua Franca Communication* (pp. 245–68). Frankfurt am Main: Peter Lang.

——(2012). 'Teaching oral skills in English as a lingua franca.' In L. Alsagoff, S. L. McKay, G. Hu and W. A. Renandya (eds), *Principles and Practices for Teaching English as an International Language*. New York: Routledge.

Hu, G. (2012). 'Assessing English as an international language.' In L. Alsagoff, S. L. McKay, G. Hu and W. A. Renandya (eds), *Principles and Practices for Teaching English as an International Language* (pp. 123–44). New York: Routledge.

Huber, M. and Dako, K. (2004). 'Ghanaian English: morphology and syntax.' In B. Kortmann, E. W. Schneider, K. Burridge, R. Mesthrie and C. Upton (eds), *A Handbook of Varieties of English Volume 2: Morphology and Syntax* (pp. 854–65). Berlin: Mouton de Gruyter.

——(2008). 'Ghanaian English: morphology and syntax.' In R. Mesthrie (ed.), *Varieties of English Volume 4: Africa, South and Southeast Asia* (pp. 368–80). Berlin: Mouton De Gruyter.

Hughes, A., Trudgill, P. and Watt, D. (2012). *English Accents and Dialects: An Introduction to Social and Regional Varieties of English in the British Isles*. New York: Routledge.

Hui, P. (2001, 29 September). '"Mother tongue" schools bow to English as best medium.' *South China Morning Post*, p. 2.

Hülmbauer, C. (2009). '"We don't take the right way. We just take the way that we think you will understand": The shifting relationship of correctness and effectiveness in ELF communication.' In A. Mauranen and E. Ranta (eds), *English as a Lingua Franca: Studies and Findings* (pp. 323–47). Newcastle upon Tyne: Cambridge Scholars.

——(2013). 'From within and without: the virtual and the plurilingual in ELF.' *Journal of English as a Lingua Franca*, 2(1), pp. 47–73. doi:10.1515/jelf-2013-0003

Hundt, M., Hay, J. and Gordon, E. (2004). 'New Zealand English: morphosyntax.' In B. Kortmann, K. Burridge, R. Mesthrie, E. W. Schneider and C. Upton (eds), *A Handbook of Varieties of English Phonology Volume 2* (pp. 560–92). Berlin: Mouton de Gruyter.

Huygens, I. and Vaughan, G. (1983). 'Language attitudes, ethnicity and social class in New Zealand.' *Journal of Multilingual and Multicultural Development*, 4(2–3), pp. 207–23.

Hymes, D. H. (1966). *Language in Culture and Society*. New York: Harper and Row.

ICAO. (2004). *Manual on the Implementation of ICAO Language Proficiency Requirements*. International Civil Aviation Organisation. Retrieved 5 September 2014 from http://caa.gateway.bg/upload/docs/9835_1_ed.pdf

Ingvarsdóttir, H. and Arnbjörnsdóttir, B. (2013). 'ELF and academic writing: a perspective from the Expanding Circle.' *Journal of English as a Lingua Franca*, 2(1), pp. 123–45. doi:10.1515/jelf-2013-0006

Ismail, M. (2012, 14 February). 'Five tips for learning to speak English like an American.' *The Seattle Globalist*. Retrieved 5 September 2014 from www.seattleglobalist.com/2012/02/14/five-tips-for-learning-to-speak-english-like-an-american/1185

James, W. and Youssef, V. (2008). 'The creoles of Trinidad and Tobago: morphology and syntax.' In E. W. Schneider (ed.), *Varieties of English 2: The Americas and the Caribbean* (pp. 661–92). Berlin: Mouton de Gruyter.

Jenkins, J. (2000). *The Phonology of English as an International Language: New Models, New Norms, New Goals*. Oxford: Oxford University Press.

——(2006). 'Points of view and blind spots: ELF and SLA.' *International Journal of Applied Linguistics*, 16(2), pp. 137–62.

——(2007). *English as a Lingua Franca: Attitude and Identity*. Oxford: Oxford University Press.

——(2009a). 'English as a lingua franca: interpretations and attitudes.' *World Englishes*, 28(2), pp. 200–207. doi:10.1111/j.1467–1971X.2009.01582.x

——(2009b). *World Englishes: A Resource Book for Students* (2nd ed.). London: Routledge.

——(2011). 'Accommodating (to) ELF in the international university.' *Journal of Pragmatics*, 43(4), pp. 926–36. doi:10.1016/j.pragma.2010.05.011

——(2012). 'English as a lingua franca from the classroom to the classroom.' *ELT Journal*, 66(4), pp. 486–94. doi:10.1093/elt/ccs040

——(2013). *English as a Lingua Franca in the International University: The Politics of Academic English Language Policy*. Abingdon: Routledge.

Jenkins, J., Cogo, A. and Dewey, M. (2011). 'Review of developments in research into English as a lingua franca.' *Language Teaching*, 44(03), pp. 281–315. doi:10.1017/S0261444811000115

Kachru, B. B. (1965). 'The Indianness in Indian English.' *Word*, 21, pp. 391–410.

——(1983). *The Indianization of English: The English Language in India*. Oxford: Oxford University Press.

——(1985). 'Standards, codification and sociolinguistic realism: the English language in the outer circle.' In R. Quirk and H. Widdowson (eds), *English in the World: Teaching and Learning the Language and Literatures* (pp. 11–30). Cambridge: Cambridge University Press.

——(1986). 'The power and politics of English.' *World Englishes*, 5(2–3), pp. 121–40. doi:10.1111/j.1467–1971X.1986.tb00720.x

——(1991). 'Liberation linguistics and the Quirk concern.' *English Today*, 7(01), pp. 3–13. doi:10.1017/S026607840000523X

——(1992a). *The Other Tongue: English Across Cultures* (p. 384). Urbana, IL: University of Illinois Press.

——(1992b). 'World Englishes: Approaches, Issues and Resources.' *Language Teaching*, 25, pp. 1–14.

——(1994). 'English in South Asia.' In R. Burchfield (ed.), *The Cambridge History of the English Language* (pp. 497–553). Cambridge: Cambridge University Press.

Kachru, B. B., Kachru, Y. and Nelson, C. L. (2006). *The Handbook of World Englishes*. Chichester: Blackwell.

Kachru, Y. and Nelson, C. L. (2006). *World Englishes in Asian Contexts*. Hong Kong: Hong Kong University Press.

Kachru, Y. and Smith, L. (2008). *Cultures, Contexts, and World Englishes*. London: Routledge.

Kamwangamalu, N. (2001). 'Linguistic and cultural reincarnations of English: a case from Southern Africa.' In E. Thumboo (ed.), *The Three Circles of English: Language Specialists Talk about the English Language* (pp. 45–66). Singapore: UniPress.

Kankaanranta, A. and Planken, B. (2010). 'BELF competence as business knowledge of internationally operating business professionals.' *Journal of Business Communication*, 47(4), pp. 380–407. doi:10.1177/0021943610377301

Kaur, J. (2009). 'Pre-empting problems of understanding in English as a lingua franca.' In A. Mauranen and E. Ranta (eds), *English as a Lingua Franca: Studies and Findings* (pp. 107–23). Newcastle upon Tyne: Cambridge Scholars.

Kelch, K. and Santana-Williamson, E. (2002). 'ESL students' attitudes toward native- and nonnative-speaking instructors' accents.' *The CATESOL Journal*, 14(1), pp. 57–72.

Khalik, A. (2010, 24 February). 'No English, no diplomacy, experts tell RI attachés.' *The Jakarta Post*. Retrieved from www.thejakartapost.com/news/2010/02/24/no-english-no-diplomacy-experts-tell-ri-attachés.html

Khan, S. Z. (2009). 'Imperialism of international tests: an EIL perspective.' In F. Sharifian (ed.), *English as an International Language: Perspectives and Pedagogical Issues* (pp. 190–208). Bristol: Multilingual Matters.

Kim, H. and Elder, C. (2009). 'Understanding aviation English as a lingua franca.' *Australian Review of Applied Linguistics*, 32(3), pp. 23.1–23.17. doi:10.2104/aral0923

Kim, H.-J. (2006). 'World Englishes in language testing: a call for research.' *English Today*, 22(4), pp. 32–39.

Kirkpatrick, A. (2007). *World Englishes: Implications for International Communication and English Language Teaching*. Cambridge: Cambridge University Press.

——(2008). 'English as the official working language of the Association of Southeast Asian Nations (ASEAN): Features and strategies.' *English Today*, (94), pp. 27–34.

——(2009). *Learning English and Other Languages in Multilingual Settings: Myths and Principles*. Hong Kong: The Hong Kong Institute of Education.

——(2010a). *English as a Lingua Franca in ASEAN: A Multilingual Model*. Hong Kong: Hong Kong University Press.

——(2010b). *The Routledge Handbook of World Englishes*. London: Routledge.

——(2010c). 'Researching English as a lingua franca in Asia: the Asian Corpus of English (ACE) project.' *Asian Englishes*, 31(1), pp. 4–18.

——(2011). 'English as an Asian lingua franca and the multilingual model of ELT.' *Language Teaching*, 44(2), pp. 212–24.

——(2012). 'English as an Asian lingua franca: the "Lingua Franca Approach" and implications for language education policy.' *Journal of English as a Lingua Franca*, 1(1), pp. 121–39. doi:10.1515/jelf-2012-0006

Kirkpatrick, A. and Xu, Z. (2002). 'Chinese pragmatic norms and "China English."' *World Englishes*, 21(2), pp. 269–79. doi:10.1111/1467–1971X.00247

Knight, J. (2003). 'Updated internationalisation definition.' *International Higher Education*, 33, p. 223.

Kobayashi, Y. (2013). 'Europe versus Asia: foreign language education other than English in Japan's higher education.' *Higher Education*, 66(3), pp. 269–81. doi:10.1007/s10734-012-9603-7

Kondakci, Y., Broeck, H. and Yildirim, A. (2008). 'The challenges of internationalization from foreign and local students' perspectives: the case of management school.' *Asia Pacific Education Review*, 9(4), pp. 448–63. doi:10.1007/BF03025662

Kortmann, B. (2008). 'Synopsis: morphological and syntactic variation in the British Isles.' In B. Kortmann and C. Upton (eds), *Varieties of English 1: The British Isles* (pp. 478–95). Berlin: Mouton de Gruyter.

Kortmann, B. and Upton, C. (eds). (2008). *Varieties of English: The British Isles*. Berlin: Mouton de Gruyter.

Krauss, M. (2007). *Native Peoples and Languages of Alaska*. Fairbanks: University of Alaska Press.

Kretzschmar, W. A. (2008). 'Standard American English pronunciation.' In E. W. Schneider (ed.), *Varieties of English 2: The Americas and the Caribbean* (pp. 37–51). Berlin: Mouton de Gruyter.

——(2010). 'The development of Standard American English.' In A. Kirkpatrick (ed.), *The Routledge Handbook of World Englishes* (pp. 96–112). London: Routledge.

Kubota, R. (2001). 'Teaching world Englishes to native speakers of English in the USA.' *World Englishes*, 20(1), pp. 47–64. doi:10.1111/1467–1971X.00195

——(2012). 'The politics of EIL: toward Border-crossing Communication in and beyond English.' In A. Matsuda (ed.), *Principle and Practices of Teaching English as an International Language* (pp. 55–69). Bristol: Multilingual Matters.

Kuhn, T. (1962). *The Structure of Scientific Revolutions*. Chicago: The University of Chicago Press.

Kumaravadivelu, B. (2012). 'Individual identity, cultural globalization and teaching English as an international language: the case for an epistemic break.' In L. Alsagoff, S. L. McKay, G. Hu and W. A. Renandya (eds), *Teaching English as an International Language: Principles and Practices* (pp. 9–27). New York: Routledge.

Kuo, I.-C. (Vicky). (2006). 'Addressing the issue of teaching English as a lingua franca.' *ELT Journal*, 60(3), pp. 213–21. doi:10.1093/elt/ccl001

Labov, W. (1969). *The Study of Nonstandard ENGLISH*. Washington, DC: National Council of Teachers of English.

——(1972). 'The social stratification of (r) in New York City department stores.' In W. Labov (ed.), *Sociolinguistic Patterns* (pp. 43–69). Philadelphia, PA: University of Pennsylvania Press.

Ladegaard, H. J. and Sachdev, I. (2006). '"I like the Americans ... but I certainly don't aim for an American accent": language attitudes, vitality and foreign language learning in Denmark.' *Journal of Multilingual and Multicultural Development*, 27(2), pp. 91–108. doi:10.1080/01434630608668542

Lambert, W. E. (1967). 'A social psychology of bilingualism.' *Journal of Social Issues*, 23, pp. 91–109. doi:10.1111/j.1540–4560.1967.tb00578.x

Lambert, W. E., Hodgson, R. C., Gardner, R. C. and Fillenbaum, S. (1960). 'Evaluational reactions to spoken languages.' *The Journal of Abnormal and Social Psychology*, 60(1), pp. 44–51. doi:10.1037/h0044430

Landry, R. and Bourhis, R. Y. (1997). 'Linguistic landscape and ethnolinguistic vitality: An empirical study.' *Journal of Language and Social Psychology*, (16), pp. 23–49.

Larsen-Freeman, D. and Cameron, L. (2008). *Complex Systems and Applied Linguistics*. Oxford: Oxford University Press.

Lasagabaster, D. and Sierra, J. (2005). 'What do students think about the pros and cons of having a native speaker teacher?' In E. Llurda (ed.), *Non-Native Language Teachers SE – 12* (Vol. 5, pp. 217–41). New York: Springer. doi:10.1007/0-387-24565-0_12

Lave, J. and Wenger, E. (1991). *Situated Learning: Legitimate Peripheral Participation*. Cambridge: Cambridge University Press.

Leung, C. and Street, B. V. (2012). 'Linking EIL and literacy: theory and practice.' In L. Alsagoff, S. L. McKay, G. Hu and W. A. Renandya (eds), *Principles and Practices for Teaching English as an International Language* (pp. 85–103). New York: Routledge.

Levey, S. (2010). 'The Englishes of Canada.' In A. Kirkpatrick (ed.), *The Routledge Handbook of World Englishes* (pp. 113–31). London: Routledge.

Lichtkoppler, J. (2007). '"Male. Male." – "Male?" – "The sex is male." The role of repetition in English as a lingua franca conversations.' *Vienna English Working Papers*, 16(1), pp. 39–65.

Lillis, T. M. and Curry, M. J. (2010). *Academic Writing in a Global Context: The Politics and Practices of Publishing in English*. Abingdon and New York: Routledge.

Lim, L. (ed.). (2004). *Singapore English: A Grammatical Description*. Amsterdam: John Benjamins.

Lippi-Green, R. (1997). *English with an Accent: Language, Ideology, and Discrimination in the United States*. London: Routledge.

Llurda, E. and Huguet, A. (2003). 'Self-awareness in NNS EFL primary and secondary school teachers.' *Language Awareness*, 12(3–4), pp. 220–33. doi:10.1080/09658410308667078

Louhiala-Salminen, L. (2002a). 'Communication and language use in merged corporations: cases Stora Enso and Nordea.' *Helsinki School of Economics Working Papers W-330*.

——(2002b). 'The fly's perspective: discourse in the daily routine of a business manager.' *English for Specific Purposes*, 21(3), pp. 211–31. doi:10.1016/S0889–4906(00)00036–3

Louhiala-Salminen, L., Charles, M. and Kankaanranta, A. (2005). 'English as a lingua franca in Nordic corporate mergers: two case companies.' *English for Specific Purposes*, 24(4), pp. 401–21. doi:http://dx.doi.org/10.1016/j.esp.2005.02.003

Louhiala-Salminen, L. and Rogerson-Revell, P. (2010). 'Language matters: an introduction.' *Journal of Business Communication*, 47(2), pp. 91–96. doi:10.1177/0021943610364510

Low, E. L. (2010). 'English in Singapore and Malaysia: similarities and differences.' In A. Kirkpatrick (ed.), *The Routledge Handbook of World Englishes* (pp. 229–46). London: Routledge.

Luke, K.-K. and Richards, J. (1982). 'English in Hong Kong: functions and status.' *English World-Wide*, (3), pp. 47–64.

McArthur, T. (1987). 'The English languages?' *English Today*, 11, pp. 9–11.

——(1998). *The English Languages*. Cambridge: Cambridge University Press.

——(2002). *The Oxford Guide to World English*. Oxford: Oxford University Press.

McCrum, R., Cran, W. and MacNeil, R. (1992). *The Story of English*. London: Penguin Books.

MacGregor, L. (2003). 'The language of shop signs in Tokyo.' *English Today*, 19(01), pp. 18–23. doi:10.1017/S0266078403001020

McIntyre, D. (2009). *A History of English: A Resource Book for Students*. London: Routledge.

McKay, S. L. (2002). *Teaching English as an International Language: Rethinking Goals and Approaches*. Oxford: Oxford University Press.

——(2012). 'Teaching materials for English as an international language.' In A. Matsuda (ed.), *Principles and Practices of Teaching English as an International Language* (pp. 70–83). Bristol: Multilingual Matters.

McKenzie, R. M. (2008a). 'Social factors and non-native attitudes towards varieties of spoken English: a Japanese case study.' *International Journal of Applied Linguistics*, 18(1), pp. 63–88. doi:10.1111/j.1473–4192.2008.00179.x

——(2008b). 'The role of variety recognition in Japanese university students' attitudes towards English speech varieties.' *Journal of Multilingual and Multicultural Development*, 29(2), pp. 139–53. doi:10.2167/jmmd565.0

Maclagan, M. (2010). 'The English(es) of New Zealand.' In A. Kirkpatrick (ed.), *The Routledge Handbook of World Englishes* (pp. 152–63). London: Routledge.

McNamara, T. (2012). 'English as a lingua franca: the challenge for language testing.' *Journal of English as a Lingua Franca*, 1(1), pp. 199–202. doi:10.1515/jelf-2012-0013

Mahboob, A. (2004). 'Native or nonnative: what do students enrolled in an intensive English program think?' In L. D. Kamhi-Stein (ed.), *Learning and Teaching from Experience: Perspectives on Nonnative English-speaking Professionals* (pp. 121–48). Ann Arbor: University of Michigan Press.

Mair, C. (2003). *The Politics of English as a World Language: New Horizons in Postcolonial Cultural Studies*. Amsterdam: Rodopi.

Maley, A. (2009). 'ELF: a teacher's perspective.' *Language and Intercultural Communication*, 9(3), pp. 187–200.

Matsuda, A. (2003). 'The ownership of English in Japanese secondary schools.' *World Englishes*, 22(4), pp. 483–96. doi:10.1111/j.1467–1971X.2003.00314.x

——(2009). 'Globalization and English language teaching: opportunities and challenges in Japan.' *The Language Teacher*, 33(7), pp. 11–14.

——(2012). 'Teaching materials in EIL.' In L. Alsagoff, S. L. Mckay, G. Hu and W. A. Renandya (eds), *Principles and Practices for Teaching English as an International Language*. New York: Routledge.

Matsuda, A. and Friedrich, P. (2012). 'Selecting an instructional variety for an EIL curriculum.' In A. Matsuda (ed.), *Principles and Practices of Teaching English as an International Language* (pp. 17–27). Bristol: Multilingual Matters.

Matsuura, H., Chiba, R. and Yamamoto, A. (1994). 'Japanese college students' attitudes towards non-native varieties of English.' In D. Graddol, J. Swann and British Association for Applied Linguistics (eds), *Evaluating Language: Papers from the Annual Meeting of the British Association for Applied Linguistics held at the University of Essex, September 1992* (pp. 52–61). Clevedon: Multilingual Matters.

Matsuura, H., Fujieda, M. and Mahoney, S. (2004). 'The officialization of English and ELT in Japan: 2000.' *World Englishes*, 23(3), pp. 471–87. doi:10.1111/j.0883–2919.2004.00369.x

Mauranen, A. (2006). 'Signaling and preventing misunderstanding in English as lingua franca communication.' *International Journal of the Sociology of Language*, 2006(177), pp. 123–50. doi:10.1515/IJSL.2006.008

——(2007). 'Hybrido voices: English as the lingua franca of academics.' In Kjersti Flottum (ed.), *Language and Discipline Perspectives on Academic Discourse* (pp. 243–59). Newcastle: Cambridge Scholars Publishing.

——(2009). 'Chunking in ELF: expressions for managing interaction.' *Intercultural Pragmatics*, 6(2), pp. 217–33. doi:10.1515/IPRG.2009.012

——(2012). *Exploring ELF: Academic English Shaped by Non-native Speakers*. Cambridge: Cambridge University Press.

Mbangwana, P. (2004). 'Cameroon English: morphology and syntax.' In B. Kortman, E. W. Schneider, K. Burridge, R. Mesthrie and C. Upton (eds), *A Handbook of Varieties of English Volume 2: Morphology and Syntax* (pp. 898–908). Berlin: Mouton de Gruyter.

Medgyes, P. (1992). 'Native or non-native: who's worth more?' *ELT Journal*, 46(4), pp. 340–49. doi:10.1093/elt/46.4.340

——(1994). *The Non-native Teacher*. London: Macmillan.

——(2001). 'When the teacher is a non-native speaker.' In M. Celce-Murcia (ed.), *Teaching English as a Second or Foreign Language* (pp. 429–42). Boston: Heinle & Heinle.

Meierkord, C. (1996). *Englisch als Medium der interkulturellen Kommunikation. Unter-suchungen zum non-native-/non-native speaker Diskurs.* [*English as a Medium of Intercultural Communication: Investigations into Nonnative-/Nonnative Speaker Discourse.*]. Frankfurt: Lang.

——(2002). '"Language stripped bare" or "linguistic masala"? Culture in lingua franca conversation.' In K. Knapp and C. Meierkord (eds), *Lingua Franca Communication* (pp. 109–33). Frankfurt: Peter Lang.

Melchers, G. and Shaw, P. (2003). *World Englishes: An Introduction*. London: Arnold.

——(2011). *World Englishes (The English Language Series)* (2nd ed.). London: Hodder Education.

Mesthrie, R. (1997). 'A sociolinguistic study of topicalisation phenomena in South African Black English.' In E. W. Schneider (ed.), *Englishes Around the World, Volume 2: Caribbean, Africa, Asia, Australasia. Studies in Honour of Manfred Görlach* (pp. 119–40). Amsterdam and Philadelphia, PA: Benjamins.

——(2004). 'Black South African English: morphology and syntax.' In B. Kortmann, E. W. Schneider, K. Burridge, R. Mesthrie and C. Upton (eds), *A Handbook of Varieties of English Volume 2: Morphology and Syntax* (pp. 962–73). Berlin: Mouton de Gruyter.

——(2006). 'World Englishes and the multilingual history of English.' *World Englishes*, 25(3–4), pp. 381–90. doi:10.1111/j.1467–1971X.2006.00477.x

——(2013). 'Contact and African Englishes.' In R. Hickey (ed.), *The Handbook of Language Contact* (p. 518–537). Malden, MA: Wiley-Blackwell.

Mesthrie, R. and Bhatt, R. M. (2008). *World Englishes: The Study of New Linguistic Varieties*. Cambridge: Cambridge University Press.

Mesthrie, R., Joan, S., Leap, D. and William, L. A. (1999). *Introducing Sociolinguistics*. Edinburgh: Edinburgh University Press.

Mey, J. (1981). '"Right or wrong, my native speaker:" Estant les régestes du noble souverain de l'empirie linguistic avec un renvoy au mesme roy.' In J. Coulmas (ed.), *A Festschrift for Native Speaker* (pp. 69–84). The Hague, Netherlands: Mouton.

Miller, J. (2008). 'Scottish English: morphology and syntax.' In B. Kortmann and C. Upton (eds), *Varieties of English 1: The British Isles* (pp. 299–327). Berlin: Mouton de Gruyter.

Milroy, J. (2007). 'The ideology of the standard language.' In C. Llamas, L. Mullany and P. Stockwell (eds), *The Routledge Companion to Sociolinguistics* (pp. 133–39). New York, NY: Routledge.

Milroy, J. and Milroy, L. (1999). *Authority in Language: Investigating Standard English*. London: Routledge.

Milroy, L. (2001). 'The social categories of race and class: language ideology and sociolinguistics.' In N. Coupland, S. Sarangi and C. N. Candlin (eds), *Sociolinguistics and Social Theory* (pp. 16–39). London: Routledge.

Mithun, M. (1998). 'The significance of diversity in language endangerment and preservation.' In L. A. Grenoble and L. J. Whaley (eds), *Endangered Languages: Language Loss and Community Response* (pp. 163–91). Cambridge: Cambridge University Press.

Modiano, M. (1999a). 'International English in the global village.' *English Today*, 15(2), pp. 22–34.

——(1999b). 'Standard English(es) and educational practices for the world's lingua franca.' *English Today*, 15(4), pp. 3–13.

——(2001). 'Linguistic imperialism, cultural integrity, and EIL.' *ELT Journal*, 55(4), pp. 339–47. doi:10.1093/elt/55.4.339

——(2006). 'Euro-Englishes.' In B. B. Kachru, Y. Kachru and C. L. Nelson (eds), *The Handbook of World Englishes* (pp. 223–39). Malden, MA: Blackwell.

——(2009). 'Inclusive/exclusive? English as a lingua franca in the European Union.' *World Englishes*, 28(2), pp. 208–23. doi:10.1111/j.1467–1971X.2009.01584.x

Mok, K. H. and Xu, X. (2009). 'When China Opens to the World: A Study of Transnational Higher Education in Zhejiang, China.' *Asia Pacific Education Review*, 9(4), pp. 393–408.

Mollin, S. (2006). *Euro-English: Assessing Variety Status*. Tübingen: Gunter Narr Verlag.

Montgomery, M. B. (2008). 'Appalachian English: morphology and syntax.' In E. W. Schneider (ed.), *Varieties of English 2: The Americas and the Caribbean* (pp. 428–67). Berlin: Mouton de Gruyter.

Montgomery, S. L. (2013). *Does Science Need a Global Language?: English and the Future of Research*. Chicago: University of Chicago Press.

Moore, B. (2007). 'Towards a history of the Australian accent.' In J. Damousi and D. Deacon (eds), *Talking and Listening in the Age of Modernity: Essays on the history of sound*. Canberra: Australian National University Press.

Morrish, J. (1999, 21 March). 'The accent that dare not speak its name.' *The Independent on Sunday*. London. Retrieved from www.independent.co.uk/life-style/focus-the-accent-that-dare-not-speak-its-name-1082144.html

Morrow, P. R. (2004). 'English in Japan: the world Englishes perspective.' *JALT Journal*, 26(1), pp. 79–100.

Mortensen, J. (2013). 'Notes on English used as a lingua franca as an object of study.' *Journal of English as a Lingua Franca*, 2(1), pp. 25–46. doi:10.1515/jelf-2013-0002

Moussu, L. and Llurda, E. (2008). 'Non-native English-speaking English language teachers: history and research.' *Language Teaching*, 41(03), pp. 315–48. doi:10.1017/S0261444808005028

Mufwene, S. S. (2001). *The Ecology of Language Evolution*. Cambridge: Cambridge University Press.

——(2002). 'Colonization, globalization, and the future of languages in the twenty-first century.' *International Journal on Multicultural Societies*, 4(2), pp. 162–93.

——(2008). *Language Evolution: Contact, Competition and Change*. New York: Continuum.

Mukherjee, J. (2010). 'The development of the English language in India.' In A. Kirkpatrick (ed.), *The Routledge Handbook of World Englishes* (pp. 167–80). London: Routledge.

Murray, H. (2003). 'Swiss English teachers and Euro-English: attitudes to a non-native variety.' *Bulletin Suisse de Linguistique Appliqué*, 77, pp. 147–65.

Murray, T. E. and Simon, B. L. (2008). 'Colloquial American English: grammatical features.' In E. W. Schneider (ed.), *Varieties of English 2: The Americas and the Caribbean* (pp. 401–27). Berlin: Mouton de Gruyter.

Neau, V. (2003). 'The teaching of foreign languages in Cambodia: a historical perspective.' *Language, Culture and Curriculum*, 16(3), pp. 253–68. doi:10.1080/07908310308666673

Nevalainen, T. and van Ostade, I.M. (2006). 'Standardisation.' In R. Hogg and D. Denison (eds), *A History of the English Language* (pp. 271–311). Cambridge: Cambridge University Press.

Newman, B. (1995, 24 March). 'Global chatter.' *The Wall Street Journal*, pp. 1, 6.

Nickerson, C. (2005). 'English as a lingua franca in international business contexts.' *English for Specific Purposes*, 24(4), pp. 367–80. doi:http://dx.doi.org/10.1016/j.esp.2005.02.001

Nunan, D. (2003). 'The impact of English as a global language on educational policies and practices in the Asia-Pacific region.' *TESOL Quarterly*, 37(4), pp. 589–613.

O'Regan, J. P. (2014). 'English as a lingua franca: an immanent critique.' *Applied Linguistics*, (2011), pp. 1–21. doi:10.1093/applin/amt045

Pacek, D. (2005). '"Personality not nationality": foreign students' perceptions of a non-native speaker lecturer of English at a British university.' In E. Llurda (ed.), *Non-Native Language Teachers. Perceptions, Challenges and Contributions to the Profession*, Vol. 5 (pp. 243–62). Springer. doi:10.1007/0-387-24565-0_13

Paikeday, T. M. (1985). *The Native Speaker is Dead!: An Informal Discussion of a Linguistic Myth with Noam Chomsky and other Linguists, Philosophers, Psychologists, and Lexicographers*. Toronto and New York: Paikeday Publishing.

Pang, T. T. T. (2003). 'Hong Kong English: a stillborn variety?' *English Today*, (19), pp. 12–18.

Park, J.-K. (2009). '"English fever" in South Korea: its history and symptoms.' *English Today*, 25(01), pp. 50–57. doi:10.1017/S026607840900008X

Park, S. J. and Abelman, N. (2004). 'Class and cosmopolitan striving: mother's management of English education in South Korea.' *Anthropological Quarterly*, 77(4), pp. 645–72.

Patrick, P. L. (2008). 'Jamaican Creole: morphology and syntax.' In E. W. Schneider (ed.), *Varieties of English 2: The Americas and the Caribbean* (pp. 609–44). Berlin: Mouton de Gruyter.

Pawley, A. (2004). 'Australian vernacular English: some grammatical characteristics.' In B. Kortmann, K. Burridge, R. Mesthrie, E. W. Schneider and C. Upton (eds), *A Handbook of Varieties of English Phonology Volume 2* (pp. 611–42). Berlin: Mouton de Gruyter.

Penhallurick, R. (2008). 'Welsh English: morphology and syntax.' In B. Kortmann and C. Upton (eds), *Varieties of English 1: The British Isles* (pp. 360–72). Berlin: Mouton de Gruyter.

Pennycook, A. (1994). *The Cultural Politics of English as an International Language*. London: Longman.

——(2007). *Global Englishes and Transcultural Flows*. Abingdon and New York: Routledge.

——(2010). 'The future of Englishes: one, many or none?' In A. Kirkpatrick (ed.), *The Routledge Handbook of World Englishes* (pp. 673–87). Abingdon and New York: Routledge.

Phillipson, R. (1992a). 'ELT: the native speaker's burden?' *ELT Journal*, 46(1), pp. 12–18. doi:10.1093/elt/46.1.12

——(1992b). *Linguistic Imperialism*. Oxford: Oxford University Press.

——(2003). *English-Only Europe? Challenging Language Policy*. London: Routledge.

——(2008). 'Lingua franca or lingua frankensteinia? English in European integration and globalisation.' *World Englishes*, 27(2), pp. 250–67. doi:10.1111/j.1467–1971X.2008.00555.x

——(2009). 'Disciplines of English and disciplining by English.' *The Asian EFL Journal Quarterly*, 11(4), pp. 8–28.

——(2012). 'Imperialism and colonialism.' In B. Spolsky (ed.), *The Cambridge Handbook of Language Policy* (pp. 203–35). Cambridge: Cambridge University Press.

Pickering, L. (2009). 'Intonation as a pragmatic resource in ELF interaction.' *Intercultural Pragmatics*, 6(2), pp. 235–55. doi:10.1515/IPRG.2009.013

Pickering, L. and Litzenberg, J. (2011). 'Intonation as a pragmatic resource, revisited.' In A. Archibald, A. Cogo and J. Jenkins (eds), *Latest Trends in ELF Research*. Cambridge: Cambridge Scholars.

Pitzl, M.-L. (2005). 'Non-understanding in English as a lingua franca: examples from a business context.' *Vienna English Working Papers*, 14(2), pp. 50–71.

——(2009). '"We should not wake up any dogs": idiom and metaphor in ELF.' In A. Mauranen and E. Ranta (eds), *English as a Lingua Franca: Studies and Findings* (pp. 298–322). Newcastle upon Tyne: Cambridge Scholars.

Pitzl, M.-L., Breiteneder, A. and Klimpfinger, T. (2008). 'A world of words: processes of lexical innovation in VOICE.' *Vienna English Working Papers*, 17(2), pp. 21–46.

Platt, J. T. (1982). 'English in Singapore, Malaysia and Hong Kong.' In R. W. Bailey and M. Görlach (eds), *English as a World Language* (pp. 384–414). Ann Arbor, MI: University of Michigan Press.

Platt, J. T., Weber, H. and Lian, H. M. (1984). *The New Englishes*. London: Routledge & Kegan Paul.

Poncini, G. (2002). 'Investigating discourse at business meetings with multicultural participation.' *International Review of Applied Linguistics in Language Teaching*, 40, pp. 345–73. doi:10.1515/iral.2002.017

——(2007). 'Communicating within and across professional worlds in an intercultural setting.' In G. Garzone and C. Ilie (eds), *The Use of English in Institutional and Business Settings: An Intercultural Perspective* (pp. 283–312). Frankfurt: Peter Lang.

Prodromou, L. (1992). 'What culture? Which culture? Cross-cultural factors in language learning.' *ELT Journal*, 46(1), pp. 39–50.

——(2006). 'A Reader Responds to J. Jenkins's "Current perspectives on teaching world Englishes and English as a lingua franca."' *TESOL Quarterly*, 41(2), pp. 409–13.

Pullin, P. (2013). 'Achieving "comity": the role of linguistic stance in business English as a lingua franca (BELF) meetings.' *Journal of English as a Lingua Franca*, 2(1), pp. 1–23. doi:10.1515/jelf-2013-0001

Quirk, R. (1985). 'Language varieties and standard language.' *JALT Journal*, 11(1), pp. 14–25.

——(1990). 'Language varieties and standard language.' *English Today*, 6(01), pp. 3–10. doi:10.1017/S0266078400004454

Rajagopalan, K. (2004). 'The concept of "World English" and its implications for ELT.' *ELT Journal*, 58(2), pp. 111–17. doi:10.1093/elt/58.2.111

——(2006). 'South American Englishes.' In B. B. Kachru, Y. Kachru and C. L. Nelson (eds), *The Handbook of World Englishes* (pp. 158–71). Malden, MA: Blackwell.

Rampton, M. B. H. (1990). 'Displacing the "native speaker": expertise, affiliation, and inheritance.' *ELT Journal*, 44(2), pp. 97–101. doi:10.1093/elt/44.2.97

——(1995). 'Politics and change in research in applied linguistics.' *Applied Linguistics*, 16(2), pp. 233–56.

Rapatahana, V. and Bunce, P. (2012). *English Language as Hydra: Its Impacts on Non-English Language Cultures*. Bristol: Multilingual Matters.

Reaser, J. and Torbert, B. (2008). 'Bahamian English: morphology and syntax.' In E. W. Schneider (ed.), *Varieties of English 2: The Americas and the Caribbean* (pp. 591–608). Berlin: Mouton de Gruyter.

Reves, T. and Medgyes, P. (1994). 'The non-native English speaking EFL/ESL teacher's self-image: an international survey.' *System*, 22(3), pp. 353–67.

Risager, K. (2006). *Language and Culture: Global Flows and Local Complexity*. Clevedon: Multilingual Matters.

Rogerson-Revell, P. (2008). 'Participation and performance in international business meetings.' *English for Specific Purposes*, 27(3), pp. 338–60. doi:10.1016/j.esp.2008.02.003

Romaine, S. (1988). *Pidgin and Creole Languages*. London: Longman.

Rubdy, R., Mckay, S. L., Alsagoff, L. and Bokhorst-Heng, W. D. (2008). 'Enacting English language ownership in the Outer Circle: a study of Singaporean Indians' orientations to English norms.' *World Englishes*, 27(1), pp. 40–67. doi:10.1111/j.1467–1971X.2008.00535.x

Rubdy, R. and Saraceni, M. (2006). *English in the World: Global Rules, Global Roles*. London: Continuum.

Rubin, D. L. (1992). 'Non-language factors affecting undergraduates' judgments of nonnative English-speaking teaching assistants.' *Research in Higher Education*, 33(4), pp. 511–31.

Rubin, D. L. and Smith, K. A. (1990). 'Effects of accent, ethnicity, and lecture topic on undergraduates' perceptions of nonnative English-speaking teaching assistants.' *International Journal of Intercultural Relations*, 14(3), pp. 337–53. doi:10.1016/0147–1767(90)90019-S

Samimy, K. K. and Brutt-Griffler, J. (1999). 'Perceptions of NNS students in a graduate TESOL program.' In G. Braine (ed.), *Non-native Educators in English Language Teaching* (pp. 129–46). Mahwah, NJ: Lawrence Erlbaum.

Saraceni, M. (2009). 'Relocating English: towards a new paradigm for English in the world.' *Language and Intercultural Communication*, 9(3), pp. 175–86. doi:10.1080/14708470902748830

Sarnoff, I. (1970). *Social Attitudes and the Resolution of Motivational Conflict*. Harmondsworth: Penguin.

Schmied, J. (1991). *English in Africa: An Introduction*. New York: Longman.

——(2006). 'East African Englishes.' In B. B. Kachru, Y. Kachru and C. L. Nelson (eds), *The Handbook of World Englishes* (pp. 188–202). Malden, MA: Blackwell.

——(2008). 'East African English (Kenya, Uganda, Tanzania): morphology and syntax.' In R. Mesthrie (ed.), *Varieties of English Volume 4: Africa, South and Southeast Asia* (pp. 451–72). Berlin and New York: Mouton de Gruyter.

Schneider, E. W. (2003). 'The Dynamics of New Englishes: From Identity Construction to Dialect Birth.' *Language*, 79(2), pp. 233–81. doi:10.1353/lan.2003.0136

——(2007). *Postcolonial English: Varieties Around the World*. Cambridge: Cambridge University Press.

——(2008a). 'Introduction: varieties of English in the Americas and the Caribbean.' In E. W. Schneider (ed.), *Varieties of English 2: The Americas and the Caribbean* (pp. 23–36). Berlin: Mouton de Gruyter.

——(ed.) (2008b), *Varieties of English 2: The Americas and the Caribbean*. Berlin: Mouton de Gruyter.

——(2011). *English Around the World: An Introduction*. Cambridge: Cambridge University Press.

The Scotsman. (2006, 18 November). 'Is Scotland turning into a call centre nation?' Edinburgh.

Seargeant, P. (2009). *The Idea of English in Japan*. Bristol: Multilingual Matters.

——(2012). *Exploring World Englishes: Language in a Global Context*. Abingdon and New York: Routledge.

Seargeant, P. and Swann, J. (eds). (2012). *English in the World: History, Diversity, Change*. Oxford: Routledge.

Sebba, M. (1997). *Contact Languages: Pidgins and Creoles*. New York: St. Martin's Press.

——(2009). 'World Englishes.' In J. Culpeper, F. Katamba, P. Kerswill, R. Wodak and T. McEnery (eds), *English Language: Description, Variation and Context* (pp. 404–21). Hounslow: Palgrave Macmillan.

Seidlhofer, B. (2001a). 'Closing a conceptual gap: the case for a description of English as a lingua franca.' *International Journal of Applied Linguistics*, 11(2), pp. 133–58.

——(2001b). 'Towards making Euro-English a linguistic reality.' *English Today*, 68, 17(4), pp. 14–16.

——(2004). 'Research perspectives on teaching English as a lingua franca.' *Annual Review of Applied Linguistics*, 24, pp. 209–39.

——(2005). 'Language variation and change: the case of English as a lingua franca.' In K. Dziubalska-Kolaczyk and J. Przedlacka (eds), *English Pronunciation Models: A Changing Scene* (pp. 59–75). Bern, Switzerland: Peter Lang.

——(2006). 'English as a lingua franca in the expanding circle: what it isn't.' In R. Rubdy and M. Saraceni (eds), *English in the World: Global Rules, Global Roles* (pp. 40–50). London: Continuum.

——(2007). 'English as a lingua franca and communities of practice.' In S. Volk-Birke and J. Lippert (eds), *Anglistentag 2006 Halle Proceedings* (pp. 307–18). Trier: Wissenschaftlicher Verlag Trier.

——(2009a). 'Common ground and different realities: world Englishes and English as a lingua franca.' *World Englishes*, 28(2), pp. 236–45. doi:10.1111/j.1467–1971X.2009.01592.x

——(2009b). 'Accommodation and the idiom principle in English as a Lingua Franca.' *Intercultural Pragmatics*, 6(2), pp. 195–215. doi:10.1515/IPRG.2009.011

——(2011). *Understanding English as a Lingua Franca*. Oxford: Oxford University Press.

Seidlhofer, B., Breiteneder, A. and Pitzl, M. (2006). 'English as a lingua franca in Europe: challenges for applied linguistics.' *Annual Review of Applied Linguistics*, 26, pp. 3–34.

Seidlhofer, B. and Widdowson, H. (2003). 'House work and student work: a study in cross-cultural understanding.' *Zeitschrift Für Interkulturellen Fremdsprachenunterricht* [online], 8(2/3). Retrieved 5 September 2014 from http://zif.spz.tu-darmstadt.de/jg-08-2-3/beitrag/Seidlhofer_Widdowson1.htm

——(2009). 'Conformity and creativity in ELF and learner English.' In M. Albl-Mikasa, S. Braun and S. Kalina (eds), *Dimensionen der Zweitsprachenforschung: Festschrift für Kurt Kohn [Dimensions of Second Language Research: In Honour of Kurt Kohn]* (pp. 93–107). Tübingen: Gunter Narr.

Selinker, L. (1972). 'Interlanguage.' *International Review of Applied Linguistics in Language Teaching*, 10, pp. 209–32. doi:10.1515/iral.1972.10.1–4.209

SGEM (Speak Good English Movement). (2011). 'About us.' Retrieved 16 April 2014 from www.goodenglish.org.sg/site/category/movement/about-us.html

Sharifian, F. (2009). 'English as an international language: an overview.' In F. Sharifian (ed.), *English as an International Language: Perspectives and Pedagogical Issues* (pp. 1–18). Bristol: Multilingual Matters.

Sharifian, F. and Clyne, M. (2008). 'English as an international language: synthesis.' *Australian Review of Applied Linguistics*, 31(3), pp. 36.1–36.19. doi:10.2104/aral0836

Shen, W. (2008). 'International student migration: the case of Chinese "sea-turtles."' In D. Epstein, R. Boden, R. Deem, R. Fazal and S. Wright (eds), *World Yearbook of Education 2008: Geographies of Knowledge, Geometries of Power: Framing the Future of Higher Education* (pp. 211–32). New York: Routledge.

Shim, R. J. (2002). 'Changing attitudes toward TEWOL in Korea.' *Journal of Asian Pacific Communication*, 12(1), pp. 143–58. doi:http://dx.doi.org/10.1075/japc.12.1.09shi

Siegel, J. (2010). *Second Dialect Acquisition*. Cambridge: Cambridge University Press.

Sifakis, N. C. and Sougari, A.-M. (2005). 'Pronunciation issues and EIL pedagogy in the periphery: a survey of Greek state school teachers' beliefs.' *TESOL Quarterly*, 39(3), pp. 467–88. doi:10.2307/3588490

Simmons-McDonald, H. (2010). 'West-Indian Englishes: an introduction to literature written in selected varieties.' In A. Kirkpatrick (ed.), *The Routledge Handbook of World Englishes* (pp. 316–32). London and New York: Routledge.

Singh, I. (2000). *Pidgins and Creoles*. London: Hodder Arnold.

Singh, M. (2005). 'Enabling transnational learning communities: policies, pedagogies and politics of educational power.' *Internationalizing Higher Education*, 16, pp. 9–36.

Smieja, B. and Mathangwane, J. T. (2010). 'The development of English in Botswana: language policy and education.' In A. Kirkpatrick (ed.), *The Routledge Handbook of World Englishes* (pp. 212–28). Abingdon and New York: Routledge.

Smith, L. (1976). 'English as an international auxiliary language.' *RELC Journal*, 7(2), pp. 38–43.

Sobkowiak, W. (2005). 'Why not LFC?' In K. Dziubalska-Kolaczyk and J. Przedlacka (eds), *English Pronunciation Models: A Changing Scene*. Frankfurt am Main: Peter Lang.

Song, M.-M. and Tai, H.-H. (2007). 'Taiwan's responses to globalisation: internationalisation and questing for world class universities.' *Asia Pacific Journal of Education*, 27(3), pp. 323–40. doi:10.1080/02188790701594067

Sowden, C. (2012). 'ELF on a mushroom: the overnight growth in English as a lingua franca.' *ELT Journal*, 66(1), pp. 89–96. doi:10.1093/elt/ccr024

Spolsky, B. (2004). *Language Policy*. Cambridge: Cambridge University Press.

Stanlaw, J. (2004). *Japanese English: Language and Culture Contact*. Hong Kong: Hong Kong University Press.

Starks, D. and Paltridge, B. (1994). 'Varieties of English and the EFL classroom: a New Zealand study.' *TESOLANZ Journal*, 2, pp. 69–77.

Stewart, M. A., Ryan, E. B. and Giles, H. (1985). 'Accent and social class effects on status and solidarity evaluations.' *Personality and Social Psychology Bulletin*, 11, pp. 98–105.

Strevens, P. (1980). *Teaching English as an International Language*. Oxford: Pergamon Press.

——(1992). 'English as an international language: directions in the 1990s.' In B. B. Kachru (ed.), *The Other Tongue: English Across Cultures* (p. 384). University of Illinois Press.

Stuart-Smith, J. (2008). 'Scottish English: phonology.' In B. Kortmann and C. Upton (eds), *Varieties of English 1: The British Isles* (pp. 48–70). Berlin: Mouton de Gruyter.

Suzuki, A. (2011). 'Introducing diversity of English into ELT: student teachers' responses.' *ELT Journal*, 65(2), pp. 145–53. doi:10.1093/elt/ccq024

Svensson, L. and Wihlborg, M. (2010). 'Internationalising the content of higher education: the need for a curriculum perspective.' *Higher Education*, 60(6), pp. 595–613. doi:10.1007/s10734-010-9318-6

Swan, M. (2005). *Practical English Usage*. Oxford: Oxford University Press.

——(2012). 'ELF and EFL: are they really different?' *Journal of English as a Lingua Franca*, 1(2), pp. 379–89. doi:10.1515/jelf-2012-0025

Tange, H. and Jensen, I. (2012). 'Good teachers and deviant learners? The meeting of practices in university level international education.' *Journal of Research in International Education*, 11(2), pp. 181–93. doi:10.1177/1475240912447849

Tardy, C. (2004). 'The role of English in scientific communication: lingua franca or Tyrannosaurus rex?' *Journal of English for Academic Purposes*, 3(3), pp. 247–69.

Taylor, J. (2000). *'I Wanna Speak Perfect English': EFL Students' Attitudes to Accents of English*. London: Birkbeck College, University of London.

TESOL. (1992). 'A TESOL statement of non-native speakers of English and hiring practices.' *TESOL Quarterly*, 2(4), p. 23.

——(2006). *Position Statement Against Discrimination of Nonnative Speakers of English in the Field of TESOL*. Retrieved 5 September 2014 from www.tesol.org/docs/pdf/5889.pdf

Thayne, D. A. and Koike, N. (2008). *Sono Eigo, eitibu Niwa Kou Kikoemasu* [*How Your English Sounds to Native Speakers*]. Tokyo: Shufutotomosha.

Thomas, E. R. (2008). 'Rural Southern white accents.' In E. W. Schneider (ed.), *Varieties of English 2: The Americas and the Caribbean* (pp. 87–114). Berlin: Mouton de Gruyter.

Thomas, J. (1999). 'Voices from the periphery: non-native teachers and issues of credibility.' In G. Braine (ed.), *Non-native Educators in English Language Teaching*. Mahwah, NJ: Lawrence Erlbaum.

Thomson-Reuters. (2012). 'The Thomson Reuters journal selection process.' Retrieved 16 April 2014 from http://wokinfo.com/essays/journal-selection-process/

Timmis, I. (2002). 'Native-speaker norms and international English: a classroom view.' *ELT Journal*, 56 (3), pp. 240–49. doi:10.1093/elt/56.3.240

Tollefson, J. (1995). *Power and Inequality in Language Education*. Cambridge: Cambridge University Press.

Tripathi, P. D. (1990). 'English in Zambia.' *English Today*, 6(3), pp. 34–38.

Trudgill, P. (1998). 'World Englishes: convergence or divergence?' In H. Lindquist, S. Klintborg, M. Levin and M. Estling (eds), *The Major Varieties of English: Papers From MAVEN 97*. Växjö: Acta Wexionensia.

——(2002). *Sociolinguistic Variation and Change*. Edinburgh: Edinburgh University Press.

——(2005). 'Native-speaker segmental phonological models and the English Lingua Franca Core.' In K. Dziubalska-Kolaczyk and J. Przedlacka (eds), *English Pronunciation Models: A Changing Scene* (pp. 77–98). Bern: Peter Lang.

Trudgill, P. and Hannah, J. (2008). *International English: A Guide to the Varieties of Standard English*. London: Hodder Education.

Tsui, A. B. M. and Bunton, D. (2002). 'The discourse and attitudes of English language teachers in Hong Kong.' In K. Bolton (ed.), *Hong Kong English: Autonomy and Creativity* (pp. 57–77). Hong Kong: Hong Kong University Press.

UNESCO. (2009). *IFAP Annual World Report 2009*. Retrieved 5 September 2014 from www.unesco.org/new/en/communication-and-information/resources/news-and-in-focus-articles/all-news/news/ifap_annual_world_report_2009_available_online-1/#.U1EWna6LHZM

Upton, C. (2008). 'Synopsis: phonological variation in the British Isles.' In B. Kortmann and C. Upton (eds), *Varieties of English 1: The British Isles* (pp. 269–83). Berlin: Mouton de Gruyter.

Upton, C. and Widdowson, J. D. A. (1996). *An Atlas of English Dialects*. Oxford: Oxford University Press.

Van Parijs, P. (2011). *Linguistic Justice for Europe and for the World*. Oxford: Oxford University Press.

van Rooy, B. (2008). 'Black South African English: phonology.' In R. Mesthrie (ed.), *Varieties of English 4: Africa, South and Southeast Asia* (pp. 177–87). Berlin: Mouton de Gruyter.

Verma, S. (1982). 'Swadeshi English: form and function.' In J. B. Pride (ed.), *New Englishes* (pp. 174–87). Rowley, MA: Newbury House.

Wagner, S. (2008). 'English dialects in the Southwest: morphology and syntax.' In B. Kortmann and C. Upton (eds), *Varieties of English 1: The British Isles* (pp. 417–39). Berlin: Mouton de Gruyter.

Walker, R. (2010). *Teaching the Pronunciation of English as a Lingua Franca*. Oxford: Oxford University Press.

Wee, L. (2008). 'Singapore English: morphology and syntax.' In R. Mesthrie (ed.), *Varieties of English Volume 4: Africa, South and Southeast Asia* (pp. 593–609). Berlin: Mouton de Gruyter.

Wee, L. H. A. (1998). 'The lexicon of Singapore English.' In A. Crilly (ed.), *English in New Cultural Contexts: Study Guide – Block* (pp. 1–14). Singapore: Singapore Institute of Management.

——(2004). 'Reduplication and discourse particles.' In L. Lim (ed.), *Singapore English: A Grammatical Description* (pp. 105–26). Amsterdam: John Benjamins.

Wells, G. (1999). *Dialogic Inquiry: Towards a Sociocultural Practice and Theory of Education*. Cambridge: Cambridge University Press.

Wells, J. C. (1982). *Accents of English*. Cambridge: Cambridge University Press.

Widdowson, H. G. (1994). 'The Ownership of English.' *TESOL Quarterly*, 28(2), pp. 377–89. doi:10.2307/3587438

——(1997). 'EIL, ESL, EFL: global issues and local interests.' *World Englishes*, 16(1), pp. 135–48.

——(2003). *Defining Issues in English Language Teaching*. Oxford: Oxford University Press.

——(2012). 'ELF and the inconvenience of established concepts.' *Journal of English as a Lingua Franca*, 1(1), pp. 5–26. doi:10.1515/jelf-2012-0002

Wilton, A. (2012). 'The monster and the zombie: English as a lingua franca and the Latin analogy.' *Journal of English as a Lingua Franca*, July, pp. 337–62.

Winford, D. (2008). 'English in the Caribbean.' In H. Momma and M. Matto (eds), *A Companion to the History of the English Language* (pp. 413–22). Oxford: Blackwell.

Wolf, H.-G. (2010). 'East and West African Englishes: differences and commonalities.' In A. Kirkpatrick (ed.), *The Routledge Handbook of World Englishes* (pp. 197–211). London: Routledge.

Wolfram, W. (2008). 'Urban African American vernacular English: morphology and syntax.' In E. W. Schneider (ed.), *Varieties of English 2: The Americas and the Caribbean* (pp. 510–33). Berlin: Mouton de Gruyter.

Wolfram, W. and Schilling-Estes, N. (2006). *American English: Dialects and Variation*. Oxford: Blackwell.

Xu, Z. M. (2010). 'Chinese English: a future power?' In A. Kirkpatrick (ed.), *The Routledge Handbook of World Englishes* (pp. 282–98). London: Routledge.

Yano, Y. (2001). 'World Englishes in 2000 and beyond.' *World Englishes*, 20(2), pp. 119–30.

Yoshikawa, H. (2005). 'Recognition of world Englishes: changes in Chukyo University students' attitudes.' *World Englishes*, 24(3), pp. 351–60. doi:10.1111/j.0083–2919.2005.00416.x

Zacharias, N. T. (2005). 'Teachers' beliefs about internationally-published materials: a survey of tertiary English teachers in Indonesia.' *RELC Journal*, 36(1), pp. 23–37. doi:10.1177/0033688205053480

Index